D1302657

IRVING HOWE—SOCIALIST, CRITIC, JEW

JEWISH LITERATURE AND CULTURE

SERIES EDITOR, ALVIN H. ROSENFELD

IRVING HOWE

SOCIALIST, CRITIC, JEW

Edward Alexander

INDIANA UNIVERSITY PRESS / BLOOMINGTON & INDIANAPOLIS

The paper used in this publication meets the minimum requirements of American
National Standard for Information Sciences—Permanence of Paper for Printed Library
Materials, ANSI Z39.48–1984.

Manufactured in the United States of America

Library of Congress Cataloging-in-Publication Data

Alexander, Edward, date
Irving Howe : socialist, critic, Jew / Edward Alexander.
p.   cm.
Includes bibliographical references and index.
ISBN 0-253-33364-4 (cl. : alk. paper)
1. Howe, Irving. 2. Jews—New York (State)—New York—Biography. 3. Critics—New
York (State)—New York—Biography. 4. Jewish radicals—New York (State)—New
York—Biography. 5. Jews—New York (State)—New York—Intellectual life. 6. New
York (N.Y.)—Biography. 7. New York (N.Y.)—Intellectual life.   I. Title.
F128.9.J5A48 1998
974.7'1004924'0092—dc21
[B]   97-27112

1 2 3 4 5 03 02 01 00 99 98

For my parents, once more

I knew that in essential goodness of soul
nothing I might ever find "out there" was likely
to surpass my parents. . . . Nothing ever has.

—Irving Howe, *A Margin of Hope*

CONTENTS

SIX

The Sixties, Decade of Controversy: The Golem Rises against Its Creator
110

SEVEN

In the Shadow of Decades: Farewell to Immigrant Jewishness
155

EIGHT

The Final Reckoning: Socialism, Jewishness, Literary Study
198

PREFACE

For more than fifty years, from the 1940s to the 1990s, Irving Howe was a kind of miracle. He wrote about politics and literature and Jews with the productivity of a major industry; and yet his scores of books and hundreds of essays not only met the demanding scholarly standards of the academy but were written with an analytical sharpness, polemical bite, and lethal irony that raised them above the level of what was (and is) generally found in journals of literary and cultural opinion. He worked for decades in the academy, and yet was never entirely of it; although he deferred to the examples of Edmund Wilson and Lionel Trilling, he may yet prove to be not only the last estimable public intellectual, but the greatest one. Even though he has been dead only a few years, a retrospective glance at his achievement may serve to remind us that the present concerns of American literary culture are neither the only possible ones nor necessarily the highest ones. For novelists who subscribed to the dictum of (for example) writer-philosopher William Gass that "life is not the subject of fiction" and for critics who took the position that literature is not the subject of literary criticism, he had little but scorn. Despite his Marxist beginnings, he was contemptuous of schemes for reducing literature and ideas to their supposed determinants in gender, class, and race. Instead, he relentlessly called us back to what Cynthia Ozick has called the great Judaic concerns of Dickens and Tolstoy and George Eliot: the nature and consequences of conduct, the forces and attitudes that give life meaning and direction, the struggle to make something *human* of our lives even in the midst of social injustices and frustrating circumstances, and the inevitability of old age, sickness, and death.

The intellectual development of Irving Howe into one of the most original, principled, and independent minds of twentieth-century America proceeded along three tracks: socialist, Jewish, and literary. My book tries to show how these three tracks usually ran parallel to each other, sometimes intersected, sometimes merged smoothly, occasionally collided. Howe's mind was a complex unity, only rarely glimpsed by either admirers or detractors. Those who attended his memorial service at the YMHA Poetry Center in New York City in May 1993 could well have come away with the impression that he had spent all of his life in the orbit of the magazines *New Republic* and *Dissent,* and that his career was essentially that of a literary critic who also held forth occasionally on politics and Jewish affairs. As a bitter former colleague of his in the Workers party remarked, there were no speakers at the commemoration from any organization that had claimed Howe's political adherence for decades, "not even Democratic Socialists of America of which he was a vice president."[1] But when I mentioned to one of my English Department colleagues that I was writing a book about Irving Howe, her response was: "Why are you writing about that socialist?" For the majority of his readers, of course, Howe was neither socialist nor literary critic but the chronicler of the immigrant Jewish world who earned his fame through the best-selling *World of Our Fathers* (1976), a book that nobody who knew him in his formative years could have imagined him writing.

Of the three tracks, the socialist one began earliest, in the 1930s. Howe was already an active socialist in his teens and never underwent the spectacular conversion from the faith that would occur in many of his contemporaries; he did not change from commissar to yogi. But although he remained a socialist throughout his life, by the fifties he had changed from an emphasis upon organizational activity to a struggle for the socialist idea, from a politics to an ethic; and by the sixties he was no longer a Marxist. His commitment to literature and its intrinsic value also began early and never wavered, despite the political onslaughts upon literary autonomy and integrity led by his fellow-leftists in the forties, the sixties, and the eighties and nineties. But his early devotion to modernism was gradually replaced or at least enlarged by a more humane and ethical conception of literature. As for Jewishness (not Judaism) Howe came to it much later than he did to socialism and literature, so that his creed of secular Jewishness was deeply influenced by both his literary sensibility and his socialism.

In one sense, even though both his ideas and his temperament changed greatly during his life, the story of Irving Howe's intellectual growth is a chronicle of lost causes, as he himself would have been the first to admit. Socialism not only failed as a political force in America, but the socialist idea was irreparably besmirched by the Soviet regime (which Howe consistently and strenuously opposed) and its satellites and sycophants. Secular Jewishness as Howe understood it—that is, the immigrant culture of Yiddish—was overtaken by Zionism, by religion, by assimilation, by the ravages of time. Literary study, as Howe often ruefully observed in his last years, was being usurped by failed sociologists and professors who didn't really like literature at all, and whose stupefyingly opaque "theorizing" about it made Howe's eyes glaze over.

I have tried to write a biography of Howe's mind. In one sense, of course, I cannot hope to be wiser on this subject than Howe himself was in his "intellectual autobiography," *A Margin of Hope* (1982). I can claim only the advantages of another thirteen years (Howe told his own story through the 1970s, and lived until 1993), greater disinterestedness and perspective, and also a willingness to supply the points of view of his numerous adversaries much more amply than it would be reasonable to expect from even so fair-minded a combatant in controversy as Irving Howe. Keeping in mind Howe's frequent complaint that amnesia is a long-standing American affliction, I have also tried to provide the background to the major literary, political, and Jewish disputes in which Howe engaged: disputes about socialism, about the racial question, about the Holocaust, about Israel, about multiculturalism, about Ezra Pound and T. S. Eliot and Hannah Arendt and Ralph Ellison and Philip Roth. (Howe enjoyed a good fight.)

Although I have some sympathy with the view that philosophy is ultimately no more than character, I have based my study of Howe's ideas on his scores of books and hundreds of articles, as well as on some archival material. Discussion of Howe's personal life has been kept to a minimum, partly because of the general uncooperativeness of Howe's wives and children, and the specific prohibition by Nicholas Howe, his son and literary executor, against my quoting from his letters. (This also means that, in this book, Howe often fights against his adversaries with one hand tied behind his back: I can quote from their letters but only paraphrase his.) A writer is primarily what he writes, and Howe wrote so much that it would require a second volume to deal with his private as well as his public life. But the reader can keep abreast of his private life with the help of the Chronology and occasional signposts in the text itself.

Perhaps it is in order for me to add that I was drawn to the subject of Irving Howe by my affection and admiration for the man. Our acquaintance began in 1972 when he sent me an unsolicited response to the first piece (which many wish had been the last) I ever wrote on a Jewish subject, an essay on Chaim Grade's story, "My Quarrel with Hersh Rasseyner." He praised the essay, which had appeared in *Judaism*, but expressed wonder about why neither the story nor the anthology in which it appeared—*A Treasury of Yiddish Stories*—ever attracted much attention in American literary circles. His last letter to me was dated 30

April 1993. In it he reported that 1992 had been a terrible year for him, with three operations close together, but that he was fine now. Five days later he died. To me (his "favorite reactionary," as he once said), he was always kind, generous, open, and liberal-minded, despite our serious disagreements on many subjects, disagreements I have not tried to hide in this book. I know that Howe has many detractors, including people— some of his own political persuasion—who, at the mere mention of his name, bark that "he was the rudest person I ever met." Perhaps I am insensible of all reproof, but I myself never felt this harshness. More important, I always felt that I was learning something by listening to Howe's voice, a kind of life-wisdom that went beyond political differences. Once, shortly after his father had died late in 1977, I was in New York to visit my own ailing father, hospitalized not far from Irving's apartment on 83rd Street. "Come over," he said on the phone, "and let's talk about life and death—no politics." Moreover, this life-wisdom expressed itself in a prose as supple and exact and analytically precise as that of any critic writing in English in this century.

In the course of writing this book, I have incurred numerous debts, which I am happy to acknowledge. For extraordinarily generous help, well beyond the call of duty, I am indebted to Ronald M. Bulatoff (Hoover Institution Archives), Werner Cohn, Morris Dickstein, Albert Glotzer, Ronald D. Patkus (Boston College Archives), Janet Rabino- witch, Alvin H. Rosenfeld, Edward S. Shapiro, Alan M. Wald, Ruth R. Wisse, and Dennis Wrong. For help and suggestions of various kinds, I am indebted to the following: Alan Adelson, Jane Arnold, Avi Bass, Mary Bell, Brenda Brown, Constantine Christofides, Lewis Coser, Sanford Dornbusch, Carl Gershman, David Gold, Melissa Hammerle (Unterberg Poetry Center), Robert B. Heilman, Andrew R. Hilen En- dowment (University of Washington), Milton Hindus, Ernest B. Hook, Irving Louis Horowitz, Larry Husten, Wayne Jennings, George Jochnowitz, Donald M. Kartiganer, Elaine M. Kauvar, Carole S. Kessner, Jacob Korg, Neal Kozodoy, Melvin D. Landsberg, Berel Lang, Rafael Medoff, Joan Mellen, Asher Z. Milbauer, Hugh Moorhead, Miriam Moorman, Robert Negin, Cynthia Ozick, Shirley Panken and the late Irving Panken, Bess G. Paper, Ross Posnock, Daniel Silver, Jay Tolson, Micael Vaughan, Chaim Waxman, and Helene Williams.

Special thanks to my wife Leah Alexander for supplying me, at the right time, with *A Margin of Hope* (the book and the thing) and for helping with the index.

CHRONOLOGY

1920   Born June 11, East Bronx, New York City, to David and Nettie (Goldman) Horenstein. David Horenstein ran a grocery store, then worked as a peddler and later as a presser in a dress factory. Nettie Horenstein also worked in the dress trade as an operator.

1930   Family grocery store in West Bronx goes bankrupt.

1933   Becomes bar mitzvah in whitewashed storefront *shul.*

1934   Becomes active in left-wing, anti-Stalinist politics.

1936   Graduates from DeWitt Clinton High School in northwest Bronx and enters City College of New York.
Begins to read Edmund Wilson's literary criticism.

1938–
1939   Still Horenstein in class, begins to use the party name of Hugh Ivan. Also acquires nickname of "Fangs" because of zest for polemics and protruding eyeteeth.

1940   Graduates from CCNY in spring as Irving Horenstein, but uses name Irving Howe for speeches and articles.

1941   Marries Anna Bader.
Managing editor, under Emanuel Garrett (pseudonym of Emanuel Geltman), then editor, of Workers party weekly, *Labor Action,* for about eight months until drafted into the army in mid-1942.

1942   Enters U.S. Army at Camp Upton, Long Island, beginning stint of about three and a half years.

1944   Visits—on last weekend leave before going "overseas" to Alaska—Clyde, Ohio, which Sherwood Anderson used as the model for Winesburg. Reaches Alaska in November, and spends last sixteen months of military service at Fort Richardson, near Anchorage, reaching the rank of sergeant.

1946   After release from army, moves back to Bronx and resumes writing for *Labor Action* and *New International.* Legally

changes surname to Howe. Divorces first wife, Anna.
Publishes first articles for *Commentary* and *Partisan Review*.
Studies toward master's degree at Brooklyn College.
Mother, Nettie Horenstein, dies.

1947 Marries Thalia Filias, an archaeologist, of Buffalo, New York.
Assistant to Hannah Arendt, editor at Schocken Books, and to
Dwight Macdonald, editor of *Politics*. Writes for *Politics* using
the pseudonym Theodore Dryden.

1948 Becomes book-reviewer (of nonpolitical books) for *Time
Magazine*, a post held for about four years. (Over half his
reviews are never printed.)
Moves to Princeton when his wife gets job teaching Greek
and Latin at Miss Fine's Day School for girls, a private school.
During Princeton years becomes acquainted with R. P.
Blackmur, Delmore Schwartz, Saul Bellow, and John
Berryman.
Edits *Essence of Judaism*, by Leo Baeck.

1949 Enters the controversy over Ezra Pound's Bollingen Award.
The UAW and Walter Reuther (with B. J. Widick).

1951 Publishes first article in *New Republic* (December 10).
Sherwood Anderson.
Daughter Nina born.

1952 Teaches summer session at University of Washington, Seattle.
William Faulkner: A Critical Study.
Resigns (October) from Independent Socialist League (for-
merly Workers party).

1953 Leaves Princeton to begin teaching at Brandeis University,
where he remains until 1961.
Son Nicholas born.
Kenyon Review fellow for literary criticism.

1954 Founds *Dissent*, publishing first issue in January. For next
forty years spends two days a week working on the maga-
zine.
Christian Gauss seminar chair; visiting professor at Princeton.
Breaks (for seven or eight years) with Lionel Trilling.
A Treasury of Yiddish Stories (with Eliezer Greenberg).

1957 *Politics and the Novel.*
The American Communist Party: A Critical History (with Lewis
Coser).

1959 Makes Richard Wright contributing editor of *Dissent*.
Divorce and breakup of family.

1961 Moves to California to teach at Stanford University.

1963 Leaves California to begin teaching at Hunter College and

Graduate Center of City University of New York, where he remains until retirement in 1986.
A World More Attractive.
Dissent organizes public forum on Arendt's *Eichmann in Jerusalem.*
Becomes active in "the moderate peace organization called SANE."

1964– Marries Arien Hausknecht, a widow and a member of New
1965 School faculty in psychology, later editor of *Social Research.*
1966 *Steady Work.*
1967 *Thomas Hardy.*
1968 Works for Eugene McCarthy's presidential campaign.
Breaks with Philip Rahv over anticommunism.
1969 *The Decline of the New.*
A Treasury of Yiddish Poetry (with Eliezer Greenberg).
1970 Named Distinguished Professor, CUNY.
1971 Bollingen Foundation Fellow.
Guggenheim Fellow.
1972 *Voices from the Yiddish* (with Eliezer Greenberg).
Attacks Phillip Roth in December *Commentary.*
Israel, the Arabs, and the Middle East (with Carl Gershman).
Joins Michael Harrington's Democratic Socialist Organizing Committee, of which he would become vice president.
1973 *The Critical Point.*
1976 *World of Our Fathers,* winner of National Book Award in History.
Fellow at National Humanities Institute, New Haven.
1977 *Ashes Out of Hope: Fiction by Soviet-Yiddish Writers* (with Eliezer Greenberg).
1978 *Leon Trotsky.*
1979 *Best of Sholom Aleichem* (with Ruth R. Wisse).
Elected member of American Academy of Arts and Letters.
1980– *Who's Who* shows IH married to Ilana Wiener.
1981
1982 *A Margin of Hope.*
1985 *Socialism and America.*
1986 Retires from City University of New York.
The American Newness.
1987 MacArthur Fellow.
The Penguin Book of Modern Yiddish Verse (with Ruth R. Wisse and Khone Shmeruk).
1990 *Selected Writings: 1950-1990.*
1993 Dies May 5, New York City, from cardiovascular disease.

ABBREVIATIONS

ACP	*The American Communist Party: A Critical History (1919–1957)*
C&A	*Celebrations and Attacks*
CP	*Critical Point*
J-A	*Jewish-American Stories*
LT	*Leon Trotsky*
MH	*Margin of Hope*
"Range"	"The Range of the New York Intellectuals"
SA	*Sherwood Anderson*
SW	*Selected Writings*
TYP	*Treasury of Yiddish Poetry*
TYS	*Treasury of Yiddish Stories*
VY	*Voices from the Yiddish*
WF	*World of Our Fathers*

IRVING HOWE—SOCIALIST, CRITIC, JEW

ONE

A Lost Paradise: Starting Out in the Thirties

*In the glow of memory, those years of hardship in
the East Bronx figure as a lost paradise simply
because they were my years of growing up, when
the world still shone with freshness and expectation. A lost paradise, also, because immigrant-
Jewish life—narrow and provincial as it could be—
gave me sensations of coherence, the persuasion
that life has shape and meaning, perhaps even
purpose, as nothing in my later years, neither
political involvement nor literary effort, quite
could. The immigrant subculture . . . was an
"organic" culture, and ever since I left it—for the
keenest impulse of my late teens was to race toward
the outer world of America—I have known doubt
and division.[1]*

Growing up in the East Bronx

Irving Howe entered the world as Irving Horenstein on June 11, 1920,
the son of David and Nettie (Goldman) Horenstein. The family lived in
the eastern section of the borough of the Bronx in New York City. The
predominant language of the neighborhood, in which it was possible to
live and die without any significant encounter with a non-Jew, was
Yiddish. The generation of Howe's parents might possess a Yiddish that

was like silk, yet stumble badly in English. Their children spoke an English that might be untainted by accent, yet had its own recognizably "immigrant" intonation and melody. (Henry Roth would capture the interplay of Yiddish and English in such neighborhoods in his novel of 1934, *Call It Sleep*, in which he makes of English, in effect, two languages.)

Although Howe would in later years refer to his childhood in this immigrant neighborhood as a lost paradise, this did not mean that his childhood was particularly "happy" or that his upbringing was all that it might have been. "My parents were very poor garment workers who bequeathed to me—it was not their fault—an ineradicable anxiety about livelihood. I still bear the distrust, even fear, of the physical that many immigrant Jews implanted in their children, as if learning to ice-skate would forever keep a nice Jewish boy from becoming a high-school teacher" ("Immigrant Chic," 76).

Irving Horenstein became bar mitzvah in a whitewashed storefront *shul*, "ramshackle and bleak with its scattering of aged Jews." It was not, however, the synagogue that captured young Irving's interest and loyalty but a loft a few blocks away, in which the secular Yiddish school run by the socialist Workmen's Circle was located. His father would not let him go there because, though not himself religious, he sensed (correctly) that what held the Jews together was located in the *shul* and not the Arbeiter Ring. But for Irving Horenstein "that loft . . . turned out to be more important in my life than any synagogue." The Jewishness that young Irving did encounter was a hollowed-out version of what had flourished in the old country. "Sometimes the family was about all that was left of Jewishness; or, more accurately, all that we had left of Jewishness had come to rest in the family. Jewishness flickered to life on Friday night, with a touch of Sabbath ceremony a few moments before dinner. . . . Our parents clung to family life as if that were their one certainty. . . ."[2]

The Horensteins were poor, but never really hungry. When David Horenstein's West Bronx grocery store went bankrupt in 1930, a year into the Great Depression, and he became a "customer peddler," selling sheets and linens from door to door, the family sank further and was forced to crowd into a small apartment with aunts, uncles, and grandmother in order to save rent. "We were dropping from the lower middle class to the proletarian—the most painful of all social descents" (MH, 7). But the circumstances that forced both his parents to find jobs in the garment industry also formed their son's strongest, most enduring political convictions. Fifty years later, Howe recalled what happened:

> I remember my mother [in 1931] coming home exhausted each evening, and ending the week with a $12 paycheck. I remember my

father who stood all day over a steaming press-iron, coming home during the summer months with blisters all over his body. When the great strike of the garment workers was called by the International Ladies Garment Workers Union in 1933, my folks, who had had no experience with unions before, responded immediately . . . they picketed, they borrowed money for food, they stood fast. The strike over, my mother brought home her first new paycheck: $27. It seemed like heaven: we felt freer, better, stronger. And there was meat on the table. After that, my folks were never active in the union, but they paid their dues faithfully, and if a strike was called, they were the first to go out. This was the ethic I grew up with, the ethic of solidarity. Almost half a century later, I still believe in it.[3]

Nevertheless, Irving Horenstein had little sense of being deprived, or victimized by social injustice. Not until he was a teenager and began to read a magazine printing Sherwood Anderson's reports about hunger in North Carolina textile towns did he react to poverty with indignation, "barely aware of the extent to which I was perhaps feeling sorry for myself. The realization of what it meant to be poor I had first to discover through writings about poverty; the sense of my own handicap became vivid to me only after I had learned about the troubles of people I did not know."[4]

Although descended from "the people of the book," Howe grew up in a home that was already more representative of what American Jews would become in this regard: namely, the people *without* the book. "My folks' reaction to school was pretty typical. They had a kind of blind, sweet trustfulness. They didn't really know what the hell it was all about. There was something like a semi-religious faith that books were good. I don't know if they could have said why. There were no books in our house—none, literally none."[5] Given the awe of Jewish immigrants before high school teachers, it is not surprising that David Horenstein dreamed that his son would become a high school teacher. But Irving was convinced he would never reach that eminence because the oral examination for teachers required pronunciation of "Long Island" without sounding the hard or doubled "g," a hurdle New York Jews were notoriously unable to leap. Instead, *faute de mieux*, at the age of fourteen, while at DeWitt Clinton High School (for boys only) in the northwest Bronx, he stumbled into socialism, the Movement. "At the age of fourteen I wandered into the ranks of the socialist youth and from then on, all through my teens and twenties, the Movement was my home and passion, the Movement as it ranged through the various left-wing, anti-Communist groups" (*Steady Work*, 350). Howe became a "Trotskyist," that is, an opponent of those whose sympathy with Soviet communism led them to justify the Moscow trials, the purges of old Bolsheviks, the glorification of Stalin and his concentration camps.

The Movement

What attracted young people to the movement? Howe believed that it wasn't primarily ideology, since few even tried to master Marxist economics: "In economics I was a complete bust. . . ."—a telling admission from a lifelong socialist. Neither was it the pull of group life. No, it was "the sense that they had gained, not merely a 'purpose' in life but . . . a coherent perspective upon everything that was happening to us." This enabled one to respond quickly and confidently to events. "One revelled in the innocence and arrogance of knowledge, for even in our inexpert hands Marxism could be a powerful analytic tool and we could nurture the feeling that . . . we enjoyed a privileged relationship to history" (*Steady Work*, 357–58). Horenstein began to think of himself as a Marxist by the age of sixteen or seventeen ("Range," 275). Marxism seemed to provide a key to all the doors of knowledge, and he was awed by the avalanche of its dogmatic language. An even more profound reason for its appeal was that "Marxism involved a profoundly *dramatic* view of human experience. With its stress upon inevitable conflicts, apocalyptic climaxes, ultimate moments . . . it appealed deeply to our imaginations. We felt that we were always on the rim of heroism, that the mockery we might suffer at the moment would turn to vindication in the future, that our loyalty to principle would be rewarded by the grateful masses of tomorrow. . . . The moment would come . . . if only we did not flinch, if only we were ready to remain a tiny despised minority, if only we held firm to our sense of destiny" (*Steady Work*, 358–59).

The language of religion that Howe uses to reflect upon his youthful conversion to the movement is highly revealing. Although he sometimes disparaged the glibness of comparisons between radical politics and religious practice, his autobiographical reflections "recognize, not very comfortably, that there were *some* parallels between the two. Everything seemed to fall into place; ordered meaning, a world grasped through theory, a life shaped by purpose. Is that not the essence of conversion" (MH, 14)? Needless to say that Howe's critics, far more than Howe himself, would later attribute his tenacious clinging to socialism to the blindness of religious faith impervious to empirical evidence.

As for Howe's inherited religion, Judaism, he barely sensed its doctrinal incompatibility with Marxism, or even the tendency of Marxism to superimpose a false identity upon his Jewish one. Once in the movement, he felt he couldn't bring friends home because he would have been "as ashamed to show them to my parents as to show my parents to them." His self-consciousness led him, in relation to his parents, "into a maze of superfluous lies and trivial deceptions. . . . I could not imagine bringing together the life that was given, with its sweet poignancy and embittered conflicts, and the life one had chosen, with its secret fellowship and sectarian vocabulary" (*Steady Work*, 354–55).

One wonders, for example, whether Howe's parents were aware, and, if they were aware, what they thought of his rejection of their name. The movement compelled its members to acquire a "party name," which by a peculiar accident nearly always meant substituting an Anglo-Saxon name for a Jewish one. (In Howe's circle, only an Italian Trotskyist named Peter Rossi took on a Jewish name.) When Daniel Bell (whose family name had once been Bolotsky) met Howe in 1938, he was Horenstein in class, but using the party name of Hugh Ivan, which combined English gentleman and Russian muzhik.[6] The CCNY yearbook for 1940 (*Microcosm*) has a picture of a very severe-looking young man named Irving Horenstein, Bachelor of Social Science, President of the Philosophy Club, resident at 763 Jennings Street, Bronx. This young man was already using the name of Irving Howe, not only for "party" purposes but also, more importantly, as his *nom de plume*. (In the CCNY Alumni Association Directory of 1946, however, he is still listed as Horenstein.) Without ever specifying his own name change, Howe in later years would repeatedly reflect critically upon this practice of Jewish Marxists in the thirties. In 1966 he contrasted the healthy attitude of the immigrant parents with the self-deceptions of their radical children. "In the thirties the ordinary New York Jew realized that Jewishness was not something one had much choice about, and in this respect his instincts were sounder, both morally and practically, than that of the radicals who chose for their 'party names' almost anything that did not sound Jewish. You might be shouting at the top of your lungs against reformism or Stalin's betrayals, but for the middle-aged garment worker strolling along Southern Boulevard you were just a bright and cocky Jewish boy, a talkative little *pisher*" (*Steady Work*, 353). In 1982 Howe again returned to the topic of name changing: "We were caught up in a historical charade, trying to don the costumes of a resurrected bolshevism. The costumes didn't fit. Unacknowledged motives were also at work, having less to do with Marxist strategy than our own confused and unexamined feelings about Jewish origin" (MH, 47). In an interview of the same year Howe explicitly said that pseudonyms expressed "a decided rejection of Jewishness" ("Range," 276).[7]

From 1936 to 1940 Howe attended City College, where he compiled a mediocre academic record, "except for an occasional course that lured me into unplanned enthusiasm" (MH, 61). He became an English major because "it struck me as the easiest major, where I could bullshit the most" ("Range," 280).[8] But even of this dubious classroom activity he could not have had much, for he rarely attended classes. Often he would go to class, wait until the teacher had taken the roll, then walk out and return at the end of the hour. He did consider CCNY a wonderful place during those years, not because of its faculty but because of its students. "The real center of life at City College was in our Alcove 1, dark-stained, murky, shaped like a squat horseshoe. . . . Alcove 1 was the home of heresy, left sectarianism, independent thought, and . . . a share of fanaticism and intolerance. Here gathered Trotskyist, Socialist, Lovestonite students . . ." (MH, 64). Alcove 2 was for the pro-Stalinist left. Irving Kristol remembers the Howe of City College days as "a pillar of ideological rectitude. Thin, gangling, intense, always a little distant, his fingers incessantly and nervously twisting a cowlick as he enunciated sharp and authoritative opinions, Irving was the Trotskyist leader and 'theoretician.'"[9] Daniel Bell, who first met Howe in Alcove 1, describes it as "the sandbox of radical politics," which Howe ruled as "commissar of the revolution" ("Remembering Irving Howe," 517).

Literary Life and the Communist Party

If Howe as a young man was a Jew by default or "accident," as he once put it ("Range," 279), and a socialist by conscious choice, he was a literary person by natural inclination. "With T. S. Eliot . . . I fell crazily in love, more with the rhythms and music of his verse than its meaning. I knew he was a reactionary but didn't really care." He also began to have an inkling of his future vocation as literary critic. "At the age of sixteen I was lent a copy of Edmund Wilson's *Axel's Castle* by a YPSL [Young People's Socialist League] friend in the Bronx. This was probably the first book of literary criticism I read through from start to finish. . . . Something about Wilson's moral gravity moved me." Although Howe might (at least then) easily ignore the fact that Eliot was a reactionary, he had a harder time sorting out his own intellectual models among American writers (Wilson included) who shared his own radical political sympathies (and had not, like Eliot, become expatriates). His decision to be a socialist rather than a Communist, a Trotskyist rather than a Stalinist, though primarily due to what he considered insufficient Communist stridency against war, was also tied up with his burgeoning sense of a literary and intellectual vocation, and his awareness of the fate of writers who had taken the Communist path, and taken it in large part because "it was Stalinism, and only Stalinism, that commanded power on 'the Left'" (MH, 56–7, 76). He received confirmation of the rightness of his decision when he was physically assaulted every time he tried to speak for Trotskyism on the CCNY campus.[10]

Howe, we need to recall, grew up during the thirties, the most important period in the history of American communism, and the one in which large numbers of literary intellectuals were turning not only leftward but in the direction of communism and Joseph Stalin. He did not follow their lead, despite the fact that many of the literary people he admired, including Wilson himself, had rushed into the arms of the Communists in the wake of the stock market crash of 1929. At this distance in time, one cannot fully comprehend the choices that faced a budding socialist intellectual with strong literary interests growing up in the thirties, but we can at least try to recreate some of the salient characteristics of the left-wing ambience.

The intellectual monthly magazine *New Masses* was founded by the Communist party in 1927, in hopes of capitalizing upon the indignation stirred in most American intellectuals by the Sacco-Vanzetti executions in August of that year. From its inception and for many years to come, the guiding spirit of the magazine was Michael Gold, of whom Howe has left a devastating portrait: "Gold was an inveterate low-brow who, if he had not turned radical, would have made a superb police reporter; he was a hater of refinements of thought, partly because he could not distinguish them from refinements of manners, which he *knew* to be a petty-bourgeois lure. He had learned once that there was a class struggle between workers and bosses, and that was all he knew or needed to know. He believed that the future of literature lay in the primitive propaganda sketches written by Communist workers or, more often, by young Communist quasi-intellectuals passing for workers. He wrote with a recklessness possible only to a man who could not even imagine that the possession of Marxism, key to all realities though it might be, did not exempt a writer from the need for knowledge and thought."[11] But this apostle of cultural Know-Nothingism was able to attract many gifted writers to *New Masses*. Between 1930 and 1936 the famous names who contributed to it included Theodore Dreiser, Sherwood Anderson, John Dos Passos, Edmund Wilson, Erskine Caldwell, James Farrell and (slightly later) Ernest Hemingway. With the exception of Dreiser, none of these writers had extended relations with the Communist party, but contributed to its journal and its "cause" out of the feeling that, as the incurably naive Anderson said in replying to his own question about the difference between a Socialist and a Communist, "the Communists mean it" (ACP, 280). In this ingenuous remark, Howe detected, even in his youth, the attraction of Stalinism for the intellectuals. The Communists alone, they suspected, had a firm grasp of ultimate reality. What else would justify their dogmatic ruthlessness? Also at work was an impulse to self-abasement that many intellectuals felt in the presence of the working class (just as their spiritual inheritors would feel in the presence of members of minority groups fifty years later).

When, in 1957, Howe came to write (with Lewis Coser) a history of the American Communist party, he analyzed the motives of both the intellectuals who turned to the party and of the party functionaries who enlisted them. Many of the former sought relief from the embarrassment and frustrations of uncertainty about their inherited values and beliefs. "The new converts, young and old, obscure and famous, came rushing in quest of a system, like hungry geese to the trough; they wanted to feel that, at the very moment the world was being shattered, they had found the key to its meaning." Howe did not deny the moral idealism of the eager converts; rather, he believed it was precisely this idealism that helped to explain the behavior of the Stalinist intellectuals as they broke from corrupt traditional authority only to surrender to corrupt untraditional authority. The party wanted these people "*because* they were intellectuals, but it did not want them *as* intellectuals. . . . And what was still more astonishing in this grandiose deception: the party persuaded the intellectuals not merely that it was their duty to submit but that submission was good and joyful and spiritually renovating. . . . They were to love Big Brother . . . as an abstraction or an absolute" (ACP, 283–84). The most famous fellow travelers were left alone, but all the others had to undergo spiritual lobotomy.

Disgusted by this spectacle of intellectual buffoonery and self-abasement, the young Howe allied himself spiritually with members of the anti-Stalinist left. These included Sidney Hook, Max Eastman, and Philip Rahv, who were gifted not only as writers but also as political polemicists. The intrinsic appeal of this combination to Howe was increased by the fact that they represented a dissent from the conformity of dissent. All left-wing intellectuals dissented from the odious capitalist system, but during the thirties the majority of them were sympathetic to Stalinism; the truly independent minds were a minority of socialist critics of Stalin that Howe aspired to join.

In 1934 *New Masses* was confronted with heresy by some of its most prominent literary supporters. After the New York Communists broke up a memorial meeting called by the Socialist party and the trade unions to eulogize the defeated Austrian Social Democrats, an open letter denouncing "the culpability and shame of the Communists" was signed by, among many others, Wilson, Dos Passos, Lionel Trilling, and Meyer Schapiro. The Communists suddenly lost the most distinguished group of intellectuals ever to have approached the party orbit. A few years later these heretics formed the anti-Stalinist group that tried to mobilize opinion against the Moscow trials. These controversies led to the founding (or refounding) of *Partisan Review* in 1937 as an intellectual center for left-wing intellectuals who had turned away from Stalinism but wished to remain Marxists. From their example the young Howe concluded that Marxism might be useful to a literary critic *if* it did not become reductive, but that the real problem was that in the Stalinist milieu no literary or any other idea could operate freely, undistorted by the demands of the party line. For the party, ideas were nothing more than convenient instruments to be used or discarded according to political need.

The most prosperous years for the Stalinist movement in the American intellectual world were those of the Popular Front, 1935–39, the very years in which Howe became a fierce anti-Stalinist. During this period, the party wanted not so much writing as famous writers, who could be "stars" in the numerous front organizations. Its influence was very strong in such journals as the *Nation* and *New Republic* and in the burgeoning industries of middle-class culture, from all of which strategic positions its dutiful followers consistently denounced writers who clung to a position of independent radicalism. The turning point for the Stalinists came in August 1939: no fewer than 300 intellectuals—among them Clifford Odets, Granville Hicks, Dashiell Hammett, Max Lerner, S. J. Perelman, and James Thurber—issued a statement denouncing the "fantastic falsehood that the USSR and totalitarian states are basically alike." A week later, the Hitler-Stalin pact was announced. Rarely have bad judgment and bad timing been so perfectly combined and suitably rewarded. The seemingly irrational tenacity of Howe's socialist faith was due in part to his sense that he had kept clear of the taint of Stalinism. Even if he eventually decided that socialism had failed in America, he could still believe in its truth. The memories of Stalinists and ex-Stalinists were much harder to bear: "It is a terrible thing to commit one's hopes to a cause that turns out to be not a failure but a falsehood" (ACP, 315, 318). Although Howe would eventually acknowledge that socialism too was a failure, he remained forever proud of the fact that he and his fellow-Trotskyists, unlike most liberals, for example, were among the few people in the thirties who had told the truth about Stalinism.

In the spring of 1940 Howe graduated from City College. "At Lewisohn Stadium I sat in my absurd black gown next to Irving Kristol and Earl Raab, and we listened to the commencement speaker, an official from the League of Nations who gravely assured us that our generation, unlike an earlier one, would not have to go to the battlefields" (MH, 69).[12]

TWO

Labor Action: Socialism and Opposition to the War

The collective mind does not penetrate below the surface, but it sees all the surface; which profound thinkers, even by reason of their profundity, often fail to do: their intenser view of a thing in some of its aspects diverting their attention from others.

—J. S. Mill

Trotskyist Journalist

By the summer of 1940, if not earlier, Irving Horenstein had, for all political (as distinct from official) purposes become Irving Howe. We know this from an ad in the July 1 number of the weekly paper *Labor Action*. It announces a "Mass Meeting" to open the National Convention of the Young Peoples Socialist League (YPSL)—4th International. For 15 cents admission, one can get to hear several speakers, among them Irving Howe, identified as "Editor, *Challenge of Youth*," which was the YPSL newspaper. (According to Phyllis Jacobson, a comrade in the movement, "Howe was an excellent speaker, forceful and interesting, both indoors and on street corners. He also spoke in Yiddish at outdoor meetings in the Bronx.")[1] In the office of *Labor Action*, nobody ever thought or spoke of him as Horenstein, but only as Howe.

Howe's political ideas between the time he left City College and the time he entered the army in 1942 are best examined in *Labor Action,* to which he contributed regularly, and the "theoretical" journal, *New International: A Monthly Organ of Revolutionary Marxism,* to which he was an occasional contributor. *Labor Action* was started in 1940 by the Workers party, later the Independent Socialist League, which had come into being when the so-called Shachtmanites (disciples of Max Shachtman) left the Socialist Workers party. Its first editor was Joseph Carter, who was succeeded in about August 1941 by Emanuel Garrett (the pseudonym of Emanuel Geltman). When the WP sent Geltman, who had been very close to Howe, to serve as an "organizer" in California, Howe took on the editorship. He was assuming control of a paper that had already set itself in sharp opposition to the war against the Axis powers, just as its sponsoring organization had set itself against the Stalinists for lapsing into "patriotic" support of Roosevelt's war policy. A 3 June 1940 issue, for example, carries on the left side of the front-page banner the slogan: "Let the Bankers Fight on the Maginot Line, Labor's Fight is on the Picket Line!" On 9 July we find, in the same front-page location: "Workers! This Is Not Our War! It Is a War for Boss Profits! Join Hands in Independent Labor Action Against the War!"

The Trotskyist character of the paper was also clearly established before Howe took it over. Most of the issue of 26 August 1940 is devoted to the murder of Trotsky, which had taken place in Mexico a few days earlier. The material on Trotsky is assembled (into a kind of hagiography) by Dwight Macdonald, a frequent contributor to the paper who would later employ Howe at *his* journal, *Politics. New International* actually carried numerous articles by Trotsky until (and indeed after) the time of his death; and, like *Labor Action,* it was preoccupied with him long after his demise.

The editorial board of *Labor Action* could have been in no doubt about the political positions or the polemical ferocity of the young man they were considering for the managing editorship of their paper in the waning months of 1941 (by which time Howe was married and living with his wife Anna in Greenwich Village). In October, for example, Howe had published in *New International* an assault on the journalist Louis Fischer which was the journalistic equivalent of a blow to the back of the head. In an article delicately entitled "The Frauds of Louis Fischer," Howe identifies his target as having in the past been "for fifteen years . . . the journalistic high priest of the left intelligentsia, . . . a Stalinist and . . . the serious and authoritative spokesman of liberalism." (This linkage of Stalinism and liberalism would continue in Howe's writing for many years.) Among Fischer's recent transgressions are the equation of Bolshevism with Stalinism, the suggestion that "socialism is not a realistic perspective," and falsification of the role of the late Leon Trotsky. Using the subhead "Fischer is a Liar," Howe relentlessly assaults him for his former Stalinism, and this with a rhetoric even more violent than what he would later use against targets in *Labor Action*. "Why, Louis Fischer, did you not say anything about the 'ugliest face' of the dictatorship in 1936? Why did you keep quiet about the first Moscow trial which you now call the 'bloodiest purge in history'? . . . Only a person like you, Louis Fischer, king of the philistines and prince of liars, could establish such a record of filth and hypocrisy." A main reason why Howe cannot give Fischer any credit for abandoning Stalinism or let him live down his "foul past" is that (Howe would deal similarly with Arthur Koestler for the same reason) Fischer is now "an hysterical supporter of the imperialist war," as bad a jingoist as Harold Laski, the English socialist.[2]

Editorship of *Labor Action*

Howe's name appears in *Labor Action*'s masthead as managing editor for the first time on December 1, 1941. This is the first one-cent issue, a reduction of two cents from the old price. Howe's byline also appears, on a report about a sedition trial in Minneapolis of twenty-three members of the (rival) Socialist Workers party and Local 544-CIO, all accused of advocating and planning the forcible overthrow of the U.S. government. This report follows several articles in previous issues on the Minneapolis affair—unsigned, but probably also written by Howe.

Within days of Howe's taking over the paper came Pearl Harbor and American entry into the war, an action stridently opposed by *Labor Action* at the time and for years to come. The 15 December issue, the third under Howe's editorial direction (by 22 December, he is the only editor listed in the masthead), carries a front-page cartoon showing "The Ultimate Victor," which is the vulture named Capitalism perched on a stone labelled "3rd Year" [of the war, presumably]. One unsigned front-page article is headed "40 Hour Week Will Be the First War Victim!" (Apparently the headline writer had not noticed the Americans killed at Pearl Harbor.) A subhead expresses worry about what will happen to time and a half pay for overtime work. But the main article, also unsigned, is the lengthy "Statement of National Committee, Workers Party." It does attack the Hitler regime for "its cruel destruction of the labor movement in Germany" and for its crimes against the Austrian, Czechoslovakian, Polish, and other European peoples (among whom the Jews are not mentioned). But, it goes on, "noble hatred of tyranny has been cunningly exploited by the imperialist statesmen of the so-called democracies for the purpose of whipping up of a pro-war sentiment among the masses of the people." The paper takes the position, which Howe would espouse for many years, that this war, like World War I, is "a war between two great imperialist camps ... to decide ... which ... shall dominate the world." It is "a war of finance capital ... a war for stocks and bonds and profits ... a war conceived and bred by world capitalism." The trade unions are also attacked for supporting Roosevelt's decision to enter this "capitalist" war.

Very few political groupings would escape Howe's lash for their sin of supporting the war. In an article of 29 December 1941 called "Liberals State Their Program of Bankruptcy," he attacks liberals for having been "sucked into the fold of Rooseveltian capitalism." (In a letter of about the same date, he alleges that Hitler and Roosevelt are doing essentially the same thing—i.e., keeping the machinery of capitalism running by mortgaging the future to provide for the present.)[3] His main targets in the article are the *Nation* and the *New Republic*, which "long ago attached themselves to the chariot of American imperialism and nobody expected them to jump off." These two ostensibly left-wing magazines are berated by Howe for their jingoism and ludicrous calls for national unity. They even dare to criticize the labor movement for selfishness, urging it not to demand wage increases in the midst of war. Liberals, always incapable of struggling for socialism, "are no longer distinct from, they are rather lost in, the pack of journalistic hyenas who screech their super-nationalistic choruses." Even Norman Thomas, of whom the mature Howe would write so reverently as the only great man he had ever met, comes in for severe criticism because he has "fail[ed] to specify the attitude of the Socialist Party toward the political character of the war." (In the 19 January 1942 issue of *Labor Action*, the tireless Shachtman fiercely attacked Thomas for jumping "into the War Camp.") By 1942 Howe's paper began to carry in the upper right hand corner of the front page of each issue the motto: "We Say—Conscript War Industries/Under Workers' Control!"

If the pro-war liberals and radicals were a constant irritant to Howe, the antiwar American fascists and Nazis were a constant embarrassment. In an article of 5 January 1942, Howe warns of the "dangerous" line of the Coughlinites with regard to the war—dangerous because to a large extent it resembles Howe's own. Howe's problem is that Father Charles Coughlin's "rag," the weekly paper *Social Justice* is, like *Labor Action*, also against the war. But it is against the war for the wrong reasons, and does not try to explain to its readers the true cause of the war: "It makes no attempt to tie up the existence of capitalism with the outbreak of war because ... it is pledged to rescue capitalism." *Social Justice*, just like *Labor Action*, attacks war-makers and profiteers, hoping thereby to "entice the people with their false 'radicalism.'" The only reason that the capitalists hold back from supporting Coughlin's fascism is, alleges Howe, that Coughlin is against their precious war. He neglects to mention that one of Coughlin's central themes was the accusation that Jews were responsible for America's entry into World War II.

One of the ironies of Howe's line in *Labor Action* is that, although he is opposed to the war, he occasionally (as in the 19 January 1942 article called "Who Are the Real Enemies of Production?") dons the cloak of patriotism to argue that individual capitalists are slowing down the very production essential for their own imperialist war "because of their wild rush for profits." Socialism could organize production better, but for peace and not for war. Despite the fact that one of the parties to the war called itself a National Socialist regime and another the Union of Soviet Socialist Republics, Howe blithely declares that "in a socialist world, that crowning and most damnable instance of capitalist greed and inefficiency—imperialist war—would be a thing of the past." Always and everywhere—Howe would repeat this line with steam-engine regularity at least through 1946—"socialism is the burning need of the hour." In an article of 26 January, he cites the Truman Report on industrial production as evidence that the auto, rubber, and shipbuilding industries, crucial for the war effort, should be taken over by the workers. The major problem of "dollar-a-year" corporation executives serving in government before returning to private industry to capitalize on their connections is one that can never be solved by Roosevelt but only by "a workers' and farmers' government."

Racial Issues and the Jewish Question

The racial issue (in America, not Europe) also preoccupied young Howe during 1942, as it would throughout his life. In a *Labor Action* article of 2 February sarcastically headed "Democracy Wins the Battle of Sikeston, Missouri," Howe recounts the lynching (i.e., shooting and burning) of a black millworker accused of attacking a white woman. He manages, in a single brief piece, to criticize the *New York Times,* Archibald MacLeish, and Roosevelt himself, for their complicit silence. Roosevelt in particular is mocked for getting so exercised over "the horrors of racial persecution . . . in Germany" while ignoring racist depredations at home.

A follow-up piece on 9 February adds yet another, more surprising and deserving culprit, the Communist *Daily Worker.* Although the lynching is, in Howe's view, "a manifestation of a rotten social system . . . an integral part of Southern capitalist society," the *Daily Worker,* displaying a "hysterical jingoism and pseudo-patriotism . . . second to none in this country," treats it primarily as a blemish on America's reputation and therefore harmful to the war effort. In what must be one of the rare instances where somebody blamed the *Worker* for being too pro-American, Howe accuses the paper of being interested in nothing except the victory of Russia and its Allies, and therefore presenting America as (at the moment) a land of "milk and honey"—apart from the occasional lynching. (The *Daily Worker* would remain a favorite target of Howe's. In an 11 May 1942 attack, he accuses it of being just like "the boss press" in whitewashing monopolists like Standard Oil for their collusion with I. G. Farben and Krupp: the *Worker* will always sacrifice the interests of workers for the sake of "national unity.")

Although Howe makes a special point of advising Negro people that they should no more support America and Britain (both "racist" countries) than Hitler, the recipients of his advice did not seem particularly grateful for it. A few weeks later, a black newspaper called *California Eagle* (eerily foreshadowing Ralph Ellison's insinuation, to be made decades later, that Howe was less American than he) attacked *Labor Action* for "play[ing] Hitler's game" and for being in favor of "letting the Japs win." Howe replied in an irate letter which he took care to publish in *Labor Action* (25 May 1942) in case the *Eagle* ignored it. "We must . . . categorically reject your insinuation that we are in favor of a victory of fascism. . . . We are in favor of the defeat of fascism. We believe, however, that an indispensable prerequisite . . . is the establishment of workers' and farmers' governments in the Allied countries. . . ." In other words, the Trotskyists are in favor of the defeat of fascism after revolutions in the Allied countries have installed the reign of socialism—which by Howe's definition is against war altogether. Not surprisingly, the *California Eagle* was not the only American journal that accused *Labor Action* of helping the other side in the war. Howe was kept extremely busy answering attacks of this sort. On 30 March 1942, he replied to the St. Louis *Star-Times'* allegation that *Labor Action* was pro-Japanese; on April 5 to the *Christian Science Monitor's* "slanderous" accusation that *Labor Action* was taking a neutral attitude toward fascism, Hitlerism, and Japanese imperialism. In fact, writes Howe, the paper is against all these things, but in its own way.

One does not have to read very far in Howe's outpourings of these years to recognize the voice and mind of a fanatically single-minded ideologue, predictably blaming all the world's evils on capitalism and prescribing a universal panacea in "the star of socialism" (18 May 1942). Strong opposition to Stalin and Stalinism was no guarantee of lucid mind and disinterested judgment. On 9 March 1942, for example, Howe reflected upon the recent suicide in Brazil of the exiled Austrian-Jewish writer Stefan Zweig. He describes Zweig as a typical example of the Viennese petty bourgeoisie, a man whose suicide was an admission of his inability to face the reality of total war, and a revelation of the blind alley of the culture he epitomized. If there was anything fine and beautiful in that bourgeois culture, it can in future find expression "only in the cultural renaissance which is the promise of socialism." Nowhere in the article does Howe mention that Zweig was a Jew or that this fact might have played some small role in his exile, despair, and eventual suicide.

Howe and *Labor Action* did, however, deal with the Jewish question in other articles. One unsigned piece of 30 March 1942 asks, in its headline, "What Will the Jews Do About the Struma Murder? / Protest or Play Diplomatic Ostrich?" The article takes a very severe line against the British, who were indirectly responsible for the sinking of the ship *Struma,* carrying 769 Jewish refugees from central Europe to Palestine. After the British refused it entry, the *Struma* sank in the Marmara Sea with the loss of all persons on board except one. *Labor Action* actually recommends a statement on the tragic episode made by a socialist-Zionist group, not because it is Zionist but because the group's socialism and anti-imperialism are similar to *Labor Action's*.

Howe himself deals with the American aspect of the Jewish question in a 5 April 1942 article contentiously entitled "The Saturday Evening Post Slanders the Jewish People." This is a critique of an article by Milton Mayer called "The Case Against the Jew" that had appeared on 28 March in the *Saturday Evening Post.* According to Howe, the article had brought into the open "the subterranean anti-Semitic currents swelling at the base of the American social structure." Mayer, a Jew, had severely criticized Jewish name changers and assimilationists, but had also subscribed to the antisemitic line on "Jewish" exploitation of Negroes, tenants, and shopworkers, and even predicted a postwar outbreak of antisemitism in America.

Howe's reply is not without merit, but reveals as much about himself as about his subject. He declares that most American Jews are working-class or lower-middle-class people, who are entirely uninterested in "assimilating" or changing their names. Having a few years earlier substituted for the "Jewish" Horenstein the Anglo-Saxon pseudonym of Howe, having taken charge of a newspaper which seemed to favor employing Jews who had taken on Anglo-Saxon names, having belonged to Trotskyist cells filled with Jews who had also taken on Anglo-Saxon pseudonyms, Howe brazenly asks, as a rhetorical question, "How many [Jews] could afford to spend $50 to change their names, even if they wanted to?" To judge from Howe and his colleagues, the answer would be: plenty. *Labor Action* was, in fact, by now being edited by an Emanuel Garrett who was really Emanuel Geltman. Those name changes probably had a motive other—and even worse—than assimilation. Despite *Labor Action*'s constant insistence that workingmen, especially socialist workers, were immune to antisemitism, they did not believe what they preached; rather, they assumed that the ordinary workingman would be far more susceptible to ideological appeals from Howe and Garrett and Gates than from Horenstein and Geltman and Glotzer.[4] Nevertheless, one wonders why they neglected to replace "Irving" and "Emanuel" with, say Nigel or Ernest, or why they invariably chose Anglo-Saxon pseudonyms when most of their intended working-class clientele, if not Jewish, was likely to be of eastern and southern European origin.

Howe goes on, more fruitfully, to accuse Mayer of "slander" (a favorite Howe epithet at this time) for identifying Jews with the small group among them who are capitalists. After all, Jews who are capitalists are just like the capitalists of any other religious persuasion. Their badness is that of the capitalist, not of the Jew. However valid this objection, it comes with ill grace and an unconvincing guise of innocent shock from a devotee of Karl Marx, who insistently equated capitalist and Jew. Also doctrinally self-interested is Howe's righteous denial of any such thing as "the Jew," for this would limit the possibilities for class war by ethnic boundaries. "There are rich Jews and poor Jews, Jewish workers and Jewish bosses." Howe also insists, as he would still be doing thirty-four years later in *World of Our Fathers*, that the basic capitalist strength in the United States is not Jewish, indeed that Jews remain far from the centers of commercial and industrial power.

Even worse for Howe than Mayer's description of the existing situation is his solution to the problem. It is deplorable partly because it is religious—urging Jews to return to the radical righteousness of Isaiah so that they may prepare for the suffering ahead by having something worth suffering for—and "vile" because it says that Jews must behave better than anybody else. This "DOUBLE STANDARD" is, says Howe, no more than an inversion of Goebbels. Although Howe's language is hyperbolic, his criticism is just. (Would that he had remembered it decades later when he became active in American Friends of Peace Now, which specialized in making Israel's sovereignty conditional on its acting as a "light unto the nations.") He concludes his rebuttal of Mayer with an all too typical assurance that antisemitism becomes dangerous "only when it is deliberately fostered by capitalism."

The most amazing thing about this article is that Howe invoked it in 1983 to refute Lucy Dawidowicz's allegation, in her *Commentary* essay of June of that year entitled "Indicting American Jews," that "Hardly any group or party along the Marxist spectrum . . . ever gave a passing thought to the fate of the European Jews."[5] Had Dawidowicz taken the trouble to look at some of the *Labor Action* articles Howe listed in his lengthy letter to *Commentary* (September 1983), she might not have mitigated her criticism to grant (however facetiously) that "I should have said: 'Some leftist groups gave a passing thought to the fate of the European Jews.'"[6] Despite Howe's protestations of 1983, a reader wading through his *Labor Action* reports and editorials of 1942, perhaps the most terrible year in Jewish history, in search of some evidence that what was happening to the Jews of Europe mattered very much to him will be sorely disappointed. Such a reader will at first be relieved to come upon an article by him (18 May) entitled "Poison Gas"; but the relief is short-lived. Not only does the article fail to mention the Jews who were then being gassed to death; it assigns blame for the use of poison gas not to Hitler at all, but to Churchill. "All that Churchill could promise the German people was . . . poison gas . . . the super-Versailles treaty to grind them down as they were ground down after the last world war, national dismemberment." Although Hitler had threatened the use of poison gas as far back as September 1, 1939—"Whoever fights with poison will be fought back with poison gas"[7]—Howe not only endorses the Hitlerian practice of projecting his own murderous schemes upon his enemies, he even implicitly endorses the Hitlerian apologia for war by blaming the Versailles treaty for humiliating the poor Germans.[8]

As usual, the terrible actuality of Hitler's war against the Jews and against the peoples of Europe is concealed in a socialist oration about how "we are living through the literal last convulsions of capitalist interminable warfare . . . both sides fight for the retention of their reactionary status quo."

Attacking the Allies

The last *Labor Action* piece signed by Howe in 1942 was "The Second Front Issue in England," which appeared on 29 June. It claims that Churchill stays in power only because of FDR's support for his "pliant puppet." Although Howe never has a kind word to say for Churchill, he is equally dismissive of what he calls the alliance between the imperial isolationist Lord Beaverbrook (British newspaper tycoon and prominent Conservative minister in Churchill's coalition government) and the Stalinists, an alliance which, he claims, now seeks to overthrow the Churchill coalition.

By 6 July 1942, Howe's name disappeared from the masthead, and Geltman (still calling himself Garrett) resumed the editorship of *Labor*

Action. If anybody on the local draft board in the Bronx thought he was doing the country a great service by drafting the twenty-two-year-old antiwar polemicist, he was mistaken. Not long after entering the army, Howe resurfaced in both *Labor Action* and the *New International* as R. Fahan, pursuing the same subjects, the same themes, the same antiwar rhetoric.[9]

One assumes that he took on this new pseudonym not only because he did not wish it to be known that he was working at his old job while he was supposed to be working for the U.S. government, but because the spectacle of a GI opposing the very war he was officially helping to prosecute might have been risky. In retrospect, it may seem surprising that their firm opposition to the war did not lead Howe and his Trotskyist friends to refuse to serve in the army. But to them it was perfectly natural and right to respond to the draft. Howe and Glotzer and Geltman and Irving Panken took the view that you went with your generation, and especially with the working classes who made up most of the draftees. (Indeed, it is surprising that Howe, in his later polemics against the New Left, not only did not contrast their draft dodging with the class solidarity of his own generation of radicals, but drew up, with Michael Harrington, a statement in support of students and others of draft age who refused to serve on grounds of individual conscience.)

In his first piece as Fahan in *Labor Action* (21 September 1942), Howe attacks President Roosevelt—also commander in chief of the armed forces—for bribing Fascist leader Franco to remain neutral for the duration of the war. The so-called "cultural" aid to Franco, he argues, is a foreshadowing of what the real "war aims" of the Allies will prove to be once the war ends: imperialism and support of dictatorships. It was no doubt easier for R. Fahan than for Private Irving Horenstein/Howe to excoriate the allegedly imperialist war aims of the United States.[10]

In 1943 Howe, disguised as Fahan, attacked the Allies from a variety of perspectives and on several fronts in the pages of *Labor Action*. (His last wartime article appeared in October 1943; he did not return to the pages of *Labor Action* until 11 February 1946, usually as Irving Howe.) On 18 January 1943 he wrote about the new "crisis" in India, endorsing the Indians' skepticism about British promises and predicting "complete victory of the Indian struggle for national independence" from British imperialism ("India: Reports Show New Crisis Is Brewing"). On 15 February, in an article called "Youth: Capitalist Society Offers Them What?," he turned his critical eye to the home front to blame the "total" war for corrupting American youth. Trotting out every liberal cliche on the subject of juvenile delinquency, he declares it "social" in origin: hooligans who beat up their teachers, for example, are "the victims of a society which has no place for them other than the battlefield." In

Harlem especially, "the Bigger Thomases are trapped by society into doing things they would never dream of doing if they were given half a chance!" Nor does he fail to add that, of course, the capitalist press exaggerates black crime in any case.

Although Howe was himself serving in the American army at the time, he is unremitting in his condemnation of radical or ex-radical intellectuals who "support the imperialist war." On February 22, 1943, his target was Koestler, the Hungarian-born English writer who had left the Communist party during the Stalin purge trials of the thirties and subsequently gained great influence as a spokesman of the ex-Communist left. Koestler had written an article in the *New York Times Magazine* supporting the war even as he admitted that it was "on the part of the Allies, as well as the Axis . . . nothing more than a conservative struggle for the maintenance of the capitalist status quo." Although Howe fiercely attacks him for his pro-war position, Koestler is offered a drop of pity because he cannot find his way back to the socialist camp ("Koestler: A Pathetic 'Knight' Who Has Lost His Armor").

With what might appear to be a fine evenhandedness, except for the fact that both targets support the Allied cause, Howe would tear into Clare Boothe Luce one week and Stalinism the next. Luce and her like are, he alleges, even worse than FDR because they make it plain that America is "in this war for world domination" ("GLOBALONY: Vital Issues Lie behind Luce 'Humor,'" *Labor Action*, 8 March 1943). The Stalinists have realized a political "methodology" that "differs in no essential respect from fascism and Hitlerism." Those on the left in Europe who point this out, like the Polish-Jewish socialist leaders Ehrlich and Alter, are promptly murdered. As always, Howe takes care to remind readers that "Stalinism is not socialism: it is the very opposite. Stalinism is . . . a workers' prison" ("STALINISM: The Murder Machine Adds Two Victims," *Labor Action*, 22 March 1943).[11]

Blindness of the Antiwar Intellectuals

Although his eight or nine months as managing editor of the four-page weekly might well have been, as Howe later said, one of the happiest periods of his life, reading what he wrote or encouraged others to write in *Labor Action* is not a happy experience. Nor was it for Howe himself when he looked back decades later: "Reading over, a mere thirty-eight years later, what I wrote in *Labor Action*, I blush at the ready-made assurance with which I wrote. . . . " He admitted that the socialist analysis of the war was almost entirely mistaken. "We underestimated the ferocious urge to total domination characterizing Nazism. We were still thinking about Nazism as the last, desperate convulsion of German capitalism, and had not yet recognized that the society created by the Nazis was something qualitatively new in its monstrousness. Nor did we anticipate that even in the 'flabby' bourgeois democracies . . . there would emerge an enormous popular will to resist, a deep, spontaneous conviction that the Nazi regime had to be destroyed at all costs. . . . We were a war behind in our thinking" (MH, 85, 87).

Howe uses "we" advisedly. Mary McCarthy, interviewed by the *Paris Review* in 1963, reflected as follows on her own blindness and that of her intellectual friends in the same period: "At the beginning of the war we [the *Partisan Review* group] were all isolationists, the whole group. Then I think the summer after the fall of France—certainly before Pearl Harbor—Philip Rahv wrote an article in which he said in a measured sentence, 'In a certain sense, this is our war.' The rest of us were deeply shocked by this, because we regarded it as a useless imperialist war. . . . In other words, we reacted to the war rather in the manner as if it had been World War I. This was after Munich, after the so-called 'phony war.'. . . Years later, I realized I really thought Philip had been right, and that the rest of us had been wrong. Of course we didn't know about the concentration camps: the death camps hadn't started at the beginning."[12] But didn't these clever people know, as did most ordinary, nonintellectual folks, about the Nuremberg Laws, and the boycott of Jewish stores, and Kristallnacht? Apparently not.

In retrospect, Howe acknowledged that although the socialists' interpretations of fascism, Nazism, and the Second World War contained "an element of truth," most were "utterly wrong," and all were scholastic and irrelevant. Nevertheless, he says that they maintained that fascism could be defeated only by socialist reconstruction that would infuse fighting energy into the European masses. "In actuality we recognized what our formal 'third camp' position failed to acknowledge adequately: that there was a deep truth in the feelings of most people that Nazi Germany signified a social evil far greater than that of traditional capitalism, and that the one had to be disposed of militarily before the other could be confronted politically. . . . We moved, I suppose, to what Marxists called a position of 'critical support' for the war, though we didn't make this explicit—and I don't want in the least to deny the deep error of not making it explicit" (MH, 88).

This description of his position during the early forties and, indeed, until 1947, is, not to put too fine a point upon it, inaccurate. The insistent demands for socialism that Howe and his colleagues made did not envision a more proficient force to fight fascism, but an international brotherhood of the working class that would make war obsolete. Saying that he and his Trotskyist comrades were not "explicit" in their support for the war is worse than an understatement; it is a prevarication.[13]

In February 1942 Howe published in *New International* a broadside against the *Partisan Review* for failing to unify its editorial board in opposition to the war. Rahv (as noted above) had in the November-December 1941 issue of *Partisan* attacked an article in the previous issue written by two other *PR* editors, Clement Greenberg and Macdonald, which had argued that the war was "reactionary" on both sides and therefore deserved no political support from the workers of America. Rahv committed, in Howe's eyes, the cardinal sin of urging (critical) support of Churchill, Roosevelt, and Stalin in the war. Given this editorial disunity with respect to the war, *Partisan Review,* Howe charges, has betrayed the purposes for which it was founded and retreated into "flaccid and timid equivocation . . . intellectually misleading and dishonest"; in other words, it has taken no editorial line on the war. Having forgotten that "the specific impulse toward its creation and its unique *raison d'etre* were essentially political . . . *PR* had no particular political position on the decisive issue of our time." Contemptuous of the magazine's evasive "sophistry," Howe relentlessly (not to say inquisitorially) presses the question: "For or Against the Imperialist War—that is the issue."

Who needs *Partisan Review* at all, asks Howe, when its literary contents are not superior to those of the *Kenyon Review* or *Virginia Quarterly Review,* and it has nothing to say on the greatest issue of the day? Worse yet, its most recent issue, albeit cluttered with "the insipid, gossipy purrings of Marianne Moore," really does have a discernible political content—and it is entirely pro-war. "There are several letters from England which are uniformly pro-imperialist. One of them, by George Orwell, even makes the assertion that 'to be anti-war in England today is to be pro-Hitler.' And this preposterous statement—fit for the garbage pails of the *New Republic* or *The Nation*—goes unchallenged by the editors!"[14] If this constitutes "implicit" support of the Allied effort against Hitler, one wonders: what did outright *opposition* sound like? In replying on behalf of *Partisan Review* to Howe's attack, Macdonald (who was, remember, one of the *anti*war editors of the journal) justly described Howe's harangue as follows: "Howe preaches the usual sermon about how sinful Rahv is and how unprincipled Greenberg and Macdonald are and how extraordinarily wicked and/or stupid everyone in the world today is . . . except members of the Workers Party" (*New International,* 8 [April 1942]: 90).

Anyone who harbors doubts about whether Howe's opposition to the war against Hitler was anything less than total can lay them to rest quickly by examining his articles in *Labor Action* and *New International* well after the war was over, in 1946–47: they still insist that World War II was nothing other than a repetition of World War I, and that "just as the Second World War was the continuation of the first, so will the third be the continuation of the second" (*Labor Action*, 18 March 1946). They excoriate anyone, especially any liberal or radical, who supported the Allied effort. By the usual standards of intellectuals, who are far less willing to take responsibility for their catastrophic mistakes than industrialists are for the flaws in their products, Howe may be said to come off fairly well in assessing, and trying to tell the truth about, his own past in *A Margin of Hope*.[15]

Nevertheless, reading his youthful work is mystifying as well as distressing. One searches in vain for the qualities of mind and of writing that would make him one of the major figures of twentieth-century American culture. Indeed, Howe himself, when he had occasion in the eighties to look back over this early work, said that he took a mild pleasure in noticing that whatever his foolishness and self-importance in those days, at least he could write a passable sentence.[16] When and why did the transformation of Irving Howe, with respect to the Jews, to Hitler's war against them, and to the Allied war against Hitler, take place?

THREE

Marxism and Modernism
at the *Partisan Review*

---

*It was Camus who said: "The great event of the
twentieth century was the forsaking of the values
of freedom by the revolutionary movements. . . .
Since that moment a certain hope has disappeared
from the world and a solitude has begun for each
and every man." That was how I felt in those
years, though I would not have put it quite so
grandly. . . . (MH, 132)*

Formerly associated with the Communist Party,
Partisan Review *strove from the first against its
drive to equate the interests of literature with those
of factional politics. Our reappearance on an
independent basis signifies our conviction that the
totalitarian trend is inherent in that movement and
can no longer be combatted from within.*

—*"Editorial Statement,"* Partisan Review,
4 (December 1937): 3

Discharge from Army; Unsettling of Socialist Orthodoxy; the Koestler Controversy and the Conflict between Literature and Politics

Early in 1946, a few months after the Japanese surrender, Howe, who had risen to the rank of sergeant while spending most of his time reading, studying (German, among other things), and taking notes on important books, was discharged from the army and boarded a ship from Alaska to Seattle. In the army, he had still officially been Irving Horenstein, but at about this time—so he told an old college friend, Werner Cohn, whom he met in Seattle—he had his name legally changed to Howe, which he had been using since at least 1940 both in Trotskyist circles and as a literary pseudonym. Soon thereafter Howe was back in the Bronx, sharing an apartment with two friends. He saw that the time had finally come to make his way in "the world," and also, of course, to earn a living. He felt that, like many others of his generation in the socialist movement, he was neither a skilled intellectual nor a worker, that (a misgiving that would follow him to the end of his days) he knew a little about everything and not very much about anything. Despite his reluctance—a kind of secular version of the traditional attitude of the Torah scholar who declines to make material use of Torah study as "a spade with which to dig"—to adopt the fatal habit of looking toward literary work as a means of sustenance, he could find no other way of earning his living than by writing (abundantly) for numerous journals. He continued to produce occasional pieces for *New International*, and he rejoined the editorial board of *Labor Action*, of which he had been managing editor before entering the army. He wrote regularly for the weekly, once again under his own name, from the beginning of 1946. Nevertheless, in February he urgently asked Dwight Macdonald to help him find part time work to tide him over; he described himself as a bright young fellow, willing to do editorial work, copywriting, book reviewing, makeup, even—if necessary—physical labor. In July he was offered a job as an organizer for the ILGWU, but turned it down because his work was being warmly received by *Commentary*, which brought him for the first time some money and fame.[1]

He now felt strongly that the time had come to break, not so much with, as out of, the socialist movement. "Grateful as I felt for what the movement had taught—even mistaught—me, it was a crutch I could no longer lean on." He had spent the last fourteen months of army service at Fort Richardson, a post near Anchorage, Alaska. There he acquired the education that had eluded him at City College. In that period, he read regularly and hard. He greatly missed the interchange of opinion and conflict of ideas which he was used to,[2] yet got what benefit he could from reading about "150 solid books, more and better ones than any time before or since." One result of this reading was to unsettle, a little anyway, his socialist orthodoxy. He remained "passionately caught up with politics, but increasingly it became an abstract passion, like a remembered love. . . . " Moreover, his political commitment was qualified by numerous new interests, especially literary ones, that led him to "that taste for complication which is necessarily a threat to the political mind" (MH, 110, 95).

One of the first instances of Howe's new "complication" of mind and how it jarred his relations with his fellow socialists was a fiery dispute of 1946–47 over the work of Arthur Koestler in *New International*. It was probably a crossroads in Howe's intellectual development, for it showed him that narrow-minded dogmatism among revolutionary literary critics was by no means confined to the Stalinists, and it helped him to define his own approach to literary criticism. Beyond this, his contributions to this sectarian fray, though confined to lengthy letters to the editor, are one of the earliest instances of the witty, polemical style, permeated by a lethal irony, that would come to characterize Howe's mature writing, most especially when he came to the defense of the integrity of literature and literary study.

The *New International* had been taken to task for the manner in which it had been reviewing Koestler's work. Neil Weiss, a member of the Workers party, responding to an August 1945 review by Peter Loumos of several books by Koestler, had charged that *New International*'s Marxist reviewers were prone to strike easy attitudes and indulge in "theological tub thumping." Howe, writing in October 1946, calls this criticism "essentially correct."[3] Nevertheless, he suggests that Weiss is mistaken to draw simple political conclusions from Koestler's essays, which are "a kind of *politics-in-metaphor*," a dangerous method in the hands of so skillful a journalist, "the glitter of [whose] metaphors often veils some very shoddy thinking" (251). Howe finds Koestler's comments on the failure of the Second and Third Internationals worthless; and the reason is that Koestler substitutes for analytical rigor in discussing politics an inadequate literary impressionism.

Still—and one can sense the joy Howe derives here from eluding not only his critics but also his allies—the question remains: "Why is Koestler so exciting to read even when we disagree with his every word? Why can he raise us to a pitch of tenseness such as no other contemporary can, except perhaps Silone" (252)? The answer lies not only in his skill but in his unparalleled ability, almost instinctive, "to *touch* the heart of the modern problem. More so than any other contemporary novelist, he writes with the crushing consciousness of being part of the generation of the left which has suffered the victory of fascism, the defeats of the proletariat and above all the triumph of Stalinism." True, Koestler is unable adequately to state the modern problem as a coherent political proposition, but his ability to "touch" it gives him unequalled relevance. Reproaching his colleagues at *New International* and taking the side of their critic Weiss, Howe warns against "the gross error of judging a novel merely by political standards." Let us, he urges, with italicized emphasis, recognize that *"there is more than one universe of discourse in human existence; politics is not the totality of life"* (252).

Howe's letter provoked an angry response from editor Albert Gates (Glotzer), whom Howe facetiously refers to in *his* reply, in July 1947, as "Comrade Gates."[4] The crudity of Gates's attack on Koestler for political heterodoxy, on Howe for "bourgeois" literary criticism, and on literature for existing autonomously at all, seems suddenly to have revealed to Howe the nature of the ideological company he had been keeping. (Gates, as noted earlier, had served as editor of *Labor Action* as well as *New International*.) Gates, like Loumos, whose attack on Koestler had originated the whole debate, cannot, Howe charges, distinguish a novel from a political analysis. He fails to understand that the task of a critic is not to denounce a novelist for the choice of his subject (in this case a Marxist who capitulates to Stalinism), but "to judge how profound a heightening of sensibility is evoked by his novel." A novel cannot be judged as a political program even though it may contain political material; the critic's obligation is not to do polemical battle with an author's political ideas but to evaluate his book as a work of art.

Howe says that he does not object to revolutionary politicians discussing literature. But he does demand that they know something about it and not simply make raids into literature in order to comdemn an author's politics. "For the Marxist method is no substitute for intelligence and knowledge." Marxism can do no more than "help explain" the link between a work of art and its social milieu, but "since it is a theory of historical analysis and social action rather than literary criticism, it contributes little to an *evaluation* of a work of art" (158–59). Earlier in the year, writing as Theodore Dryden in *Politics*, Howe had gone so far as to assert that all Marxist criticism, even the skillful kind, is reductive: "The sociological approach to art . . . almost always—whatever the disclaimers of its practitioners—ends up as a reduction, which is why it so often clarifies things *about* literature or art but so seldom illuminates their specific manifestations."[5]

Howe is scathing in his mockery of Gates's dismissive attitude toward "bourgeois critics" as plodding empiricists without method or aim, unlike the Marxist theoreticians. Bludgeoning his provincial fellow-Trotskyist with all the literary erudition at his command, Howe asks: "*What is Gates talking about?* Which 'bourgeois critics?' Coleridge's *Biographia Literaria* without method or aim? Is Empson's *Seven Types of Ambiguity*? Or Taine's *History of English Literature*? Or Matthew Arnold? Or John Dewey and Edmund Wilson and Parrington and Sainte-Beuve?—all 'bourgeois critics.'" Gates may not be as crude as the Stalinists, says Howe, since he doesn't judge a novel by party interests. But judging it by political content is almost as deplorable. For a work of art cannot be viewed "as a container in which one finds what one already knows in politics . . . it is not essentially a means for the propagation of political or any other ideas." Everything in this dispute leads Howe to the melancholy but also liberating conclusion that "being a socialist revolutionary does not necessarily prevent one from being a cultural philistine" (159).

The Intellectuals' Flight from Politics

If, as this dispute with Gates would seem to indicate, Howe was becoming more and more literary, he nevertheless feared some of the contaminations that often accompanied the literary life and the life of intellectuals in general. It is a tribute to the increasingly complex unity of his mind that, just three months after vindicating the claims of literature as against the imperialism of revolutionary politics, Howe published, again in *New International* (October 1947), a sharp attack on "The Intellectuals' Flight from Politics."[6] In it he expresses fear that the retreat from Marxism of the late thirties is now leading to a flight from politics in general. Reactionary ideas are reappearing among the intellectuals, along with a loss of the spirit of rebelliousness. Most of them are settling down "to the security of the good life," (242) (a typical Howe lament that would survive even his employment by *Time* magazine). Gone is the sensitivity to the world's sufferings that was an admirable trait of the intellectuals fifteen years earlier. "So immersed are they now in *man's* cosmic sufferings that they maintain their silence about the here-and-now sufferings of *men*; so fascinated are they by their private problems that they are indifferent to the social catastrophe which tortures all humanity."

Howe traces four main routes of "flight" from politics: religion, absolutist moralism, psychoanalysis, and existential philosophy.

Although he concedes that the causes of any individual's "conversion" are often complex and puzzling, he is nevertheless smugly condescending toward writers who have turned (or turned back) to religion. "Each age of defeat and dissolution sees similar developments. Where men fail, miracles are needed. . . ." He depicts those who have reverted to religion as having repudiated the whole tradition of modern thought running from the Enlightenment to the twentieth century, and as having rejected rational inquiry, scientific method, and "the conception that man need seek no sanction for his quest for dignity and meaning outside of himself." Although religion may give emotional nourishment and mythic symbols to a Robert Lowell, it is for the most part a "hard crust on the social organism shutting off the breath of freedom, generosity and experimentation" (242).

The central and most representative figure among the fugitives from politics is T. S. Eliot, whose poetry had meant so much to the young Howe. But Eliot has done something worse, really, than flee politics: he has transmuted church values not only into his literary criticism but also into a political scheme. Howe is particularly severe on Eliot for *The Idea of a Christian Society,* not—as would be the case in later (*much* later) years—for its implicitly exclusionary attitude toward Jews but because it argued that "the practice of church politics is a merely transient *aspect* of Christianity while the *idea* of a Christian society is its indestructible *essence."* (Ironically, Howe failed to see that "this bland dismissal of actuality in the name of a formal ideal" of which he accused Eliot was precisely what he himself was perpetually guilty of in writing about the *idea* of socialism. Not only did he consistently declare that Stalinism had nothing to do with socialism; he also—most notably in a *Labor Action* piece of 1 April 1946—insisted that the nationalization program of the British Labor party "has nothing in common with socialism.") But even in the midst of his onslaught against Eliot and his epigones—among whom Howe includes Aldous Huxley, Evelyn Waugh, and W. H. Auden—Howe reminds his socialist readers that Eliot remains a major voice in contemporary poetry, one whose achievement "should warn us against too easy correlations between religiosity and cultural sterility" (243).

A second group of intellectuals, Howe complains, has expressed its sense of impotence before the social problems of the world by turning to an absolute or extra-historical set of moral values. Surprisingly, Howe singles out as chief example of this tendency Macdonald, the Trotskyist for whom he was working at a magazine called—*mirabile dictu*—*Politics*! Macdonald is here "the man who went from Karl Marx to Paul Bunyan" and whose social wisdom consists of telling people to turn the other cheek. (Macdonald may well have remembered this reproach when, about a year later, he took the occasion of a Howe article in *The Progressive* [December 1948] on Walter Reuther to warn his young colleague that "you are in danger of becoming a liblab. . . . [Your] style is full of liblab cottonwool orotundities . . . [and] dreary cliche.")[7] Howe's essay further accuses Macdonald's coconspirator, Paul Goodman, of urging men simply to ignore society, to stop working for wages, and to quit their jobs when they find their work uninteresting.

The third group of apolitical miscreants, the psychoanalytic escapists, is epitomized by Wilhelm Reich, the Austrian-born psychiatrist and biophysicist. Reich, linking political authoritarianism to sexual suppression, has concluded "that before people can become genuine revolutionists they must first restore their orgastic potency." Briefly dropping his mask of puritanical severity, Howe mockingly notes that "the tyro of the bedroom is not necessarily the hero of the barricade . . . and vice versa" (244). Besides, if it is really true that you can't make a truly liberating revolution unless the revolutionaries are first sexually liberated, how did the French, Cromwellian, American, and Russian revolutions come to pass? Ultimately, this theory of Reich's is for Howe a sexual variant of the theory of absolute morality which says that the individual must save himself before he can save society. (The young Howe obviously takes it for granted that the moral individual is the one who wants to make other people good rather than to be good himself.)

The last group of would-be escapees from politics, according to Howe's taxonomy, is the existentialist school. Their essential characteristic, but also their essential error, is to extrapolate the moods of a whole generation from their social matrix "by constructing them into a set of attitudes with which to counter the conditions from which they arose." They forget that their obsessive concern with "anxiety" is the result of specific historic conditions, namely "the *death-politics* of totalitarian society" (245). Existentialism is for Howe "essentially a reflection of a period of social defeat and decay." It purports to cure the conditions from which it arose by applying the baneful results of those conditions. In any case, it suffers from the generic fault of all the fugitives from politics, which is the tendency to tell man what to be, not what to do. (An odd complaint, one might add, from a devotee of modernist literature.)

Howe expects little in the way of recovery from these wayward intellectuals. They are probably lost to the socialist movement, especially if the next depression that Howe confidently predicts (just as, in these years, he was confidently predicting a third world war) bursts upon them. The only hope lies in the younger intellectuals of tomorrow, from whom "a new leftward trend" can be expected. Howe, at age twenty-seven, might consider himself a member of this new cohort, on whom "we can try to build the kind of movement which is sympathetic to the needs and problems of young intellectuals and which by its democratic nature and its lively and undogmatic attitudes to ideas will be able to attract them" (246).

Partisan Review, the New York Intellectuals, and "Cleansed" Marxism

In November 1946 Howe began contributing to *Partisan Review*, "the vibrant center of our intellectual life" (MH, 117). Decades later, he told an interviewer that the first thing people said, when introducing him to an audience in the late 1940s, was "Mr. Howe writes for *Partisan Review*!" "That didn't totally define me," added Howe, "but it was almost sufficient."[8]

Partisan Review was a revival of a defunct Communist journal of the same name. Its opening statement of purpose, published in December 1937 (and reprinted in 1986) declared a double commitment to modernism and to (anti-Stalinist) Marxism. "Marxism in culture, we think, is first of all an instrument of analysis and evaluation; and if . . . it prevails over other disciplines, it does so through the medium of democratic controversy."[9] By implication, the magazine was committing itself to both Eliot and Leon Trotsky, and expressing its belief that the literary avant-garde and the political left could be partners, joining critical consciousness and political conscience in the struggle against bourgeois society. To criticisms that it lacked a definite political program, *PR* replied that "Our program is the program of Marxism, which in general means being for the revolutionary overthrow of capitalist society, for a workers' government, and for international socialism. In contemporary terms it implies the struggle against capitalism in all its modern guises and disguises, including bourgeois democracy, fascism, and reformism (social democracy, Stalinism)" (quoted by Howe in "The Dilemma of *Partisan Review*"). "*Partisan Review*," Howe would later write, "was the first journal in which it was not merely respectable but a matter of pride to print one of Eliot's *Four Quartets* side by side with Marxist criticism."[10] Contributors to the first issue were mainly literary figures with leftist leanings, such as Delmore Schwartz, Edmund Wilson, James T. Farrell, and Lionel Trilling. At least two contributors, Schwartz and the philosopher Sidney Hook, were connected with *The Marxist Quarterly*, of which Hook was an editor.

In his seminal essay on "The New York Intellectuals," published in *Commentary* in October 1968, Howe traced the social roots of the group. With a few exceptions, they came from the immigrant Jewish world, children of workers or petty bourgeois. Really, Howe admitted, "New York intellectuals" meant "the intellectuals of New York who began to appear in the thirties, most of whom were Jewish." Among the prominent Jewish figures in the original group were Sidney Hook, Lionel and Diana Trilling, Meyer Schapiro, Harold Rosenberg, and Clement Greenberg. Coming later were younger Jewish writers like Saul Bellow, Isaac Rosenfeld, Schwartz, Leslie Fiedler, and Howe himself. (Non-Jews in the original group included F. W. Dupee, Mary McCarthy, Macdonald, and Farrell.) They came together at a moment in the development of immigrant Jewish culture when there was a strong drive not only to escape the ghetto but to abandon Jewishness itself. These intellectuals were, according to Howe, the first group of Jewish writers from the immigrant milieu who did not define themselves through a relation (whether nostalgic or hostile) to memories of Jewishness: ". . . Precisely at the point in the thirties when the New York intellectuals began to form themselves into a loose cultural-political tendency, Jewishness as idea and sentiment played no significant role in their expectations . . . " (SW, 241).

Although the New York intellectuals aggressively espoused modernism and Marxism, and—whether they liked it or not—had to be viewed as a phenomenon within Jewish American life, Howe in retrospect saw them as participants in a tripartite ending, an ending which might also turn out to be his own: "The New York writers came at the end of the modernist experience, just as they came at what may yet have to be judged the end of the radical experience, and as they certainly came at the end of the immigrant Jewish experience . . . *they came late.*"[11] Their radicalism especially was already in a state of decay when they adopted it. When *Partisan Review* was conceived in 1936, its central figures—Rahv, William Phillips, Hook—had given up their Stalinism and were desperately casting about for "some cleansed version of Marxism." They did not succeed because "the politics of this century, notably the rise of totalitarianism, called into question Marxist categories" (SW, 243).

What exactly did the *Partisan Review*'s "cleansed version" of Marxism consist of? The editorial statement of purpose in the first issue of the resuscitated journal had made clear that *PR* was breaking with the Communist party and opposing the party's drive to equate literary interests with those of party politics. Howe always maintained that, whatever their other shortcomings, the New York intellectuals achieved something of substantial value in the history of American culture by helping to destroy Stalinism as a force in our intellectual life—though he often neglected to add that many of them were responsible for creating this force in the first place (just as, it might plausibly be argued, their adored hero Trotsky had helped to create the Stalinist monster that destroyed him).

But the magazine's Marxism was also "cleansed" or sanitized in a less admirable way: Marx's ferocious and obscene antisemitism was neither examined nor mentioned (any more than Eliot's was). In *A*

Requiem for Karl Marx (1996), Frank E. Manuel has demonstrated that Marx's deep-seated, unrelenting antisemitism permeated everything that he wrote. Yet somehow the Jews at *Partisan Review* managed to avert their eyes from this little problem. The Jewish convert (at age six) to Lutheranism who referred to Polish Jews as "this filthiest of all races"; who described capitalism as the Talmud written in the language of the Jews, which is to say, haggling; who derided his rival socialist Ferdinand Lassalle as a degenerate "Jewish nigger"[12]—this Marx never appears in the *Partisan Review*. "Cleansing" of a sort, no doubt, but the failure even to mention Marx's consuming antisemitism hardly redounds to the credit or integrity of the Jewish Marxists, including Howe, who would prove so sensitive to the antisemitism of Ezra Pound. If antisemitism was at the center of Pound's poetry, how could its pervasiveness in Marx's social theories be ignored? And yet it was.

The main element of the New York intellectuals' "cleansing" of Marxist socialism in the thirties and early forties, according to Howe, was their insistence upon a *democratic* radicalism (in opposition to Soviet totalitarianism) and their struggle against Stalinism in American intellectual life. They may be said to have taken as their motto the saying of Jean Jaures, the French socialist who insisted that "There is more in common between two parliamentarians one of whom is a socialist, than between two socialists one of whom is a parliamentarian."[13] By the forties and fifties, however, most of the New York intellectuals—"to their serious discredit," in Howe's view—gave up the effort to find a renewed basis for socialism and left it to Howe doggedly to maintain faith in what they saw as the oxymoron called "democratic socialism." He claimed that the writers for *Dissent,* the magazine he founded with Lewis Coser in 1954, not only cut all ties to Bolshevism but "made the indissoluble connection between democracy and socialism a crux of their thought" (SW, 258). (If the connection was really indissoluble, however, why did Howe find it necessary compulsively to affix the label "democratic"? Did this not suggest that socialism was inherently *un*democratic?)

A good instance of *Partisan's* anti-Stalinism in the realm of culture was Howe's own evisceration, in the October 1948 issue, of the Harvard literary critic and revolutionary, F. O. Matthiessen. "The Sentimental Fellow-Traveling of F. O. Matthiessen" is a merciless polemic against the scholar of American literature who would influence a whole generation of teachers of American studies, and was among the few literary intellectuals who in the postwar period continued to be actively engaged in politics. As "the most distinguished literary fellow-traveler in the country," says Howe, "his political writings acquire an uncommon, quite symptomatic interest." After remarking, acidly, on Matthiessen's "slightly sad, slightly ridiculous eagerness to sidle up to 'the people,'" Howe points out the crucial difference between Matthiessen and fellow-travelers of a decade earlier. The latter, naive and idealistic, actually believed Russia was a democracy; Matthiessen knows it is a dictatorial, corrupt, and brutal regime, but does not care. Dictatorship and brutality are for him minor matters in comparison with state ownership of industry, which he views, with sentimental befuddlement, as an expression of "the right of all to share in the common wealth." Howe mercilessly mocks Matthiessen's praise of the Russians for recognizing this "right" as "a priceless instance of how the progressivist mind can entangle itself in a semantic coil." After all, every freshman could tell Matthiessen that this "right" must be recognized by all societies if they are not to be depopulated.[14]

Howe, examining Matthiessen's *From the Heart of Europe,* a statement of his attitude to European Stalinism and to the Henry Wallace movement in America, notes that the professor is ready to acquiesce in the most brutal political behavior so long as it calls itself socialism. In this attitude, he is a loyal follower of Wallace and his supporters, who will not countenance even the mildest criticism of the Russian dictatorship.[15] Those who believe that the study of literature is conducive to humane values, writes Howe, would do well to recognize that Matthiessen is "a man of literary refinement insensitive to half a continent of victims and charmed by the pseudosocialist rhetoric of those who grind these victims; an American intellectual who would join the French Communist party because it is large but not the American Communist party which is small, even though their aims are identical. . . . " Should not literary intellectuals who become violently partisan about matters relating to the structure of poetry pay close attention to a Matthiessen— and there are "thousands of European Matthiessens"—whose supposedly good intentions may one day bring about the downfall not only of himself but of his fellow literary critics? "I could not help thinking," Howe concludes, "that if some of us ever end our days in a 'corrective labor camp' it might well be because of the . . . good intentions of intellectuals like F. O. Matthiessen" (1129). (Twenty years later Howe would express fear of being sent to a labor camp by the Students for a Democratic Society leader Tom Hayden.)

No one can doubt the genuineness of the anti-Stalinism of Howe and his comrades. Indeed, it is so intense and unrelenting that a naive American politician might easily have thought of them as "staunch anti-Communists" if he read only what they wrote of the Soviet Union and its American apologists. But just how much courage was required of Howe and the others at *Partisan Review* to espouse their de-Stalinized version of Marxism is still a matter of dispute. Ruth Wisse has alleged that the image they presented of themselves as embattled dissenters from totalitarian communism was overblown and self-flattering. "It was not," she writes, "to any *political* reality (such as a state) that the group mounted its active opposition, but rather to an ideology that had limited their freedom of expression and creativity. In real terms, *their* polity, the state in which *they* lived, allowed them to put out any magazine they liked. . . . Thus, though it undoubtedly required courage to make a public disavowal of Stalinism in the intellectual climate of the time, the liberty the *Partisan Review* writers championed was a liberty they already enjoyed."[16]

Partisan Review's Modernism

The second element of the *Partisan Review* program for opposing and reversing the values of bourgeois America was modernism. *Partisan Review,* Howe later wrote, "sanctioned the idea—perhaps the most powerful cultural idea of the century—that there existed an all-but-incomparable generation of modern masters who represented for our times the highest reaches of the imagination" (MH, 149). For a succinct definition of the modernist sensibility that the New York intellectuals embraced, we may turn to Howe himself. In a textbook introduction to Dostoyevsky's *Notes from Underground,* Howe enumerated the following characteristics of the distinctively "modern" sensibility that had dominated Western culture since the 1860s: (1) the replacement of religious certainty and moral absolutes by skepticism, doubt, agnosticism, relativism; (2) stress upon estrangement or alienation from prevalent social standards, which are derided as materialistic, bourgeois, hypocritical; (3) a feeling that religion is defunct and man, left spiritually homeless, consumes himself with fruitless introspection; (4) increasing doubt as to the value of rational thought; (5) a feeling that, in the absence of moral certainties, men must create a new order of values in personal relations and in the creation of art and destruction and rebuilding of society; (6) doubt as to the purpose or even value of human life, a doubt often culminating in nihilism, denial of meaning in life, perhaps denial of life itself.[17]

Elsewhere, in more leisurely reflections on modernism (not to be confused with the contemporary), Howe embellished this portrait. Modernism rejects traditional "wisdom" as not transferable; it cultivates what Thomas Mann called "a sympathy for the abyss"; it proposes "the one uniquely modern style of salvation: a salvation by, of, and for the self." Modernism assumes that human nature has changed, if not as recently as December 1910—the date confidently given out by

Virginia Woolf—then probably a few decades earlier. Modernism despairs of human history, yet is committed to constant change. It defines itself by questions rather than answers, for it sees the human lot as inescapably problematic. Because of its nihilism, it is terrified by the prospect of "meaningless and eternal death" (SW, 142, 165).

Howe also defined the formal, literary attributes of modernism. Modernist writers express a new cultural style that reflects the interaction between literary dynamics and historical pressures. They discard the formal procedures and decorums of their Romantic predecessors. They reject the idea of literary tradition as a nuisance or even tyranny. They question not only the Romantic faith in transcendence through individual ego or pantheism but also the belief of some Romantic poets that the poet should be engaged in militant liberalism (SW, 149–50).

The contempt of both right- and left-wing intellectuals for liberal democracy, starting in the nineteenth century and continuing until World War II, was for a political animal like Howe a major impediment to the complete embrace of modernism. Modernist writers, Howe frequently noted with chagrin, have been powerfully attracted to authoritarian political ideologies and regimes. "Yeats and Pound, on the right; Brecht, Malraux, and Gide, on the left: all succumbed to the glamour of ideology and party machines, invariably with painful results. Fruitful as avant-garde intransigence was for literature itself and inescapable as it may have been historically, it did not encourage a rich play of human feelings. On the contrary, *in every important literature except the Yiddish*, the modernist impulse was accompanied by a revulsion against traditional modes of nineteenth-century liberalism and by a repugnance for the commonplace materials of ordinary life . . . " [emphasis added] (SW, 152). Reactionary writers like Pound, Eliot, and Yeats knew little about what fascism really meant and what it would bring; and only Pound supported and was actively involved with fascism once it came to power. In this respect, the left wing of modernism was worse, for many of its writers "continued to defend Stalinism long after its criminal brutality had become obvious" (SW, 225). Despite his own commitment to "commitment," Howe was reluctantly forced to acknowledge that it would have been better for both literature and society if the modernist writers had kept aloof from politics.

But he never fully faced the question of why, if modernism really believed in salvation exclusively "by, of, and for the self," its high priests were incessantly drawn to political projects at all, much less to political projects that aspired to obliterate the self in the interests of the state. Nor could he answer the question of how to relate the assumptions of (mainly) liberal and democratic readers to the authoritarian politics of the high modernists (with the exception of Joyce).[18] Was it just remarkably bad luck that the favorite modernist writers of the *Partisan Review* Marxists espoused political views that were anathema to them, or was there a deeper problem? "We read the late novels of D. H. Lawrence or the cantos of Ezra Pound aware that these are works of enormously gifted writers yet steadily troubled by the outpouring of authoritarian and fascist ideas." And what of Brecht's justification of the Stalin dictatorship? "How are we to respond to all this? The question is crucial in our experience of modernist literature. We may say that doctrine is irrelevant . . . and that would lead us to the impossible position that the commanding thought of a poem need not be seriously considered in forming a judgment of its value. Or we may say that the doctrine, being obnoxious, destroys our pleasure in the poem . . . and that would lead us to the impossible position that our judgment of the work is determined by our opinion concerning the author's ideology. There is . . . no satisfactory solution . . . " (SW, 156).

The T. S. Eliot Problem

For Howe as for many other New York intellectuals in the forties the chief exemplar of modernism was Eliot. "Even in my orthodox Marxist phase," Howe confessed in 1968, "I felt that the central literary expression of the time was a poem by a St. Louis writer called 'The Waste Land'" (SW, 247). Eliot was the supreme "culture hero" (Schwartz's label) for Howe and his friends. "Eliot," he recalled, "wrote poetry that seemed thrilling in its apprehension of the spirit of the time, poetry vibrant with images of alienation, moral dislocation, and historical breakdown. . . . Reading Eliot's poetry a half-century ago I felt so strongly (if not always lucidly) attuned to its inner vibrations that I had little desire to be critical. . . . "[19]

Howe and the other Jews clustered around *Partisan Review* saw (or thought they saw) similarities between Eliot's situation and their own. If he had traveled from provincial St. Louis to cosmopolitan London, they had made a similar journey from Brooklyn or the Bronx to Manhattan. If they were alienated from the Jewish community, he seemed alienated from the entire modern world, if not from the world altogether. Their pride in rootlessness seemed to be mirrored in Eliot's poetry. But all these young Jewish intellectuals deceived themselves.

In fact, of course, Eliot proclaimed himself a proud and very devout Christian. Contrary to the image of modernism that the New York intellectuals had conjured up, Eliot did not feel that religion was defunct or that it had been replaced, among "thinking" people, by agnosticism or atheism, or that nihilism was orthodoxy. On the contrary, Eliot had declared himself unequivocally in favor of a distinctly Christian society. Moreover, as early as 1933, in *After Strange Gods*, he had said that the one group which could not, should not, be included in the "ideal Christian society" was precisely the "modernist" Jews (like Howe and his friends) who were so deeply devoted to his poetry. In the society which this avatar of modernism envisioned in a series of lectures at University of Virginia, "the population should be homogeneous; where two or more cultures exist in the same place they are likely either to be fiercely self-conscious or both to become adulterate. What is still more important is unity of religious background; and reasons of race and religion combine to make any large number of free-thinking Jews undesirable. There must be a proper balance between urban and rural, industrial and agricultural development. And a spirit of excessive tolerance is to be deprecated."[20] Later, in a letter of 1940, Eliot defended himself by saying that the free-thinking European, or "American of European race," retains many of the moral habits and conventions of Christianity, whereas the free-thinking Jew is "much more deracinated" than his Christian counterpart, and "it is this deracination that I think dangerous and tending to irresponsibility" (quoted in "An Exercise in Memory," 30). Eliot, like many cruder modern antisemites, was more perturbed by the free-thinking Jews who had shortened their hair and their coats and their memories—and who adored his poetry—than by traditional, religious Jews.

Although the New York Jewish intellectuals might have pleaded in their defense that Eliot very rarely made straightforward declarations about Jews, they surely knew that his poetry is replete with ugly images of Jews. In "Sweeney Among the Nightingales," "Rachel nee Rabinovitch [which happens to be the actual surname of Sholom Aleichem] / Tears at the grapes with murderous paws." In "Burbank With A Baedeker: Bleistein With A Cigar," Eliot writes that "The rats are underneath the piles. / The jew [sic] is underneath the lot." In "Gerontion," the speaker's "house is a decayed house, / And the jew [sic] squats on the window sill, the owner, / Spawned in some estaminet of Antwerp, / Blistered in Brussels, patched and peeled in London." From all this vileness, as well as the strong possibility that antisemitism was an animating force in Eliot's poetry,[21] Howe and most of his Jewish colleagues averted their eyes at the time. (A partial exception was Schwartz, greatly admired by Howe in the late forties, who became "obsessed with T. S. Eliot's anti-Semitism" to the point of paranoia. Also, Rosenfeld, whom Howe dubbed "our golden boy, more so than Bellow" (MH, 133), impudently translated Eliot's "Love Song of J. Alfred Prufrock" into Yiddish, but only for private consumption.)[22]

Looking back from the perspective of 1991, Howe wondered "why were we so hesitant (as I am convinced we were) to confront the matter of Eliot and anti-Semitism?" Why were they so embarrassed when Jewish community leaders attacked gentile writers who made contemptuous references to Jews or presented them unsympathetically in novels? Was it because they deplored a strained defensiveness and a philistine insensitivity to literature? Or was it because "the young Jewish writers starting to appear in print between the late 1930s and the early 1950s wanted to discard narrow habits of response and to embrace universalist values" ("An Exercise in Memory," 31)? Eager to be rid of the inherited burdens of religious and ethnic ties, aspiring to membership in the republic of letters, they chose to ignore the numerous antisemitic passages in American writing. Opportunism and discomfort over their Jewishness won an easy triumph over self-respect. The division between the aesthetic and the ethical, which ought to have been the special province of writers who aspired to be social critics of literature, eluded them in the very realm—their own Jewishness—where it should have been most readily evident. Very few were able to acknowledge, as Martin Greenberg did in *Commentary*'s 1949 symposium on "The Jewish Writer and the English Literary Tradition" that "'Full participation and integration' in a literary tradition is not one of the Rights of Man; it is not only Shylock and Fagin who debar me from it, but my own consciousness of being a Jew."[23]

In looking back at the New York Jewish intellectuals, one wonders whether they ever really believed in the ultimate integration of modernism and Marxism. One pillar of their declared faith, Marxism, exuded confidence in a method that claimed to have plotted the progressive course of "historical necessity," to be in possession of the truth, to have the capacity to explain every social, political, human phenomenon in accordance with a single set of rational axioms; the other pillar, modernism, embraced agnosticism, uncertainty, tentativeness, questions without answers, sincerity rather than truth, antirationalism, despair of human history. For Howe himself, what may finally have united modernism and Marxism was their shared incapacity to respond adequately to the Jewish debacle. For it was not the T. S. Eliot "problem" of old-fashioned Jew-hatred but, as we shall see, the Ezra Pound affair, deeply entangled with modern antisemitism and memories of the Holocaust, that brought into focus for Howe the conflict between literary modernism and his ethical and political values.

FOUR

The Reconquest of Jewishness

We were living directly after the holocaust of the
European Jews. We might scorn our origins; we
might crush America with discoveries of ardor; we
might change our names. But we knew that but for
an accident of geography we might also now be
bars of soap.[1] At least some of us could not help
feeling that in our earlier claims to have shaken off
all ethnic distinctiveness there had been something
false, something shaming. Our Jewishness might
have no clear religious or national content, it
might be helpless before the criticism of believers;
but Jews we were, like it or not, liked or not. (SW,
264)

Howe versus "Stalinophobia" and Sidney Hook

Although the first piece by Irving Howe to appear in *Partisan Review*
was a review of a collection of Sholom Aleichem stories (translated by
Julius and Frances Butwin) called *The Old Country,* that was not his first
submission to the magazine. Howe first offered himself to Philip Rahv
as a contributor by submitting to him, in 1946, "a slashing attack on
Partisan Review's postwar retreat from Marxism." It was by no means
Howe's first skirmish with the *Partisan Review.* Back in February 1942,
as we have seen, he had in *New International* savaged the magazine for
failing to oppose the "imperialist" war in Europe. Rahv of course re-

jected Howe's latest "slashing attack" on the magazine, archly pointing out to him that as a Marxist he ought to have understood why the journal would not act against its own interests (MH, 117–18). Instead, he invited the aspiring critic to choose a book to review, and Howe, in a piece of symbolic action whose meaning would not fully reveal itself for several years, chose the volume of translations from the Yiddish.[2]

Unfortunately, Howe did not toss the rejected piece into the wastebasket but published it in April 1947, *faute de mieux,* in the very magazine where he had attacked *Partisan* five years earlier, *New International.* "How *Partisan Review* Goes to War: Stalinophobia on the Cultural Front" is a distressing performance, especially in its revelation that, even at this late date, Howe was thoroughly convinced of the correctness of his opposition to the war against Hitler, who happened to be conducting a war against the Jews. Ostensibly an attack on what he calls the "Stalinophobia" of the *Partisan Review,* the article is notable for an almost fanatical fixation on the "wrongness" of those liberals and radicals who had supported the Allied cause eight years earlier.

The editors of *Partisan,* Howe alleges, have allowed their (fully justifed) hatred of Stalinism to impede their political analysis of it. Their complaints about the insufficient firmness of the United States in facing up to Stalinist Russia "are in no essential way different from the complaints which filled the pages of *The Nation, The New Republic* and *PM* . . . about U.S. foreign policy *vis-à-vis* Hitler."[3] Summoning the same arguments that they had once used to hasten "the already inevitable imperialist war between the Allied bloc and Germany"—and Howe quotes the (to him) outrageous declaration from *Partisan*'s summer 1946 editorial that *"Hitler might have been permanently checked had he been firmly opposed at his very first steps toward aggression"* (109) as confirmation of his charges—the *Partisan Review* now accuses the Trotskyists of placing democratic capitalism and Stalinist totalitarianism on the same plane. Howe heatedly repudiates this charge—not without some snide comments about how the *PR* does not show the same verbal precision in political as in literary matters—by insisting that although Stalinism and democratic capitalism are different social systems, "they are both *reactionary* social systems and a choice between reactionary systems would be necessary *only if one abandoned the socialist perspective"* (110). Is it possible, he accusingly asks, that *Partisan Review* has given up hope that the "masses" will overthrow both democratic capitalism and Stalinism?

None of these Trotskyist pieties is particularly surprising. But what is shocking—yet again—is Howe's compulsive return (in 1947!) to the old argument over whether to join the war against Hitler. Indeed, at one point, he asks how it is that Rahv and William Phillips, apparently the editors of *Partisan Review,* allow their editorials to be written by "Freda

Kirchway, Max Lerner and Bruce Bliven—1938 versions, to the very phrase" (111). Exactly when Howe got around to changing his mind about the war it is hard to say. Both Lewis Coser and Dennis Wrong have suggested to me that it was when Howe gave up the hope that the war would be followed by revolutions across Europe of the kind that had followed World War I.

However foolish Howe's "Third Camp" position with respect to the war that had ended two years earlier, there is no reason to question the good faith of his protest against "Stalinophobia." He took arms against what he viewed as its extremes once more in 1949 in a dispute with Sidney Hook (long a *bête noir* of Howe's)[4] occasioned by an incident at the University of Washington in Seattle. Three of its professors had been fired and three placed on probation because of alleged membership in the Communist party. Hook, then a teacher of philosophy at New York University, had, in an article in the *New York Times* of 27 February called "Shall Communists Be Allowed to Teach?," argued that the professors were indeed guilty of violating academic liberty because they belonged to a political party which insists on absolute intellectual discipline of a kind that prevents free and honest functioning in the classroom. Hook maintained that the Communist party laid down and enforced a line "in every area of thought from art to zoology." Although Hook did not favor expulsion of Stalinist teachers in all circumstances, he argued that such expulsions were justified in principle.

Howe wrote two essays in rebuttal of Hook's position, one ("Washington Case Raises Civil Liberties Issue: Should Stalinist Be Permitted to Teach?") in the guise of R. Fahan in *Labor Action* for 14 March 1949, and a more detailed one, under his own name, called "Intellectual Freedom and Stalinists," in *New International* for December 1949. Although Howe does not consider the question of legislation to prevent Stalinists from teaching quite so "open-and-shut as the civil libertarians seem to think," he nevertheless opposes Hook's defense of such legislation. What he finds most distressing in the whole debate, however, is what it reveals about his own comrades, the intellectuals of the anti-Stalinist left: "The truth seems to be that most of these intellectuals are rapidly losing their capacity for political action on any issue but opposition to Stalinism. . . . Only Stalinism rouses their feelings, only Stalinism can jolt them into making an occasional political response. And this is a great danger—not least of all because it is so certain a way of helping Stalinism."[5] Howe felt that he, unlike his old Trotskyist allies, knew how to wage a two-front war, against Stalinism and against what he calls Stalinophobia. (In view of Howe's dispute with Albert Gates over literature and with the "Stalinophobes" over Stalinism, it comes as no surprise to find him telling Dwight Macdonald in August 1948 that he no longer considers himself a Trotskyist in any strict sense of the word.)[6]

One of Howe's main arguments against Hook's position in this debate was that Stalinists are not the only group of teachers whose professional functioning is adversely affected by doctrinal impositions of organizations to which they belong. What of Catholics, he asks; and he does so with some acerbity because Hook, reporting on a European philosophical congress in the March 1949 issue of *Partisan Review*, had expressed pleasurable surprise at how several of the philosophical priests there had, in contrast to the Stalinist intellectuals, "lined up solidly with the democratic forces." Hook's complimentary remarks about these clerical philosophers, "deriving from orders not conspicuous for their defense of philosophical freedom in previous centuries," provoked Howe to a vitriolic response.

Using his old pseudonym of R. Fahan, Howe published in the 28 March issue of *Labor Action* a fierce polemic called "Sidney Hook: His New Friends in the Vatican?" In it he claims to recall overhearing a conversation about four years earlier between Max Shachtman and Hook on the subject of the threat to intellectual liberties represented by the Catholic church; and he notes that at that time Hook had a considerable reputation as an anti-Catholic polemicist. Nevertheless, "Fahan" recalls, Shachtman predicted that, before the end of the decade, Hook would find himself in political partnership with the Catholics. The reason for Shachtman's prediction was—no surprise here—that Hook had abandoned the perspective of socialism for that of capitalism, and was therefore likely to align himself with the one force that could be relied on always to oppose Stalinism: the Catholic church. Fahan proceeds to take Hook's *Partisan Review* report on the philosophical congress as sufficient proof that Shachtman knew whereof he spoke, that indeed Hook is on the verge of going over to the enemy a year earlier than Shachtman had predicted. The venom of Fahan's remarks is a throwback to the Howe of the early forties: "The italicized [by Fahan] phrase 'in previous centuries' is precious. It can only imply that while the Catholic orders were not conspicuous for their defense of freedom for the first 19 centuries of Christendom, something different has been the case for the 20th century. Please specify, Professor Hook, not merely with evidence that Catholics voted for certain resolutions but with evidence of how they behave in the countries where they have either state or educational power." Fahan concludes the article by taunting Hook: "Where are you going, Sidney Hook? Why such haste in fulfilling Shachtman's prediction?"

Within days of the article's appearance, Howe heard from Clement Greenberg of Hook's fury. This arose, he was told, not only from the content of the article but from Howe's use of a pseudonym to (as Hook viewed the matter) evade responsibility. Howe at once wrote two letters to Hook, an explanatory one of 30 March and an apologetic one of 2 April. In the first, he told Hook that he had been using the pseudonym for some time, and this mainly because of the attorney general's unpleasant habit of compiling lists of subversives. As for the article itself, Howe claims that it had tried to make the objective point that Hook's politics led him to an ambiguous relation to the Catholic church, but had not been a personal attack. If the tone had been excessive, Howe regretted that, especially if it would make difficult the personal meeting with Hook to which he had long looked forward. Surely, he proposed, people in the anti-Communist left should be able to preserve civility while disagreeing sharply with each other. In the second letter, written three days later, Howe apologized without qualification: in rereading his *Labor Action* article, he had found its tone nasty and its conclusions far-fetched; this was not the kind of writing he really wanted to do, and he regretted its unpleasant polemical tone.

But Hook was not mollified:

> I should be less than frank with you if I concealed the fact that I regarded your first letter of March 30th as extremely disingenuous. First of all, you have been writing under your own name in *Labor Action* at a date subsequent to the Attorney General's proclivity for compiling lists. Secondly, there is nothing in the subject matter you wrote about that required an anonymity, and thirdly, I cannot believe that you are so devoid of political wisdom as not to know that there are no secrets in politics and that your pseudonym was revealed by your friends immediately after you used it.
>
> I have no objections to your silly criticisms. After all, your press has attacked me as a Fascist and you can hardly improve on that. But it was the double dealing that was so repulsive, and so genuinely Leninist in manner.... It was because you screened yourself behind an anonymity that you dared to invent facts. There was no such conversation as that to which you refer between Shactman [*sic*] and me.... I have never been a Trotskyist nor have any members of the Trotsky organization ever referred to me as one.... I do not know whether it is your politics or your character which makes it constitutionally impossible for you to do elementary justice to people with whom you disagree.

Howe followed up on the very next day (mail service seems to have been better in those days), April 5, with a very lengthy apologia. Starting with the touchy matter of the pseudonym (it is a good thing that Hook, one of the few New York Jewish intellectuals who died with the surname he was born with—though the family's original spelling, in

Moravia, was Huk—did not know that Howe was itself a pseudonym), Howe says that if he had wanted to hide, he could simply have left his piece unsigned. He offers (convincing) substantiating details of the meeting between Shachtman and Hook, argues that Hook was surely in general agreement with the Trotskyist position during the mid-thirties even if not a party member, and reiterates his apology while expressing regret that Hook insists on creating a mental ogre with Howe's name attached to it. This exchange of letters (which continued for another round) was the inauspicious beginning of a tortured, disputatious, but ultimately friendly relationship between Howe and Hook that would continue for four decades. From the perspective of 1997, it is also a curious prefigurement of the recent dispute between Jewish liberals and Jewish neoconservatives over the dangers of the latter's pragmatic political alliance with Catholic and other religious conservatives.[7] The acerbity of the Hook-Howe argument shows just how difficult to attain was the goal of civility, much less unity, among the factions of the anti-Communist left, or between anti-Stalinists and "Stalinophobes." It shows too how much more skilled was Howe than Hook in the rhetoric of concessiveness, even if his actual concessions are hard to specify.[8]

Postwar Inattention to the Jewish Question

Howe has acknowledged that, prior to the Second World War, he had been indifferent to Jewishness and to the Jews. During the 1930s and 1940s he, like Lionel Trilling and Rahv, was primarily interested in the progress of socialism (especially in America), not in the difficulties the Jews were having in Europe and Palestine. Like most of his comrades in the Trotskyist movement, Howe, as we have already seen, had argued strongly against American participation in the war against Hitler, taking the position that this was a war between two imperial and capitalist systems. Although, as we noted previously, he later referred to this position toward the war as a grave error, it is hard to dissent from Midge Decter's judgment that "for a Jew, any Jew, to have proclaimed World War II merely a war between two 'imperialisms' . . . had to have been a significant and haunting act."[9] According to Phillips, Howe "was haunted by the question of why our intellectual community . . . had paid so little attention to the Holocaust in the early 1940s. . . . He asked me why we had written and talked so little about the Holocaust at the time it was taking place." When Howe was working on *A Margin of Hope,* he looked through the old issues of *Labor Action* to see how, or indeed whether, he and his comrades had responded to the Holocaust. He found the experience painful, and concluded that the Trotskyists were only the best of a bad lot of sects, people who had been disabled by their virtues.[10] He told Phillips that this inattention to the destruction of European Jewry was "a serious instance of moral failure on our part" (*A Partisan View,* 123).

But if we look at Howe's writings in the years just after the Second World War when everybody knew about the destruction of European Jewry, we find a similar "inattention." We might take as an instance the 5 August 1946 issue of *Labor Action,* to whose editorial board Howe had now returned. It contains two articles by him, both dealing with the subject of "terror." One concerns "Terrorism in Palestine." It purports to assess "the use of terror by the extreme nationalist wing of the Jewish community," in particular the Irgun attack on British military head-quarters in the King David Hotel. Howe expresses some considerable degree of sympathy and even admiration for these "men of great hero-ism and daring" who risk their lives without flinching.[11] But he shows no sympathy for the specifically Jewish nature of their aspiration, an affirmation that, in spite of the Holocaust, the Jewish people are deter-mined to live. Rather, he scolds them for being "exclusively nationalist" in their struggle, and putting Jewish unity above the great desideratum of working-class unity. What is wanted in Palestine, says Howe, is not a nationalistic union of Jewish workers with Jewish capitalists but a socialistic one of the Jewish and Arab "masses" against British imperi-alism. So much for Holocaust awareness: millions of Jews had recently been murdered because they had no Jewish homeland to which they could flee; yet in 1946 the devout Trotskyist finds Jewish nationalism less compelling than the chimera of socialist universalism. Ten days later Howe boasted to Macdonald (who was no doubt pleased to hear it) that he was quite immune from any Jewish nationalism.[12]

Elsewhere in the same issue of *Labor Action* we find one of the most bizarre articles Howe ever wrote. Called "Terror—The Barbaric Master of Europe," it features a large reproduction of a drawing done by a boy of thirteen who had been in one of Hitler's concentration camps and miraculously survived death. From the drawing, Howe surmises, "we can understand the fate of society under capitalism." Why? Because the boy has numbered the prisoners' huts, thereby reminding us (just how, it is not clear) of the identity of totalitarianism and capitalism. The picture does not call to Howe's mind the fate of the Jews (who go un-mentioned) under Nazism. In fact, without missing a beat, he launches into an attack on Stalinism for now terrorizing ethnic Germans by sending them "back" to Germany.

The Jews of Europe are more visible in Howe's article in *Labor Action* of 26 August which discusses the Jews who are fleeing westward from the antisemitic terror of Poland and Stalinism in general. These homeless, still-persecuted Jews, amounting to about a million people, form the core of the DP problem, according to Howe. "Most of them," he admits, "yearn for Palestine." The article is a peculiar and precarious mix of general sympathy for Jews (including insistence that the doors not only of Palestine but of America and any other country they wish to go to be thrown open to them) and the predictable whine about "the fruit of [Roosevelt and Churchill's] imperialist war and capitalist society."[13]

On October 14, again in *Labor Action*, the tireless Howe returns to the subject of the war's aftermath in a piece entitled "Why Schacht and Von Papen Were Freed at Nuremberg." He notes with pleasure that some Nazi war criminals, such as Hermann Goering, have been sentenced to death. But just what was their crime? He describes them as having "danced on the graves of Europe's workers and [given] to the world the names of Maidoneck [*sic*] and Buchenwald." After offering the predictable explanation of the exoneration of Hjalmar Schacht and Franz Von Papen—that they were spokesmen for those German capitalists who "played ball with Hitler" and so are favored by the Anglo-American imperialists who preside over Nuremberg—Howe says that the proper judges at Nuremberg should have been the German working classes, for they were "the real victims of Nazism." Apparently Howe's socialist zeal still led him to overlook not only the chief intended victims of Hitler's war—the Jews—but also the little problem inherent in his proposal for replacing the judges: namely, that German workers had been among the murderers of the Jews. (It seems odd that Howe should have still embraced the pious fiction that all workers are innocent of racial prejudice when he knew very well that, in Detroit, the Poles and southern whites drawn to the auto industry by Henry Ford were seething with race-hatred, so much so that the United Auto Workers [UAW] found it expedient to invite the antisemite Father Charles Coughlin to speak to the union's first convention in 1936 to attract Polish and Irish workers.)[14]

Even a year later, in September 1947, we find Howe writing about concentration camps in *New International* without saying a word about the Jewish identity of most of their inmates. "The Concentrationary Universe" is mainly a review of *The Other Kingdom*, by David Rousset, the French Trotskyist who had been in Buchenwald for sixteen months. Howe approves Rousset's "explanation" of Nazi atrocities as the logical result of the disintegration of capitalist society but attacks him (somewhat arbitrarily) for his failure to express opposition to Stalinism or to equate the Stalinist and the Nazi camps. "[Rousset] writes of them [Stalinists] as if they were the Communists rather than as a movement in the service of a totalitarian state as vile as that of the Nazis and one which maintains to this day concentration camps as terrible as those of the Nazis."[15] The place of the Jews in the Nazis' "concentrationary universe" goes unmentioned.

And so we are once more driven to ask: just when and why did Howe change his perspective on his own people, on the Jews?

Stirrings of Jewishness

As late as 1945, even while still in uniform, Howe had been actively involved in organizing efforts for the Workers party, especially in Akron and Youngstown, Ohio. But once out of the army, he had begun to move into the bourgeois, philistine, intellectual, and commercial worlds. Such a move, however reluctantly made, meant leaving not only the socialist ambience, but also the confines of the Jewish family.[16] In retrospect, Howe claimed to have sensed that "in essential goodness of soul nothing I might ever find 'out there' was likely to surpass my parents and my comrades. Nothing ever has" (MH, 112).

At the time, however, Howe's conflict with the Jewish world of his father (his mother died late in 1946) appears to have been turbulent, though probably subterranean. This conflict is openly acknowledged in the first piece that Howe published in *Commentary* (August 1946), a review of Isaac Rosenfeld's novel, *Passage from Home*. The hero of the novel is a precocious fifteen-year-old named Bernard who suffers the particular form of alienation that is the heritage of the son of an immigrant Jewish family. Although Howe always admired Rosenfeld's novelistic gifts, he was drawn to this book partly for very personal reasons: "It involves the eternal pattern of conflict between father and son given concreteness in the immigrant Jewish family where that conflict takes on especially sharp form. (I recall with emotion, for it impinges upon my own life . . . a scene at the end of the novel where, after Bernard's return, his father faces him in judgment and confession and begins by a summary symbolic act. . . . "[17]) The father stops before his son's bookcase, looks at the books as symbols of his son and therefore related to himself (he had, after all, paid for them), yet simultaneously alien and hostile, strange and remote, just as his son had become.

In an unusually personal passage for the book review section of *Commentary*, Howe asserts that "nobody who has been brought up in an immigrant Jewish family and experienced the helpless, tragic conflict between the father, who seeks in his son the fulfilment of his own uninformed intellectuality, and the son for whom that very fulfilment becomes the brand of alienation . . . can read this passage without feeling that here is true and acute perception . . . " (191). This confessional outburst gains in poignancy when set alongside Howe's remark, quoted in Chapter One, that "There were no books in our house . . . " ("Range," 270). Nevertheless, Howe subscribes to Rosenfeld's paradigm of the Jewish immigrant workers as "intellectualized" because, as urban, restless, and rootless people, they found sustenance in internalized, intellectualized experiences, which they consequently overvalued. Whatever intellectual aspirations the father may have had were stifled by circumstances, and therefore could be realized only in the favorite son. Yet the more the son did what his father wished, the more distant from him he would grow.

Encouraged by *Commentary* editor Greenberg, who commended him for having shown the ability to be flexible and undogmatic despite his Marxist loyalties, Howe published, two months later (October 1946), a full-fledged essay on the hero of Rosenfeld's novel, now appearing as a nameless abstraction, the type of the "lost, young (Jewish) intellectual," a marginal man, twice alienated. Whereas the reviewer of Rosenfeld's novel was identified by nothing except his name, here *Commentary*'s editors, no doubt after having consulted with the author, describe Howe as a young writer active in radical politics, studying for a master's degree (never conferred, by the way) at Brooklyn College, and contributing to *Tomorrow* and *Politics*. They also add, ironically, that "any implied resemblance between him and the young intellectuals described in this article is, we are assured, quite unwarranted."[18]

But we are not far along in this piece before we understand just the opposite to be the case. Among the things which this new social type on the American Jewish scene may be are: a reviewer of books for obscure magazines; a Yiddishist; a young American Jew whose interests "fall into two main categories: cultural activity or radical politics" (361). This young man has largely lost his sense of Jewishness, and of belonging to a people with a meaningful tradition; but he has also failed to find a place for himself in the American tradition. Hence he has a marginal status and a feeling of estrangement in relation to both American society at large and his own Jewish background. He may think he has detached himself entirely from Jewish life, yet he still shows the "restless, agonizing rootlessness that is the Jew's birthmark" (361). In a formulation as mawkish as it is self-pitying, Howe describes this young intellectual as having inherited only the agony, but not the joy of his people. He has lost the shelter afforded by both family and home. A little like Matthew Arnold's wanderer "between two worlds," this contemporary intellectual finds that *"it is difficult to be a Jew and just as difficult not to be one"* (362).

If Jewishness is no longer part of the life of this abstract figure conjured up by Howe, that is not his fault, not a matter about which to moralize. Whether his family is still observant or has already drifted away from tradition, this fellow is made uneasy by religious observance. But always his feelings are defined in relation to his father. Once upon a time, he watched "the vigor and sweep of his father leading the family in Passover songs . . . "; but now, twenty years later, "he sits on the sidelines while his father watches him out of the corner of his eye, acutely aware of the existence if not the cause of the son's alienation . . . " (363). The family is inevitably the center of his struggle between past and present, for "what is . . . the Jewish world to him but his family?" (363). The story of Rosenfeld's *Passage from Home* is constantly being reenacted. Typically, the father hopes to see his own frustrated intellectual ambition realized in his son, who "shouldn't have to work in a shop." But the father cannot separate intellectual achievement from professional success, whereas the son, a rebel against the standards of bourgeois capitalist society, if not on principle committed to "failure," is at least indifferent to professional success.

If, halfway through this lengthy piece, the reader is still inclined to believe the disclaimer about "any implied resemblance" between Howe and the young intellectual described, he is now prevented from doing so by the author's recourse to personal experience to confirm the rootedness of the father-son conflict in early childhood. Howe recalls (as he would do more than once in subsequent writings decades later) two childhood incidents involving humiliation by the taint of Yiddish. The first came at age five when he knew Yiddish better than English. On his first day of kindergarten, the teacher asked the children to identify certain everyday objects. When she held up a fork, little Irving proudly identified it by its Yiddish name: "*a goopel.*" This brought a gale of laughter from the other children. In consequence, "That afternoon I told my parents that I had made up my mind never to speak Yiddish to them again, though I would not give any reason" (364). The second incident came a few years later, at age eight or nine, when his parents had their grocery store in the West Bronx. Young Irving neglected to come home at supper time from playing baseball at a lot one block from the store, and his father came to call for him, shouting "Oivee!" Shamed at hearing his name "mutilated" (into Yiddish, so to speak) in the presence of amused onlookers, he ran home well ahead of his father "as if to emphasize the existence of a certain distance between us" (364). Writing in 1946, Howe wondered how he would react if his father were again to call him "Oivee" in, say, Washington Square. But writing in 1982, Howe said of the incident involving his "unloved name" (the one he did *not* change) that "half a century later, I still feel shame"—shame, that is, for having been ashamed (MH, 114).

Jewish mothers are not entirely neglected in this portrait of the lost young Jewish intellectual, but they are presented even less favorably than the fathers. The "typical" Jewish mother is depicted as inhibiting the normal urges of her son toward athletic activity (for fear he will be hurt) and instead burdening him with such a variety of "lessons" that he has no time for normal childhood games. Worse, she "constantly hovers over him, developing in him . . . the sense of dependence on her which he is later to find so difficult to overcome." As if this were not stereotype enough, Howe endorses the view of a psychoanalyst that "Jewish women show an overstressed oral-motherly giving toward their children . . . and . . . much solicitude about their food" (365). No wonder that Philip Roth's alter ego Nathan Zuckerman (as we shall see later) was overwhelmed by the "wisdom" of this composition by the young Howe.

Howe himself took a dimmer view of the essay, which he never reprinted. He dismissed it as "badly written" and indulging the then fashionable taste for Jewish self-examination and chatter about "alienation." It is likely that he also felt embarrassed by the assumption that it was always other people who were responsible for the "angst" of the young Jewish intellectual. He was always a victim, even *"a victim of his own complexity of vision"* (366), which deprived him of spontaneity and the capacity for direct action. (If you are going to be miserable, why not identify yourself with Hamlet?) Nevertheless, even in this generally dreary essay Howe hints that he, for one, understands the need to cease contemplating his own navel and turn outward to the world and work: "a writer . . . who cannot lift himself out of the pitfalls and swamps of his own ego can hardly expect to reach the plane of objectivity essential to sustained and valuable work" (366). As for specifically Jewish solutions to the dilemma of the young Jew, however, Howe is decidedly negative. For Zionism, for a return to traditional Judaism, for Jewish education, for a reconstruction of the Jewish community and Jewish culture, he has only a dismissive skepticism.[19]

Strangers in America

Ultimately, Howe concluded, in a passage anticipating his mature view that nothing has worked for Jews in the twentieth century except America, only a renovated American society could solve the problems of the Jewish intellectual and the Jewish people. But how did the young Howe, becoming ever more literary, perceive the America that he now encountered? He had, after all, become a socialist partly as a way of expressing distaste for the peculiarly American Emersonian delusion of self-reliance, in place of which he affirmed a heritage, a Jewish heritage, "of communal affections and responsibilities." For the immigrant Jews, everything revolved around the family, as could be seen in virtually all the significant fiction produced by American Jewish writers. But—as Howe would observe in later years—"where . . . is the family in Emerson, or Thoreau, or Whitman?" On the other hand, pressures of a very different kind drove Howe back toward American literature. Although they were not immigrants or Jews, Whitman and Melville had also, like Howe and his friends, regarded themselves as strangers; and Melville was actually a worker, "perhaps the only authentic proletarian writer this country has ever known."[20]

In the postwar period, aspiring young Jewish writers like Howe felt their connection with traditional Jewish culture to be tenuous. They were aware of a double sense of loss. The immigrant experience itself was but "a thinned-out residue of the complex religious culture that had been built up over the centuries by the East European Jews"; the immigrants wanted to receive the blessings of the New World and yet maintain what Howe called "a moment of identity neither quite European nor quite American." From this mere residue of the old country and the old culture the young Howe, like most of his contemporaries, was estranged. The estrangement was compounded by sheer ignorance of the deeper religious currents of East European Jewish life such as Cabalism and Hasidism. "The truth is that most of the American Jewish writers are painfully ignorant of the Jewish tradition" (481, 490).

Howe's preoccupation in the postwar years with the "stranger" status of American Jews is evident in a lengthy *Commentary* essay of August 1949 called "The Stranger and the Victim: The Two Stereotypes of American Fiction." Novels about American Jews, he writes, are, with few exceptions, based upon stereotyped characterizations; rarely do they show the Jew as an individual. Whether treated with hostility or with sympathy, the Jew is denied the one "right" he needs most: his human uniqueness. Modern American representations of the Jew reflect the two great historical myths that have always dominated fictional characterizations. Either the Jew is Judas, devil, alien (as in Chaucer, Shakespeare, Marlow); or he is the benign and prophetic darling created by such philo-Semites as George Eliot in *Daniel Deronda*. Howe notes, acerbically, that most Jewish writers also order their novels according to these myths: "The stigmatized help perpetuate their own stigma." Whether denunciatory or apologetic, novels tend to assume that Jews are not like other people, not susceptible to the pressures that move other human beings.[21]

The essay proceeds to define the prevalent stereotypes in which the two major myths about the Jews are expressed in modern American fiction. They are: Rags to Riches; The Great Romance; The Father as Patriarch; The Bohemian Rejection; Through Native Eyes; Nothing to Lose but Your Chains; The Artist as Businessman; The Jew as Placard. The writers who come in for Howe's sourest remarks are Samuel Ornitz and Michael Gold ("caricatures . . . all the more malicious in that their creators intend no malice"); Sholem Asch ("combines the melodrama of a Second Avenue tear-jerker with the contrivances of American soap opera"); Ben Hecht ("the first to attack Jewish group existence from a standpoint close to fashionable Bohemian anti-Semitism"); Thomas Wolfe ("never saw individuals; where there lived a person, he saw a 'race'"); Budd Schulberg and Jerome Weidman ("the terrible vicious- ness of their portraits of Jewish businessmen [may] be an index less of their 'self-hatred' as Jews than of their feelings about their own status as artist"); and Arthur Miller ("the Stalinoid mentality") (148, 150, 152, 154).

Only a very few writers earn Howe's praise. Abraham Cahan, in *The Rise of David Levinsky* (1917), expressed an equilibrium that would never come again. He "was in both worlds, the Jewish and the American, and since he believed strongly in their continuity and contiguity he felt no need to apologize for one to the other. His viewpoint was that of a socialist and his cultural medium was Yiddish. . . . " Henry Roth in *Call It Sleep* was the one American Jewish writer who had raised the stereo- type of the Jewish mother, "the most celebrated contemporary heroine of the Oedipal myth," to a genuine characterization. F. Scott Fitzgerald had created in Monroe Stahr, the Jewish film producer who is the hero of *The Last Tycoon* (1941), "one of the few genuinely tragic heroes of American literature." Ernest Hemingway, among all the American writ- ers who approached the Jew as a stranger, had depicted him best in the portrait of Robert Cohn in *The Sun Also Rises* (1926). Though not admi- rable, Cohn is a triumphant characterization because he is "a Jew who is both a Jew and a human being. And once a Jew has been granted truly human status, he has been granted everything." Fainter praise is ac- corded to John Dos Passos, for having—in contrast to the "now happily forgotten 'Marxist' novels"—created a convincing characterization of a Jewish radical (Ben Compton) in *USA* (1937). In the penultimate paragraph of the essay, Howe quickly reels off the names of (mainly) younger writers who have tried, "with some success," to create genu- ine Jewish characters: they are Daniel Fuchs (about whose three novels Howe had published a lengthy essay in *Commentary* a year earlier), Michael Seide, Delmore Schwartz ("the most accomplished"), Ros- enfeld, and Saul Bellow. He concludes the essay, in something of a *non sequitur*, by saying that "the Jew cannot reach full human status in

American literature and life because modern man cannot reach that status." Thus does Howe suddenly make the Jew an extreme version of everyman (148, 149, 152, 153, 156).

What is notable about these early excursions into the Jewish dimensions of American literature is both their (justified) confidence in literary judgment and lack of it in relation to Jewishness itself. Just how great was Howe's unease at these tentative excursions into "Jewishness," mostly carried out in *Commentary*, is indicated by the fact that, at the very time he was writing them, he could complain—but under the pseudonym of Theodore Dryden in Macdonald's *Politics*—that although *Commentary* was a magazine of many virtues, it was "given to the unwarranted attempt to discover a 'Jewish angle' in everything."[22]

The Ezra Pound Controversy

At the same time that the burgeoning literary critic was trying to work out the relation of the Jew as "stranger" both to and within American literature, a far more compelling and morally tangled problem, one which seemed to set Jewish as well as ultimate human values in opposition to literary values, thrust itself upon him. In 1949 the jury for the prestigious Bollingen Award for excellence in poetry, a jury which included such writers as T. S. Eliot, Allen Tate, W. H. Auden, and Robert Lowell, voted to give its coveted prize to Ezra Pound for his *Pisan Cantos*, a work permeated by antisemitic and fascist sentiment and idea. Indeed, insofar as the Cantos had an organizing idea, it was Pound's belief in fascism. Typical of Pound's moral style in the *Cantos* were such lines as "Pétain defended Verdun while Blum/Was defending a bidet" or "the yidd is a stimulant, and the goyim are cattle/in gt/proportion and go to saleable slaughter/with the maximum of docility." Even Tate, who staunchly defended the jury's decision, candidly admitted that "the disagreeable opinions are right in the middle of the poetry."[23]

Pound had also made wartime speeches on Mussolini's radio in Italy in praise of fascism and antisemitism—this at a time when the ideology of antisemitism was being realized in the destruction of European Jewry. In one broadcast (23 April 1942), he had said: "any man who submits to Roosevelt's treason to the public commits a breach of citizen's duty. . . . Had you the sense to eliminate Roosevelt and the Jews . . . at the last election, you would not now be at war." In another (10 May 1942), he declared: "England will certainly have nothing whatever to say about the terms [of the next peace]. Neither . . . will simple-hearted Joe Stalin, not wholly trusted by the kikery which is his master." Yet again (26 May 1942) Pound urged that "every sane act you commit is committed in homage to Mussolini and Hitler. . . . they are your leaders, however much you think you are conducted by Roosevelt or told up by Churchill. You follow Mussolini and Hitler in every constructive act of your government" (CP, 110–11).

In the same year that he received the Bollingen, Pound was tried for treason, but judged to be of "unsound mind" and confined to St. Elizabeth's Hospital, where he would remain for the next twelve years. Some of his defenders argued that since he had been ruled of unsound mind, not much significance should be attached to his wartime broadcasts. The negative implications of this apologia did not, apparently, occur to them. For how could a madman have written as much verse as Pound did without his mental "unsoundness" leaving its marks on the poetry?

The Pound controversy (which would resurface in 1972 when the American Academy of Arts and Sciences rejected a subcommittee's recommendation that Pound be given its Emerson-Thoreau Award) raised questions about the relation between art and morality with a sharpness they could never have had prior to the Holocaust. George Orwell put the matter with characteristic bluntness: "One has the right to expect ordinary decency even of a poet."[24] Wallace Stevens wrote, in a similar vein, to Charles Norman that "I don't consider the fact that [Pound] is a man of genius as an excuse. Surely, such men are subject to the common disciplines. . . . If his poetry is in point, then so are Tokyo Rose's singing and wise-cracking."[25] But there were more subtle questions to be considered. Are terms of aesthetic judgment adequate to assess literary works that carry a heavy ideological freight? Why did many major twentieth-century writers embrace totalitarian ideologies?

In the years following the war, Howe, like many of the group upon whom he would bestow the sobriquet "New York Intellectuals," embraced literary modernism, one of whose tenets was the autonomy of the literary text and aesthetic judgment, a version of Oscar Wilde's famous dictum that "There is no such thing as a moral or an immoral book. Books are well written, or badly written. That is all."[26] But now the Pound controversy brought out the rift between the two wings of modernism: the New York critics (mostly Jews) and the (mostly Southern) New Critics.[27] It also released the feelings of uneasiness that the New York intellectuals had long harbored about the modernist poets and novelists they championed. Above all, it brought literary and moral values into sharp conflict. It was one thing, Howe wrote, to acknowledge Pound as the poet of "the right wing of modernist culture," but "to render him public honor a few years after word of the Holocaust reached us was unbearable." Howe now wondered about the mental processes that had led the judges, all men of the highest literary sensibility, to make their decision in total disregard of the pain it might cause to their Jewish literary colleagues, and indeed to non-Jewish colleagues to whom it might have occurred that the Holocaust was not entirely a "Jewish" concern. "When John Berryman, author of an affecting story, 'The Imaginary Jew,' sent a letter to Meyer Schapiro asking him to support the Bollingen Award, couldn't Berryman imagine the feelings of a real-life Jew?" (MH, 152)

Howe found himself confronted by two different, but intertwined questions. One was the propriety of honoring a fascist and antisemite whose poetic achievement of 1948 was highly esteemed by some discerning poets and critics. The other was the more complicated question of whether or how fascist and especially antisemitic matter can find a home in poetry taken to be great. To the first question Howe proposed the following answer in his contribution to *Partisan Review*'s May 1949 debate on the issue: "To give Pound a literary prize is, willy-nilly, a moral act within the frame of our social world. To honor him is to regard him as a man with whom one can have decent, normal, even affectionately respectful human and intellectual relations; it means to extend a hand of public fraternity to Ezra Pound. Now a hand to help him when he is down, yes. But a hand of honor and congratulations, no. For Pound, by virtue of his public record and utterances, is beyond the bounds of our intellectual life. If the judges felt that he had written the best poetry of 1948, I think they should have publicly said so—but not awarded any prize for the year."[28]

Not to be outdone by *Partisan Review*, *Commentary* ran in October 1949 a symposium on the general subject of "The Jewish Writer and the English Literary Tradition." Howe's contribution stressed the antisemitism of Theodore Dreiser, who also—not coincidentally—was a radical and a member of the Communist party. Seeing a parallel to the far more celebrated Pound case, Howe asks why, "in all the tributes paid Dreiser, has this vicious, not exactly secret, streak of prejudice so seldom been mentioned?" Howe also argues that, although the gross caricatures of Jews in older English literature "make it impossible for one to be totally at ease with its tradition," the antisemitism of a Dreiser is far more reprehensible than that of Chaucer, who was only expressing the point of view universally accepted in the Christian Middle Ages. Howe does not propose any specific action to be taken with respect to literary antisemitism, but insists that one must not allow "notions about the inviolability of literature or the sacredness of art [to] sway us from expressing our spontaneous passionate feelings about those contemporary writers who succumb . . . to anti-Semitism." To refrain from expressing distaste is to fall prey to what Greenberg called "the culture-sickness of this age, the sickness which permits people to excuse or justify the most dreadful behavior and the most vicious ideas in the name of culture."[29]

But how could people who had long affirmed the principle of the autonomy of literature—exactly the principle on which the award to Pound was being justified—people who had defended literature, as Howe himself had done, against the depredations of Stalinist commissars, now repudiate that principle when confronted with poetry expounding the antisemitic ideology that led to the Holocaust? Howe did not arrive at a firm answer to this question. But the quarrel over the Pound award had broad and lasting implications for American letters. It made critics like Howe think more carefully than they had ever done before about their motivating views of literature and history:

> We were forced back to a reconsideration of what could be meant by aesthetic autonomy. We had meant, I think, that a work of literature has distinctive properties and must be perceived and judged according to categories distinctive to its kind. So far . . . so good. Troubles began when we tried to specify the relation between the literary work acknowledged to be autonomous and the external world to which nevertheless it was related—the relation between literature and history. . . . Autonomy, for us, did not signify a severance between moral precepts in criticism and in ordinary experience, though the modes of application must surely be different. . . . We had to conclude, as did Karl Shapiro, the one Bollingen judge to vote against the award, that "the poet's political and moral philosophy ultimately vitiates his poetry and lowers its standard as a literary work." We had to agree, uneasily, with William Barrett that "the category of the esthetic is not the primary one for human life. . . . " And we had to cultivate, increasingly, a wariness regarding the claims of the formalist aesthetic. (MH, 154–55)

A few years later, in the essay "Anti-Semite and Jew," Howe would upbraid his Brandeis colleague Milton Hindus for his inability to see the truth about the French fascist novelist Louis Ferdinand Céline because he overvalued literature and "culture" at the expense of immediate personal and social experience. As a result, Hindus forgot that "A writer who provides us the deepest aesthetic satisfactions can also hold the most repugnant opinions and values. . . . "[30]

The Holocaust and the Reality of Evil

The Pound controversy, ignited in large part by the guilt that critics like Howe were beginning to feel over their indifference to the Holocaust while it was taking place, had wide reverberations, whose full importance would not be recognized, even in Howe's own criticism, until many years later. His tenacity in opposing the Bollingen award to Pound because of the contradiction it revealed between aesthetic standards and central human values may be viewed, though it brought him into collision with numerous literary "conservatives," as, paradoxically, a function of his increasingly conservative view of human nature.

This view was a result, albeit neither direct nor timely, of the Holocaust, which disabused Howe of his liberal assumptions about human nature and turned him, hesitantly and unwillingly, in a different direction. He, like other radicals, had long espoused the malleability of human nature, mainly in order to oppose those conservatives who had argued that the inherent limits of human nature made grandiose proposals for social change implausible and irrelevant. "How small of all that human hearts endure," Dr. Johnson had declared, "that part which laws or kings can cause or cure." If George Orwell could argue in *1984* (1949) and Hannah Arendt in *The Origins of Totalitarianism* (which started to appear in *Partisan Review* in July 1948) that totalitarianism was capable of changing human nature—but for the worse, not the better—then Howe felt it imperative to switch sides in the old liberal-conservative debate. "Now, backs to the wall, we found ourselves stressing the intrinsic recalcitrance of human nature, its ultimate refusal of the transformations exacted through ideology and terror." He even felt forced to reconsider a matter that he had previously dismissed or minimized: namely, "the actuality of 'radical evil,' an evil rooted, incorrigible, irreducible, not to be explained or explained away by social analysis, but part of the very nature of things. A phrase from one of Saul Bellow's novels—'evil is as real as sunshine'—lodged itself deeply in my mind" (MH, 203). Just how deeply is evident from the fact that, decades later, Howe would speak of "that sense of evil which for cultivated people has become a mark of wisdom and source of pride, indeed the very sun of their sunless world."[31]

Howe kept repeating Bellow's sentence to himself as a means of checking "the arrogance of an earlier radicalism acknowledging no limit to its claims." It reminded him of the need to restrain and resist socialist authority, which would be inherently flawed in the same way as capitalist authority. Reluctantly, Howe (still, it is worth recalling, under thirty) was constrained "even to see some wisdom in the conservative idea that politics should not be allowed to engulf the whole of human existence" (MH, 203). Recognition of the incorrigible nature of evil did not lead Howe to adopt the then current literary versions of the distinctly Christian doctrine of "original sin," the political applications of which, as we shall see, he strongly censured.[32] But to this "conservative idea" of the limits of politics we may attribute Howe's regret over the extent to which his polemics against leftist totalitarianism had deprived him of "the composure needed for serious intellectual work. A writer who devotes himself exclusively to politics courts the dangers of dryness, the mental undernourishment of journalism" (MH, 198). It is also likely that the more conservative view of human nature which he adopted in the aftermath of the Holocaust led a few years later to his remarkable sympathy with the "reactionary" school of Southern New Critics, who—paradoxically—had been Howe's sharpest antagonists in the Pound controversy. Once again, he would succumb to that taste for complication which is alien to the political mind.

The Sartre Debate and Jewish Identity

The debate over Pound took place while another, and specifically Jewish, controversy was under way, one which would prove to be a more crucial turning point in Howe's reconquest of Jewishness. Immediately after the downfall of the Nazis, the French existentialist philosopher Jean-Paul Sartre had written a work called *Réflexions sur la question juive* (*Reflections on the Jewish Question*). Sartre took it upon himself to depict the antisemite as a danger to all Frenchmen, to urge gentiles to oppose antisemitism, and to welcome French Jews back into the French nation from which they had been expelled by the Nazis and their ardent French collaborators. The three "characters" of Sartre's work were the vicious and psychopathic antisemite, the "inauthentic" Jew trying (and failing) to disguise himself, and the "authentic" Jew proudly turning against his persecutors. In 1948, Sartre's three essays on antisemitism and the modern Jew were published in English in the April, May, and June issues of *Commentary,* where they became the most widely debated articles that had ever appeared in the magazine. They were to form the larger part of the volume subsequently published by Schocken Books under the title *Anti-Semite and Jew.*

Howe seems to have recognized at once that Sartre's small book, though a deeply flawed and often confused piece of writing, would ignite a debate that would ultimately be useful in raising the level of thought on the whole subject of Jew and antisemite. To the noisy conflict of debate, the collision of half-truths, Howe was always attracted, sensing that it kept his own convictions from becoming complacent and dogmatic. The retort to Sartre which was of most importance to him was the essay by Harold Rosenberg that appeared in *Commentary* (January 1949) under the title "Does the Jew Exist? Sartre's Morality Play about Anti-Semitism."

Although one might have been impressed by Sartre's good inten-

tions when the book appeared in French shortly after the downfall of
the Nazis, writes Rosenberg, an American Jew coming upon it in 1948
cannot but be critical of it. Although Sartre wished to distinguish his
view of the Jews from the liberal one which looks forward to the assimilation (and disappearance) of the Jews into *man*, the distinction does
him no credit. All it amounts to, says Rosenberg, is something worse:
namely, that the Jew should dissolve into a Frenchman. Sartre "does not
say a word about dissolving the French identity. For Sartre it is enough
that *the Jews* should be assimilated."[33] Like the liberals, Sartre antici-
pates that under the blessings of socialism both Jew and antisemite will
disappear; unlike them, he does not anticipate the disappearance of the
Frenchman (or German or Englishman). He also assumes that all Jews
really share his view that their disappearance into the nations in which
they live would come to pass if not prevented by antisemitism.

According to Sartre, the Jew exists only as a reflection: "It is the anti-
Semite who creates the Jew." Both the Jew's inner life and his relations
to other men are the product of the antisemite's glare. The Jew is
nothing in himself; rather he is "one whom other men consider a Jew."
The Jew does not even have a historical identity except the one arising
from antisemitism. Antisemitism, on the other hand, is for Sartre the
unmoved mover, free, autonomous, uncaused. One of Sartre's most
remarkable formulations was that "It is the Christians who have created the Jew." Rosenberg remarks, somewhat mildly given the provocation, that "The opposite is, of course, the case: the Jews created Christianity" (11). Sartre, who saw no objection to basing his generalizations
about Jews entirely upon the Jews of France (and especially those who
had been in concentration camps), cut the Jews off from their history,
blithely taking it for granted that the Jew originated not in Abraham but
in the antisemite. Without saying just when the Jew of former times
ceased to exist, Sartre claimed that the Christian created the Jew by
putting a stop to his assimilation.

Sartre, Rosenberg points out, barely seemed to be aware of the most
elementary facts about Judaism, among them the destiny of the people
Israel to occupy a special land ordained by the deity. He failed therefore
to see the continuity of the modern Jew, even in Paris, with the Jews of
the Hebrew Bible. Sartre defined history in such a way as to deny that
the Jews, though they had persisted for more than three thousand years,
even had one. The Jews, said Sartre, "have no history . . . twenty
centuries of dispersion and political impotence forbids its [the Jewish
community's] having a *historic past.*" The Jews, he maintained, were
bound together solely by the hostility and disdain of the societies that
surrounded them. The very fact that they were unable to resort to arms

to defend themselves but always remained passive is itself reason to deny them a history.

Sartre's thesis, alleging that antisemitism itself creates Jewish consciousness, Jewish peoplehood, and Jewish persistence, can, in its broad outlines, be traced back to Spinoza. Nevertheless, as writers ranging from Arendt to Robert Alter have pointed out, it entirely fails to explain why other peoples in the ancient Near East who suffered misfortunes similar to those of the Jews interpreted them as proof that their national god had failed them and chose to surrender their religious loyalties in order to assimilate into the surrounding cultures. The Jews, also conquered, banished, and persecuted, chose to cling to their religion and national identity in exile. The real question, therefore, should have been not how antisemitism created Jewish consciousness but, on the contrary, what inner compulsion led the Jews, unlike other unfortunate nations, to remain loyal to their god—to God—*despite* persecution.

Rosenberg answers the question by arguing that two thousand years of statelessness and powerlessness did not annul a people's history or its right to survive. Howe was impressed by the way in which Rosenberg demonstrated that the Jews, in Howe's words, "had lived in the narrow spaces of an autonomous history and a self-affirmed tradition" (MH, 255) and had survived because of an inner necessity derived from collective memory. "The Jews," Rosenberg argued, "have shown that without being a race, a nation, or a religion, it is possible for people to remain together in a net of memory and expectation" (13). Rosenberg might have added that (in Simon Rawidowicz's famous formulation) a people dying for thousands of years is a living people.[34]

The English translation of Sartre's book appeared in 1948, the year in which the state of Israel was born (or the year in which, according to a certain Zionist formulation of Sartre's thesis, the Jews returned into history).[35] This fact gives a certain poignancy to the eagerness (in 1949) of Rosenberg (and Howe as well) to confute Sartre's contention that the host nation need only welcome the Jew without reserve and he will make that nation's history his own. However dissatisfied young Jews like Howe and Rosenberg were with Jewish tradition, they did not want to become merely "Americans." Given the Zionist claim that Jewish life was being eroded everywhere in the Diaspora, either by antisemitism or—in postwar France and America—by assimilation (by gentiles who wished not to kill Jews but to marry them), they were eager to assert the possibility of an American Jewish identity. Hence, in replying to Sartre's claim that the Jews "cannot take pride in any collective work that is specifically Jewish," Rosenberg dismissively refers to the momentous events in Palestine by remarking that "If [Sartre] means a Jewish post-office system or a Jewish army, he *was* correct." It is not the newly created state of Israel that gives the lie to Sartre's denial of anything of importance that is specifically Jewish but rather the Jews' creation, over the centuries, of a unique type of human being, the "Jewish intellectual," who springs from the tradition of the *talmid chacham,* the lifelong student. "For two thousand years," Rosenberg retorts, "the main energies of Jewish communities in various parts of the world have gone into the mass production of intellectuals" (14).

Although Howe saw (or rather claimed to have seen when he looked back from the vantage point of 1982) that Rosenberg, like Sartre, failed to weigh the significance of the emerging state of Israel—a powerful declaration of the Jewish people's will to live—he felt that Rosenberg's essay was a turning point in his own development as a Jew. Rosenberg, in his "insistence upon the integrity of the inner history of the Jews, despite the absence of governments, armies, and diplomacies," spoke for him and other "partial Jews," who believed that, without being a race or a nation or a religious community, Jews could nevertheless remain together as a people "in a net of memory and expectation." The latter formulation was strikingly similar, Howe sensed, to that of non-Zionist Yiddishists who celebrated the two thousand years of *galut* as the very opposite of a historical emptiness, indeed as a higher form of Jewish civilization than had existed in the Land of Israel. And yet, in the very moment of identification with Rosenberg's affirmation of a Jewish identity rooted in history rather than religion or homeland, Howe introduced a devil's advocate into the midst of his cherished belief. He conjectured that, had Sartre troubled to reply to Rosenberg, "he could have raised the question of whether the present historical condition of the Jews would long permit them to claim or keep ties with their 'ultimate beginnings.'" There might be a net of memory and expectation, but "what if the net grows increasingly full of holes?" (MH, 257). That is to say, how far could the Jews drift not only from religious observance but from religious literacy without losing their memories and their national (or, according to Howe's view of the matter, international) unity?

The debate provoked by Sartre's book meant, for Howe, that the "Jewish question" could no longer be dismissed by intellectually serious people with jejune Marxist slogans about the inherent disorders of capitalist society (the very slogans, one might add, that Howe had used to blur the distinction between Hitler and the Allies in World War II). "Jewishness" was now at least recognized as a subject of serious inquiry. Howe was forced to admit to himself that his earlier failure to face Jewish problems candidly had made him one of Sartre's "inauthentic"

Jews. Yet already, in 1948, he recognized that he had limited assets with which to embark on the quest for new possibilities. "It is true that Jews who did not believe in Judaism as a traditional faith had serious problems: they were left with a residual 'Jewishness' increasingly hard to specify, a blurred complex of habits, beliefs, and feelings. This 'Jewishness' might have no fixed religious or national content, it might be helpless before the assault of believers. But there it was, that was what we had—and had to live with" (MH, 258). As for the returns to Judaism itself by Rosenberg, Irving Kristol, and others, Howe continued to view them as sickeningly sentimental.[36]

Howe claims that he kept away from the controversies in which rabbis and various Jewish leaders began urging intellectuals to come home, back to the synagogue, back to the Jewish community. He did so in part because he felt that he had almost nothing coherent to say on Jewish themes. "At the time my main intellectual journey, difficult enough, consisted of a break from an earlier orthodox, anti-Stalinist Marxism. Yet I also read the newly 'Jewish' writing of friends like Rosenberg and [Clement] Greenberg with an intensity that suggested they had touched some unresolved personal involvement" (MH, 259–60).

Failure to Respond to State of Israel in 1948

Although Rosenberg's rejoinder to Sartre failed adequately to take account of the significance of the birth of Israel, it did, as noted above, at least imply the possibly ancient origins of the modern state by referring to the Jew's repeated "acts of turning toward the Promised Land in his crises" (12). Howe, by contrast, gave even less serious attention than Rosenberg to an event still more central to Jewish history than the Holocaust: namely, the foundation of the State of Israel. Howe's old nemesis Winston Churchill said in 1947 that the creation of the State of Israel would in time be considered the major historical event of the twentieth century. "The coming into being of a Jewish state . . . is," he declared, "an event in world history to be viewed in the perspective not of a generation or a century, but in the perspective of a thousand, two thousand or even three thousand years."[37] Yet Howe at the time seems not to have viewed it as anything more than an instance of the struggle against British imperialism. In this respect he was not much different from the rest of the New York (Jewish) Intellectuals. One may search the pages of *Partisan Review*, edited by William Phillips and Philip Rahv (born William Litvinsky and Ivan Greenbaum) for the years 1947–49 without finding a single article on the emerging State of Israel—the same *Partisan Review* that neglected to mention Nazism or Hitler between its founding in 1937 and the issue of Summer 1939. There is one article in June 1949 about Jewish problems in the Middle East: it is by H. J. Kaplan and discusses the embarrassments a Jewish tourist may feel while traveling in Egypt. Howe was tremendously pleased with himself for having taken a sharper political jab at *Partisan Review* in the magazine's very own pages than anyone had ever done; but when viewed in retrospect his attack resonates with unintended irony: "In recent months, there has been a spate of attacks on PARTISAN REVIEW, all for the wrong reasons. . . . As one reads these attacks, one cannot help wishing that they were true, that PARTISAN were really as bold, as dissident as its critics make out. . . . " ("Magazine Chronicle," *Partisan Review*, 16 [April 1949]: 425).[38]

No more damning comment on the indifference of the New York Jewish intellectuals to the fate of twentieth-century Jewry is to be found than that of Ruth Wisse, Irving Howe's collaborator on several of his anthologies of Yiddish literature. "Rather than exposing themselves to the storm, the New York intellectuals . . . spent the 1940's as a Jewish *arrière-garde*, sheltered by the conviction that they were serving a higher purpose. Only decades later did some of them suddenly discover the Jewish state, which had meanwhile transformed world politics and culture" ("The New York [Jewish] Intellectuals," 36). She notes too that the studied indifference of the *Partisan Review* crowd was by no means the only possible reaction of American Jewish intellectuals. While *Partisan* was following the twists and turns of Marxism and modernism in 1942, the *Jewish Frontier* became the first American publication to report on the Nazi campaign to destroy the Jews of Europe. Another student of American Jewish letters, Carole Kessner, has compiled an anthology of essays on those she calls *The 'Other' New York Jewish Intellectuals*, writers like Marie Syrkin, Ludwig Lewisohn, Ben Halpern, Charles Reznikoff, and Maurice Samuel. In contrast to Howe, Rahv, and Trilling, intellectuals "who happened to be Jewish," these "proudly affirmative Jews" in the 1930s and 1940s riveted their attention upon (and put their pens at the service of) the embattled Jews of Europe and Palestine. Their now far more famous contemporaries in the world of intellectual Jews were immersed in the fate of socialism in the Soviet Union and America, and of themselves.[39]

Howe, at the very time that he was starting to chastise himself for having opposed American participation in the war against Hitler, for having been far more interested in the progress of socialism than in the troubles of the Jews in the 1930s and 1940s, above all for having paid virtually no attention to the Holocaust while it was taking place, was in danger of becoming guilty of a still more egregious inattentiveness. Here again, an observer inclined to censoriousness might say that Howe's repentance for a thoughtlessness bordering on immorality came rather late. In 1982, he wrote:

> The reconquest of Jewishness . . . had some positive aspects, and one of these was a growth of feeling for the new state of Israel. It didn't happen quickly, or quickly enough; I wasn't one of those who danced in the streets when Ben Gurion made his famous pronouncement that the Jews, like other peoples, now had a state of their own. I did feel an underglow of satisfaction, but my biases kept me from open joy. Old mistakes cling to the mind like pitch to skin. . . . It took some time to realize that being happy about the establishment of Israel—perhaps the most remarkable assertion a martyred people has ever made— didn't necessarily signify a conversion to Zionist ideology. (MH, 276)

Howe is fuzzy about dates when referring to the slow growth of his sympathy for the state of Israel, and it is probable that it reached its full development (which was not much) only at the time of the Six-Day War in 1967. In an interview of 1982, he said: "I would be lying if I said I was tremendously excited by the formation of Israel in 1948. It didn't, at first, touch me very much per se—it got to me only later, when it was in danger. I was for the state; I thought it was okay. But I wasn't so deeply stirred emotionally as I would be in the last fifteen years" ("Range," 286). When he was working on his autobiography in the late seventies, he knew that the subject of Israel would be an awkward one for him to treat. In fact, he asked Albert Glotzer if he could go through the files of *Labor Action* in order to refresh his memory not only, as we have seen, on how these Jewish socialists had responded to the Holocaust but also on what attitude the paper had taken in 1948 to the founding of Israel.[40] He was also torn between embarrassment for "having finally acknowl- edged what it would have been better never to have denied" and retro- active apologias based on the socialist "sensitivity" in 1948 to the al- leged symmetry between Arab and Jewish claims to the Land of Israel (the same socialist sensitivity, the same proclivity to false moral equiva- lence that had proved so catastrophically mistaken in its analysis of World War II as a conflict between two "imperialisms"). Howe also alluded to his over-refined revulsion from the "simple-hearted nation- alist sentiment" that swept over American Jewry in the years after formation of the state. He admitted overreacting, "perhaps because pre- disposed to overreact, against the public image Israel soon acquired— the image of a sunny paradise with stern pioneers on kibbutzim, rows of young trees, and the best hospitals in the world" (MH, 276–77). This remark calls to mind the Yiddish critic Shmuel Niger's bitter observation about the American Jewish literati who in 1944 still repudiated any special responsibility for their fellow Jews being doomed to death in Europe: "We suffer not only from Jews who are too coarse, but also from Jews who are too sensitive."[41]

FIVE

The Fifties: Age of Conformity, Age of Dissent

In the fifties, for better or worse, almost everything
began that would dominate our life in the following
decades. (MH, 246)

Becoming a Literary Critic

In 1948 Irving Howe succumbed to temptation and accepted the offer of
T. S. Matthews to become a book reviewer for *Time Magazine,* the very
center of "money, power, and misuse." As recently as spring of 1947,
using his Theodore Dryden pseudonym, he had contemptuously referred to "the capsulizing, English-twisting, high-speed, omniscient-
reporter approach of *Time.*"[1] Yet he now allowed himself, like Balzac's
Lucien and Dickens's Pip, to be "lured by Satan's finger of gold." Every
one of his Marxist comrades held *Time* in contempt for its chauvinism
and bad English and (this Howe does not mention) the presence of
Whittaker Chambers as a senior writer, "and everyone was right. But I
went" (MH, 122). (Nor was Howe the only distinguished writer who
"went." His literary colleagues at *Time* included Robert Fitzgerald,
James Agee, Nigel Dennis, and Louis Kronenberger.) He took a part-
time job as book reviewer, doing one piece of no more than 800 words a
week for seventy-five dollars, a princely sum at that time. (*Labor Action*
paid its regular writers twenty-five dollars a week if they were single,
forty dollars a week if they were married and had children.) Not having

a Ph.D., Howe rationalized, he could not get a university job; but now he believed his financial troubles would be over. He worked as a *Time* reviewer for about four years, during which time he wrote intently on his own as well, coauthoring (with B. J. Widick) a book on Walter Reuther and the UAW, writing his critical biography of Sherwood Anderson, and starting the essays that would make up *Politics and the Novel.*

Howe's feverish immersion in literary journalism was a means not only of supporting himself—benefits of the GI Bill could not last forever—but of defining his profession as a literary critic and a writer. "Becoming a literary critic seemed fairly easy: it was something one might pick up in a few months. Becoming a writer seemed very hard: it would take several decades." With excessive modesty, Howe later defined the obligations of literary criticism as reading attentively, pencil in hand, charting the patterns of a novel or poem, locating the distinctive nuance or voice of a text. For theories of criticism Howe never had any use, either in the forties or the nineties. "Decidedly more interesting than theories of criticism was the act of writing. I knew that my prose had a certain vigor, but was deficient in nuance, ease, modulations of tone and pace. . . . I played with mixtures of high seriousness and street colloquialism . . . 'New York Baroque'" (MH, 144). He also developed, relatively early in his career, humor, wit, a gift for the occasional lyrical rise, and a nearly perfect balance of emotion and control.

Among the writers Howe chose consciously to imitate were George Orwell, Matthew Arnold, and Edmund Wilson. Orwell embodied an incisiveness of style as well as a conception of criticism as open-ended humanist discourse; and for good measure, of course, he was a socialist, a free-thinking one. Arnold, especially in his classic essay of 1865, "The Function of Criticism at the Present Time," defined for Howe the ideal of "disinterestedness," of a mode of speech and writing free of sect and party, committed above all to seeing the object as in itself it really is, regardless of practical considerations. "Ever since Arnold found that reflecting upon the place of poetry in an industrial society led him to worry about 'a girl named Wragg,' the most valuable critics have often doubled as cultural spokesmen, moral prophets, political insurgents" (MH, 147).

Above all, Howe tried to model himself as critic and intellectual upon the "breadth of interest and lucidity of style" of Edmund Wilson. Wilson, who looked "like a cross between Henry James and W. C. Fields" (MH, 168), first became known to Howe when, as noted earlier, he read Wilson's magisterial *Axel's Castle* (1931), the book which anointed Valéry, Proust, Joyce, Yeats, Eliot, and (even Wilson could blunder) Gertrude Stein as the high priests of the modernist canon. To the mature Howe, Wilson represented an emphasis on literature as a pleasurable activity that was bound up with other disciplines and passions, and a conception of criticism as "a conversation among peers in which exegesis can be little more than a preliminary to the main business of comparing and refining tastes. . . . "[2] Wilson was also profoundly democratic in his eagerness to share every pleasure of literary discovery, and he made discoveries across the whole range of world literature. In Wilson's determined commitment to the *idea* of the man of letters and his insistence upon speaking his own mind, there was for Howe a trace of the heroic. Like Arnold and Orwell, Wilson offered no critical "method" for the young Howe to follow. On the contrary, Howe already believed, and would continue to believe, that "the best prescription for criticism has been given by T. S. Eliot: 'the only method is to be very intelligent.'"[3] Of course, Howe did not emulate Eliot's traditionalism. Looking back over his career as a critic from the perspective of 1984, he would write:

> [Henry] Fielding is unhappy that the world of letters is becoming "a democracy or rather a downright anarchy" and that "the offices of criticism" are being taken over by "a large body of irregulars" admitted into the realm of criticism "without knowing one word of the ancient laws."[4]

Howe was from the outset, and would always remain, an "irregular," but he would soon become an irregular in a most unlikely place, within the walls of academe.

Sherwood Anderson (1951)

It is not easy to fit Howe's first book of literary criticism, his biographical and critical study of the Ohio writer Sherwood Anderson, into an account of his own intellectual development and the complex unity of his writing. Yet the book reveals not only intellectual mastery of Anderson's work but an involved and intimate relationship with it. Howe had read *Winesburg, Ohio* (1919) in his adolescence with the sense of a new world opening to him; and on his last weekend before sailing overseas (to Alaska) with the army, he hitchhiked through Ohio in order to visit Anderson's hometown of Clyde, the model for Winesburg. Howe never claimed that Anderson was more than "a minor writer," yet insisted that he ought to be of special interest to Americans because in his stories he evoked "aspects of our experience—those feelings of loneliness, yearning, and muted love—which lie buried beneath the surface of our culture."[5]

Neither of Howe's dominant interests in 1950—socialism and literary modernism—could explain his deep engagement with Anderson. True, there was a kind of political arc in Anderson's own story: he had moved from the literary Babbittry of his formative years—churning out advertising copy, singing the praises of "business," operating a paint factory, writing explicitly antisocialist fiction—to political radicalism in the 1930s. But Howe was far too discriminating a radical to be impressed by Anderson's belated conversion to communism, especially in its mindless Stalinist form. He refers to the Amsterdam Peace Congress to which Anderson went as an American delegate in 1932 as "one of the innumerable gatherings of the innocent arranged by the not-so-innocent" (SA, 220); and he dismisses Anderson's radicalism as lacking in responsibility, dignity, and mind—an instance of the intellectual laziness that permeated his life. Thus the radicalism of Anderson in the 1930s did almost nothing to redeem him of the political taint that, in Howe's view, had attached to him since *Marching Men* (1917), in which his populism showed a distinctly totalitarian bias, a programmatic mindlessness, and a whiff of antisemitism. That early novel "represents the price Anderson was to pay, and which he never quite reckoned, for his failure to assume the responsibilities of the mind; a price he would pay again and again" (SA, 88). Howe would credit Anderson's radicalism with but one virtue: "his never-diminished feeling for the Southern workers" (SA, 224).

Far more likely than political motives for Howe's attraction to Anderson are geographical and aesthetic ones. For Howe to write of Anderson, of the Midwest, of the "Chicago Renaissance" (which receives detailed attention in the book) was to declare his independence (temporary, at least) from the insufferable provincialism of the New York intellectuals and to embrace "America." To some extent he had already done this in 1945 as a Workers party organizer in Ohio and in 1949 with the book on the UAW, which devotes a great deal of attention to life in the factory town of Detroit. To now tell the story of Anderson's effort to reverse, through honesty and creativity, the abuse of language induced by advertising was to recount an American's struggle to raise himself "from the mire of inarticulation [including struggles with syntax and spelling] to the ambiance of art" (SA, 80); it was, or so it seemed, to engage sympathetically, yet again, the plebeian struggle of ordinary Americans.

Nevertheless, the core of the book is Howe's fine analysis of Anderson's oral narrative method and of the unifying strand of action in such works as *Winesburg, Ohio*. Howe reads this collection of stories as a fable of American estrangement, centered upon the loss of love. Returning to the theme he had stressed in his 1946 discussion of Isaac

Rosenfeld, he finds *Winesburg* permeated by instances of people's alienation from the sources of emotional sustenance: from their natural surroundings; from the fertility of their farms; from the community which, according to American myth, should bind men in fraternity but now proves external to their lives; from their work, now a mere burden; most of all, from each other. Here we have a gentile American version of what in the earlier essay had seemed a Jewish affliction. The unifying strand of action in about half the book's stories is the effort of what Anderson calls "grotesques" to overcome their alienation by establishing some intimate relation with George Willard, a young reporter.

For Howe, *Winesburg* was both an aesthetic and a moral triumph. It complemented the underlying sense of oral narrative with "the stiffened superimposed beat of a prose almost Biblical in its regularity" (SA, 108). But what ultimately made this prose effective was something notably absent from the modernist writers whom Howe would so often elucidate and celebrate: a tone of tender inclusiveness, that register of love to which he would also respond in the Yiddish writers. "The ultimate unity of the book is a unity of feeling, a sureness of warmth. . . . Many American writers have taken as their theme the loss of love in the modern world, but few, if any at all, have so thoroughly realized it in the accents of love" (SA, 109). To such generosity by a writer toward his own fictional creations, Howe would always respond with warmth.

Jews in English Departments

All three of Howe's models of literary criticism—Arnold, Orwell, and Wilson—had worked outside the academy (although Arnold did the occasional series of lectures in the honorary position of professor of poetry at Oxford). His most immediate exemplar, Wilson, even seemed to Howe to epitomize virtues that in America could flourish *only* outside the academy. Yet despite the fact that Howe and most of his friends tended to view the academic world with contempt and suspicion, the pressure of circumstances now forced him to beg admittance to it. Indeed, he later likened the intensity of his "own" writing during the four years he wrote for *Time* to the diligence of a young professor trying to write his way out of a provincial university into more comfortable and prestigious academic quarters. He convinced himself that the time for his serious writing, which reviewing books for *Time* had afforded him, enabled him to break loose not only from the magazine but from all the capitalist, bourgeois wickedness it symbolized. In any case, he had decided by 1952 to escape from *Time,* and to escape in the direction of a university. He got his first taste of college teaching at the University of

Washington in Seattle, where he taught in the summer session in 1952 and was warmly welcomed by his ideological opponents, the New Critics Robert Heilman and Arnold Stein. The following summer he taught at the Indiana School of Letters in Bloomington. He was ready to enter the academic world.

For a Jew, especially one aspiring to a post in an English department, this was by no means a simple matter at that time. In his 1949 dispute with Sidney Hook over the dismissal of University of Washington professors linked to the Communist party, Howe had remarked that "if the mere holding of anti-Semitic opinions were enough to warrant the expulsion of teachers, there would have to be a considerable cleansing of the American universities" ("Intellectual Freedom and Stalinists," 236). Yet the situation had improved considerably in the half century that had elapsed since Ludwig Lewisohn, a Berlin-born Jew who had made himself into a Southern Christian gentleman in Charleston, South Carolina, had to leave Columbia in 1903 without his doctorate because he was a Jew. Like many Jewish students after him, Lewisohn was told that he should not (or could not) proceed in his studies because the prejudice against hiring Jews in English departments was insuperable. When he eventually did finish his graduate work at Columbia, his own professor sent him a note remarking on "how terribly hard it is for a man of Jewish birth to get a good position."[6] Reflecting on his rejection years later, Lewisohn wrote in 1922:

> There are a number of Jewish scholars in American colleges and universities. . . . The older men got in because nativistic anti-Semitism was not nearly as strong twenty-five years ago as it is to-day. . . . In regard to the younger men . . . they were appointed through personal friendship, family or financial prestige or some other abnormal relenting of the iron prejudice which is the rule. But that prejudice has not . . . relented in a single instance in regard to the teaching of English. (Klingenstein, 98)

The study of English, after all, was far more bound up with the particularities of culture than was the study of philosophy, for English literature expressed the spirit of Western Christianity. As Tennyson wrote in "The Hesperides," "the treasure / of the wisdom of the West" needed to be guarded well and warily "lest one from the East come and take it away."

In the hands of Lewisohn, the Victorian ticket of admission was not honored. It was left to another Victorianist (like Lewisohn the author of a book on Matthew Arnold), Lionel Trilling, to conquer Morningside Heights without paying the price of complete intellectual assimilation. Trilling, the son of a mother who had been born and educated in the East

End of London, discovered that even in 1936 the American academic world was not ready to grant Jews full and unequivocal citizenship. In that year, four years after he had been appointed an instructor of English at Columbia College, Trilling was dropped by the department because "as a Freudian, a Marxist and a Jew" he was not, and could not be, "happy" there. Diana Trilling has written that the documentation produced by the department to justify its decision—that is, *their* unhappiness with Trilling—"revealed that Jews were people who made the Columbia faculty uncomfortable, Freudians were people who made the Columbia faculty uncomfortable, Marxists were people who made the Columbia faculty uncomfortable. It is in this sense, circumscribed but charged enough, that in dismissing Lionel, Columbia can be accused of anti-Semitism. . . . "[7]

The story, as everyone knows, ended "happily." Trilling's protest of the department's decision resulted in his retention until the time he completed his dissertation, the magisterial book on Arnold that so impressed Nicholas Murray Butler, Columbia's president, that he personally appointed Trilling an assistant professor of English, the first Jew to become a member of that department's faculty. Neither did Butler fail to draw the apparent moral of the story for the benefit of the chairman of the English department by remarking, in his presence, that at Columbia, unlike the University of Berlin (which had recently refused to receive a visiting Jewish professor from Columbia), "we recognize merit, not race" (46).

Many such stories have by now been told of young Jews who in the 1920s, 1930s, and 1940s were discouraged from entering graduate English studies or excluded from employment after they had completed them. In *World of Our Fathers* Howe observed that for American Jews one of the most "treacherous" paths to professional advancement was the teaching of English literature. "Jews, it was often suggested, could not register the finer shadings of the Anglo-Saxon spirit as it shone through the poetry of Chaucer, Shakespeare, and Milton. (Christians did not seem to be similarly incapacitated with regard to the Old Testament.)"[8] *Partisan Review,* after all, represented something new in American cultural history partly because its intellectual core refused to acknowledge the primacy of this Anglo-Saxon spirit and the authority of Christian tradition.[9]

Trilling, who by the 1950s was as much at home at Columbia as in the pages of *Partisan Review,* must have represented for Howe both the difficulties and the dangers of acceptance in the English departments of the more prestigious universities. Most of the New York writers expressed derision for the gentility of the Anglo-Saxon English department ambience, a gentility that made them squirm. But also "we repaid with contempt, as well as a rather ungenerous suspicion toward those of our own, like Trilling, who had mastered the art of manners . . . " (MH, 139). The uncomfortable paradox of Jewish English professors like Trilling may be epitomized by an incident of 1950, the very time when Howe had begun to think about entering the academy. The year 1950 was the centenary of Wordsworth's death, which was commemorated at Princeton University. Trilling, one of the invited lecturers, chose to speak on "Wordsworth and the Rabbis." Howe was at the time living (in a small house financed by a GI loan) in Princeton, where his wife Thalia taught Greek and Latin at a private school. He was in the audience.

Whatever it may have become since, the English department of Princeton was not in 1950 famous for its receptivity to Jewish persons or Jewish intellectual interests. Yet throughout the lecture, Trilling—one of the most civilized, indeed courtly men in the academic profession— went out of his way to flaunt his Jewish background and identity, as if it had become a point of honor for a Jew in whom, by his own admission, Judaism had shrunk to a very small status, to be defiantly Jewish among the gentiles, and to be Jewish in dealing with one of the great poets of a pervasively Christian literature. At the time Howe was not impressed by such gestures of defiance.[10] He objected, right after the lecture, to the strain of passivity and quietism that Trilling claimed to discover in both Wordsworth and the rabbis, and later referred to the lecture as highly strained in the way it dragged Jews into the midst of the Wordsworth ambience. Once, referring to the lecture, Howe said to me that "Lionel had a habit of being Jewish among the gentiles and gentile among the Jews." An instance of the latter pose, and a cause of Howe's lingering resentment, was Trilling's sniffiness toward Yiddish: When Trilling heard that Howe was (by 1953) working on Yiddish literature, he told him that he was altogether suspicious of Yiddish literature. This deeply hurt and angered Howe, who never forgave Trilling for it, especially since he knew how ignorant Trilling was of the whole subject. Nevertheless, they became friends.[11]

In 1950, the year that Howe first became acquainted with both Diana and Lionel Trilling, Trilling published his great collection of essays entitled *The Liberal Imagination,* which went a long way toward establishing him as what Howe called "the most subtle and perhaps most influential mind in the culture of the fifties" (MH, 229). Although Trilling was writing essays in literary criticism rather than politics, his ruling intention was to save liberalism from its own smugness and the flabbiness to which unchallenged dogma is prone. "It has," wrote Trilling, "for some time seemed to me that a criticism which has at heart the interests of liberalism might find its most useful work not in confirming liberalism in its sense of general rightness but rather in putting under some degree of pressure the liberal ideas and assumptions of the present time."[12] Although Howe admired the attempt to save liberalism from deteriorating into inert dogma, he was nevertheless disturbed by what he felt was Trilling's tendency to supply American intellectuals with an apologia for their increasingly accommodating mood. He also was troubled by the extent to which Trilling tried to judge politics by literary and aesthetic standards. By so doing he conferred a mantle of nobility upon a less than courageous tendency to evade action in the public, political world. Trilling's critique of the liberal imagination, Howe complained, "eased a turning away from all politics, whether liberal, radical, or conservative" (MH, 231).

And yet, if Howe was troubled by this element in Trilling's thought and sensibility, he was also strongly drawn to it. His work is full of Trillingesque references to "that taste for complication which is necessarily a threat to the political mind" (MH, 95). He might bridle at the notion that the literary life was nobler than the political, which he always considered an essential part of his being, and yet he knew it had a kernel of truth too, one which helped to explain his inner divisions. Emanuel Geltman recalled that when Howe was writing his book on Faulkner, which came out in 1952, "he complained—why am I writing this when I should be writing about politics? By the same token, when he wrote political books, he chided himself because he should be writing about literature" ("Remembering Irving Howe," 530). Howe himself acknowledged that "Perhaps also a part of me was drawn to the claims for 'the relaxed will' that Trilling spoke about. Had not, after all, so entirely political a man as Trotsky once remarked that for him the world of letters was always 'a world more attractive'" (MH, 232)? This phrase would supply the title for Howe's 1963 volume of essays on literature and politics; and indeed it expressed his lingering regret that although literature was indeed a world more attractive, it was a world to which he could not, and must not, yield totally.

Brandeis University, 1953–61

Unlike Trilling, Howe was to find his first academic home in an atmosphere far different from both Columbia and Princeton (where he had lived since 1948). After a comic misadventure in an interview at Sarah Lawrence College, Howe was invited to be interviewed at the new, putatively Jewish Brandeis University, founded in 1948. Brandeis, in its early days, was sufficiently adventurous to consider appointing bright and literate people who did not have doctoral degrees, or displaced Europeans with credentials not usually honored in America. One of its original faculty was none other than the aforementioned Lewisohn, who was (along with the Jewish historian Simon Rawidowicz and the French scholar Joseph Cheskis) among Howe's interviewers when he visited Waltham, Massachusetts. The interview seemed to be going badly until Howe mentioned that he was collaborating with the Yiddish poet Eliezer Greenberg on an anthology of Yiddish stories in English translation. "Faces broke into smiles. Rawidowicz began 'correcting' my overestimation of Peretz; everyone started talking Yiddish. I relaxed happily, sure I was going to get the job. Is there another professor of English in the country who can say that his first job interview was conducted in Yiddish?" (MH, 184).

The Brandeis faculty, which Howe joined in 1953, was in its early years broadly divided into two kinds of Jews. On the one side were intellectuals like Howe and Philip Rahv, who happened to be Jewish, and on the other side were people like Marie Syrkin, Lewisohn, and Ben Halpern, intellectuals deeply immersed in Jewish affairs, particularly the Zionist movement. Some of the tensions between them are evident from the initial resistance by Howe to the appointment of Syrkin as a professor of English literature on the grounds that she was more a journalist than a scholar. (Later Howe became her friend and admirer, but probably opposed her tenure at Brandeis.) Rahv, nastier as usual, charged (absurdly, as anyone who knew her would recognize) that Syrkin was not an intellectual, and that she thought *The Great Gatsby* was merely a book about bootleggers (Kessner, 66). There is little evidence that the physical proximity of these two groups led to fruitful interchange, unless we count such matters as Howe—in later years—inducing Syrkin to sign his "Peace Now" petitions.

If one may judge from Brandeis President Abram Sachar's recollections of Howe, he caused the Brandeis administration some discomfort, even though it was glad to have him. "A major coup," writes Sachar, "was achieved in 1953 with the arrival of Irving Howe. . . . When he disagreed—and he disagreed more often than not—his sharpness rarely cut superficially. It left deep gashes. . . . He reserved tolerance and patience only for his students, and then only for the ones who demonstrated genuine promise."[13] Howe found the experience of teaching at Brandeis "exhilarating and terrifying." The students were more important to the school's intellectual vitality than the faculty. They were what would prove to be the last, or next to the last, bumper crop of the immigrant Jewish culture. Classrooms were scenes of lively debate between teachers and students, and between students and students. Howe found that he rarely lectured, but did better to plunge directly into the hardest and darkest questions about literary classics. Reportedly intimidating to many students, Howe was himself sometimes (if only secretly) intimidated. "What in the name of heaven could I teach them? I had still to learn that the best teaching consists in letting such young people move ahead on their own . . . " (MH, 186).

But there was more than this to Howe's pedagogy. It has been best described by John Hollander, who was Howe's student at the Indiana School of Letters in the summer of 1953, just before he took up his post at Brandeis. "What he was always, implicitly but pointedly, reminding his students is that the primal scene of the teaching of literature . . . does *not* consist in imparting information (as in those days), or installing correct sentiments (as, alas, more and more today). . . . Rather, it involves a reader, overflowing with apprehension of some moment in a book, asking someone else to 'Listen to this!' and then reading it aloud. And then . . . being prepared to point out just how, and why the passage is either marvelous or dreadful. . . . The voice that called me to listen, and then to listen why . . . as student, reader and colleague . . . was always his."[14]

Few of Howe's students at Brandeis forgot his courses. One, Jeremy Larner, recalled Howe at age thirty-four: "Some of us judged Irving harshly for his sharp Ivy League clothes and mocked his habit of fondly curling and re-curling a forelock of hair with his index finger. He had little time for fools and delighted in drawing some piece of cant from a too-assured pupil. . . . He didn't linger to smooth hurts, but unlike a few others, he was too high-spirited to teach by humiliation." Larner also remembered that the intensely political English professor "demonstrated line by line, if need be, that a writer's politics, however important to understand, could not finally dictate the worth or power of his story" ("Remembering Irving Howe," 540). In retrospect, Howe feared that he might have been too cutting in making some students aware of their deficiencies without supplying the means of overcoming them. One woman, who, despite her "fear," took his full-year course on eighteenth- and nineteenth-century English literature, found that "he was demanding and critical and sometimes his comments hurt. . . . Professor Howe disliked pretension and always insisted on concise, direct language. Reading aloud one day from one of our papers, he stopped to ask: 'Why would anyone want to "span a hiatus" when it is so much easier to "jump a gap"?'" Nevertheless, this student (who went from C's and B–'s in her first semester to B+'s and A's in the second), remained forever grateful to Howe for "develop[ing] insights that I'd previously thought were impossible in someone whose reading preferences were non-fiction."[15]

A still livelier ambience for Howe at Brandeis was the student-sponsored debate or public meeting. Here students could watch the faculty and especially the variegated species of "radicals, semiradicals, pseudoradicals, and ex-radicals" (MH, 187) act out the conflicts (both American and European) of an older generation, and—equally important—indulge the intellectual's habit of expressing ideas without having to take responsibility for their translation into action. Among Howe's own more memorable debates were those with the Marxist ideologue of antidemocracy, Herbert Marcuse, with Oscar Handlin over the Israeli capture of Eichmann (which Howe defended), and with Howard Fast, the novelist and defender of Stalinism, to whom Howe declared: "You have blood on your hands!" (Quoted by Larner, "Remembering Irving Howe," 540).

Howe left Brandeis in 1961, not long after a romantic misadventure led to the breakup of his second marriage and his family. Looking back from the distance of more than twenty years, he regretted that the university had eventually retreated into "academic respectability" (MH, 189). He expressed no regrets about Brandeis's retreat into garden-variety academic leftism or its failure to become a Jewish university in any meaningful sense. Whatever complaints he might have about university life, he was now inured to its routine comforts (not unlike those of the welfare state he admired), and headed west to Stanford.

A Treasury of Yiddish Stories (1954): The Sacred Texts of Secular Jewishness

The project that helped to get Howe his appointment at Brandeis in 1953 appeared in 1954 as *A Treasury of Yiddish Stories*. It was to prove a turning point in his career, and the necessary prelude to his massive history of the immigrant Jewish world, *World of Our Fathers,* the book for which (paradoxically) he is now best known. The Jewish belletrist, the third member of what John Simon would later call the "one-man triumvirate"[16] named Irving Howe, had now arrived, asking to be integrated with the socialist and the literary critic.

In 1953, after he had published an essay about Sholom Aleichem in *Commentary* for September 1952, Howe was invited by the Yiddish poet Eliezer Greenberg to "become partners" with him in the work of editing and translating Yiddish literature. "We began with a book of Yiddish stories. Once a week Lazer would haul up a briefcase of crumbling old books and we'd spend three or four hours reading, trying to imagine how a story that sounded good in Yiddish might sound in English . . . wondering whom we could cajole into the back-breaking work of translation . . . " (MH, 260–61). Greenberg would select the material to be considered, would describe the author and work to Howe, and proceed to read aloud. If Greenberg succeeded in reading the story through to its end, that usually meant it would go into the anthology. (Howe used to remark that he knew poor Yiddish writers better than the good ones because he had had to sit through so many offerings before the right one came along.) He apparently wrote all of the introductions to the Yiddish anthologies, both the six he coedited with Greenberg and the ones he did with Ruth Wisse and Chone Shmeruk as well as the anthology he did on his own of Isaac Bashevis Singer in 1966.

Howe thought of himself as a rescuer. "When Lazer and I started working together, some major Yiddish writers were still alive in New York. But the truth . . . was that we were dealing with a literature close to its historical exit. . . . There were no young writers in Yiddish. In compiling our anthologies we were not merely exercising personal tastes, we were undertaking an act of critical salvage" (MH, 260–61). And what, beyond this admittedly important motive of rescue, moved Howe to commit himself at this time to Yiddish literature? Partly it was the attempt to respond to the Jewish catastrophe of World War II. (The book is dedicated "to the six million.") "I cannot prove that my own turn to Yiddish literature during the fifties was due to the shock follow-ing the war years. But it would be foolish to scant the possibility" (SW, 264–65). It is safe to assume that he was also profoundly affected by the murder of all the Russian Yiddish poets on an August night in 1952 in the cellars of Moscow's Lubyanka prison. But there was a yet deeper, if unconfessed, motive.

In the late forties, as we have seen, Howe's feelings of "Jewishness" grew stronger but lacked shape and coherence. These feelings could not, for him, find satisfaction or expression in the synagogue or the Jewish community or in "literary raids on Hasidism" of the sort mounted by some of his acquaintances.[17] In order to lend these inescap-able Jewish feelings coherence, in order to provide for secular Jews like himself a substitute for Torah, he hit upon the idea of establishing what we might call an objective body of sacred texts for the creed of secular Jewishness. In doing so, he was acting in a more traditionally Jewish way than he was aware. Robert Alter has written that "the Jewish approach to truth, for better or for worse, has been decisively focused on textuality (rather than, say, on empirical investigation)"; and David Roskies, in a lecture on Howe, has observed that the anthology is "the ideal form of Jewish self-expression," especially for defining and estab-lishing tradition.[18] These canonical texts would be the stories, poems, and essays of that most secular body of Jewish writing, Yiddish litera-ture. Editing and translating this body of literature would become one of Howe's major activities for the remainder of his life. "This wasn't, of course, a very forthright way of confronting my own troubled sense of

Jewishness, but that was the way I took. Sometimes you have to make roundabout journeys without quite knowing where they will lead to" (MH, 260). One might add, too, that in order to make a return journey you must first leave.

Although Howe had read a great deal about Nazi atrocities during his years in Alaska, he admitted that it was "only later, by the early fifties, [that I began] to grasp that I had been living through the most terrible moment in human history" (MH, 247). For someone grappling with the implications of the Holocaust, Yiddish was a natural (although not inevitable) place to turn. It had been the language of the majority of Jewish victims of Nazism. As a character in Cynthia Ozick's story "Envy; or, Yiddish in America" (1969) laments: "A little while ago there were twelve million people . . . who lived inside this tongue, and now what is left? A language that never had a territory except Jewish mouths, and half the Jewish mouths on earth already stopped up with German worms."[19] Yiddish was also the language of many of Stalin's victims, most particularly the Soviet Union's Jewish writers. If misgivings over his failure to attend to the fate of European Jewry led Howe to Yiddish literature, so too did his guilty awareness that an entire "generation of gifted Yiddish novelists and poets came to its end in the prison cells or labor camps"[20] of the state whose "experiment" in transforming human nature had been for Howe a major distraction from the struggles of the Jews in the thirties and forties, a distraction so great that it made him forget that from which he had been distracted.

Yiddish literature had begun, in the mid-nineteenth century, as an intensely secular enterprise, a result of the disintegration of the traditional world of East European Judaism. Its main "religious" aspect was what Howe liked to call the "religious intensity"[21] with which its practitioners turned to the idea of secular expression. Singer recalls how, when he was a young man in Warsaw in the twenties, religious Jews "considered all the secular writers to be heretics, all unbelievers—they really were too, most of them. To become a *literat* was to them almost as bad as becoming a *meshumed*, one who forsakes the faith. My father used to say that secular writers like Peretz were leading the Jews to heresy. He said everything they wrote was against God. Even though Peretz wrote in a religious vein, my father called his writing 'sweetened poison,' but poison nevertheless. And from his point of view, he was right."[22] But in the aftermath of the Holocaust this largely secular literature could easily take on a religious aspect. Traditionally, in the bilingual Jewish cultural household, Hebrew had been the sacred tongue, Yiddish the *mame-loshen* or vernacular; but now Yiddish became for many the "dead" yet sacred language of martyrdom while Hebrew was being used, in Tel Aviv and even Jerusalem, for distinctly secular and often un-Jewish purposes. As Jacob Glatstein, whose poetry Howe championed above that of all other post-Holocaust Yiddish poets, wrote: "Poet, take the faintest Yiddish speech, / fill it with faith, make it holy again."[23]

In retrospect, we might view Zionism and Yiddishism as competitors for the loyalty of those Jews who have, in this century, believed that Jewish life could be perpetuated in secular form: the Zionists insisted that this miracle could take place only in the Land of Israel; the Yiddishists believed it could happen in the Diaspora. For Howe, as we have already seen, Zionism was not a serious option because of his ingrained "socialist" disapproval of nationalism and his "cosmopolitan" refusal to rejoice at the rebirth of a Jewish polity.

In what sense, then, did he think of Yiddish literature as a seminal source for the secular Jewishness toward which he now seemed to be moving? He first undertook to tell its "brief and tragic history" in his lengthy and ambitious introduction to *A Treasury of Yiddish Stories,* a crucial document in his intellectual history because it is the first public expression of his "reconquest" of Jewishness. It is at once a celebration and a mourning. The survival of Yiddish over the centuries, he says, "reflects the miracle of Jewish survival itself." Yet Yiddish literature began at an ending, and this long before the Holocaust. Yiddish literature deals with the *shtetl* when Jewish life there still has a culture and an inner world of its own but is under fierce attack from modernizing and external influences. "Yiddish reaches its climax of expressive power," he asserts, "as the world it portrays begins to come apart."[24] Yiddish literature flourished in the historical interim between the dominance of religion and the ascendance of nationality; hence it "became a central means of collective expression for the East European Jews, fulfilling some of the functions of both religion and the idea of nationality" (TYS, 30). Unwittingly, perhaps, Howe here suggests the eventual triumph of Zionism—for which, as we have seen, he had very little affection in the fifties—over Yiddishism; or at least he intimates that once Yiddish has served the purpose of keeping Hebrew alive in a kind of warm storage over the centuries, it would retreat and leave the two real adversaries— religion and nationalism—to contend against one another.

At the same time, Howe praises Yiddish literature and the culture it reflected most warmly for the very characteristics that made the opposing camp of secular Jews, the Zionists, reject it. "The virtue of powerlessness, the power of helplessness, the company of the dispossessed, the sanctity of the insulted and the injured—these, finally, are the great themes of Yiddish literature" (TYS, 38). So eager is Howe to encourage this view that he ignores the counterevidence in the anthology itself, including (most notably) Peretz's satire of the grotesqueness of passivity and silent suffering in the story "Bontsha the Silent." Neither does Howe take up the question of whether pride in powerlessness is justified when there is no alternative to it. To a Zionist writer, of course, it seems the obvious question: "We Jews have been unique among the peoples of the earth," says Hillel Halkin, "for having lifted our hands against no one; yet is it not belaboring the obvious to point out that being so downtrodden ourselves, there was no one to lift them against? . . . It makes as much sense to take pride in such a record, or to attribute it to our superior moral instincts, as it does for a man starving for lack of money to buy food to boast of his self-control in keeping thin."[25]

Writing at a time when the young state of Israel had already for six years been under what would prove a permanent state of siege by the Arab nations, Howe defiantly set the sacred texts of Yiddish literature in opposition to the imperatives of Zionism: "the prevalence of this [anti-heroic] theme may also help explain why Zionists have been tempted to look with impatience upon Yiddish literature. In the nature of their effort, the Zionists desired to retrieve—or improvise—an image of Jewish heroism; and in doing so they could not help finding large portions of Yiddish literature an impediment. The fact that Yiddish literature had to assume the burden of sustaining a national sense of identity did not therefore make it amenable to the needs of a national ideology" (TYS, 39).

Among the founding fathers of Yiddish literature, the figure most immediate to Howe's own concerns and most congenial to his sensibility was I. L. Peretz, the Polish writer who believed in and strove for Jewish national revival—a mainly cultural revival in Poland, not a political one in Palestine. Peretz, like Howe after him, was strongly opposed to religious orthodoxy: "Pious Jews are a suppressing majority. To the pious Jew everything is holy. The pettiest law recorded in Hebrew lore, the most insignificant and foolish custom—the entire Diasporal rope that winds from generation to generation around his neck and throttles and almost chokes him out of his breath—he regards as holy!" And yet Peretz was reluctant to undermine the foundations of traditional faith: "Yet one must confess—tragic as it may be and strange as it may sound—that this shortening of breath, this opiating of the Jewish life-pulse, has greatly helped the Jews to withstand and to endure the coal-black and blood-red times of the Inquisition, the massacres, and the like periods of woe that no other nation could survive. . . ."[26]

Howe was like Peretz in searching for a secular version of Jewishness which would not only stiffen the Jews' collective will to survive, despite the price to be paid for survival, but also the individual's will to live and to adhere to an ethical code. He was attracted to George Eliot, the

English novelist, for example, partly because, though she was deemed the first great godless writer of English fiction, "her 'godlessness' . . . kept prompting her to search for equivalents to belief that would give moral weight to human existence" (SW, 350). One should not confuse Howe's frequent disparagement of organized religious life or the virtual absence of synagogues, yeshivas, and rabbis from the later *World of Our Fathers* with a contempt for religion itself. True, he complained that during the fifties there was in the American Jewish community "little genuine faith, little serious observance, little searching toward belief. The temples grew in size and there was much busywork and eloquence, but God seldom figured as a dominant presence" (MH, 278). But this is hardly the snarl of a dogmatic atheist. In later years, he would chide socialists for their obtuse disregard for the unexpected difficulties that the weakening of religious belief, a development to which they themselves had greatly contributed, brought to the lives of skeptics. "No matter how alien we remain to the religious outlook, we must ask ourselves whether the malaise of this time isn't partly a consequence of that despairing emptiness which followed the breakup in the nineteenth century of traditional religious systems; whether the nihilism every sensitive person feels encompassing his life like a spiritual smog isn't itself a kind of inverted religious aspiration . . . and whether the sense of disorientation that afflicts us isn't due to the difficulties of keeping alive a high civilization without a sustaining belief . . . " (CP, 16, 27).

Peretz, the central figure in Howe's secular Jewish design, was not a praying Jew; he rarely went to a synagogue; he never put on prayer shawl and *tefillin* at home. Maurice Samuel wrote of him that "Peretz paid no attention to the dietary laws, and he never made the benediction before eating a piece of fruit or drinking a glass of water—or of brandy. But what the benediction before food and the grace after it meant to a Chassid, he alone makes the non-Chassid understand. . . . If we who resemble him in these matters want to understand with what intimate joy they were invested for the Chassidim, we shall do best to go to Peretz."[27] Convinced that large portions of the Jewish community in Poland were turning away from religion to a secular European perspective, Peretz sought (as Arnold and Eliot had done within Christendom somewhat earlier) to establish, through literature, worldly equivalents for values that the religious tradition, in his view, no longer could sustain.

Howe singled out, as a revealing instance of both the promise and the limits of Peretz's secular Jewishness, the story called "If Not Higher." In it an anti-Hasidic Litvak, skeptical of claims that the great Hasidic rabbi of Nemirov disappears during the penitential season before Rosh

Hashanah to intercede in heaven for the Jewish people, hides himself under the rabbi's bed to observe his rival. He discovers that at the time when the rabbi's followers suppose him to be ascending to heaven to conciliate the invisible powers he is, in fact, in the guise of a peasant, felling a tree to supply a sick woman with firewood. While he lights the fire for her, he recites the penitential prayers. Witnessing this, the Litvak is "converted" to Hasidism. The rabbi really has been ascending to heaven, "if not higher." That is, he impresses the doubting Litvak as a saint after all, but a secular saint, whose religion is justified because it inspires him to selfless ethical behavior. Howe interprets the story as "a parable of [Peretz's] own literary situation," making the Litvak a *persona* of Peretz himself, who can say nearly everything in favor of Hasidism—it is conducive to joy, to morality, to Jewish survival—everything except that it is true. "From Hasidism," Howe concludes, "Peretz tried to extract its life-strength, without finally crediting its source. The attempt was impossible. . . . " Yet Peretz was able to transform Hasidic material into "fascinating parables of a dilemma that was not his alone" (TYS, 58). It was the dilemma of Howe himself and, so he believed, of growing numbers of Jews no longer willing to credit or be controlled by religious tradition. But if Peretz's attempt to substitute literature for religion was "impossible," how much more so was Howe's attempt, given his readership of Jews without Jewish memories (and, of course, without Yiddish)? At the very outset of his project to establish Yiddish literature as the spiritual source of secular Jewishness, Howe sounded a note of skepticism.

Peretz's ambivalent relation to Hasidic materials and Hasidic faith became for Howe the paradigmatic emblem of late nineteenth-century writers (gentile as well as Jewish) convinced of the utility of a faith they no longer believed in. "He had abandoned strict faith, yet it must be remembered—this is perhaps the single overriding fact in the experience of Yiddish writers at the end of the nineteenth century—that *faith abandoned could still be a far more imperious presence than new creeds adopted* [emphasis added]. Like such Western writers as George Eliot and Thomas Hardy, he found himself enabled to draw upon traditional faiths and feelings precisely *through* the act of denying them intellectually; indeed, the greatest influence on the work of such writers is the rich entanglement of images, symbols, language, and ceremonies associated with a discarded belief."[28]

Yiddish literature, as Howe viewed it, flourished in an age of equipoise that could never come again. Had haskalah (enlightenment) and Zionism and socialism not encouraged secularism among Eastern European Jews, Yiddish literature could not have developed or survived. But if secularism had succeeded in *obliterating* traditional faith and rabbinical authority, Yiddish literature would have withered and died, or—a subject we shall turn to later—"evolved" prematurely into something like American Jewish writing in the Yiddish language. Instead, there was a "wonderful interregnum" in which "the opposing impulses of faith and skepticism stand poised, locked in opposition yet sharing a community of culture. This interregnum, which began about the middle of the nineteenth century and has not yet come to an end, found its setting in czarist Russia, Poland between wars, and in various points of Western exile and immigration, notably the United States."[29]

The literature of secular Jewishness to which Howe directed American Jewry in his volumes of translated stories, poems, and essays was redolent not of a self-confident golden age but of a precariously balanced one, with the forces of permanence and progression represented in creative tension: "You could denounce religion as superstition and worse, but the Yom Kippur service shook the heart and the voices of the Talmud lured the mind. You could decry the secular writers as apostates and worse, but no one with a scrap of Yiddish could resist Mendele's acrid satires or Sholom Aleichem's sadly ironic stories" (VY, 5).

But if the great Yiddish writers like Peretz already stood at one considerable remove from the faith which they celebrated without crediting, and Yiddish literature was itself a major break within, even from, the Jewish tradition, could modern Jews derive strength and identity from that faith by reading the Yiddish writers?[30] That Howe himself did we cannot doubt, despite his protestations that he would not let his work in Yiddish literature "become an unearned substitute for a defined Jewishness—especially at a moment when undefined Jewishness was too readily becoming a substitute for traditional Judaism." He was strongly attracted to the idea of a Jewishness split away from, yet dependent upon traditional Judaism, and the poems and stories helped him to renew his bond with his father as an embodiment of immigrant Jewishness. He claimed to have no thought of making his work in Yiddish a basis for some program that younger Jews might follow, especially those younger Jews "pinched into the narrowing sector of Jewish secularism" (MH, 267–69). Yet, given the permanently problematic condition of American Jewish life, the increasing unlikelihood either of a full return to religious faith or of a total abandonment of Jewish identification, who can doubt that Howe for a long time thought of his numerous volumes of Yiddish translations as offering a third way of being Jewish, neither religious nor nationalistic?[31]

The introduction to *Treasury of Yiddish Stories* also seems to go out of its way to discover in Yiddish literature a foil to the modernism in which Howe had been immersed—an aesthetic foil, an ethical foil, a democratic foil. Certain modernists and the literary critics who championed them had (somewhat contradictorily, to be sure) laid great stress on tradition in literature. "But," Howe now argues, "if by traditional we mean not merely a writer's sense of continuity with the writers who have preceded him but also his sense of being part of a living culture and intimately related to an active audience, then it is in Yiddish literature—far more so than in modern English or American literature—that tradition has been a sustaining force." Sholom Aleichem lived, in a sense, next door to the people who lived in his stories. The organic society that T. S. Eliot aspired to (partly by excluding Jews from it) Sholom Aleichem already had, and so could count on resources of implicit communication among members of a coherent group. "*The Waste Land* is far more recondite than any of Sholom Aleichem's stories, but the footnotes T. S. Eliot felt obliged to append suggest that he was writing in a society where tradition had been disrupted, where tradition had become a problem, *a subject for discussion*" (TYS, 42). Who can imagine Sholom Aleichem adding footnotes to explain to his readers how, for comic purposes, he had mangled quotations from Bible and Talmud? Who, we might add, can imagine any critic but Irving Howe with the daring and brilliance and competence to set Sholom Aleichem in triumphant opposition to T. S. Eliot?

Yiddish literature also, according to Howe, embodies "a moral poise, a security of values" (TYS, 37) that stands in sharp contrast to the qualities valued by "serious people" in 1954, qualities embodied best in the chief progenitor of literary modernism, Dostoyevsky. His was the genuine voice of crisis, the voice proposing that the possibilities of life may be glimpsed only through ultimates, prophecies, final judgments, catastrophes. In such a writer as Sholom Aleichem, by contrast, "there is a readiness . . . to value those milder virtues which can cause only impatience in many modern minds." The Yiddish writers do not assume evil to be the last word about man; neither do they "condescend to the ordinary, or scorn the domestic affections, or suppose heroism to be incompatible with humbleness" (TYS, 37). Here lay the kernel of a moral code for secular Jews who either no longer believed in, or considered themselves morally superior to, the Torah.

Finally, the Yiddish writers were embraced by their culture in a way inconceivable for the modernists. Although, as noted earlier, Delmore Schwartz had spoken of Eliot as a culture-hero, the term was far more applicable to Sholom Aleichem. "He is," Howe defiantly asserts, "the only writer of modern times who may truly be said to be a culture-hero . . . far more so than T. S. Eliot, about whom it should be said that the claims entered by his admirers have yet to be recognized by his culture" (TYS, 53). Sholom Aleichem's fiftieth birthday was a public event, and at the time of his death in 1916 hundreds of thousands of people filled the streets to watch his cortege make its way through the Bronx and Harlem, through lower Manhattan and eventually into Brooklyn for burial. Who could imagine a comparable tribute to Eliot or even to Howe's favorite modernist, James Joyce? In Howe's mind, then, the Yiddish writers served not only Jewish purposes. They also afforded a fully realized image of what was lacking in modernism, the very modernism to which he had given, and still in 1954 continued to give, his allegiance.

The intensity with which Howe stressed the contrasts between the Yiddish writers upon whom he was conferring a second life and the chief figures of modernism being studied in the English departments lends some plausibility to the interpretation of his motive for the anthology proposed in Philip Roth's novel, *Zuckerman Bound,* where the critic Milton Appel is obviously based upon Irving Howe:

> Though Appel's initial motive for compiling his Yiddish anthology was, more than likely, the sheer excitement of discovering a language whose range he could never have guessed from the coarseness of his father's speech, there seemed a deliberately provocative intention too. Far from signaling anything so comforting and inauthentic as a prodigal son's return to the fold, it seemed, in fact, a stand *against*: to Zuckerman, if to no one else, a stand against the secret shame of the assimilationists, against the distortions of the Jewish nostalgists, against the boring, bloodless faith of the prospering new suburbs— best of all, an exhilarating stand against the snobbish condescension of those famous departments of English literature from whose impeccable Christian ranks the literary Jew, with his mongrelized speech and caterwauling inflections, had until just yesterday been pointedly excluded.[32]

Whether out of sheer ignorance and parochialism or out of an astute recognition that Howe's Yiddish writers implied a criticism of their own assumptions and loyalties, the American literary establishment ignored the book. Almost twenty years after the event, Howe still expressed resentment that the anthology was never reviewed in any American literary magazine. The only explanation he could propose (this in a conversation with me) was that "in the warmest of hearts there's always a cold spot for the Jews."

This Age of Conformity (1954)

"In the fifties, for better or worse, almost everything began that would dominate our life in the following decades" (MH, 246). This balanced retrospective view of Howe's is probably true, and yet he himself is one of the people largely responsible for the negative view of the fifties that has now become so fashionable. For it was he who attached to it the label of "This Age of Conformity" in a highly influential essay in *Partisan Review* at the beginning of 1954 (January-February issue).

This seminal essay is, by the standard of urbanity Howe was beginning to develop, a throwback to his fierce, ragged, unkempt style of the forties, a "scatter-shot piece" in its author's own words, a polemic that Rahv "got me to write . . . in which I attacked almost everyone for the growing conservative mood of the moment."[33] Its socialism is not much more than attitudinizing; it refrains from proposing alternatives to policies of which Howe disapproves; it constantly (in the crudest Marxist style—and it is worthwhile, if disconcerting, to remember that as late as 1952 Howe could write that "Marxism seems to me the best available method for understanding and making history")[34] tries to invalidate intellectual positions by imputing to opponents material motives. In its sour condemnation of the fifties as a time when idealism slumbered, materialism flourished, and conformity threatened to blight everyone, it invites the reaction of Joseph Epstein to the standard jeremiad against the "silent generation" of that decade: " . . . What it really means is that the 50's were not a good time for left-wing politics. Whether this is the same as not being good for the country is rather a different question."[35]

Nevertheless "This Age of Conformity" is not without its illuminating (and occasionally hilarious) moments. The stated aim of the essay was "to trace a rough pattern from social history through politics and finally into literary ideology, as a means of explaining the power of the conformist impulse in our time" (SW, 42). Most social critics, he charges, have failed to recognize the social developments that have enabled capitalism in its most recent phase to find an honored place for the intellectuals, who have now become all too comfortable in their return to the bosom of the nation. Having, less than two years earlier, completed his stint with *Time Magazine*, Howe grudgingly grants that the pressures of conformism affect everyone in tandem with "the need to earn one's bread." But even if everyone bends under the weight of such pressures, it would be better if people offered at least some resistance; instead, too many now take pleasure in learning to enjoy their acquiescence.[36]

Howe insists that, despite his complaints about "Marx-baiting" by ex-Marxists in the academic journals, he is not bemoaning merely the abandonment of radical causes. If radicalism were to again become fashionable, the same intellectuals who now trumpet the ideology of capitalism would again become radical, perhaps too much so. No—what he most deplores is the loss of the intellectual vocation, a life dedicated to values that cannot be realized by a commercial civilization. Like John Stuart Mill in the Victorian period, Howe, who by this time was employed by Brandeis University, insists that whenever intellectuals become absorbed into accredited social institutions, they both lose their rebelliousness and cease to function as intellectuals.

Howe accepts Trilling's statement from the December 1949 preface to *The Liberal Imagination* (1950) that liberalism has become not merely the dominant but the sole intellectual tradition in the United States. But this means, he argues, that liberalism itself has now become conservative (as in some sense Trilling hoped it would): "in America there is today neither opportunity nor need for conservatism (since the liberals do the necessary themselves)" (SW, 34). Thus the dominance of liberalism itself contributes heavily to American intellectual conformity, but not to American freedom. This, he alleges, has been under severe attack, and intellectuals have been insufficiently militant in defending it. The chief culprit, in his view, is *Commentary*, a magazine in which Howe had published articles every year from 1946 to 1953. In its pages, he charges, "liberalism is most skillfully and systematically advanced as a strategy for adapting to the American status quo" (SW, 36). Singled out for special blame, as he would be for many years to come, is Howe's old CCNY classmate and former friend, Irving Kristol. Kristol's great offense is to have written that the American people do not know, as at least they do know about the deplorable Senator Joseph McCarthy, that American liberalism is unequivocally anti-Communist.

The debate over "anti-anti-communism" would involve Howe for a good part of this decade. At its core was the question of whether the domestic threat posed by Senator McCarthy was of an order of magnitude comparable to that of the global Communist campaign led by the Soviet Union. In the abstract, Howe did not dispute the primacy of the Soviet threat to world freedom, but he took the position that although Stalinism was the major danger internationally, in domestic affairs the correct focus of energy was the struggle against McCarthyism. He was censorious of *Commentary* (and also, to a lesser degree, of *Partisan Review*) for emphasizing the battle against anti-anti-Communists. "The country may have worried about McCarthy, but *Commentary* worried about those who profited from the struggle against McCarthy. It was all a matter of proportion" (MH, 215).

Although, in this discourse on conformity, Howe considers the *Commentary* position so outrageous that he does not even condescend to offer a substantive response to it, it is by no means clear that he is the victor in the dispute. Hook also thought it was "a matter of proportion," but his measuring rod was far different from Howe's. Writing to a historian, Hook asked: "If these victims [of McCarthy] had been members of a Nazi party and as fervent supporters of Hitler and his practices as they were of Stalin and Stalin's practices, would you still feel the same compassion for them?"[37] Indeed, Howe's recollection of the matter from the perspective of 1982 tends to substantiate the position of Kristol and *Commentary* rather than his own. In *A Margin of Hope* he recalls how Rahv and other Marxists and ex-Marxists tended to view McCarthyism as an incipient fascist movement. Howe grants that they were wrong to do so, and in fact that the McCarthy years were very far from being a reign of terror. "In a reign of terror people turn silent, fear a knock on the door at four in the morning, flee in all directions; but they do not, because they cannot, talk endlessly in public about the outrage of terror" (MH, 223), which is precisely what Rahv and his hysterical colleagues did. Moreover, Howe readily acknowledges that "When we printed violent denunciations of McCarthy in *Dissent* [begun in 1954] during these years nothing happened to us. . . . We had no sense we were taking any great risks in attacking McCarthy" (MH, 224). But if so many of the liberal attackers of McCarthy really believed they were living in a country on the verge of fascism, and therefore morally indistinguishable from the Soviet Union, was not Kristol right in saying that Americans had some reason for doubting the anti-communism of American liberalism? Indeed, had not Howe himself on countless occasions since the early forties derided American liberals for their apologias for Stalinism?

From social history and politics Howe's essay moves to consider the plague of conformity in literary ideology. Turning to the New Critics, then at the height of their influence, he blames some of them not for practicing formal criticism but for failing to do so consistently, surreptitiously weaving ideological assumptions into their writing. He inveighs against the prominence of words like "orthodox" and "traditional" in literary criticism, noting parenthetically that "literary tradition can be fruitfully seen as a series of revolts, literary but sometimes more than literary, of generation against generation, age against age" (SW, 39). He also gripes about the high prestige of Original Sin in the literary world. What, he wonders, does it portend? Do its users mean only to remind us that man is capable of evil, or do they wish to suggest that when Eve bit into the apple, she predetermined that her progeny could progress no farther in social organization than capitalism? Howe links the literary prestige of the doctrine to the deplorable turn to religion and the battle weariness of intellectuals yearning to abandon the arena of historical action and choice, "which necessarily means, of secular action and choice" (SW, 42).

Although Howe is surely right about the licentious resort to the doctrine of Original Sin by some influential critics of the fifties, he is partisan and parochial in linking it to an espousal of "capitalism." Several of its literary advocates were conservative agrarians, who, as we shall see (and as Howe himself often observed), were as severe critics of capitalism as he was, but not from a socialist perspective. One wishes too that Howe had in 1954 observed that Original Sin is a specifically Christian doctrine[38] and that it was possible (especially for a Jew) to believe in the existence and tenacity of evil without espousing the doctrine. After all, Howe himself, in the wake of the revelations about the Holocaust, repeatedly said that socialism depends upon the possibilities of human nature: if those are shown to be severely limited, socialism is probably doomed. How different is this, really, from invoking Original Sin as an argument against socialism?

Howe also, in an important foreshadowing of sentiments that he would forcefully expound in the last decade of his life, expresses misgivings about the growing arrogance, ignorance, and narrowmindedness of literary criticism. A careful examination of the graduate students in literature departments indicates their powerful desire to be "critics," not as a sideline to writing poems or changing the world or studying man and God, but just critics—"as if criticism were a *subject*, as if one could be a critic without having at least four nonliterary opinions, or as if criticism 'in itself' could adequately engage an adult mind for more than a small part of its waking time" (SW, 43). Literature in the hands of these practitioners of criticism becomes merely raw material for working up into schemes of structure and symbol, in disregard of the fact that literature is mainly concerned with human experience. A compendium of what ails literary criticism in the age of conformity is, Howe contends, the work of Stanley Edgar Hyman, in whose mind "criticism comes to resemble Macy's on bargain day: *First floor, symbols; Second floor, myths (rituals to the rear on your right); Third floor, ambiguities and paradoxes; Fourth floor, word counting; Fifth floor, Miss Harrison's antiquities; Attic, Marxist remnants; Basement, Freud; Sub-basement, Jung. Watch your step, please"* (SW, 44).

"This Age of Conformity" was a kind of rearguard effort by Howe to salvage the avant-garde in letters and resurrect the old *Partisan Review* link between literary avant-gardism and "independent" leftist politics. But its results were different from what he intended. By 1960 he was already blaming himself "for the endless chatter about 'conformity' that has swept the country." How could he have known, when he polemicized against intellectuals cowed by McCarthyism, that "unintentionally, I was helping to make the outcry against conformity into a catch-word of our conformist culture."[39]

Another unintended result of the essay was that it severed, temporarily, his relationship with Trilling. Early in the essay, Howe had mocked Trilling's view that wealth and intellect were now getting along well in the United States, and that the American cultural situation was better now than it had been thirty years earlier (Howe's golden age of the twenties). He accused Trilling of "indulging in a pleasant fantasy," mocked his use of "such stately terms as 'wealth' and 'intellect,'" and labelled the whole drift of his remarks "disastrous" (SW, 30). Trilling, who had helped Howe to publish his book on Sherwood Anderson,[40] was reported to have been angered by the polemical sharpness (and *ad hominem* insinuations) of Howe's remarks, and for the next seven or eight years the two men did not see each other, though they did exchange letters (MH, 213). Their relations could not have been helped by the acerbic exchange between Howe and Diana Trilling in 1956. In the July *Commentary*, she had referred to "the spectacle of a magazine like DISSENT, whose polemic is based not upon intellectual cogency but upon the emotional intimidation of its readers." Howe replied in the fall issue of *Dissent* with matching delicacy: "As a leading official of the American Committee for Cultural Freedom . . . , an organization largely devoted in this country to cold-war publicity among intellectuals, Mrs. Trilling seems often to behave like the 'general secretary' of a radical sect whose main joy in life is hunting for deviations among the other sects and chastising those who stray from the proper 'line.'"[41] In her autobiography, Mrs. Trilling includes Howe in the lengthy list with which she ends her book of "the strange difficult ungenerous unreliable unkind and not always honest people who created the world in which Lionel and I shared. . . . "[42] This suggests she remembered better the ungenerous Howe of the fifties than the far more gracious one who eulogized her husband in the seventies.[43]

The Founding of *Dissent* (1954)

In 1951 Howe and Stanley Plastrik tried to persuade the Independent Socialist League (formerly the Workers party), the sponsor of *Labor Action*, to sponsor as well a quarterly journal somewhat along the lines of Dwight Macdonald's now defunct *Politics*. When the ISL refused, Howe and Plastrik—already at odds with the organization because of its failure to support the Marshall Plan and align itself with the democratic West against Stalinism—resigned. But they returned a few years later to the idea of a little magazine of the socialist movement. In the very same month of January 1954 that Howe published "This Age of Conformity," he founded, along with Lewis Coser, Travers Clement, Meyer Schapiro, Plastrik, and Harold Orlans a journal that was supposed to offer the antidote to the blight of conformity rotting the coun-

try (and which tried to raise funds—$6,000 to insure a year's publica-
tion—by using the old *Politics* subscribers' list to solicit support). In
their opening "Word to Our Readers" the editors of *Dissent* declared the
purpose of their journal to be "dissent from the bleak atmosphere of
conformism that pervades the political and intellectual life of the United
States." They also proposed to dissent from the support of the *status quo*
which they imputed to many former radicals and socialists, and from
"the terrible assumption that a new war is necessary or inevitable, and
that the only way to defeat Stalinism is through atomic world suicide."[44]
But they also announced that they would attack all forms of totalitarianism, including the Stalinist. They would be distinct from liberalism, yet
engage in a frank and friendly dialogue with it.

Dissent declared its receptivity to a broad range of opinion, but made
clear that it would exclude "Stalinists and fellow-travellers on the one
hand, and those former radicals who have signed their peace with
society as it is, on the other." Having indicated what it would dissent
from, the new journal also announced what it would positively affirm:
"the belief in socialism." But it was less clear what this socialism meant.
It seemed to have little to do with ideas about state ownership of the
means of production, or the replacement of a free market with a regu-
lated one, or a solidarity of the working classes that would supersede
national loyalties (once a central theme of Howe's writing). The socialism to which *Dissent* would devote itself was "the ethos and the faith in
humanity that for more than 100 years have made men 'socialists.' . . . a
belief in the dignity of the individual . . . a refusal to countenance one
man's gain at the expense of his brother . . . an intellectual conviction
that man can substantially control his condition if he understands it and
wills to" (4). How these commitments distinguished socialism from a
generalized commitment to enlightenment or liberalism or ethical idealism or the views of Fulton J. Sheen was not evident, except for the
blurred reference to the labor theory of value. Norman Podhoretz later
asserted that by the time he founded *Dissent*, Howe was no longer even
a Marxist except in the most general way, and that his socialism had no
discernible content, even though he persisted in a stubborn religious
loyalty to the word and the idea.[45]

Howe's own declaration of purpose for the magazine is called "Does
It Hurt When You Laugh?" Its stress is almost entirely on the state of
civil liberties in America and is even more devoid of socialist content
than the editors' "Word to Our Readers." Citing a few instances of what
in the fifties might have been fearfulness of the wrath of Senator
McCarthy, Howe complains of the inadequacy of response by "those
sophisticated liberals who read *Commentary* and think of Sidney Hook
as their intellectual spokesman."[46] True, Howe reproves the *Nation* for

constantly crying wolf about American "fascism," for "never troubling to make elementary distinctions between native know-nothingism and full-fledged fascism," and for "quasi-appeasement of Stalinism." But he blames *Commentary* for allowing *The Nation*, by default, to present itself as the journal most deeply concerned with violations of civil liberties. *Commentary* is good at spreading awareness that "certain Stalinoids" are exploiting the McCarthyite threat for their own purposes, but shows little interest in exposing the seriousness of the threat itself. Since the liberals decline to mount a counterattack against the reactionaries, it must fall to American radicals, gathered together at *Dissent*, to "raise the traditional banner of personal freedom that is now slipping from the hands of so many accredited spokesmen of liberalism" (7).

Howe returned so compulsively to *Commentary* in his indictment of liberals who fail to take seriously the threat to civil liberties that he came close to giving the impression that *Dissent* was founded less as a tribune of socialism than as an anti-magazine designed to combat *Commentary* (just as Michael Lerner's *Tikkun* would become in 1986).[47] The challenge (no doubt to Howe's satisfaction) was quickly taken up in a devastating review of *Dissent*'s first issue by the sociologist Nathan Glazer in the February 1954 issue of *Commentary* (then edited by Elliot Cohen). He pronounced the new project "an unmitigated disaster as far as what is left of socialist thought in this country is concerned."[48] The editorial statement and Howe's essay provided, Glazer charged, sufficient explanation of why socialism has failed in America. He looks through the entire first issue to find evidence of the poisonous blight of conformism and finds virtually nothing apart from Howe's claim that the *Nation* magazine provides "more necessary information about violations of civil liberties than any comparable American journal." Glazer argues (convincingly, it should be added) that more often than not the *Nation*'s information about civil liberties has turned out to be misinformation. Could it have been otherwise with a journal that, as Howe himself readily admits, is still in thrall to Stalinism?

Glazer also mocks the new journal's pronouncements on foreign policy and war. Who exactly, he asks, are the people who believe a new war necessary and inevitable? And who, apart from inmates of insane asylums, are those agitating for "world atomic suicide"? In effect, Glazer accuses Howe and his colleagues of still being in the grip of the high-minded confusion that had kept them neutral in the conflict between Nazism and the "bourgeois" democracies. He finds in *Dissent*'s statement of purpose the familiar historic position of socialism about war: "it does not ask whether war is ever necessary or unnecessary, avoidable or unavoidable—it's simply against it, and assumes that the fact of war is decisive proof of the immorality of 'capitalism'" (204).[49] Glazer even charges that *Dissent*'s adversary position toward American foreign policy reminds one of Orwell's remark that "if the radical intellectuals in England had had their way in the 20's and 30's, the Gestapo would have been walking the streets of London in 1940" (204).

However vague Howe and *Dissent* may be in their enunciation of socialist principles, they are, says Glazer, at least traditionally Marxist in their vituperative intemperance toward opponents, especially those who are viewed as renegades and those who are closest to them in first principles. They invariably imply that former radicals and socialists who support the status quo have sold out, thus reducing their opponents' ideas to material and egoistic motives. *Dissent*'s editors take much less interest in the far more intense support of the status quo evinced by the remaining 98 percent of the population.

Glazer himself concludes on rather a personal note. He remarks that many of *Dissent*'s leading figures (Howe writing for *Partisan Review* and *Commentary* is the obvious example here) had themselves benefited by the discipline of writing for magazines that disagreed with what they had to say: "such pushing against opposition forces you to moderate your claims, strengthen your arguments, and be as concrete as possible. *Dissent* represents what happens when all the oppressive wraps are off" (206). Glazer might well have pointed to the disparity between Howe's literary criticism—work distinguished by flexibility, variousness, tolerance, and analytic incisiveness—and his strictly political writing, especially in *Dissent*. The quarrel between *Dissent* and *Commentary* had been joined, and would continue for decades to come.[50]

The new magazine was also attacked from the left. In Howe's old paper, *Labor Action* (22 February 1954), Hal Draper, now the paper's editor, excoriated the heretical journal. He singles out for condemnation Howe's article on "Stevenson and the Intellectuals," which epitomized both Howe's "political retrogression" (to the Democratic party) and an intellectual irresponsibility similar to "the way in which he had announced his break with the Third Camp antiwar position." Although we may find it astonishing that Howe took as long as he did to repudiate his opposition to the war against Hitler, Draper attacks *Dissent* precisely because its first issue avoids "the battle for the world between the two imperialist camps." Whereas Glazer blames Howe and his colleagues for repeating the same disastrous neutrality that led them astray during World War II, Draper blames them for having forsaken the antiwar position and fallen in line with the West. But Draper joins Glazer in objecting to the vague, amorphous quality of *Dissent*'s socialism: "Here 'socialism' is reduced to liberalism at best; to the liberal *mood* at something less than the best; and to nothing much at all, if one insists on being rigorous." Perhaps most egregious, from Draper's point of view, is Howe's attempt to subsitute a forum of "ideas" for an organization. Both Howe's break with ISL and his founding of *Dissent* declare, in effect, that "those who sympathize with his 'ethos' must likewise abandon any *organized* socialist movement, which is to be replaced by such a center for thinkers as his magazine seeks to make itself." The ISL even passed a motion prohibiting its members from contributing articles to *Dissent* unless they received a special dispensation.[51] Howe's rejoinder to Draper in the 15 March issue of *Labor Action* alludes condescendingly to the posturing of Draper and his colleagues: "I know this way of thinking, having suffered from it myself for a good many years." He insists on the importance of honestly admitting that there is no longer a socialist movement in the United States, only individual socialists, and that "'we' have no political significance whatsoever."

Although Howe's socialist ideas might seem to Glazer amorphous and to Draper worm-eaten with liberalism and to Howe himself unlikely to be realized in his lifetime, he was prepared to expend a tremendous amount of time and energy to diffuse them. Coser, his coeditor, recalls how "when Irving and I would talk about the chances of creating a magazine of the democratic socialist left during the McCarthy years, we both felt that its chances to live for more than a year or two were very slim. But Irving argued that it was worthwhile to devote a big chunk of his time to the magazine . . . because the idea of socialism should remain an image of our desire even though the reality of socialism, in the East but also largely in the West, was not something that could inspire a new generation of intellectuals and activists. One had to try. And try he did for over forty years" ("Remembering Irving Howe," 527). During all that time Howe spent at least two days of every week on the magazine. Money was a constant problem, and Howe found it galling that *Dissent*'s total expenditure in the year 1958 was a third of the salary that Kristol was said to be getting at the *Reporter.*[52] Howe worked for the magazine without any material reward, and all for what he seemed to sense at the outset, and certainly declared later on to be, a lost cause. He wrote for nearly every issue of the magazine until he died, and in his will bequeathed whatever in his estate had not been left to his or his wives' families to *Dissent* and to the Democratic Socialists of America.

Over the years Howe recruited for *Dissent* such writers as Ignazio Silone, Harold Rosenberg, Paul Goodman, Erich Fromm, Norman Mailer (whose "The White Negro" was one of the magazine's most disgraceful publications),[53] Richard Wright, Andrei Sinyavsky, and George Lichtheim. At the outset of the magazine, he felt at once beleaguered by enemies and abandoned by friends. "When DISSENT first appeared, it was attacked with a violence which surprised even those of us who knew we had no reason to expect popularity. Among prominent intellectuals only C. Wright Mills came to our defense. . . . " But a decade later he could express satisfaction that the magazine had managed not only to survive but to send both its radical contributors and its radical ideas into "mainstream" journals and discourse. This success did not, however, mean that *Dissent* had lost its original *raison d'etre*, for the gap between radical journalism and radical politics—i.e., the rebuilding of a radical political community—remained. *Dissent* could never be content to have its leading writers place an article or two in the *New Yorker* or *Partisan Review*; no, it had to develop its outlook with an eye toward a distinctly political, socialist end.[54] Whatever its shortcomings, *Dissent* not only published a great deal of first-rate political writing, but gave a distinction to radical journalism that stood in sharp contrast to magazines like the *Nation*, already sinking into what William Buckley called "the cesspool of opinion journalism."

The Southerners: New Critics and William Faulkner

Howe wrote, in "A Memoir of the Thirties," that he became a socialist through recognition of what poverty was, but that it was the poverty of the rural South that brought it home to him, not the poverty of the Jewish slums of the East Bronx in which he lived in the midst of the Depression. Once he told an interviewer that "Now, I don't know if the life of the North Carolina textile workers was any more wretched than the life of the garment workers in the East Bronx; but it was to the wretchedness of the workers of North Carolina that I responded with great imaginative urgency. I remember shedding tears about their conditions while taking utterly for granted the conditions I lived in" ("Range," 268). Thus, from an early stage, Howe was magnetized by reading of the South and by the writing of Southerners.

Although, as we have seen, the young Howe felt estranged from such classic American writers as Emerson, Thoreau, and Whitman because the family did not exist in their imaginative world, the Southern writers seemed to him very different. In the sense of the family as an inviolable institution, "we were closer to the Southern than to the New England writers. . . . With Faulkner, despite all his rhetoric about honor, we might feel at home because the clamp of family which chafed his characters was like the clamp that chafed us" (SW, 329). Howe believed that in this century it was Southern writing that was the most important regional culture to break into the national awareness but not the only one. He thought of Jewish American writing too as part of a regional culture, not only because it deals mainly with a single locale (the streets and tenements of the immigrant Jewish neighborhoods or the better neighborhoods to which the immigrants' children have moved), but also because "it comes to us as an outburst of literary consciousness resulting from an encounter between an immigrant group and the host culture of America."[55]

Between these two regional literatures Howe saw striking similarities. In both cases, just as in Yiddish literature, "a subculture finds its voice and its passion at exactly the moment it approaches disintegration." (Howe was coming to view this morbid trait as a touchstone of literary value.) This moment of intense self-consciousness offers to both the Southern and the Jewish writers the advantages of an inescapable subject—Howe always believed that the best subjects are those which choose the writers rather than being chosen by them. In both literatures we find the complex of emotions the writers bring to the remembered world of their youth, and also the psychic costs of their struggle to tear themselves away from that world. Both regional literatures offer "the emotional strength that comes from traditional styles of conduct— honor for the South, 'chosenness' for the Jews—which these writers seek to regain, escape, overcome, while thereby finding their gift of tongue." Both literatures are permeated by old stories remembered and retold, "whether by aging Confederate soldiers or skull-capped grandfathers recalling the terrors of the Czars. [They offer] the lure of nostalgia, a recapture of moments felt to be greater in their emotional resonance, perhaps more heroic than the present, all now entangled with a will toward violent denial of the past" (J-A, 3).

If the Southern writers seemed akin, in their literary qualities, to the Jewish ones, their social and political ideas presented a more complicated problem. Socially, both groups of writers were cut off from the "mainstream" of American culture and assertive in affirming the splendor of their minority status (MH, 141). Allen Tate, the southern poet and critic, had written that "the distinctive Southern consciousness was quite temporary. It has made possible the curious burst of intelligence that we get at the crossing of the ways, not unlike . . . the outburst of poetic genius at the end of the sixteenth century when commercial England had already begun to crush feudal England." Tate, "a kind of swashbuckling Quixote with a Southern accent" (C&A, 164), and his friends were also, like Howe, albeit for different reasons, uncomfortable with American liberalism. "No wonder conflict melted into a gingerly friendship, plight calling to plight, ambition to ambition" (MH, 141). No wonder, too, that Howe resisted Rahv's summons to battle: "Oiving, why don't you smash . . . this Tate?" ("Rahv: A Memoir," 490).

Howe of course understood that the Southerners' rejection of liberalism was done on behalf of conservatism, not socialism. The only American conservatism of which he spoke respectfully in these years was the literary conservatism of people like Tate, John Crowe Ransom, and Robert Penn Warren, who rejected an industrial economy and yearned for an ordered, rural, hierarchical society. But he respected it largely as myth, not policy. These writers envisioned a self-sufficient agrarian economy in which the small farmer, proud and independent, would be the dominant social type and the cultural ideal as well. Howe was convinced that these literary agrarians (many of whom, like Tate and Warren, had left the South to teach and write in northern cities like Minneapolis and New Haven) recognized the hopeless and utopian character of their political ideas, which could flourish in the imaginative work of Faulkner and others, but not in the hands of political writers obliged to deal with questions of practice and power (SW, 35; MH, 225–27).

The southern agrarians may well have contributed to Howe two favorite ideas that he would develop and embellish throughout his career. One was that a utopian myth affords both a revealing perspective and a powerful instrument for criticism of existing American society. He referred to the agrarian vision as "an idyll reflecting their desire" (C&A, 163), just as throughout his career he (and his epigones) would refer to socialism as "the image or the name of our desire." He also likened the literary fruitfulness of "the decomposition of their [agrarian] ideology" (C&A, 164) to that of the Marxists of the thirties. Howe was ever wont to believe that our most splendid yearnings derive from the impotence of decline.

Howe encountered Southerners and Southern ideology mainly in the person of the New Critics, many of whom were from the South. He gave them credit for a largely salutary revolution in the study of literature, one which returned the reader's attention from historical "background" and biography to the particular strategies of the poetic text, to nuances of language, form, rhetoric, and tone. Although Howe did not subscribe entirely to their program—how could he, given his historical and social bent?—he admitted that when he began teaching at Brandeis in 1953 he used "a loosened version of the New Criticism almost as a matter of course" (MH, 179). As noted earlier, he chastised the New Critics for not being aware that, despite their commitment to formalism and spurning of "relevance," their work too was (inevitably) tainted by political and theological bias. How could it have been otherwise with writers who started their careers with a burning social passion, and then set up as models for pure, formalistic criticism? Yet he was drawn to them by forces that went beyond ideas.

Although populists and vulgar Marxists attacked people like Tate and Ransom as reactionaries, Howe and several of the New York intellectuals felt a bond based on shared predicaments. "The problem of teaching, with which the New Critics began, became the problem of civilization, with which the best of them ended. For us in New York it was perhaps the other way around, but no matter—whoever has taken this journey in one direction will soon find a way back in the other" (MH, 180). Whatever doctrinal matters divided them, Howe found in the New Critics a keenness, commitment, and vividness in dealing with literature and ideas that he highly valued. In the Southern contingent he also responded to a special charm, civility, gallantry, even grandeur. He once told Heilman, a New Critic from Pennsylvania who became a kind of honorary Southerner by virtue of thirteen years at Louisiana State University, that, polemical disputes apart, there was a kind of largeness of spirit among almost all the New Critics he got to know in the fifties, which he had seldom found in the intellectual world since then.[56] He would also, in later decades, invoke the example of the New Critics in his battles with New Leftists who thought of literature mainly as an "instrument" subserving political ends. "Men like Tate, [R. P.] Blackmur, Warren and Ransom were honorable intellectual opponents, and thereby our teachers too. All they finally demanded, of ally or opponent, was that one should care passionately about literature *in its own right* and find the study of it worthy of a mature intelligence" ("Literary Criticism and Literary Radicals," 116).

The chief expression of Howe's interest in the South in the 1950s was his book *William Faulkner: A Critical Study,* published in 1952. Southern writing might be "regional," and yet it had been a major conduit for the entry of the international movement of modernism into America. "Yoknapatawpha County and all its brilliant figures thrive upon local myth, indeed, are inconceivable without the obsessive Southern stories; but the local myth rises to art through a sensibility shaken and stimulated by European modernism. Faulkner as mere provincial would not be very interesting" (J-A, 2). In his book, Howe argued that the more intense Faulkner's treatment of the South, the more readily did the reader forget that he was writing "about" the South. Thus Faulkner's masterpiece, *The Sound and the Fury,* emerges as a powerful criticism not only of the recent South, but of the whole life of the modern era. "To the extent that *The Sound and the Fury* is about modern humanity in Mississippi, to the same extent is it about modern humanity in New York and in Paris."[57]

Howe's *William Faulkner* was one of the first book-length studies of Faulkner's fiction. It would go through four editions, and remains in print to this day. Its scheme is simple. In Part One Howe tells what Faulkner's work is "about" in a series of compact sections (such as "The Southern Tradition" and "Faulkner and the Negroes") that describe the social and moral themes of the novels; then, in Part Two, he analyzes and evaluates the more important novels, starting with *The Sound and the Fury*. Howe, irritated by the tendency of later Faulkner critics to relegate the book to the "social" approach to literature, claimed that he had no programmatic intent in writing it and that, especially in Part Two, he had emphasized distinctly literary issues.

The lengthiest chapter of the book is "Outline of a World," in Part One. Since Faulkner was alone among twentieth-century American novelists in creating an imaginary world nearly complete in itself, Howe devotes minute attention to showing the inseparable link between locale and theme in the world of Yoknapatawpha County, believing that "merely to describe this world with some fullness and accuracy is to approach the central motives of his work." This county, Faulkner's imaginative recreation of Mississippi and parts of Tennessee, became, according to Howe, "the setting for a complex moral chronicle in which a popular myth and an almost legendary past yield something quite rare in American literature: a deep sense of the burdens and grandeur of history . . . " (4).

Howe, despite his commitment to "progressive" politics, here grants that social backwardness and even failure can yield great literary advantages. Just as the Russian writers of the nineteenth century had exploited Russia's backwardness as a vantage point to observe the "advanced" life of Western Europe, so too did the Southern writers exploit the "perspective from the social rear" (23) and still more the perspective of the defeated. Howe views Faulkner and the other Southern writers as creators of a literature that began at an ending, just as he viewed Yiddish literature and American-Jewish literature. He observes that it was not until the First World War that serious Southern writing began to appear, for it was only then that Southern regional consciousness began to decay. Tate was correct in saying that Southern literature took on seriousness and grandeur only when the South began to die (26). Southern writers were driven by the grim circumstances of twentieth-century life to a regional past that in happier circumstances they would have learned peaceably to forget. "The mottoes of Southern agrarianism which became popular some decades ago were hardly to be taken seriously as social proposals for the most industrialized country in the world; but as signs of a fundamental quarrel with modern life, an often brilliant criticism of urban anonymity, they very much deserved to be taken seriously" (24–25). In such praise of the Southern ideology as myth rather than political program, one finds an eerie foreshadowing of Howe's later definition of his own chief lost cause: socialism in America.

Although Faulkner's work rises, so to speak, upon the ruins of the old South, Howe claims that Faulkner nowhere in his voluminous work offers a copious and lively image of the old South. "It remains forever a muted shadow, a point of reference rather than an object of presentation." Even in *The Unvanquished*, where he does offer a glimpse of the old South, he begins at the point where its demise is certain. Nevertheless, Howe argues, this absence of the old South is no weakness at all; rather it shows Faulkner's sense of reality triumphing over his preconceptions, "wisdom as omission" (42), a notion Howe would use many years later in writing about Aharon Appelfeld's novels of the Holocaust.

The chapter called "Faulkner and the Negroes" is one of the early instances in Howe's criticism of his sureness of touch and (un-Marxian) disinterestedness in dealing with political issues in literary works. Needless to say that Howe, as a socialist, a Jew, an intensely political creature, was deeply concerned with America's racial divide. Yet it is clear that his main concern in this book is not with Faulkner's explicit views on the racial question but rather with how those views affect the novels. Faulkner's views matter only when they are absorbed into his art, "there to undergo transformations of a kind that justify our speaking of literature as a mode of creation" (116).

Howe argues that Faulkner has no single view on the Negro question, but multiple perspectives. One strong motif of his work, for example, to which Howe responds with undogmatic sympathy, is the conviction that "fraternity is morally finer than equality" (123), a conviction that would repeatedly find expression in Howe's later work.[58] On the other hand, Howe thinks that perhaps the "endurance" of the Negroes, of which Faulkner makes so much, is no more than one of the masks they use in order to find their way in a hostile world. Stressing that Faulkner is not a systematic thinker, has no strictly formulated views on the "Negro question," and as a novelist is not obliged to have them, Howe nevertheless tries to trace an upward trajectory, from novel to novel, in Faulkner's grasp of the racial problem. A particularly interesting instance, he asserts, is the portrait of Lucas Beauchamp in *Absalom, Absalom*. Howe praises this character as "a member of an oppressed group who appears not as a catalogue of disabilities or even virtues, but as a human being in his own right. He is not a form of behavior but a person, not 'Negro' but a Negro" (129). Such praise for literary creation of an oppressed person whose character and culture are not reducible to the terms of oppression would seem to run counter to the position that Howe later (1963) would take in his heated dispute with the writer Ralph Ellison.

The Faulkner book may be viewed as a kind of declaration of independence by Howe from the narrow-minded dictates of Marxist, progressive literary criticism. He defiantly states that "whoever wants a precise platform or a coherent sociology for the Negroes had better look elsewhere. Faulkner's triumph is of another kind, the novelist's triumph: a body of dramatic actions, a group of realized characters" (134).

Politics and the Novel, 1957

Not long after the Faulkner book, Howe embarked on a series of essays about politics and the novel which demonstrated still more powerfully a disinterestedness of mind and fineness of discrimination entirely at odds not only with Marxist modes of thought but even with Howe's own strictly political writing. Indeed, it is nearly mind-boggling to recognize that Howe's essays on Conrad, Stendhal (in part), James, now usually read as chapters of the 1957 book, grew out of his teaching at the Indiana School of Letters in Bloomington, in the summer of 1953[59] and were published in late 1953 and early 1954, almost simultaneously with the intensely partisan and contentious essays on "This Age of Conformity" and on the program of *Dissent*. The chapter on Orwell's *1984*, a book that, if not quite "conservative," is nevertheless very critical of certain key socialist tendencies, is essentially the essay that Howe had published in *New International* back in 1950.[60]

No principle of organization enunciated by Howe for this book about what happens to the novel when subjected to the pressures of politics and political ideology reveals as much about its nature as his ranking of Dostoyevsky's *The Possessed* as "the greatest of all political novels." From a crudely political perspective, Dostoyevsky might be thought to have represented all that Howe deplored. Dostoyevsky wrote this novel with the explicit purpose of excoriating, even cursing, all beliefs in salvation outside of Christianity. Dostoyevsky himself was quite candid about his polemical intention: "I mean to utter certain thoughts whether all the artistic side of it goes to the dogs or not . . . even if it turns into a mere pamphlet, I shall say all that I have in my heart." Knowing this, how does a socialist literary critic approach *The Possessed*? First, of course, he must conclude (rightly in this case) that the novelist has not after all deteriorated into a pamphleteer or suppressed his "artistic side," but has probed corners of the mind and heart not mapped out in the original plan. But then he must recognize that the task of persuasion in which the political novel engages is not really its main or distinctive purpose. "I find it hard to imagine . . . a serious socialist being dissuaded from his belief by a reading of *The Possessed*, though I should like equally to think that the quality and nuance of that belief can never be quite as they were before he read *The Possessed*."[61]

Politics and the Novel was an attempt by Howe to bring together two aspects of his own sensibility, the literary and the political, and to integrate them in the act of criticism. He selected a number of major novels that had been shaped by one of the dominant varieties of modern thought in order "to see what the violent intrusion of politics does to, and perhaps for, the literary imagination" (15). He believed that historically the political novel came into being when the novelist could no longer take society for granted in the way that a writer like Jane Austen had done. When the novelist was forced to shift his attention from distinctions of class and manners within society to the fate of society itself, the political novel came into being. Howe grants that in practice the distinction is less sharp than in theory: *Middlemarch*, for example, seems to encompass both categories.

At the center of political novels, as Howe defines them, is the tension between ideology, which is abstract, and immediate experience, which is sensuous. From this conflict the political novel gains its peculiar interest and high drama. Howe does not take the view that abstract ideas violate or contaminate works of art; on the contrary, they are indispensable to serious novels. But they must be transformed by the novelist into something other than the ideas of a political program. "At its best, the political novel generates such intense heat that the ideas it appropriates are melted into its movement and fused with the emotions of its characters. George Eliot . . . speaks of 'the severe effort of trying to make certain ideas incarnate, as if they had revealed themselves to me first in the flesh'" (21).[62] The successful political novelist endows ideas with the power to stir characters into life. But always he faces the task of demonstrating the relation between theory and experience, between the preexisting political ideology and the individual feelings and social relations he tries to present in his narrative.

A major paradox of Howe's conception of the political novel is his premise that it is always on the verge of becoming something other than itself. This is because it is in a state of internal conflict between the imperious and impersonal claims of ideology and the pressures of private emotion. Just as Irving Howe, Marxist-socialist ideologue, is wise enough to recognize that the chemistry of human motive complicates the application of political abstractions, so does the political novel confront "the purity of ideal with the contaminations of action" (23). In consequence, the novels Howe selects as exemplars of the genre typically turn to apolitical temptations, just as the archetype of the form, *The Possessed*, abandons politics for the belief that redemption comes only to sinners who have suffered greatly.

The greatness of political novels cannot, Howe declares, be determined by political standards. Rather, they must satisfy the criteria used for assessing any other novel: how much of our lives do they illuminate? how inclusive a moral vision do they suggest? But given the fact that political novelists and their readers are more sensitive than ordinary people to political opinions, especially political opinions they hate, such novels pose a special challenge or test. "For the writer the great test is, how much truth can he force through the sieve of his opinions? For the reader the great test is, how much of that truth can he accept though it jostle *his* opinions?" (24) In the course of *Politics and the Novel* that anonymous political reader becomes Howe himself; and a good part of the book's interest lies in seeing how this particular ideologue can accommodate his convictions to his literary integrity as he examines novels that call those convictions into question. Nor is it far-fetched to suppose that, in the process of testing his opinions against the imagined life of the novels, he was going through a process of refinement, discrimination, and selection whereby he altered his political ideology. Marxism, for example, is so frequently modified by the adjective "vulgar" in Howe's literary discussions that one may begin to wonder whether there is any other kind, despite his constant protestations of loyalty to the creed.

Let us illustrate Howe's critical method in this early book by examining his treatment of two novels, one written by the conservative Joseph Conrad, the other by his fellow-socialist George Orwell.

Although Howe looked upon Conrad's conservatism as in large part a psychological reflex as much as a full-fledged ideology, and perhaps not organic to his work, he recognized it as deeply felt and fervently adhered to by the transplanted novelist, whose politics (on both the positive and negative sides) was rooted in Polish nationalism. Conrad's conservatism pitted itself, of course, not against Howe's Marxian socialism so much as against anarchism. Yet Howe suggests, mischievously, that nineteenth-century anarchism and nationalism were only apparent opposites, were in fact more like each other than either was like Marxian socialism. Showing perhaps too keen an appetite for paradox, he says that "conservatism is the anarchism of the fortunate, anarchism the conservatism of the deprived. Against the omnivorous state, conservatism and anarchism equally urge resistance by the individual" (84). Moreover, unlike socialism, they both reject industrial society and express a rural bias.

The Secret Agent (1907) has at its center a group of stupid, vicious, yet largely harmless anarchists. Conrad treats them and virtually everyone else in the story, including their adversaries in the British police and the Czarist infiltrators, with corrosive irony. The only character who escapes this irony, according to Howe, is Stevie, the idiot boy who is the brother of the novel's heroine, Winnie. "He is meant to convey a purity

of pathos and to represent the humanitarian impulse in its most vulnerable form; but a character for whom one feels nothing but pity can
hardly command the emotion Conrad intends" (97). But one wonders
whether this gingerly dismissal of a symbolically central character does
not conceal on Howe's part a certain recognition that Conrad has cut
closer to the bone of his own political organism than he liked. Stevie,
readers of the novel will recall, is characterized by "the anguish of
immoderate compassion . . . succeeded by the pain of an innocent but
pitiless rage" (chap. viii). Thus, deranged though he be, Stevie is symbolically linked with most of the would-be world betterers in the novel.

Howe also objects to Conrad's "cartoon"-like depiction of the anarchists, especially the bomb-laden professor (of terror), as manifestations of what Conrad calls "human nature in its discontent and imbecil-
ity." His objection, Howe insists, derives not from sympathy with the
anarchist movement but from aesthetic and historical reasons. The
actual anarchists—Kropotkin and Bakunin, for example—were surely
motivated by something more than, as Conrad puts it, "dislike of all
kinds of recognized labor." If Conrad really wants to get at the complexities of the radical mind, why does he present radicals as shams
who don't actually believe what they profess, or else are crazy?

One might here be tempted to charge that Howe's objection to
Conrad as, so to speak, unfair to radicals betrays a personal unease not
fully acknowledged. But Howe, with that critical honesty that was
always to distinguish his literary work, beats us to the accusation.
What, he asks, is the relation between a political novel and the actuality
it purports to describe? Can such a book as *The Secret Agent* be read, in
a "fiercely partisan age," without fiercely partisan emotions? No matter
the author's intention, such novels work eagerly to persuade readers of
some point of view: "And the critic too had better acknowledge that he
comes to the political novel with an eye that is partial and perhaps
inflamed" (98). This is done with true Arnoldian disinterestedness, and
it compels the reader's admiration.

Although it does not pose the challenge of dealing fairly with a
conservative novelist, the book's final essay, "Orwell: History as Nightmare," merits a similar accolade. Orwell, in 1949 (just a year before his
death) gave the world the classic nightmare vision of the revolutionary
betrayal of freedom in the anti-utopian fiction called *1984*.[63] From
Howe's perspective, Orwell came to his task with impressive credentials (despite the blemish of having supported the war against Hitler).
He had declared in an autobiographical essay of 1947 that "every line
of serious work that I have written since 1936 [the year of his experience
of Communist betrayal in the Spanish Civil War] has been written,
directly or indirectly, *against* totalitarianism and *for* democratic Socialism. . . . "[64]

Howe found *1984* impressive and also appalling because in it Orwell had conveyed the unwelcome truth that totalitarian terror was not inherent in the human condition but peculiar to the twentieth century, a result of conditions that might have been avoided. The uneasy balance which *Partisan Review* (which included Orwell among its contributors) tried to maintain between the aesthetic and the political was tipped sharply toward the latter by Orwell's book; and Howe approved. He writes that those who derided the style of *1984* as drab, uninspired, sweaty, had "succumbed to the pleasant tyrannies of estheticism; they had allowed their fondness for a cultivated style to blind them to the urgencies of prophetic expression." When Orwell wrote *1984*, Howe defiantly declares, "the last thing [Orwell] should have cared about, was literature" (237).

Howe read Orwell's book as an attack on the totalitarian system for its destruction of individuality and personality through an assault on contemplativeness and "purposeless" sexual passion. The book, he argues, offers a model of the totalitarian state in its pure form and a vision of what this state does to human life. Like most political novels, it stresses the conflict between ideology and emotion, but in a particularly twentieth-century version—by setting politics in opposition to humanity, and the state in opposition to society. Howe readily concedes that this theme expresses the "conservative side of Orwell's outlook," a side which the first name of the hero, Winston Smith, fixes in the reader's mind. Neither does Howe conceal the importance of Orwell's casting Trotsky (in the guise of Emmanuel Goldstein) as the counter-image to Churchill. *1984* is for Howe an assault upon the Russian travesty of socialism, whose actual campaign to obliterate individuality and expunge memory was merely carried one step further, to extreme and radical form, in the fictional Oceania. Oceania's physical atmosphere was also derived in part from "the modern Russian cities with their Victorian ostentation and rotting slums" (243). Howe is careful to include in his essay Orwell's disclaimer: "My novel *1984* is *not* intended as an attack on socialism, or on the British Labor Party, but as a show-up of the perversions to which a centralized economy is liable . . . " (240).

Howe praises Orwell for having recognized Stalinism as a more advanced and subtle form of totalitarianism than the Nazi version: "Hitler burned books, Stalin had them rewritten." The destruction of social memory, the euphemization and perversion of language, the exploitation of popular culture: all these characteristics of totalitarian regimes have, in Howe's view, been masterfully conveyed by Orwell.

Nevertheless, Howe has reservations about the book's assumption that totalitarianism can transform human nature itself; in these reservations lurks a paradox. Howe often asserted that socialism rests ultimately upon the possibilities for transforming human nature (e.g., MH,

106). Yet now he recoils in horror from the recognition that totalitarianism had succeeded as a vast laboratory experiment in the transformation of man—but into a form of animal. The main fault of Orwell's book, Howe believes, is that his totalitarian society is more *total* than can be imagined; that is to say, it transforms human nature itself. For example, Orwell depicts the sexual impulse as so weakened among the members of the Outer party that the rulers of Oceania are able to transform sexual energy entirely into political hysteria. This Howe finds implausible, and for a reason that sounds very "conservative": namely, that not even the most powerful terrorist regime can radically alter "the fundamental impulses of man." There is, he insists, "a constant in human nature which no amount of terror or propaganda can destroy." Are there not certain "indestructible human needs" that no regime can break down? In a rare surge of optimism, Howe espouses the "animal drives" of man as among "the most enduring forces of resistance to the totalitarian state" (245–47).

Howe is also skeptical about Orwell's portrayal of the party oligarchy in Oceania as having dispensed with ideology. O'Brien, the Inner party spokesman, says in a key speech of the novel that "the Party seeks power entirely for its own sake. We are not interested in the good of the others; we are interested solely in power." In discarding ideology, the rulers of Oceania claim to have gone beyond the Nazi belief in race and the Stalinist devotion to Marxism. But if this were possible, Howe asks, what would be the "ultimate purpose" of totalitarian rulers? "Why do they kill millions of people, why do they find pleasure in torturing and humiliating people they know to be innocent?. . . What is the image of the world they desire, the vision by which they live?" (249–50) To such questions Howe cannot supply an answer any more than Orwell could, but he knows that Orwell has demonstrated irrefutably how the rise of totalitarianism called into question (if it did not entirely explode) the capacity of Marxist categories to encompass the twentieth-century debacle.

Howe's essay on *1984* provides, in the framework of *Politics and the Novel,* a kind of completing counterpart to the book's lengthy discussion of *The Possessed* in chapter three. There he argues that Dostoyevsky, starting out with the deliberate purpose of making a reactionary case, was moved by the play of his imagination and the reach of his sympathies to make the novel something far larger than the "tract" he had intended. With Orwell, Howe shows how a writer of the left found himself criticizing the mistakes, myths, and foolishness of the left. Indeed, Howe in later years would grant that "a neoconservative of subtle literary habits" might reasonably claim for *1984,* "not that it was written with the intent of supporting conservatism but that, in its penetration and honesty regarding the total state, it necessarily comes down on the conservative side. . . . "[65] Howe does not quite endorse such an interpretation, of course, but the penetration and honesty of his own approach in *Politics and the Novel* helped to make such interpretations possible and plausible, just as they made the book the exhilarating and enlarging experience that it still is.

SIX

The Sixties, Decade of Controversy: The Golem Rises against Its Creator

---

> *We race along from dizzy decade to decade. We hurry from the tepid conservatism of the '50s to the utopian frenzies of the '60s. . . . Professors who only the day before yesterday were the milkiest of liberals or who declared themselves above "mere" politics, now lash themselves into a revolutionary intoxication. They denounce people like myself as barriers to the gathering popular upsurge. . . .*[1]

> *By about 1960 most of us no longer thought of ourselves as Marxists. At times we seemed to have almost nothing left but the animating ethic of socialism, and we knew that an ethic, no matter how admirable, could never replace a politics. But if you took that ethic seriously and persisted in struggling for modes of realization, you could have enough intellectual work for a lifetime. (MH, 238)*

Early Sixties: Public Optimism, Private Despair

The early 1960s seemed to Howe to bring a new atmosphere of liberal openness. He was delighted that *Commentary* had found itself a new editor, Norman Podhoretz, who was steering the magazine sharply to the left and unashamedly espousing visionary, utopian ideals. "*Com-*

mentary, once the center of the more embittered, sophisticated anti-radicalism, is these days [1963] a new magazine, receptive to a wide range of opinion, including that of writers on the democratic left." He believed that the Cold War had "run its course of futility."[2] He was pleased that Americans now actually had, in John F. Kennedy, a literate as well as reasonably liberal president. The nascent civil rights movement brought the fresh ideas of nonviolent resistance and civil disobedience to American society. Young people were turning in small yet significant numbers to the peace movement. The old radicals saw hope of resurrection: "Just about all of us who had experienced the debacles of the thirties and the dryness of the next two decades were tempted to seek political renewal through forming ties with the insurgent students" ("Rahv: a Memoir," 495). Howe and his friends admired the energy of the young radicals, and shared much of their criticism of American society. There was, it seemed, only one problem: "we could not go along with their pastoral simplicities" ("Historical Memory," 26).

Howe's *Dissent* essay of winter 1960 called "A Mind's Turnings" appears, in retrospect, almost complacent in its (relative) optimism, especially when we recall what was soon to come. Howe begins with the small apology, noted in the previous chapter, for having helped to encourage the obsession with "conformity" that is sweeping the country. He now thinks that the most striking trait of American culture during recent decades has been neither conformity nor conservatism but "an unprecedented capacity for assimilating—and thereby depreciating—everything on its own terms, both lavish praise and severe attacks" (31). It is almost as though Howe is complaining that he cannot take yes any more than no for an answer from capitalist culture.

But if radical ideas were being adulterated through bland assimilation, this did not absolve intellectuals from promoting them. Espousing a form of limited liability for intellectuals, Howe says that "we can be responsible only for what we say, not for what 'happens' to it later. . . . " By way of explanation, he offers this humorous yet also discomfortingly pious illustration: "If Jesus were to deliver His sermon on the mount next week, Ed Murrow would interview Him in His gracious suburban home, Khrushchev would announce that in Russia they have 'things just as good,' *Time* would sorrowfully warn its readers against His gnostic heresies, Jean-Paul Sartre would publish in a special number of *Temps Modernes* a 60,000-word preface to the French edition, and Dwight Macdonald . . . would write that while 'Mr. Christ makes some telling points' they suffer from syntactical confusion and 'a woolly pretentious style'" (33).[3]

Even though his Marxism is by now "vestigial" and his socialism "primarily a commitment to a value and a problem," Howe insists that he and his colleagues must continue to regard themselves "not merely as radicals but also as socialists" (32). Moreover, as intellectuals they must be pledged to freedom as the highest, though not only, value. They must not hire themselves out as servants to any cause—History, Progress, or Plans—except the cause of truth freely pursued. All intellectuals, including socialist intellectuals (a label in which Howe recognizes an uneasy tension between noun and adjective), who are true to their calling "tend finally toward a kind of non-political anarchism." For that reason, Howe feels himself spiritually closest not to American liberals or European Social Democrats but to "conservative" writers like Conrad, Melville, and—above all—Dostoyevsky; and he makes it clear that he is talking not of Dostoyevsky the novelist so much as Dostoyevsky "the thinker whom radicals used uneasily to belittle" (34). At the very moment when Howe suspected that radical ideas were infiltrating the culture at large, his mind turned back once more to the reactionary thinker "who foresaw a situation in which the movement of history would drive men into a fearful choice between the risks of freedom and the security of a false collective" (34). At the very moment when he concluded (contrary to his post–World War II obsession) that "there will not be a war within the next few decades" (35) and could "envisage a world in which material wants will be moderately satisfied" (35), Howe was driven by some deep-seated conservative intuition back to the bosom of Dostoyevsky, who feared that society, precisely by its desire to be beneficent, could rob us of our freedom. Thus did Dostoyevsky become in Howe's mind the forerunner of Camus and his lament, quoted earlier, about the betrayal of freedom by modern revolutionary movements.

Howe's public optimism, however qualified, about the state of America at the beginning of the sixties was in sharp contrast to his private gloom and personal difficulties. Although it should have been bliss in that dawn to be alive, Howe now suffered (and probably also contributed to) the collapse of his second marriage and consequent breakup of his family. "To get up each morning became an ordeal of the will. Everything I had striven for seemed pointless. . . . Stumbling in private life, I was soon overcome by doubts about vocation. I could not reconcile my desire to be a writer with remembered fantasies about public action. I had written books just good enough to mark the limits of my talent. I chafed under the crossed frustrations of literary critic and socialist editor." Had he belonged to some larger, vital community, this crisis would have been less painful. Even in the sanguine essay just discussed, he acknowledged that "our [we *Dissenters'*] main difficulty is that we are not related to a living movement about which we could steadily and with loyalty complain, and . . . no such movement is in sight" (37). No such communal life—neither socialist, nor literary, nor Jewish—was available to him; and so his pain had to be endured privately, "quite in the American way" (MH, 287–88).

Howe spent two unhappy years, 1961–63, at Stanford University. He brought with him urban New York parochialism and a prejudice against the whole state of California as second-rate, mind-softening, smug, and self-adoring. Celia Morris, in her fine memoir of Howe, recalls how "Irving hated Stanford. He found those sunny, healthy, surf-boarding California students bland and appallingly polite, and it was an awful time in his own life because of his bent for romantic misadventures. Irving once said . . . that he might have been a great critic if it hadn't been for women. . . . He had this Woody-Allen way of mocking his own gracelessness that made me forget most of the time that for a deeply cultured and sophisticated man, he was the most parochial person I'd ever known."[4] Robert Heilman recalls that Howe told him he eventually decided to leave Stanford because nobody there could understand his Jewish jokes. When a job offer came from the City University of New York, Howe accepted it with alacrity and went back home, thereby (as he liked to joke) saving himself from the dangers of becoming a dope dealer or transcendental guru or beat poet had he remained in California. In 1963 he began to teach at Hunter College. He no longer loved New York, but felt it was his natural habitat. "In the discords of this city I could again listen to myself. Even when heartsick, I knew it was my heart's field" (MH, 291).

The New Radicalism

At first, the new wave of radicalism struck Howe as innocent and sweet-tempered; but he soon discovered that it was neither. In 1962 several of the leading figures of the ironically named Students for a Democratic Society, including Tom Hayden, paid a visit to the editorial board of *Dissent*. Quickly Howe and his colleagues discovered, to their dismay, that the SDS slogan of "participatory democracy" was conceived of as the antithesis to, not the completion of, "representative democracy." (Thirty years later, in an essay on Walter Scott, Howe would refer to a chapter in *Old Mortality* "depicting a clutter of demented fanatics exhorting a rebel gathering of Scottish Presbyterians in an exercise of 'participatory democracy' unnervingly similar to some I witnessed in the 1960s.")[5] The older generation of radicals could not but recall the old Stalinist slogans about the need to suppress "mere" bour-

geois democracy. Equally troubling was the readiness of the SDS leaders to applaud such Communist tyrannies as Cuba. Their most contentious member, Hayden, might seem brilliant, but also struck Howe as
rigid and fanatical, somebody with the makings of a commissar: "And
I felt . . . that if he had the power and believed it necessary, he wouldn't
hesitate to put me up against the wall and have me shot. That done, he
might shed a tear for my miscreant social democratic soul" ("Historical
Memory," 26). The meeting ended badly, portending the hostility that
would grow between Howe and the younger generation of radicals he
had helped to create.

Podhoretz has described Howe's brief embrace of the nascent radicalism and the reasons for his break with it:

> Like me, but unlike Trilling, Howe had welcomed the appearance of a
> new radicalism in the early sixties. Like me too, he had developed
> serious doubts about its attitudes toward democracy on the one side
> and communism on the other, and he had expressed those doubts
> forcefully enough to provoke Philip Rahv and others into charging
> him with having deserted "genuine radicalism" altogether. When,
> therefore, my younger *Commentary* colleague Neal Kozodoy . . . and I
> decided that the time had come to declare full-scale war [against the
> Movement], we had good reason to expect Howe's enthusiastic coop-
> eration, and we got it—for as long, that is, as he continued to worry
> about the Movement's claim to have supplanted "democratic social-
> ists" like himself as the true heir of the radical tradition. (*Breaking
> Ranks*, 304–305)

Howe felt slightly more comfortable in the "moderate" peace organization called SANE (Committee for a Sane Nuclear Policy), which he
joined in 1963. Its members, unlike those of SDS, were neither all radical
nor all young; and they impressed Howe because of the personal,
conscientious nature of their opposition to American intervention in
Vietnam. They were, however, the spiritual children of Thoreau, never
one of Howe's favorite authors. Ever inclined to dissent from the conformity of dissent, he did not much like these people, even if he did
admire them: "they carried themselves with an air of righteousness not
very far from fanaticism" (MH, 300).

Howe's open combat with the New Left would come later in the
decade. Meanwhile, there were other struggles to be joined. In 1963 he
became embroiled in two controversies ultimately more crucial to his
intellectual development than the battle with the New Left. The first
concerned the nature of Jewish behavior during the Holocaust; the
second the role of the Negro writer in what was then called the Negro
Revolution. Both brought Howe into conflict with people who in "nor-

mal" circumstances would have been his allies: Hannah Arendt and Ralph Ellison.

The Eichmann Controversy: 1963–64

In 1961 the *New Yorker* sent the eminent political thinker Arendt to Jerusalem to cover the trial of Adolf Eichmann. Her account and analysis of the trial first appeared in the February and March 1963 issues of that magazine. The articles were published as a book in May of the same year, with the contentious title *Eichmann in Jerusalem: A Report on the Banality of Evil.*

The book aroused a terrific storm of controversy primarily because it alleged that the Jews had cooperated significantly in their own destruction: "Wherever Jews lived, there were recognized Jewish leaders, and this leadership," Arendt maintained, "almost without exception, cooperated in one way or another, for one reason or another, with the Nazis."[6] Except among her most passionate disciples, it is now generally accepted that Arendt was woefully and willfully mistaken in this central assertion. At the time she wrote, very little serious historical research had been done on the subject of the *Judenrate,* the Jewish councils that the Germans established to help them administer the ghettos of Eastern Europe until they were disbanded and their inhabitants deported and murdered. But even to the meager historical material available she paid little attention, preferring to use secondary sources that would lend support to her accusation of Jewish collaboration with the Nazis. The abrasive effect of the book was increased by the fact that it first appeared in the *New Yorker*—the discussions of mass murder alongside the ads for perfume, mink coats, and racing cars—and that the sections on the Jewish leaders were in a tone that the great scholar Gershom Scholem, Arendt's old friend, characterized in a letter to her as "heartless, frequently almost sneering and malicious."[7]

Also subjected to widespread, albeit far less withering, criticism was the book's depiction of Eichmann not as a monster at all, but as the most ordinary of men. The deportation of the Jews from every corner of Europe to the death camps in Poland was, according to Arendt, "for Eichmann a job, with its daily routine, its ups and downs" (153). Typical of the criticism of her interpretation of Eichmann's character is the outburst of the hero of Saul Bellow's novel, *Mr. Sammler's Planet* (1970): "What better way to get the curse out of murder than to make it look ordinary, boring, or trite?" Arendt, according to old Artur Sammler, was duped, for the banality that she purported to discover in these murderers and their evil deeds was merely camouflage. The Nazis, he argues, never forgot their old, normal knowledge of what is meant by murder. No one should believe that the abolition of conscience is a trivial or banal matter unless she believes that human life itself is trivial. Arendt stands accused of "making use of a tragic history to promote the foolish ideas of Weimar intellectuals."[8]

Howe, who had already publicly defended the Israeli capture of Eichmann in Argentina as a necessary moral act by the victims of the Holocaust, was deeply troubled by Arendt's articles, both by their content and by their location in the *New Yorker,* a magazine then infamous for not allowing letters to the editor challenging or refuting articles it had published.[9] The articles, Howe wrote in *Commentary* in October 1963, "roused in me such strong sentiments of disagreement that for the moment I put aside the problem of their appearance in the *New Yorker.* Time went by, and most of what had to be said in criticism . . . was said by Marie Syrkin, Lionel Abel, and Norman Podhoretz; so that, in my mind, I could turn back to the feeling of resentment I had had upon first seeing them in the pages of the *New Yorker.*"[10] Syrkin, one of Arendt's most trenchant critics, had urged Howe to consider: how many *New Yorker* readers had ever before cared to read a word of the vast literature about Jewish resistance, martyrdom, and occasional survival during the Holocaust? How many of these readers would ever know that the distinguished Jewish historian, Jacob Robinson, had discovered a huge number of factual errors in Arendt's articles? (He later enumerated them in a page-by-page refutation of her book entitled *And the Crooked Shall Be Made Straight,* 1965.)

Howe was outraged by the fact that Arendt's articles, which had brought the most serious charges against the European Jews, against their institutions and leaders and character, had been distributed to a mass audience unequipped to judge them critically, and had then been sealed shut against criticism in the *New Yorker* itself. "For the *New Yorker,* as for the whole cultural style it represents, the publication of Miss Arendt's articles disposed, in effect, of the issue: there was nothing more for it to say or allow to be said in its columns, except to defend Miss Arendt in a lugubrious editorial against those who had presumed to notice that she wrote with insufficient scholarship or humane sympathies" (319). Arendt had branded the Jewish leadership in Europe as cowardly, incompetent, collaborationist; she had accused it of helping the Nazis destroy the Jews of Europe; and she had alleged that if the Jews had not "cooperated" with the Nazis, many fewer than six million would have been killed. Responsible and scholarly opponents disputed her factual statements and her conclusions; yet as far as the imperious *New Yorker* was concerned, "Miss Arendt has the first, the last, the only word" (319). Thus Howe saw in the Arendt controversy not only a

Jewish problem, but one in social controls and the nature and power of modern journalism.

The debate that did not take place in the *New Yorker* did come to pass in the *Partisan Review*. Both Arendt and her ardent supporter Macdonald tried to stop William Phillips from printing Abel's attack on the book. Pressured in the opposite direction by coeditor Philip Rahv, he printed the review but then opened the question to wider discussion in subsequent issues. Comments were published by Mary McCarthy, Macdonald, Syrkin, Robert Lowell, Harold Weisberg, Phillips himself, and Howe. This too, of course, failed to satisfy Arendt, who proceeded to excommunicate Phillips as well (*A Partisan View*, 109).

The Eichmann controversy was by no means Howe's first encounter with Arendt. Back in 1947 he had earned $150 a month as her assistant when she was the editor of Schocken Books. He wrote copy for book jackets, improved translations, and so forth. In addition to the $150, he received the privilege of visiting the great thinker at her office every week. He found her attitudes toward modern Jewry "hopelessly mixed. She breathed hostility toward established Jewish institutions, especially Zionist ones. . . . She felt impatient with what she took to be their intellectual mediocrity, their bourgeois flaccidity—oh, she could be very grand in her haughtiness." When the Eichmann book came, what struck Howe most painfully in it was her supercilious contempt for everyone and everything connected with the trial, and especially "those coarse Israelis" (MH, 270–71).

The dispute over *Eichmann in Jerusalem* simmered, splitting the New York intellectuals into opposing camps. Howe's magazine, *Dissent*, organized a public forum on the book early in the fall of 1963 in the Hotel Diplomat in midtown Manhattan. Nearly five hundred people were in attendance, to witness the debate between Arendt's primary critics, Abel and Syrkin, and her defenders, Raul Hilberg and Daniel Bell. Howe presided as chairman; Arendt ignored the invitation to attend; so too did Bruno Bettelheim, whose views resembled hers (and whose anti-Zionism, expressed in Macdonald's *Politics* as far back as 1948, exceeded hers). When Arendt met Howe a year later at a party, she refused to speak to him, though relations improved slightly after a lapse of four or five years.

Just what happened at the forum has been a subject of contention for decades. Although Howe awarded the accolade for the "most judicious words in the whole debate" to Podhoretz, who portrayed Arendt's book as a flagrant example of applying higher moral standards to Jews than to everybody else, Podhoretz's wife, Midge Decter, later accused Howe of arranging a "lynching" in the form of a public meeting. "It did not then and does not now [1982] occur to Mr. Howe that gathering a mob against a book is not a proper form of intellectual manners" (Decter, 30). Dispute about Howe's conduct of the meeting began early and continued for a mere eighteen years. In winter 1964, in the pages of *Partisan Review*, Mary McCarthy, who had not attended the forum, alleged (in a generally disgraceful article) that the one voice from the audience raised in Arendt's defense had been shouted down, and that the atmosphere of the meeting was "remote from that of free speech." Howe replied sharply in the spring 1964 issue that, as chairman, he had twice asked for speakers from the floor to speak in support of Arendt, and none arose. Only after he announced that discussion from the floor was over did Alfred Kazin jump up to speak. "Though I regarded this intervention as irregular, I gave him the floor and he spoke his piece."[11]

When Howe's autobiography appeared in 1982, he once more found himself defending his conduct of the forum on *Eichmann in Jerusalem*, now in the pages of *Dissent*. Arendt's biographer and apologist, Elizabeth Young-Bruehl, had included in her book a jaundiced account of the evening, repeating, for example, McCarthy's claim that Kazin had been kicked out. Howe, in a letter dated 21 March 1982, rebutted her accusation, insisting that "We of *Dissent* have made it a point of principle, and honor, that whenever we hold a public forum, the floor is granted to whoever wishes to participate in the discussion period. We have a record of tolerance and freedom on such matters that we cherish. . . . "[12] Howe granted that the atmosphere of the meeting more closely resembled a contentious session of the House of Commons than a typical faculty meeting, but insisted that everybody who wished to speak had been heard out. That a majority of those who spoke turned out to be critics of Arendt was not part of a stratagem by the sponsors of the meeting. In *Commentary*, Syrkin came to Howe's defense, scoffing at the notion that Arendt could ever have been a defenseless lamb set upon by a frenzied mob. The symposium, she argued, was not a mere literary controversy about a book, but an examination of widely disseminated allegations of the Jews' guilt for and complicity in their own destruction. Howe had performed a notable service by involving a previously aloof sector of the Jewish intelligentsia in a consideration of the greatest crime of the century. The forum, she believed, had marked a turning point in bringing awareness of the catastrophe to a once indifferent group.[13]

About two years after Howe's death, it became evident that neither he nor Syrkin nor Abel nor even Robinson had dealt as severely with Arendt as she deserved. For when the correspondence between her and Martin Heidegger, the Nazi philosopher with whom she had had a love affair for four years in the 1920s, was published, it revealed that they had resumed their friendship after World War II. She then, from 1950 onward, according to Professor Elzbieta Ettinger, devoted herself to popularizing his philosophy in the United States by finding publishers, negotiating contracts, and selecting translators. "Above all, she did what she could to whitewash his Nazi past."[14] In 1971, for example, on the occasion of Heidegger's eightieth birthday, she wrote in *The New York Review of Books*, in what Richard Wolin calls "flagrant defiance of the truth," that Heidegger (by neglecting to read *Mein Kampf*) had escaped "from the reality of the Gestapo cellars and the torture hells of the early concentration camps into ostensibly more significant regions":

> By showing that Arendt was busy exculpating Heidegger even as she was busy inculpating the victims of Nazism, Ettinger's book casts an even darker shadow over *Eichmann in Jerusalem*. The tone of that book seems even uglier. Arendt appears to have been raising herself above those Eastern European Jewish ghetto-dwellers who willingly cooperated in being collectively led to the slaughter. She, after all, had imbibed, and now exemplified, certain higher European traditions; and she had studied with, and loved, the great modern tribune of *Geist*. Could it have been those old loyalties that in some way led her to purvey such calumnies about the Jews in the Eichmann book? Could the offensive passages of the book have been meant somehow to absolve the magician of Messkirch of his crimes by showing that his victims were also guilty?[15]

No wonder, then, that Arendt contemptuously dismissed critics of her book as part of a conspiracy against her by the "Jewish Establishment," an odd appellation for Irving Howe. All in all, it is not a pretty picture. But whatever else may be said about the dispute over Arendt's book there is no doubt that it played a tremendous role in Howe's consciousness of himself as a Jew, disturbing him more than any subsequent event. "Unwittingly," he later recalled, "it served a great purpose. The book was like a therapeutic session where you discover that, welling up within you, there is a great mass of feeling that you have not known, that had been suppressed" ("Range," 286).

The Negro Revolution and the Ralph Ellison Controversy, 1963

At the very time that the Eichmann controversy was raging, Howe was writing passionately and extensively on "The Negro Revolution." In fact, the second of his two articles with that title appeared in the very issue of *Dissent* (Autumn 1963) that carried Syrkin's devastating attack entitled "Hannah Arendt: The Clothes of the Empress"; the same issue also included Howe's essay on Richard Wright, James Baldwin, and Ellison: "Black Boys and Native Sons."

As if to stress the supreme importance of the subject, *Dissent*'s Summer 1963 issue printed on its front cover the opening words of Howe's lengthy essay on "The Negro Revolution": "These are great and stirring days in America. A social transformation, as vast in scope and at least as significant in morality as the rise of industrial unionism in the thirties, has begun to sweep the country." Like much else of Howe's at this time (and perhaps up to the Kennedy assassination in November) it is a hopeful, even effervescent statement of confidence that, "with or without anyone's help, the Negro people are on the way up to freedom" in a great social movement the prospect of whose triumph must make "decent men feel profoundly glad."[16]

Although expectant excitement is the dominant mood of the essay, its prosaic center enumerates four reasons for the confidence and intensity with which the Negroes have begun to fight: the rise of a new Negro leadership, centered in the formerly passive churches; the success of the tactic of nonviolence in the South; the disillusionment among many Negroes with the government, the white liberals, the "white power structure"; and the profound crisis in Negro morale arising from a frustration given notable voice in "the feverish urgency of James Baldwin's recent writings" (208). Following this analysis of the reasons for the eruption of the long-simmering Negro revolt, Howe turns savagely upon President Kennedy and his attorney general, brother Robert, for their vacillation, pusillanimity, and failure to exert moral leadership on behalf of the Negroes in the South. "The White House minds," he quips, "are very shrewd; they miss nothing except the fundamental trends of modern society. . . . The Kennedys seem very bright at winning primaries . . . but they are not so good at spotting social revolutions" (212). Howe also calls for a long-range plan to improve the socioeconomic condition of American Negroes. He sneers at those who think equality of opportunity is a sufficient goal, and demands equality of result, even though this will mean "the Negroes must be given special help, special privileges . . . in jobs, in the unions, in the universities" (214). Already, in 1963, Howe was adumbrating the rationale for what came to be called affirmative action by its proponents, affirmative or reverse discrimination by its opponents. Anticipating the objection that once such special privileges are extended, they can no more be removed than can meat from the cage of a tiger, Howe insists that they "should remain in effect until the Negroes themselves declare the time has come when they are no longer needed" (214).[17]

The second, shorter segment of "The Negro Revolution" appeared three months later, and includes reflections on Martin Luther King's March on Washington, sour remarks about the failure of the AFL-CIO executive board to endorse the march, and censorious comments on "Summer-patriots" in the Negro movement, "genteel Toms" who are now "leaving the masses of poor Negroes in the lurch."[18] Elsewhere in the same issue, in "Black Boys and Native Sons," Howe took it upon himself to identify some of these defectors in the black literary world, thereby precipitating a mammoth controversy. Although Howe relished controversy (and liked to quote William Dean Howells's dictum that anybody could make enemies, but the real achievement was to keep them), he usually knew when he was entering a fight. In the case of his extended dispute with Ellison, however, he seems to have been surprised by the acrimony and ferocity of the novelist's reaction to his critique.

"Black Boys and Native Sons" starts from the assumption that black American writers form a distinct genre in American literature and are to be considered mainly in relation to one another rather than to, say, Thoreau and Emerson (for whom Ralph Waldo Ellison was named), Faulkner and Hemingway. Howe recounts Baldwin's polemic of 1949 ("Everybody's Protest Novel") against Wright and the school of naturalistic fiction he represented. Baldwin had argued that such fiction, by presenting the Negro as social victim or mythic agent of sexual prowess, confined him to the very atmosphere of violence in which he already found himself. Baldwin aspired to prevent himself from becoming *merely* a Negro; "or even, merely a Negro writer" because the world "tends to trap and immobilize you in the role you play" (SW, 119–20). Howe shows little sympathy with Baldwin's rebellion against the older Wright, and alleges that his insistence on sharply separating literature from sociology evades the difficult issue of the link between social experience and literature.

If, as Baldwin acknowledged in *Notes of a Native Son,* a writer can write only of his own experience, then his disavowal of Wright's militancy made no sense to Howe. In a statement that was to irritate Ellison as much as anything in this essay, Howe asks: "What, then, was the experience of a man with a black skin, what *could* it be in this country? How could a Negro put pen to paper, how could he so much as think or breathe, without some impulsion to protest, be it harsh or mild, political or private, released or buried? The 'sociology' of his existence formed a constant pressure on his literary work, and not merely in the way this might be true for any writer, but with a pain and ferocity that nothing could remove" (SW, 120). This is not the kind of remark Howe had made about Sholom Aleichem and the other Yiddish writers, who had also experienced some formidable difficulties from the "sociology" of their existence.

Wright's *Native Son* (1940) represented for Howe the condition to which all black writing should aspire. It struck at "the most cherished of American vanities: the hope that the accumulated injustice of the past would bring with it no lasting penalties." It also told whites the one thing even white liberals preferred not to hear: namely, that Negroes were neither patient nor forgiving, were scarred by fear, and *"hated every moment of their suppression even when seeming most acquiescent"* [emphasis added]. Wright's novel also, according to Howe, declared that Negroes "hated *us*, the decent and cultivated white men who from complicity or neglect shared in the responsibility for their plight" (SW, 121). Thus does Howe identify himself as a white liberal (in the broad sense), but not—either here or anywhere else in the essay—as a Jew.

Whereas Kazin had complained of Wright's obsession with violence, Isaac Rosenfeld is praised by Howe for pointing out that "part of [Wright's] humanity found itself only in acquaintance with violence, and in hatred of the oppressor." This is probably as close as the mature Howe ever comes to "excusing" the violence of the oppressed, and even here he enters a strong *caveat*: "To say this is not to propose the condescension of exempting Negro writers from moral judgment, but to suggest the terms of understanding, and still more, the terms of hesitation for making a judgment" (SW, 126).

Nevertheless, in taking the side of Wright, Howe was chastising Baldwin and Ellison (and even Saul Bellow) for espousing "a postwar liberalism not very different from conservatism." Instead of Wright's "clenched militancy," Baldwin—in 1955 if not in 1963, when he published *The Fire Next Time*—was in Howe's view recommending stoical acceptance, and Ellison spoke of America's "rich diversity and . . . almost magical fluidity and freedom." All were tainted by that fifties spirit of conformity. Wright, on the other hand, had told Howe in 1958 that "only through struggle could men with black skins . . . achieve their humanity. It was a lesson, said Wright . . . , that the younger writers would have to learn in their own way and their own time. All that has happened since bears him out" (SW, 127).

Howe does concede one major point to Baldwin. His complaint that Wright's fiction, stressing black struggle against whites, cuts away the whole dimension of the relationship that Negroes bear to one another, is a just one: "the posture of militancy . . . exacts a heavy price from the writer. . . . " The implication, of course, is that there are certain things more important than good writing (something Howe would hear from an angry Jacob Glatstein about Cynthia Ozick in the next decade).

Howe adds that the refusal of militancy may exact an even greater price, but he does not say of what kind.

After brief comment on Baldwin's novels and on the general question of how one can stress degradation and oppression at the same time that one celebrates creativity and achievement, Howe turns to Ellison, the Negro writer who has come closer than Baldwin himself ever did to following Baldwin's precepts and carrying out his program. He treats *Invisible Man* (1952) as "a brilliant though flawed achievement," whose most astonishing feature is its apparent freedom from the ideological and emotional scars that America inflicts upon its Negro citizens. He praises Ellison for writing with "an ease and humor which are now and again simply miraculous" (SW, 129), calls him "richly, wildly inventive," and says that "no other writer has captured so much of the hidden gloom and surface gaiety of Negro life" (SW, 130).

Nevertheless, Howe has strong reservations, which can fairly be described as ideological more than aesthetic. He objects to Ellison's depiction of his Stalinist figures, who are "so vicious and stupid that one cannot understand how they could ever have attracted him or any other Negro." But far more troublesome to Howe is the "implausible assertion of unconditioned freedom with which the novel ends" and the hero's discovery that his world has become one of infinite possibility. Once again, Howe detects the pseudo-liberal ideology of the fifties, "the unqualified assertion of self-liberation" (SW, 131). This idea is as much a falsification, he insists, as the determinism of the thirties.

These few remarks about Ellison in an essay mainly devoted to the tortured intellectual relationship between Baldwin and Wright touched a raw nerve of anger in the novelist, who "replied" at inordinate length in the *New Leader* for December 9, 1963. In a fierce, exaggerative, but often shrewd essay entitled "The World and the Jug," Ellison describes Howe as a "sociology-oriented critic" who knows little of the variety of Negro life and rates literature so far below politics and ideology that he "would rather kill a novel" than modify his presumptions about reality.[19] He claims that Howe misses the irony (or assumes that Ellison did) in the reference to "infinite possibilities" while inhabiting a hole in the ground. As for Howe's confident description of the experience of a black man in the United States as requiring a black writer to protest, Ellison acerbically refers to "Howe, suddenly appearing in blackface," i.e., claiming to know what he could not possibly know. Howe, Ellison alleges, "feels that unrelieved suffering is the only 'real' Negro experience, and that the true Negro writer must be ferocious" (119).

Had Howe known more of Negro experience, he would have been aware, says Ellison, of the American Negro tradition "which teaches one to deflect racial provocation . . . which abhors as obscene any trading on one's own anguish for gain or sympathy." This tradition does not deny the harshness of existence but confronts it with the fortitude of a man or of an artist. The real question about the sociology of the Negro artist's existence is "how much of his life the individual writer is able to transform into art." Howe, he charges, forgets that the life of the oppressed is not only a burden but also a discipline, "teaching its own insights into the human condition, its own strategies of survival." In the interests of political dogma and revolutionary posturing, Howe has been forced to deny that possibilities of human richness exist for others, "even in Mississippi." In doing so, he has both denied the Negro's humanity and betrayed the critic's commitment to social reality. "Critics who do so should abandon literature for politics" (119). Howe prefers to see the Negro writer—or so Ellison charges—as a product of his sociopolitical predicament, and leaves out individual will and the "broader American cultural freedom in which he finds his ambiguous existence" (120). Ellison might have added that Howe was now, in effect, taking the position toward the Negroes that he had once attacked Sartre for taking toward the Jews, as people who were defined entirely by the external hostility directed against them. Ellison now claims for blacks, as Harold Rosenberg and Howe fifteen years earlier claimed for Jews, an autonomous culture that could not be understood merely as a response of protest against oppression.

But the sharpest thrust of Ellison's rejoinder is his accusation that Howe is a segregationist, albeit an intellectual one. He has offered up "the Northern white liberal version of the white Southern myth of absolute separation of the races. He implies that Negroes can only aspire to contest other Negroes . . . " (122). Howe forgets that no matter how strictly Negroes have been segregated socially and politically, their capacity for imaginative freedom is limited only by their individual will, insight, energy, aspiration. Wright and Baldwin, for example, were not the "products" of Mississippi or of the Negro storefront church but of the library. Ellison himself was released from any "segregated" idea he might have had of his human possibilities by books that rarely, if ever, mentioned Negroes. He was freed not by the example of Wright, but by the composers, novelists, and poets who revealed to him more interesting and free ways of life than he had known.

Pursuing a line of thought that would a quarter century later be invoked by critics (including Howe) of the cramped, confining notions of "multiculturalism," Ellison asserts that he understands himself better as a Negro precisely because literature has taught him something of his identity as Western man and political being. Howe, he declares, must suffer from poverty of imagination if he believes that Negroes can only learn about the varied possibilities of life from other Negroes. In the first hint of the Negro-Jewish theme that will move to the center of his argument in the second part of this very lengthy essay, Ellison reminds Howe that the Negro slaves re-created themselves out of "the images and myths of the Old Testament Jews" (124). Howe is no more justified in supposing Wright the spiritual father of Ellison than Ellison would be in supposing that Marx had "spoken the final word" for Howe (125).

Ellison concludes Part One of his rejoinder to "Black Boys and Native Sons" by alleging that Howe "designate[s] the role which Negro writers are to play more rigidly than any Southern politician." By insisting that they express "black" rage and promote ideological militancy above good writing, he forecasts a social order which Ellison finds more fearful than that of the state of Mississippi.

Howe began his three-page reply in the *New Leader* of 3 February 1964 by quoting a remark from Kafka he was wont to invoke in writing about books on the Holocaust, none of which could be called enjoyable: "You can hold back from the suffering of the world," Kafka had written, "you have free permission to do so and it is in accordance with your nature, but perhaps this very holding back is the one suffering you could have avoided."[20] This is very nearly Howe's sharpest rebuke to Ellison, for most of his reply rejects Ellison's definition of the dispute and insists that "Ellison has wildly twisted the meaning of what I wrote" (12). His approach, he protests, had been analytic, not hortatory, descriptive rather than prescriptive. He had not insisted that anyone, including Ellison, plunge actively into the Negro freedom struggle: any pressure Ellison may have felt to do so has not come from Howe. Neither did Howe ever say that Negro writers should not become too interested in literary craft, or that they must choose between good writing and active, militant citizenship: "No such absurdities can be found in my essay." As for Ellison's declaration that Mississippi is more palatable to a black writer than what Howe represents: "If I thought Ellison were in control of himself when he wrote this, I would regard it as a slur upon my honor" (13). This was perhaps as close as Howe would come to challenging an adversary to a duel (as Allen Tate had done during the Ezra Pound controversy).

Howe contends that he did not say that plight and protest were the whole of Negro experience, but only that they were "inseparable" from it. Serious discussion ought to have been begun by Ellison only in response to Howe's asking in what ways a Negro writer or any Negro can achieve "personal realization" while American Negroes remain oppressed. It is an empirical fact that no serious Negro writer, including Ellison, has yet dealt with the experience of his people without including the elements of "plight and protest" (14).

In reply to Ellison's accusation of segregationism, Howe says that he had no wish to imprison his adversary in the jug of Negro-ness, apart from the world of common humanity or Western culture. Still, Howe asks pointedly, why does the influence of Hemingway seem to Ellison more desirable and attractive than that of Wright? Moreover, even if Ellison achieved a personal realization by reading the great "white" writers, he could still not attend the white man's school or movie house in Macon County, Alabama, for that kind of realization requires a *social* action.

By way of conclusion, Howe adduces the example of Yiddish literature, his first indication in this controversy that he writes as a Jew rather than yet another "white liberal." In the Yiddish tradition, he notes, the dominant tradition has been one of national outcry, social protest at the perennial plight of the folk. Some Yiddish writers, like Glatstein and Abraham Sutzkever, rebelled against this constriction—Glatstein by writing a poetry of personal introspection, Sutzkever by celebrating the natural world. But history itself, in the form of the Holocaust, dragged them back to the subject of the Jewish people. This resulted in some disadvantages to them as poets, but also brought tremendous gains. "The great themes of writers," Howe admonishes Ellison, "are not those which they choose, but those which choose them" (14). This is an adumbration of a conception of Yiddish poetry as permeated by the struggle between individual autonomy and national-social themes that Howe would develop more fully in the 1969 *Treasury of Yiddish Poetry*. It is striking that it should make its first appearance in debate over the nature of Negro American literature.

In the same issue of *New Leader* Ellison responded with an elaborate rejoinder to Howe's rejoinder. He had, he insisted, never been one of those described by Kafka as "hold[ing] back from suffering." On the contrary, he yelled when it hurt most; but what hurt most was not legal segregation in the South—"about which I could do nothing except walk, read, hunt, dance, sculpt, cultivate ideas"—but notions like those of Irving Howe, which distorted the reality of his situation and his reactions to it. He could escape the reduction of his human status imposed by unjust laws and customs, but not that resulting from ideas "which defined me as no more than the *sum* of those laws and customs" (128). For Ellison to leave the South was not to leave the field of struggle and the need to protest, "for how could I leave Howe" (129)? Mental chains forged by such Northern intellectuals were harder to break than physical ones.

Howe's reply had criticized Ellison for facilely defining the debate as one between the "knowing Negro writer" and "the presuming white intellectual." But Ellison wants it to be understood that he is an *Ameri-*

can writer, free to recognize those aspects of his role as writer "which do not depend primarily upon . . . racial identity" (131). Moreover—and Ellison's linguistic assertion here ironically prefigures Howe's own mocking reference (in 1977) to Gore Vidal's proprietary claims upon proper English[21]—he is "as writer no less a custodian of the American language than is Irving Howe" (132).

At this point the dispute takes a strange and unexpected turn, in which Ellison, as if pricked to awareness on this point by Howe's use of the Yiddish writers, raises the question of Howe's "own racial identity." Many Negroes, he says, including himself, make a distinction between "whites" and Jews:

> If I would know who I am and preserve who I am, then I must see others distinctly whether they see me so or no. Thus I feel uncomfortable whenever I discover Jewish intellectuals writing as though *they* were guilty of enslaving my grandparents, or as though the *Jews* were responsible for the system of segregation. Not only do they have enough troubles of their own . . . but Negroes know this only too well.

Having reproached Howe for not identifying himself and speaking as a Jew in his essay on Negro writers, Ellison then turns what at first appears a compliment to Jews in general into a reproach against Jewish intellectuals, of whom Howe is made representative. Their "guilt," Ellison charges, lies in their "facile, perhaps unconscious, but certainly unrealistic, identification with what is called the 'power structure.'" Irving Howe claiming to be part of the power structure? Could one imagine a more bizarre turn to Ellison's argument? Although Howe apparently thought the fact irrelevant, Ellison considers Howe's Jewish identity of the first importance, and therefore sharply criticizes him for passing as merely a "white intellectual" (132).

It is almost as if Ellison is turning Howe's criticism of the younger Baldwin and Ellison against Howe himself: that is, if Ellison construes Howe to be saying that he, Ellison, is not "black" enough, not enough of a "race man" in his writing, then he insists on saying that Howe is not Jewish enough in his. There is also, however, a discomforting two-sidedness in Ellison's depiction of what he calls the American Jews' "special forms of dissent." On one side he is praising them for making their own perennial victimization a stepping-stone to identification with other victim groups and enlisting in the struggles of those groups. But on the other side, he accuses them (as represented by Howe) of identifying with the white power structure and "passing for white" (132).

According to Ellison, Howe makes of "Negroness" a negative metaphysical condition which virtually engulfs the mind of the individual

Negro writer. Howe cannot rebut the charge that he makes unrelieved suffering the basic reality of Negro life just by quoting his favorable comments about *Invisible Man*. Neither can he charge Ellison with unfairness in saying that Howe believes ideological militancy is more important than writing well so long as he maintains that "there may of course be times when one's obligation as a human being supersedes one's obligation as a writer . . . " (138). The potentiality for conflict between art and morality was, of course, a besetting dilemma for Howe; and his inability to resolve it left him open to Ellison's barbs. A writer, Ellison says (with perhaps excessive aesthetic piety), best fulfills his obligation in the general struggle precisely by adhering to the highest requirements of his art. Howe's defense of Wright's resort to old-fashioned images of violence is either a defense of bad writing or an expression of an "irresponsible attitude toward good writing."

So far is Ellison from responding to Howe's conciliatory suggestion that he was not in control of himself when he said that his adversary's outlook was worse for Negro writers than the State of Mississippi, that he repeats it: "I fear the implications of Howe's ideas concerning the Negro writer's role as actionist more than I do the State of Mississippi" (140). The reason is that the repression in Mississippi is relatively crude and leaves the world of literature alone. Had Howe momentarily forgotten that William Faulkner, about whom he had written a book twelve years earlier, was himself a Mississippian?

Without being entirely aware of what he is doing, Ellison finds himself defending some aspects of the Southern social order in order to defend himself. Howe, he scolds, must learn more about the South and about Negro Americans before he can speak with any authority on these subjects. He does not understand the extent of choice and will available to the Negro in the South. He is too rigidly committed to the liberal dogma of integration to recognize that a Ralph Ellison had no need to attend a white university to get what he needed for his development as a man and an artist. "I went to the movies to see pictures, not to be with whites. I attended a certain college because what I wanted was there" (141).

Ellison claims that Howe should not have dragged him into the quarrel between Wright and Baldwin at all. He, after all, has always known that the source of the "inadequacy characteristic of most novels by Negroes" is "the simple failure of craft, bad writing." The "protest" theme is typically used by inferior writers to perform the difficult tasks of art, as if racial suffering and social injustice could by themselves make literature. Ellison brings his extended rejoinder to a close by insisting that his artistic ancestors were Hemingway, Malraux, Dostoyevsky, and Faulkner. At the same time he implicitly (perhaps spitefully?) insists that he is more American than Irving Howe. Hemingway was more important to Ellison than Wright not because he was white but because he loved and appreciated all those things which Ellison himself loved and which the driven and inexperienced Wright did not: "weather, guns, dogs, horses, love *and* hate" (145). Howe too, it goes without saying, did not know guns, dogs, and horses; in that sense he was less the American than Ellison, though he is "white" and Ellison "Negro." Thus does Ellison make his very reply to Howe a part of the Negro "struggle for freedom" because it expresses the desire to break out of the "jug" of Negroness into the world of art.

Howe never really replied to Ellison's reply to his reply to Ellison's attack. He did, however, when he reprinted "Black Boys and Native Sons" in 1969, offer a low-keyed, conciliatory addendum to the debate. In it, he writes that he will leave it to others to judge how accurate or valid Ellison's attack had been. Mainly he now wishes to note how the cultural atmosphere has changed. When the essays first appeared, early in the decade, the literary world was overwhelmingly on the side of Ellison's defense of creative autonomy as against the critical exhortation to protest and militancy. Now, however, white literary intellectuals, especially devotees of the New Left, are only too eager to declare their uncritical acceptance of Black Power ideology. Some of them would no doubt dismiss both Howe and Ellison as antiquated liberal advocates of integration. The fashion among Negro writers, Howe notes, has changed to Ellison's disadvantage, but also to some extent to Howe's own. For most have been caught up in separatist and nationalist ideology. They are contemptuous and dismissive of Ellison's claim that he, as much as any white writer, shares in the heritage of Western culture.

Extending a friendly hand, Howe stresses what he and Ellison (both now besieged by a new barbarism) have in common: "both of us believe in the unity of experience and culture, both of us believe that the works of literature produced by black men should be judged by the same aesthetic criteria as those produced by white men, both of us resist attempts by whoever it may be to reinstitute a new version of social and cultural segregation, and both of us believe in the value of liberal discourse" (SW, 138). In a contemporaneous essay in *Harper's* on the younger black novelists, Howe again stressed that the reality of a distinctive black experience did not portend a black nationalist or separatist literature. These black writers still wrote in English, or American-English, and remained American writers: "in ways far deeper than choice or consciousness is likely to determine, they work within the American literary tradition."[22] This too was a gesture of conciliation toward Ellison.

Acrimonious as the dispute between Howe and Ellison had been, no one thought of it as potentially murderous until Ozick, in a 1972 essay on "Literary Blacks and Jews," argued that in fact it was "an adumbration" of the conclusion to Bernard Malamud's novel *The Tenants* (1971), in which a black writer and a Jewish writer kill each other. Ozick asserted, with her usual flair for paradox, that what made Ellison's side of the argument especially valuable was that it was "a remarkably useful notation in the history not so much of black as of Jewish self-understanding." For Ellison's was essentially "the response of one profoundly gifted black writer to 'Jewish concern,'" i.e., concern for the condition of being black in America.[23]

Ozick sees the quarrel between the aesthetic principle and the principle of political engagement as a foretoken of one of Malamud's principal concerns in *The Tenants*, even though in the novel it is the Jewish writer who takes Ellison's position on behalf of artistic freedom and the black writer who expresses Howe's political commitment. But to see this "reversal" in perspective, she says, requires one first to examine Ellison's consideration of Howe as Jew. Howe, as we have seen, was severely criticized by Ellison for not declaring in his essay that he was a Jew and instead merely passing as a "white intellectual." Ozick thinks this just up to a point—that Ellison wants to see others distinctly. Yet he objects to Howe's desire to see *him* distinctly, which is to say as a man inheriting the social predicament of being born black in America. And why, she asks, after attributing so many praiseworthy qualities to Jews, does Ellison turn around and describe the special quality of their concern as "passing for white"? Her own answer is that it is Ellison, not Howe, "who fails to nail down the drift of distinctive experience, who imagines the Jew as naturally identifying with the white 'power structure'" (100). For what Howe was in fact doing in his essay was responding naturally as a Jew, through specifically Jewish forms of dissent, to the racial crisis of modern America. Ellison's refusal to grant the Jew a plausible commitment to the black cause gave a truer picture of black-Jewish relations than Malamud's optimistic story of 1958, "Angel Levine," with its embrace of the possibility of black-Jewish unity. Rather, it anticipated "the warlike actualities of *The Tenants*" (1971) [101]. One reason it did so is that Ellison went out of his way to say that he, the black man, is more at ease in America than Howe because he is a Gentile, not a Jew, not a man who had never picked up a gun (to hunt or to fight) and can only live among ideas.

Ozick also notes a further paradox in Ellison's position, which "simultaneously denies and affirms universality" (105–106). Ellison keeps saying that he considers himself a writer rather than a Negro writer, a man before he is a Negro. But he also, as a Negro, denies that any white man can understand Negro life. In this sense—and perhaps this only—

he can be linked with the ferocious Willie Spearmint of *The Tenants*, who is otherwise a foreshadowing of Leroi Jones and the later, "enraged" Baldwin, writers who exploit the "con-game" of militancy that Ellison deplored. For, Ozick glumly concludes, "It is curious, horrible, and terrifying to take in what Malamud in *The Tenants* openly posits: that the Jew in America, beginning as Howe did with a cry of identification with black suffering, is self-astonished to find himself responding . . . in the almost forgotten mood of *zelbshuts*—the *shtetl's* term for weaponry stored against the fear of pogroms" (111).[24] The Jew in Malamud's novel, so far from having white Gentile allies from that power structure Ellison claimed Howe was seeking to identify with, fights alone against his black adversary.

In January 1990, in yet another reprinting of "Black Boys and Native Sons," Howe added a brief coda to the by now epic saga of his dispute with Ellison. He describes the "black aesthetic" which has developed since 1963 and he rejects it. (Incomprehensibly, he says that it "seems to have faded.") A distinctive black experience, he maintains, no more warrants the claim for a distinctive black aesthetic than a distinctive Jewish experience would warrant a special Jewish aesthetic. More importantly, he finally concedes a major point of the debate to Ellison: namely, "the charge that I underestimated the capacity of oppressed peoples like the American blacks to create a vital culture apart from social protest" (SW, 138). Nevertheless, he holds to his central contention that protest, for better or worse, is an inescapable literary theme for black writers.

Mid-Sixties: Vietnam Protest, the New Left, "Confrontation Politics"

The sanguine mood of Howe in the early years of the sixties disappeared steadily in the wake of the assassination of President Kennedy, the burgeoning of the Goldwater movement, the expansion of the Vietnam War, the moral deterioration of the peace movement, and the turbulence at the universities. As late as 1966, in a lengthy (and surprisingly dreary) essay in *Partisan Review* called "Radical Questions and the American Intellectual," he could still be cautiously optimistic about the revival of radicalism, the end of the "suffocating complacency of the fifties," the possibility of envisaging a world in which, thanks to the growth of technology, "material wants will be moderately satisfied," and even "the essentially healthy student protests."[25] But by 1967 he was capable of writing an essay seriously asking the question "Is This Country Cracking Up?" His quick answer is "*No, of course not. But there* are signs and portents." Among them are the distrust of a significant minority of Americans in the veracity of their government, the steady escalation of the Vietnam War, the unfitness of Johnson to be president, and—not least of the evil portents—the hysteria of the left, "the apostles of nose-to-nose 'polarization,' the secret sharers of Ronald Reagan." These "leftist" dabblers in apocalypse, Howe warns, should ponder the Yiddish proverb: "*Come for your inheritance and you may have to pay for the funeral.*"[26]

The second half of the decade was largely a time of bitter, strident, sometimes violent debate over American involvement in Vietnam and the direction of the civil rights movement. Howe had three primary interests in this debate. The first, and most obvious, had to do with American foreign and domestic policy, judged from a democratic socialist perspective; the second concerned the role and limits of social protest within a democratic society; the third, which would ultimately prove the most important and lasting, involved the nature of the university, which was becoming the center of militant protest against the war.

Howe supported the protest movement against the Vietnam War but was uneasy about some of its methods and allies, and would not join protests or petitions which included pro-Communist supporters of the Vietcong. His public statements in 1965 stressed the need "to end a cruel and futile war, not to give explicit or covert political support to the Vietcong." If the movement embraced or seemed to embrace the Communists, then it would neither get nor deserve the support of large numbers of Americans. In principle, Howe endorsed civil disobedience as a legitimate means of expressing dissent and conscience in a democratic society; but he insisted that it should be used only as a last resort. He questioned, for example, efforts to stop troop trains in California: here a small minority revoked through its own decision the policy of a democratically elected government (*Steady Work*, 95, 97).[27]

Howe professed to welcome the new radical mood of the sixties, on the campuses and in the civil rights movement. Yet he was disturbed by certain segments or aspects of it, especially the undemocratic values, the moral absolutism, the blindness to shading and nuance in political thought. He cast about for the right name for the nastier elements and personalities of the Movement, calling them, at various times, guerrillas with tenure, or kamikaze radicals, or black Maoists, or—the term which stuck—"New Leftists." In a major *Dissent* essay of 1965 called "New Styles in 'Leftism,'" he expressed his uneasiness about the New Left in what he later called its second phase,[28] and did so in a tone of polemical sharpness that offended his targets at least as much as the substance of what he said. But Howe was always impervious to the shrieks of sensitive plants: "In the political tradition from which I derive, it has been common to write with polemical sharpness . . . and then to expect one's opponent to reply in kind. You argue, you let some heat come through, you don't pretend that gentility is the ultimate virtue; and then, a little later, it may even be possible to come to agreement, or work together, or accept the fact of difference" (*Steady Work*, 39–40).

He starts "New Styles in 'Leftism'" by praising the new radical mood as better than that of the 1930s, which suffered from excessive tolerance of scoundrels and fools as leaders whose bad behavior was excused in the name of an unquestioned ideology. He also applauds the movement for opposing the chauvinism, hysteria, and demagogy of the "conformist" fifties. But now the time has come to deplore those radicals who fly to the opposite extremes: "revulsion seldom encourages nuances of thought or precise discriminations of politics" (SW, 196). If you are disgusted with the rationales given for every American power move, then respond by condemning everything American. If you have become weary of Sidney Hook's warnings against communism,[29] then respond as if any talk about Communist totalitarianism is irrelevant or fraudulent. Howe consistently pointed out that although New Leftist students might be justified in revulsion against deceit and crime in the name of the Cold War, some of them lapsed by reaction into the denial that communism remained—as it did—a worldwide menace to freedom; and they tended to equate any kind of anti-communism with McCarthyism (*Steady Work*, 38). Howe also observed that the young radicals unwittingly echoed the very prejudices of their hated elders by worshiping youth as if it were a good in its own right and by remaining ignorant of the past. Lacking a historical sense, the New Leftists didn't recognize that the desire to shock had its own long and largely disastrous history.

"New Styles in 'Leftism'" offers an analysis of the New Left in the form of an elaborate essay in classification. The two major groups are Ideologues and Desperadoes. The white Ideologues include The Remains of Stalinism, True Believers (in Marxism-Leninism), and Authoritarian Leftists (who believe socialism is a combination of authoritarianism and nationalization of the means of production). Negro Ideologues include Black Nationalists like Malcolm X, Caricatures like Leroi Jones, "a burlesque double of whatever is significant in Malcolm" (SW, 201) and a frequent target of Howe (who would later, in "The Case of Ezra Pound," dub him "a racist hoodlum"). Desperadoes among the New Left also come in white and black varieties. The former adopt a style of "alienation" which for Howe is merely a token of self-pity and a rationale for marginality and withdrawal. The Negro desperadoes act out of social and psychological motives similar to those of late nineteenth-century Russian terrorists.

Howe's sketch of a composite type of the New Leftist forms the core of his essay. This fellow's first characteristic is a certain cultural style involving speech, dress, work, and manners. He rejects not just the middle-class ethos but all the things he too hastily links with it, among them things Howe valued highly: "the intellectual heritage of the West, the tradition of liberalism at its most serious, the commitment to democracy as an indispensable part of civilized life." So eager is the New Leftist to shock and assault the sensibilities of a world he cannot overcome that he unwittingly traps himself in a "symbiotic relationship with the very middle class he rejects, dependent upon it for his self-definition" (SW, 204–205). Like the class and the father he wishes to outrage, he assumes that values can be inferred from such externals as dress, appearance, furnishings, and hairdos.

Next in importance after cultural style is the domestic politics of the New Leftist. This, Howe charges, amounts to little more than a "strategy of lonely assault, which must necessarily lead to shock tactics and desperation" (SW, 207). Since the New Left sees virtually everybody (liberals, churches, unions, intellectuals, Negroes, all but a few students) in the grip of "the Establishment," its members are finally a mere handful, who "must end . . . in despair, exhaustion, burning themselves out in the all-too-characteristic rhythm of American radicalism, which too often has tried to compensate for its powerlessness in reality by ferocity in words" (SW, 209).

As self-destructive as its exclusiveness is the New Left's indifference to freedom in its basic political values and commitments. This is why it is attracted to such "third world" dictatorial heroes as Castro, Nasser, and Sukarno. It displays (as, we know, Howe himself once did) extreme hostility toward liberalism, about which it knows little, even though that tradition is invaluable for any democratic socialist. It is indifferent to the nature of Stalinism and post-Stalinist communism, serious problems that deeply concerned the older generation of radicals. It revels in theoretic, vicarious indulgence in violence, especially when it turns its attention to the nonviolent strategy of the Negro movement, whose actual needs and experience are less important to the New Left than ideological prescriptions.

Perhaps the most salient bad characteristic of the New Left, as Howe perceives it, is its "unreflective belief in 'the decline of the West.'" Two decades in advance of the onslaught of "multiculturalist" barbarism (in collusion with academic cowardice) against "the West," Howe calls attention to this bizarre and dangerous tendency among leftists. It is bizarre because the hostility to Western thought has in the West previously been a slogan of reactionaries opposed to modern rationality, democracy, and sensibility. It is dangerous because the West represents modernism in culture, a great power of recovery in economics, and a strong commitment to personal freedom that makes it "virtually alone as a place of hope" (SW, 215). Yes, Howe grants, the West is guilty of racial prejudice, but what area of the world is not? More importantly, the critical judgment we make of racism draws precisely upon values nurtured in the West more than anywhere else. Howe also makes the sensible point, which would be repeated many times in the 1980s and 1990s by conservative defenders of the study of Western civilization, that it is childish to talk of the West as if it were an indivisible whole to be accepted or rejected without amendment.

After adding to the list of New Left characteristics "a crude, unqualified anti-Americanism" (SW, 216) and a growing identification with the most violent and dictatorial segments of both the Communist and "third" worlds, Howe tries to end his essay on a positive note, by way of saying what a radical ought to be for as well as what he is against. Ironically, however, what he offers here is Leszek Kolakowski's 1957 statement entitled "What Is Socialism?," which consisted of a series of twelve epigrams stating what socialism is *not*.[30] Of course, Howe adds, "these negatives imply a positive, and that positive is a central lesson of contemporary history: the unity of socialism and democracy" (SW, 219). But here one is tempted to ask: what unity? Where does such unity exist except in the mind of Irving Howe? Would it not be more accurate to suggest that democratic socialism is an oxymoron, given the experience of socialism in Russia and the regimes of Eastern Europe? One is also tempted to fault Howe for not remarking on the fact that the Polish Solidarity revolution in which Kolakowski had been involved was probably the first revolution in modern history made by the working rather than the middle class, and that it was made precisely against what nearly everybody except Howe would call a socialist government.

Subsequent years brought further critiques of follies encouraged by, if not the exclusive property of, the New Left. In 1968, for example, Howe published a piece called "Why Should Negroes Be Above Criticism?" in which he blamed liberals, radicals, and academics for a new kind of condescension toward blacks, which "takes the form of acquiescing in almost anything said by a man whose skin is black and whose voice is loud." Howe recognizes the pattern of sympathetic condescension as one that the Communists had initiated in the thirties. He is particularly irked—and rightly so—by the tendency of Jewish liberals to rush to the defense of certain well-known blacks who steadily indulge in antisemitism. A prime example was the statement in the *New*

York Review of Books of 25 April 1968 praising the versified antisemitic diatribes of Leroi Jones; its signatories included several Jews, among them Allen Ginsberg and Denise Levertov. Howe also questions, tentatively to be sure, the university policy—a product of New Left ideology—of moving black students who have not done well scholastically up the academic ladder. "How," he asks, "can a black student know whether his A or B has been deserved, or is a token of mere sympathy? Might it not be that absolute candor and color-blindness in grading together with sustained help for disadvantaged students, would be the best policy?"[31] Despite his frequent attraction to radical nostrums—in his "Negro Revolution" essay of five years earlier, we recall, he had specifically endorsed "special privileges" for Negroes at the universities—Howe was shrewd enough finally to see that the only sure way to enforce the values of equality was for whites to start treating Negroes as real equals.

Never, during the turbulent sixties, was Howe's ability to dissent from the conformities of dissent more clearly displayed than in his lucid yet angry essay of 1968 entitled "The New 'Confrontation Politics' Is a Dangerous Game." Nineteen sixty-eight had seen spectacular eruptions of "confrontation politics" in the form of violent demonstrations, among them the Columbia University riots in late April and May and the demonstrations at the Democratic National Convention in Chicago in August. American leftists had developed new tactics of protest that went far beyond democratic methods yet fell short of full-fledged revolution. Howe describes them as "the equivalent in public life of Russian roulette in private life."[32] The self-righteous minorities, whether Negro militants or white middle-class students, who choreograph these explosions have little interest in winning large numbers of people to their views. On the contrary, they view the mass of Americans as poor fools who have been brainwashed by the media—"the very media," Howe pointedly notes, "which give them vast amounts of publicity."[33] Their only discernible politics is the politics of desperation: to administer a series of moral shocks and nihilist irritations that would destroy the complacence of "corporate liberalism" (28).

In the "historical" part of his lengthy essay, Howe proposes that the source of confrontation politics is the strategy of the civil-rights movement in the South during the fifties. But the success (and justification) of the civil-rights confrontations depended on several conditions, none of which obtained at Columbia or Chicago in 1968: (1) in the South the demonstrators were demanding rights which had already been recognized, both in law and moral consensus, by the nation as a whole; (2) the unconditional nonviolence of Martin Luther King and his followers was a principle that at least parts of the middle-class South—especially those still bound by the Christian idea of turning the other cheek—had to respect; (3) while the civil-rights demonstrators sometimes broke local ordinances, they could justify their actions by democratic standards, both because they had long been deprived of the vote, and were breaking ordinances that were blatantly unconstitutional; (4) the civil-rights protestors derived power from an alliance with major forces in the North, including liberals, unionists, churches, academicians, all working on behalf of civil-rights legislation. By contrast, the New Left rioters at Columbia and the Democratic Convention lacked clearly defined goals, did not act on behalf of moral-political opinions shared by a large majority of Americans, were not significantly deprived of their right to organize and protest, and—of course—did not act out of a principled devotion to nonviolence (28–29).

The more sinister (and genuine) precedent for the New Left riots was in the Communist movement. Howe mentions the ultra-left German Communists' "theory of electrification" (29), according to which the party, by endless and reckless demonstrations, would "electrify" the masses into revolution. Of this group Trotsky remarked that the probable consequence was that the electrifiers would burn themselves. Still worse was the Communist confrontation politics of the pre-Hitler period, when the party came up with "the insane notion of 'social fascism,' according to which the Social Democrats, and not the Nazis, were the main danger in Germany" (29). A corollary to this idea was the Stalinist slogan of "the worse, the better," and "*Nach Hitler, uns.*" What "social fascism" was to the Communists in the thirties, liberalism was to the New Leftists of the sixties. Perhaps that would explain why they broke up rallies for Humphrey[34] but not for Nixon. These Communist tactics, Howe observes, "helped the Nazis come to power" (133). What will those of the New Left bring?

The chief intellectual guru of the New Leftists was Herbert Marcuse, once Howe's colleague at Brandeis. They had adopted his line that the values of liberalism, such as tolerance, free speech, electoral activity, were merely devices for maintaining the status quo. His doctrines justified those radicals who scorned both Leninism and social democracy in favor of a series of raids upon established power, carried out with total contempt for democratic process. They envisioned a series of desperate and provocative actions to "keep the society in a state of constant turmoil and the university in a state of constant chaos" (133).

Having by now become a believer in the virtues of the American university system, which he had entered *faute de mieux* early in the previous decade, Howe was especially aggrieved by the assumption of "confrontation politics" that the university largely resembles the surrounding society, or is even identical to it. Within the university, needless to say, the leftists were now met with largely liberal faculties. But when the universities on occasion—as had happened at Columbia— did not respond to the demonstrators with the flabby indulgence of the liberal, middle-class parent, the students cried foul. How could the universities call the police to a place which tradition had established as a cloister of the intellect? In other words, the leftists wanted to eat their cake, yet have it too. Howe puts the matter with startling clarity: "If they believed it proper to transform the campus into a training ground for revolutionary action, they could hardly complain when the powers-that-be retaliated with force" (134). If the leftist students really believe that the campus should be a center of learning, then how can they keep treating it as if it were no more than a microcosm of capitalist society? The truth, of course, is that the politics of confrontation at the universities depends on a friendly or indecisive response from the very liberal professors whom the New Left treats with utter contempt.

Wrong in principle, the New Leftists are also obtuse about practical realities and likely results. While they are whipping themselves into self-righteous outrage against Social Democrats and "liberal fascism," they seem to have neither memory nor awareness of what real, "fascist" fascism is like. They advocate political polarization without stopping to think what the likely outcome of it might be in the United States, without understanding that their gratuitous anti-Americanism, their calling white men "honkies" and policemen "pigs" may be preparing a backlash, perhaps named George Wallace. Likewise, they seem wholly unaware that "the first victim of a new reaction in America would be the universities in which they now find shelter" (137). But if the student radicals really do believe that worse is better, perhaps they genuinely would prefer Wallace to the liberals whom they denominate their main enemy. Indeed, Howe notes, "some of them have even said that they would find attractive an alliance between far left and far right" (137). Howe himself, on the other hand, would not like to face a choice between an America symbolized by Wallace and one symbolized by Tom Hayden. He strongly suspects that the young man whom he had met six years earlier in the offices of *Dissent* would now send him off to a labor camp.

Advocates of "confrontation" have not, Howe charges, been disturbed by the fact that their actions set precedents that could undermine American democracy, and the very institutions which radicals have the most interest in preserving. Earlier in 1968 he had delivered a stinging rebuke to SDS spokesmen who contemptuously dismissed "bourgeois civil liberties," testily asking if they could offer some examples of *non*bourgeois civil liberties ("A Word about 'Bourgeois Civil Liberties,'"

10–11). As was so often the case in his disputes with the New Left, Howe was in reality criticizing it for not having learned from *his* past mistakes. "We did not realize then [in the thirties] how sheltering it was to grow up in this world . . . how the 'bourgeois democracy' at which we railed was the medium making it possible for us to speak and survive" (*Steady Work,* 354). Having himself been disastrously wrong about the difference between the Axis and the Allied powers in World War II, Howe in 1966 would say that "it seems to me both intellectually facile and morally disastrous to affirm an identity between the societies of East and West" ("Radical Questions," 318). Constantly, Howe saw the sixties radicals repeating the errors and crimes of the Communists, who also used to declare that civil liberties were convenient under capitalism but could be disposed of once they took power. In their casual drift from antidemocratic elitism to the rhetoric of violence, they reminded him of George Orwell's caustic remark that a certain kind of infantile leftism is "playing with fire on the part of people who don't even know that fire is hot" (139). While the New Left continues to talk blithely about revolution, he observes, it is the police who will do most of the shooting. Howe concludes with a warning that the lack of a principled basis for arguing against existing institutions, as well as the use of unprincipled methods to fight injustice, will give "the opponents of liberty an occasion for destroying both the struggle for justice and the procedures of liberty" (140).

Howe's critique of the New Left remains one of the shrewdest and sharpest that exists; that it reached its target is evident in the fact that no socialist, with the possible exception of Orwell, ever incurred so much hatred and abuse from other socialists as he did. In later years, Howe took note of the "wounding" quality of New Left attacks on older liberals and radicals like himself. "I felt that some of its spokesmen wanted not just to refute my opinions—that would have been entirely proper—but also to erase, to eliminate, to 'smash' people like me" (MH, 314). It did not occur to Howe that some of their fury toward him was akin to that of Frankenstein's monster toward the utopian genius who created and then disowned him. By the end of the decade, he had become a favorite target of New Left hecklers. "Repeatedly I found myself hissed down at campus meetings, and it was not just my opinions that were under assault . . . but my very being, my claim to some measure of persistence and integrity" ("Rahv, A Memoir," 496). But the experienced street fighter was by no means a helpless victim. On one occasion, in 1969, he turned on an SDS heckler, saying: "You know what you're going to end up as? You're going to end up as a *dentist*" (MH, 306).

The New Left and Israel: 1967–

One of the major targets of the New Left, especially in the aftermath of the war which the Arab nations started (and lost) in June of 1967, was the state of Israel. Howe had been involved with leftist movements long enough to know that sooner or later they turn against the Jews. He seems first to have become aware of the gulf between himself and other people on the left with respect to Israel shortly after the outbreak of the third Arab-Israeli war in June 1967. On 7 June the *New York Times* carried an advertisement which, written before the war actually began, called on the United States "to act now with courage and conviction, with nerve and firmness of intent, to maintain free passage in those waters [of the Gulf of 'Aqaba, which Egypt, in an act of war, had blockaded]— and so to safeguard the integrity, security, and survival of Israel and its people. . . . " The signatories included several people (including Howe, Macdonald, Kazin, Arendt, Podhoretz) who had been sharp critics of American intervention in Vietnam. But, Howe observed, numerous leftists refused to sign the statement because it would be inconsistent with their opposition to the Vietnam war.

Howe therefore felt it necessary to clarify the grounds on which he, at any rate, urged American support for Israel. He did this in two pieces, one coauthored with Stanley Plastrik (who formerly operated, in *Labor Action* days, as Henry Judd) that was written about a week after the conclusion of the war in June and was published in *Dissent* in the July-August 1967 issue, and a second, by Howe alone, called "Vietnam and Israel." The earlier essay makes a special point of declaring that its two authors "are not Zionists; or Jewish nationalists; or by any means un-critical of the state of Israel." Nevertheless, their first reaction to the imminent war of annihilation by Nasser against the Jewish state was "concern for the survival of Israel." Despite their innocence of Zionist or Jewish nationalist taint, they believed that "the destruction of Israel, coming after the holocaust of this century, would be intolerable." This statement constitutes a rare failure of tact in the mature Howe, even if Plastrik is to be held partly responsible for it. Would Israel's destruction have been tolerable if it had *not* been preceded by the Holocaust? At least there is no attempt to conceal their Jewish identity, for Howe and Plastrik go on to say that only an accident of geography had kept them "from ending as bars of soap" and that they had been stirred by the creation of a modern, democratic society in large part by Holocaust survivors.[35]

Despite the nervous, apologetic tone of this first response in the aftermath of the war, the essay does have firm hold of some facts which in later years would slip from Howe's grasp. The writers indicate that "a peace settlement does not depend on Israel alone" (388), a premise obviously denied by the very name of the organization which would call itself "Peace Now"; they refer to the Palestinian Arab problem as "the problem of the Arab refugees," not as a problem of national identity and the need for another Palestinian Arab state (in addition to Jordan); above all, they take seriously the Arabs' intention to destroy Israel. Nine years later, in a review of Bellow's *To Jerusalem and Back*, Howe would condescend to the novelist for "seeing the Arabs as ineluctably bent upon the destruction of Israel," and even add the astonishing observation that even if they are, "they can't."[36]

The second essay, "Vietnam and Israel," appeared in a collection which Howe coedited with Carl Gershman. Acccording to Gershman, "the book was undertaken as a political act to separate himself and the democratic left clearly from that part of the left that was anti-Israel in addition to being anti-Vietnam."[37] In the essay Howe again enumerates the reasons why he urged American support of Israel during the 1967 crisis. Primary among them were "the social-political achievement of the Israelis" and his strong personal conviction that it is "inconceivable that after Auschwitz the last remaining concentration of Jews outside the United States should be destroyed."[38] Oddly, Howe feels it necessary to justify the second reason—"I would be lying if I were to claim that the Jewishness of Israel seems a trivial matter" (342)—but not the first, even though it seems discriminatory to imply that a *Jewish* nation's continued existence should be predicated on its "social-political achievement." Yet Israel's democratic and socially progressive character is, according to Howe, a crucial, if not the only, reason why he and his colleagues say "yes" to support for Israel and "no" to support for the Vietnam war.

Such distinctions, he continues, are of no importance to that segment of the peace movement which follows Noam Chomsky in taking the view that anything the United States does abroad must be reactionary and deplorable. Politely avoiding all mention of Chomsky's pathological hatred of Israel, Howe refers to him as a person of "goodwill" who has nevertheless failed to ask himself whether he is prepared "*to take responsibility for the consequences of an Arab victory*" (348). This pointed thrust again reminds us that Howe, before he became a devotee of Peace Now in the late seventies, took the Arabs at their word when they vowed to drive the Israelis into the sea. Indeed, he refers to Israel's ability and desire to defend itself as the chief impediment to "a holocaust" in the Middle East.

He takes up the subject once more in a *New York Times* op-ed piece of about the same time [13 March 1971]. In it Howe seeks to explain (though not justify) the growing hostility of leftist academics and intellectuals toward Israel. He says that he does not believe it is Israel's shortcomings which explain this increasing hostility. Part of it may be due to that most durable of twentieth-century ideologies, antisemitism—although he does not actually use the word. Rather, he says—as we have seen he was wont to do in moods of despair—that "as someone has remarked, in the warmest of hearts there's a cold spot for the Jews."[39] He refrains from saying "in the warmest of gentile hearts" not so much out of delicacy as out of the awareness that many of the most passionate Israel-haters among the New Left were themselves Jews.

Yet the explanation he settles on is not Jewish antisemitism but the left's distaste and contempt for democracy. The New Left despises Israel not because of her flaws but because of her virtues, one of which is democracy. Nor is it merely democracy in the American mode, but the very kind that, according to Howe, the left should most respect. The left heaps contempt "upon a country which, under extreme difficulties, remains about as good a model as we have for the democratic socialist hope of combining radical social change with political freedom" (429).

This is an explanation both peculiar and unsettling. It is peculiar because it does not explain why leftist hostility intensified after Israel won a war which, if lost, would have meant her extinction. Was Israel more democratic after 1967 than before? Or was the real reason for the change in leftist sympathies the change in the Arab propaganda line, from right to left? Before 1967 the Arabs had openly expressed their imperialist aspirations, and vowed to throw the Israelis into the sea, declaring (as Nasser did in the months prior to the Six-Day War) that Israel's existence was in itself "an aggression." But not long after the war they decided on a different tack, one that specifically appealed to the prejudices of liberals and leftists. Ruth Wisse has succinctly summarized the new approach: "Having refused to admit a Jewish state in what they designate as their exclusive region, Arab countries accuse the Jews of refusing to accept an Arab state. Having launched against it successive wars, terrorist raids, and boycotts, Arab countries accuse Israel of aggression for defending its territory against attack." Moreover, the new vocabulary of the anti-Zionist assault "claim[ed] to replace the Jews . . . [by] systematically usurping all the symbols and terms of Jewish history and national consciousness."[40] But Howe blithely ignores all this.

His explanation is unsettling, or should have been to friends of Israel, because it seems to make support of Israel's very existence contingent on its being commendably "socialist." (Never mind that Israeli "socialism" depended for its existence on American economic aid, or that the economy it nurtured was long considered an incurable basket case of monstrous government bureaucracy.) Someone reading Howe's 1971 "defense" of Israel as a model of democratic socialism might well have wondered how staunch his support would be if the Israeli Labor party should ever lose its monopoly of government and be replaced by a nonsocialist opposition. The answer would be forthcoming after 1977, when Labor was turned out of office by Menachem Begin and the Likud.

Conserving the Universities from the Insurgents

The place where Howe encountered the most immediate pressure from the radicalism of the sixties was, of course, the place where he worked: the university. Although he began his teaching career at Brandeis for the most mundane of reasons, he gradually came to regard the profession of teaching with high seriousness and a good deal of affection. He would make the complaints that professors typically make—too much teaching, too much administrative bureaucracy, boring colleagues, mediocre students—but he came to think of teaching as "*good* work" which involves one with materials of beauty, ideas of importance, literary masterpieces, history, science. "And sometimes," he wrote in 1964, a year after he had begun teaching at Hunter College and the Graduate Center of the City University New York,[41] "teaching even yields the pleasure of stirring a young mind to knowledge and thought" (*Steady Work*, 101). That he did his job very well indeed is evident not only from the testimonials of countless students but also from the shrewd and eminently useful teaching guides that he prepared for the *Classics of Modern Fiction* anthologies that he edited. He also appreciated the complete freedom that he had always been given by his employers, even during the McCarthy years.

The traditional university was, therefore, one institution that Howe very much wished to *conserve*. By the sixties, he found himself, if only by force of circumstance, representing the old guard. "For the first time in several decades," he wrote in 1966, "the generation of intellectuals associated with the thirties . . . seems in danger of losing its dominant position in American intellectual life" ("Radical Questions," 323–24). The younger generation of intellectuals and semi-intellectuals came armed with self-assurance, a lust for power, and a contempt for, and eagerness to consume, their elders which Howe found at once admirable and disturbing—and the disturbing aspect rapidly became dominant. "How could it happen," he asks in an essay called "Universities and Intellectuals," "that a radical writing about the role of the university in modern society should find himself expressing somewhat—or what might appear to be—'conservative' views?" (*Steady Work*, 100). This statement of 1966—which he would repeat in essence in 1991 when defending the value of the literary canon—is one of the earliest explicit acknowledgments by Howe that in certain crucial respects he could be deeply conservative. Implicitly, he had already acknowledged this fact in committing himself to the preservation of Yiddish literature. In autumn of 1965 he had written a curious elegy for Adlai Stevenson, the first nonsocialist presidential candidate for whom Howe (in 1952) had voted. He praised the recently deceased politician as "the most attractive human being to figure prominently in American politics since the second world war" although he was neither a socialist nor a liberal but represented "the cultivated conservatism of the nineteenth century trying to cope with the realities of the twentieth."[42] Later, Howe would write to Professor Samuel Hux that "the tradition from which people like myself come, though it was disastrously mistaken and worse on many counts, nevertheless did share with serious conservatives a feeling for the past, a respect for inherited culture. . . . "[43]

Believing that "a part of our hope for the good, or at least a better, society lies in conserving what the university stands for," Howe found himself in the tumult of the sixties caught in a tension between his activist and contemplative selves, between "my belief that serious men must be involved in the political struggles of their day and my belief that the university . . . should serve as a center of intellectual detachment, a place devoted to scholarship and disinterested thought." Using the language of two traditionalist Victorians, one of them intensely conservative, Howe wrote on behalf of Arnoldian "disinterestedness" and of John Henry Newman's conviction that knowledge is capable of being pursued as an end in itself. He saw this old-fashioned conception of the university as a center of intellectual detachment, scholarship, and disinterested inquiry threatened from two sides. The managers of the "multiversities" wanted the schools to serve the "practical" purposes of a practical age, funneling students into industry and bureaucracy; and the student rebels against these managers wanted to turn the universities upside down and make them training schools for revolution. During the student riots at Columbia in 1968, Howe found himself ranged upon the side of the "reactionaries," i.e., those who wished to protect the university from becoming instruments of radical politics. Two decades after he had criticized Robert Lowell for joining the intellectuals' "flight from politics," he found himself, in a paradoxical reversal of roles, satirized by Lowell for the same transgression.[44]

With his characteristic idealism, Howe believed that disinterested pursuit of truth and the milieu of political protest could coexist at the university. "Why not?" he asks. The answer, alas, is that the commitment to truth and the commitment to active citizenship do not readily coexist for very long in more than a tiny minority of human beings. Perhaps Howe was one of the exceptions that test the rule. For the sake of radicalism itself, he argues, the accumulated wisdom of the past has to be treated with respect, even reverence. " . . . For the radical who wishes to see a new and better world: of what can that world be made if not—together with the work of the future—the conserved heritage of the past?" (*Steady Work*, 102).

Howe admits that it had formerly been the habit of liberal and leftist writers to mock the sterility and apolitical distance of many academics. Especially was this the case when these writers contemplated the failure of German professors to resist Hitler. He grants too that the majority of professors in the sixties are not all that different in outlook from what they had been in the thirties: parochial, timid, snobbish, indifferent to human suffering. Perhaps a certain inertia is fundamental to social and intellectual life, and it would be unrealistic to deny this.

But whereas a decade earlier Howe had mocked intellectuals who sought shelter (and sustenance) in the universities, he now sees in them the hope of salvaging the true ideal of liberal education: that there is a value to the life of the mind apart from utilitarian or national ends. He invokes Cardinal Newman's principle of "the high protecting power of all knowledge [which] maps out the territory of the intellect, and sees that . . . there is neither encroachment nor surrender on any side" (*Steady Work*, 109). In an age of "mass culture" (which Howe deplored), the democratic ideal of mass education (which he favored) is endangered precisely by such "encroachments." Intellectuals are better suited than scholars to demonstrate that knowledge is capable of being an end in itself, that its value is intrinsic, not extrinsic, coextensive with the activity of mind rather than consequent upon it. Above all, being more intimately related to the crises of the present, the intellectual is better suited than the scholar himself to search for the idea of the past.

If American students grow more skeptical of the intellectual value of a college education the more its utility is preached to them, this is partly due to the belief of American young people (a belief they share with Americans generally) that the past no longer matters. Here again Howe speaks in a markedly conservative manner. The past, he insists, is the very matter upon which the life of the mind subsists. The central task of the intellectual in the American university is not to subvert the past whose reality is the substance of the scholar's being, but—on the contrary—to validate this past, "to insist upon its organic relationship with the present, to deny that America is exempt from history" (*Steady Work*, 111). Precisely because American society has lost much of its historical sense, the intellectual, especially the liberal or radical intellectual concerned with a better future, must take upon himself a conserving task. If this sounds paradoxical, it is nevertheless true that "being a radical in politics enforces a certain conservatism in regard to education" (*Steady Work*, 112). The idea of the future to which radicals are committed will not survive if a living sense of the past does not survive.

Howe's intensely democratic and egalitarian conservatism with respect to education and culture is very much in the spirit of Matthew Arnold, like Howe "a Liberal, yet . . . a Liberal tempered by experience, reflection, and renouncement, and . . . above all, a believer in culture." At the end of the first chapter of *Culture and Anarchy*, Arnold had proclaimed that culture did not try to teach down to the level of inferior classes, but to do away with classes altogether: "to make the best that has been thought and known in the world current everywhere; to make all men live in an atmosphere of sweetness and light. . . . This is the *social idea*; and the men of culture are the true apostles of equality . . . those who have had a passion for diffusing, for making prevail, for carrying from one end of society to the other, the best knowledge, the best ideas of their time." Arnold's words of 1869 are a wonderfully precise definition of Howe's argument in the sixties for the integrity of education and a nobility of inclusiveness, an argument to which he would return with yet greater passion in the last decade of his life.

Thomas Hardy, 1967

Thomas Hardy is the only English literary figure to whom Howe devoted a full-length critical study. One wonders why. Hardy showed little interest in politics, and whatever political relevance his novels and poems have is largely tangential and accidental. Like Faulkner, the subject of Howe's earlier book, Hardy created a self-sufficient fictional world, and—like the Zionist he potentially was[45]—made attachment to the soil of a particular place a starting point for a self-conscious nostalgia and the basis for a rich interplay between past and present. But Hardy's Wessex was far more remote from Howe's political concerns than was Faulkner's Yoknapatawpha County. That Hardy was an acknowledged "classic" of English literature was not the kind of distinction likely to attract Howe; but that he was a classic under attack by numerous critics, especially the (to Howe) ever-inflammatory T. S. Eliot, because he was an auto-didact uncurbed by institutional attachments or "objective" beliefs, aroused Howe's combative instincts. It also afforded the opportunity, which he always welcomed, "to encounter uncertainties, embarrassments, challenges and revisions."[46]

Hardy must also have struck Howe as a contemporaneous English and Christian instance of the classic Yiddish writers, especially I. L. Peretz. What Hasidic Judaism was to Peretz, Christianity was to Hardy; what Jewish folk material was to Peretz, Wessex folklore was to Hardy. Although he does not mention Peretz in this book, Howe cannot but have thought of Hardy's paradoxical mixture of skepticism and regret, as a lapsed Christian, as similar to Peretz's emotional attachment to a religious system whose premises he rejected and whose leaders he often (outside of fiction) attacked. "Even after Hardy turned away from Christianity, its modes of perception remained fixed in his consciousness. What he had ceased to believe influenced his work at least as much as what he now felt obliged to think" (25).

Although Hardy may have begun as, and to some extent remained (until his last novel, *Jude the Obscure*), a novelist of provincial rootedness, he would not, in Howe's view, have become a novelist of universal interest unless, like Faulkner, he had chosen or been driven to uproot himself. Howe tends to view Hardy's work as (in the language of that most formidable of English conservative thinkers, S. T. Coleridge) a balance between the interests of permanence and progression. The former is embodied in the experience of Dorset (recreated as Wessex in the novels and poems) and the latter in the pressures of nineteenth-century thought. One part of Hardy is the lover of Wessex, an ordered existence, natural, rooted, tested; this Hardy is the traditionalist writer attached to the farmlands, animals, rocks, hills, and the simple people who inhabit them. He recognizes as essential in life "that which is repeated," and his novels gain their unique quality by suggesting a time before, and a space beneath, history, a non- or supra-historical permanence. The traditionalist Hardy is—and who but a critic with some deeply conservative instincts could define this motif so exactly?—"patient before the monotony of change and the sameness of novelty" (19). On the other hand, the decisive intellectual influences upon Hardy were distinctly "progressive" thinkers: J. S. Mill, Herbert Spencer, and T. H. Huxley. Their religious skepticism tended (in collusion with a kind of country fatalism or "pessimism") to undermine Christianity.

Not for the last time, Howe finds the center of a writer's work in his ability to balance opposed forces in a creative tension. He treats Hardy's writing—when it is at its best—as a "fruitful entanglement" of traditional and modern. "The pessimistic anxieties of a modern intellectual rub against the stoic bias of a country mind; 'modern nerves' . . . against 'primitive feelings'; skepticism against superstition" (30). Hardy, as Howe sees him, achieves a sense of inclusiveness by balancing the natural and the historical, the timeless and the time-bound, the permanent limitations of all life with the particular troubles of the moment. Hardy also exemplified Howe's axiom, articulated in the Ellison dispute, that a writer's best subject is not the one he chooses, but the one that chooses him. Hardy composed under the pressures of "an inescapable subject—the fate of Wessex . . . a subject he had . . . merely [to] submit to." When this principle of order, along with the balance of antitheses enumerated above, began to crumble in *Jude the Obscure* (1895), Hardy ended his career as a novelist and returned to his first love: poetry.

Howe's discussion of Hardy's last novel is probably the most frequently reprinted chapter of this book, even though nothing in it quite equals the impact of the sentence that opens the chapter on *Tess of the D'Urbervilles*: "As a writer of novels Thomas Hardy was endowed with a precious gift: he liked women" (108). He did not, however, like the institution of marriage, and his animus toward it impels the "reformist" side of *Jude*. This last novel appealed to Howe as Hardy's most distinctively "modern" work, one that incorporated several of the modernist assumptions—that men of any sensitivity must live in permanent doubt and intellectual turmoil; that life without traditional beliefs is inherently problematic; that loneliness and anguish are inevitable; that excessive intellection dries up the springs of life; that courage consists only of the ability to live without certainty. Yet Howe understood that Hardy could no more be at his best as a modernist alone than he could be as a traditionalist alone; hence the special difficulties of *Jude*.

At least one element of the uprooting of traditional life depicted in Jude Fawley was bound to appeal to Howe: Jude was a rural cousin of the self-educated worker who had begun to emerge in late nineteenth-century England. By making Jude a restorer of old churches who hires himself out for wages, Hardy placed him socially in between the old-fashioned artisan and the modern worker. More immediate to Howe's concerns was the "enormous sympathy" with which (along with critical irony) Hardy presents Jude's disinterested desire for learning. The novelist's balance of sympathy and distance made Jude a thoroughly individualized figure, but his personal drama was skilfully woven from the materials of historical change.

The novel's heroine, Sue Bridehead, was for Howe a still more startling instance of newness in fiction, someone who could not have appeared in a novel by Austen or Dickens or Thackeray. "She is the first major anticipation in the English novel of that profoundly affecting and troublesome creature: the modern girl" (138). Like Jude, she has her social dimension as a representation of the situation of women in the last third of the nineteenth century; but she is more important as an instance of psychological portraiture: "Sue is that terrifying spectre of our age, before whom men and cultures tremble: She is *an interesting girl* . . . Promethean in mind but masochist in character . . . all intellectual seriousness . . . all feminine charm, but without body, without flesh or smell, without femaleness" (142). One can already detect in Howe's analysis of Sue as a sick (albeit "charming") woman the (somewhat Lawrentian) tone that would later (for example, in the essay on Kate Millett) give offense to the more doctrinaire feminists.

Howe saw in *Jude* both an ending and a beginning. It marked the end of Victorian idealism. In such novels as *Middlemarch*, for example, the protagonists, Dorothea Brooke and Tertius Lydgate, struggle for the realization of ideals that both their circumstances and their society oppose. They know their struggle will be difficult, but don't regard it as impossible; and Dorothea is granted a limited success at the novel's end. "But by *Jude the Obscure* there is neither enclave nor retreat, evasion nor grasped opportunity for resistance. Jude and Sue are lost souls: they have no place in the world they can cherish or to which they can retreat" (139). Moreover, the ideals themselves—for Jude, the church and the university; for Sue, Hellenism and Millite individualism—prove to be brittle, unworthy.

But *Jude* was also, in Howe's reading of literary history, part of the beginning of that literary modernism which would dominate the twentieth century. This was true both of Hardy's distinctive sensibility, especially his bleak pessimism, and of his transformation of the realistic novel into a dramatic fable that sacrificed the accepted aesthetic criteria of unity and verisimilitude to the exaggerations of expressionism. Moving away from the older notion of character as something fixed in nature and knowable through actions, Hardy, Howe argues, depicts human character as inherently problematic, open to speculative inquiry, and perhaps beyond knowing at all. The novel was also, in Howe's view, distinctively modern in narrative structure. It dispensed with the traditional plot, which reveals and acts out a major destiny, and offered instead a series of situations or moments rather than a sequence of actions. Hardy did not move so far in this modernist direction as the fiction of Kafka, Joyce, and Faulkner, but far more so than in all his earlier novels. Within the boundaries of the traditional English novel he could not have found the formal means to give expression to "the grey poetry of modern loneliness" (146).

A Treasury of Yiddish Poetry, 1969

In 1969 Howe, again in collaboration with Eliezer Greenberg, brought out a companion volume to his *Treasury of Yiddish Stories*, published fifteen years earlier. It was the second large building block in the canon of secular Jewishness he was constructing in the form of anthologies.

Since it was a volume of poetry, the business of enlisting and consulting with translators was much more arduous, just how arduous we may learn from Ozick's account of her "struggle" with Howe over a single line in a poem by David Einhorn.[47] This volume too was preceded by a lengthy, carefully conceived, and finely nuanced introduction. It repeated some of the historical material of the earlier introduction, but was much more concerned with the evolution of Yiddish poetry into a kind of modernism and with the claim of American Yiddish poetry to be a branch of American literature.

Howe begins by noting the contrast between Yiddish fiction and Yiddish poetry. The former found its fulfillment almost at its beginning, with the appearance of the three masters of Yiddish: Mendele Mocher Seforim, Peretz, and Sholom Aleichem. Nearly everything which followed them was a variation on the opening "classical" phase. But Yiddish poetry came to its maturity later, more gradually. Much of its development came in the twentieth century, when it went through a series of abrupt convulsions; it also bore the imprint of the American immigrant experience more strongly than Yiddish fiction did. This was especially the case in the aftermath of the Holocaust. With the destruction of European Jewry, the life of the Jews in Eastern Europe was little more than a memory to Yiddish writers in America, who also, with rare exception, lacked the knowledge needed to write about Jewish or non-Jewish life in this country. For the writers of prose, this often brought paralysis. But for the poets the very loss of their subject and their audience could be, indeed was, made into a fruitful, albeit tragic, theme.

Although Howe places his usual stress upon the international nature of Yiddish literature, and devotes sections of his introduction (really a monograph) to Yiddish poetry in the Soviet Union and in Poland, the core of his discussion is the development of Yiddish poetry in America. The first generation of Yiddish poets reflected its origins in the Jewish working class that grew up in the wake of the massive immigration of Eastern European Jews in the 1880s. These were the sweatshop or labor poets, sometimes called the rhyme department of the labor movement. Despite his socialist commitment, Howe makes no excessive claims for them. But he does point out that the tremendous popularity of their work—the socialist poet Morris Rosenfeld was the most popular Yiddish poet ever to write in America—was natural and organic. "The sweatshop poets are naive writers, but naive in ways that yield, within the Jewish tradition, a certain cumulative strength. Arising out of the immigrant experience . . . these poets must be read with a greater tolerance for sentiment and a stronger belief in the idea of the poet as collective spokesman than many readers are now likely to possess" (TYP, 22). Nevertheless, Howe—ever ready to rebuke false socialism parading as populism—distinguishes these Yiddish poets, who always wrote out of their own experience, from the so-called "proletarian" writers (in English and Yiddish) of the thirties, middle-class intellectuals engaged in poetic slumming who pretended that they were sacrificing their poetic gift to a virtuous political cause.

Although Howe grants, near the end of his essay, that he has, for purposes of expository clarity, imposed a linear development on events that came almost simultaneously, he has the sweatshop poets "followed" by a group of "transitional" poets (Abraham Lyessin, Yehoash, and Abraham Reisen) who joined socialist and national themes (less clearly distinguished then than they would subsequently become). These were poets of greater self-consciousness than the sweatshop poets, more critical of the slogans of socialist internationalism, more knowledgable in Jewish tradition. Reisen was for Howe the most important of the group, the first major lyricist in Yiddish poetry, the celebrator of the sanctity of the poor, above all the complete master of the inner world of the inhabitants of the shtetl.

The third wave of Yiddish poets defined in Howe's survey of the history of the genre exemplified a paradox that might be thought of as the existential realization of his own blend of socialism and modernism. In 1907 *Die Yunge* (The Young Ones) began to publish a small periodical called *Yugend* (Youth), in which they declared their independence from Jewish communal responsibility and the obligation to speak on behalf of national ideals. They would not subordinate aesthetic ideals to political journalism and the needs (often rather pressing) of the folk. Their Jewishness was cultural rather than ideological and political; and they stressed the importance of the poet's individual voice apart from Jewish problems and Jewish fate. Rejecting the traditional subjects of Yiddish poetry—social justice, ethical idealism, Jewish suffering—meant, and this they understood, cutting themselves off from the mass of Yiddish readers upon whom their predecessors had been able to rely. Like many of their European contemporaries in the first decades of this century, they aspired to a "pure" poetry, free of the taint of ideas and polemics and paraphrasable doctrine.

But what Howe relished most about *Die Yunge* was that, *un*like European devotees of an autonomous poetry, the Yiddish modernists (or would-be modernists) were poverty-stricken immigrants who would remain workers for most of their lives. As Howe puts it, with great jubilation and entire disregard of the way in which the paradox confutes Marxist ideology: "Imagine in any other literature the turn to impressionism and symbolism being undertaken by a shoemaker [Mani Leib] and a house painter [Zishe Landau], a paper hanger [H. Leivick] and a waiter [Moishe Leib Halpern]; the dismissal of the social muse led by men who themselves labored in factories every day! Proletarian aesthetes, Parnassians of the sweatshop—this was the paradox and the glory of *Die Yunge*" (TYP, 30–31).[48] Had Ellison read this song of praise, he might well have asked: if the paradox and the glory of this imaginative freedom from social circumstances were good for the Yiddish poets, why were they unsuitable for black writers, for me?

Die Yunge did not, in Howe's view, quite succeed in becoming full-fledged modernists. But this "failure" was to their credit, for it meant, as he had already written two years earlier, that they had not entirely dispensed with the commonplace materials of everyday life. *Die Yunge* "could never fully turn away from the realities of Jewish experience and the pressures of Jewish tradition. They were modern poets, but more important, modern *Yiddish* poets. . . . they shared in the experience against which they rebelled" (TYP, 32). One aspect of Jewish tradition was embodied in Leivick's mystique of martyrdom, his view that violence does even justice unjustly. Although this introduction does not have the slightly anti-Zionist polemical tone of the 1954 introduction, with its stress on the virtue of powerlessness, Howe nevertheless—and this just two years after the Six-Day War—makes a point of asserting that "in the spectrum of Jewish values [Leivick] stands at the opposite pole from the *sabra*" (TYP, 37).

Closer than *Die Yunge* to genuine literary modernism in their experiments with form and theme were the *In Zich* or introspectivist group of poets who rose to prominence shortly after World War I. Chief among them, and for Howe probably chief among twentieth-century Yiddish poets, was Jacob Glatstein. Glatstein and his colleagues turned to free verse and declared aesthetic principles similar to those of the imagists in America and modernist groups in Europe. They sought to free themselves, even more than *Die Yunge* had done, from the national-social obligations of the Yiddish poet. In their manifesto of 1920, they defiantly announced that "for us there does not exist the sterile question as to whether the poet should write about national or social or personal problems. We make no distinction between poetry of the heart and poetry of the mind. In regard to our *Yiddishkayt*, we would point out that we are Yiddish poets by virtue of the fact that we are Jews and write in Yiddish. Whatever a Yiddish poet may write about is *ipso facto* Yiddish. One does not need specifically Jewish themes . . . " (TYP, 42). According to Howe's encapsulated history of Yiddish poetry, the *In Zich* group came closest to bringing Yiddish into the mainstream of twentieth-century world poetry. What prevented it from doing so was the ghastliness of twentieth century Jewish history. "Yiddish modernism," Howe would later write, "precisely because it is Yiddish and therefore tied to a particular destiny, can never be as free, unburdened, gratuitous (or irresponsible) as the modernism of Europe and America."[49] Once again, the "Jewish question" obliged Howe to qualify his own estimate of, and adherence to, modernism.

Glatstein, for example, was by all appearances a modernist poet. Yet the very compulsiveness with which he insisted upon individual sensibility testified to the irresistible tenacity of Jewish collective fate. Glatstein's profound ties to the Jewish traditions against which he rebelled are, Howe argued, evident even in his early poems. How much more so, then, in the poems he wrote in the aftermath of the Holocaust, when only a few major Yiddish poets remained, and Glatstein felt compelled to speak for his culture, his people, above all for the Yiddish language. In his Holocaust poems, championed by Howe as among the few bodies of literary work that seriously cope with the subject, Glatstein retained the personal voice with which he had begun as an *In Zikh* poet, but also returned, says Howe, to "the Yiddish tradition of direct speech with God, a blindingly affectionate quarrel in which the demand for justice, or at least for explanation, is never allowed to lapse" ("Journey of a Poet," 77).

Ultimately, Glatstein was for Howe more a moral and cultural exemplar, a distinctively Jewish one, than a major Yiddish poet. He believed passionately that Yiddish, by virtue of the fact that it was now the language of martyrdom, had in a way displaced Hebrew as the sacred tongue of the Jews. (It is regrettable, perhaps revealing, that Howe fails to mention that Glatstein, despite his attachment to Yiddish, did not fall into line with those Yiddishists who never "forgave" the Jewish state for choosing Hebrew over Yiddish. On the contrary, he was a strong supporter of Zionism.)[50] Glatstein's attachment to the lost cause of Yiddish was by itself sufficient to endear him to Howe, who already sensed that he was accumulating plenty of lost causes of his own. Though a major, even a great, poet, Glatstein was neither known nor likely to be known in the world. But his doggedness in upholding the Yiddish tradition could, Howe maintained, teach young people a great deal about "the courage men can have in standing by their values." In the presence of Yiddish writers like Glatstein and Greenberg, Howe could feel about the Yiddish world of his youth "as if it all had come alive, and would never end" ("Journey of a Poet," 77).

In the conclusion of his study of Yiddish poetry, Howe, in a beautiful peroration, makes a case for this body of writing in the (New Critical) language of paradox, as a precarious balance of opposed forces held together in creative tension, a stability in conflict, a kind of *discordia concors*. Yiddish poetry is both universal and provincial. It bears the stamp of a deeply religious culture; yet its very existence signaled the breakup of religious faith. It cannot break away from the integrated worldview which it helped to destroy. "It yearns for what it denies, it denies what it yearns for" (TYP, 58). Its major figures tend to rebel against the burdens of the folk and the costs of Jewish history, yet are dragged, often kicking and screaming, back to the subject of Jewish fate, the themes of the fathers against whom they have rebelled. The wisest of the Yiddish poets move away from the invisible boundaries of Yiddish culture and then return to them, "move away in order to return" (TYP, 61). In that sense, they foreshadow the career of Irving Howe himself, who would also return, not as a poet but as a socialist in quest of secular Jewishness. That quest and its difficulties were described in one of the poems of Glatstein himself: "It's as hard to return to / old-fashioned words / as to sad synagogues, / those thresholds of faith. / You know exactly where they are. / Troubled, you can still hear their undertones. / Sometimes you come close and look longingly / at them through the windowpanes. / You who still take your ease in the shadow of biblical trees, / O sing me the cool solace / of all you remember, all that you know."[51]

SEVEN

In the Shadow of Decades: Farewell to Immigrant Jewishness

*Try to retrieve the seventies and memories crumble
in one's hand, nothing keeps its shape. I can
summon a roster of Presidents and politicians,
recall hours spent watching the Watergate hearings
on television, patch together a sequence of public
events. But the decade itself lacks a distinctive
historical flavor. It's as if the years had simply
dropped out of one's life and all that remains are
bits and pieces of recollection. (MH, 328)[1]*

Political Terrorism on the Left

Early in the new decade the verbal violence of the New Left turned into actual violence, with the verbal bombs being replaced by real ones, as if to confirm Howe's direst sixties predictions of the fate of the New Left extremists, fanatics mistaking themselves for saints. In the wake of bombings in New York City (which had taken the lives of the bombers themselves), Howe wrote a sharp condemnation both of the rationale given by the New Leftists for terrorism, and of the liberal "explainers" of and apologists for the terrorists. "Political Terrorism: Hysteria on the Left" expresses impatience with the bogus claim that these young idealists "have tried everything" and, in their frustration and shock "that the centuries-long struggle for social justice did not come to instant triumph in 1969," have turned to bombs.[2] Indeed, Howe, like a job counselor for do-gooders, offers a list of names to which they can apply if they want "to change society."

Although Howe in the sixties had resisted the strong temptation to observe that the most extreme elements of the New Left were the spoiled children of affluence, he does so now: "Let us also remember that a large percentage of the New Left are the children of the middle class and the rich" (27). Were these self-styled Marxists inclined to perform a class analysis of themselves, they might pause to ask why New Leftism appeals almost exclusively to spoiled brats rather than to young proletarians. But of course they know neither themselves nor what American workers might think of their cause and methods.

Aggravating the evil of New Left sloganeering for terror are the mass media and the intellectuals. "Living in California last year," Howe writes, "I sometimes felt the S.D.S. was a creation of TV, providing it with an unfailing flow of usable items; on reflection, I concluded it was a phantom dreamed up by Ronald Reagan to insure his re-election" (124). Even worse than the irresponsible trumpeting of the terrorist cause by the mass media is the behavior of the intellectuals, "too many of whom have proved susceptible to the delights of being 90-day campus heroes" (124). Without ever naming names, Howe alludes obliquely to (among other culprits) Herbert Marcuse, Andrew Sarris, Norman Mailer (in the "White Negro" essay Howe had himself published in *Dissent*), and the *New York Review of Books*, which had run a diagram on its cover describing how to make a Molotov cocktail, "perhaps as part of an adult-education program" (124). Now, better late than never, Howe repudiates his old view that ideas are radically defenseless against the uses to which they are put, and sternly insists that "at some point sorcerers must take a bit of responsibility for their strayed apprentices" (124). The intellectuals with whom the New Left terrorists had gone to school (often literally) in the sixties had planted the elitism, the authoritarianism, the hatred of democracy and love of dictatorship, and the mystique of violence which were now sprouting in terrorism.

Howe also ventures a prediction about the political consequences of continued terrorism, one which proved true: "The first and mildest consequence would be Reaganism. 'The one indispensable element in Reagan's political survival,' says Jesse Unruh, who ought to know, 'is campus unrest'" (125). Another, perhaps graver consequence might be to arouse authority, which still acts with some measure of restraint, to brutally smash its New Left opponents. Indeed, Howe adds in a markedly "patriotic" vein: "it speaks rather well for the people of this country that, despite what they consider to be provocations and outrages, they have thus far refrained from letting themselves be stampeded into hysterical and repressive moods" (125–26). If the government should eventually lose its patience with bank burners and bomb throwers and their apologists, the worst losers would be the whole American left, the congeries of radical movements which had spent decades dissociating themselves from a small group of anarchist bomb throwers. But the radical young, innocent of history as of everything else, know nothing of how terrorists hurt the socialist movements of both Europe and America.

But Howe does not wish to rest his argument against terrorism mainly on grounds of its dreadful practical results. Terrorism, he asserts, "is wrong because minorities in a democratic society, as long as their right to dissent and protest is largely protected, do not have the right to impose their will upon the majority through violence or terror. This has always been a central argument of democratic socialism . . . " (127–28). It is also wrong in a yet more profound sense. Ask yourselves, he urges the New Left terrorists, what kind of people you will become if you use such methods. Repudiating the Marxist view that morality is a consideration not of the present but only of the long run of the historical process, Howe warns that the torturers in Stalin's prisons had also started as idealists murdering on behalf of "the revolution," devoutly believing they would ultimately be vindicated by "history." Remember, he pleads, "what matters is the quality and discipline of the life one leads at a given moment . . . " (128).

Perhaps the most poignant aspect of this essay, written as Howe was delving into the history of the immigrant Jewish community, is its grief over the full flowering of the antisemitic impulse in the New Left, most particularly in its Jewish tribunes:

> Jewish boys and girls, children of the generation that saw Auschwitz, hate democratic Israel and celebrate as "revolutionary" the Egyptian dictatorship. Some of them pretend to be indifferent to the anti-Jewish insinuations of the Black Panthers; a few go so far as to collect money for Al Fatah, which pledges to take Tel Aviv. About this I cannot say more; it is simply too painful. (124)

Kate Millett and the Feminist Masquerade, 1970

It comes as something of a surprise, in reading *A Margin of Hope,* to find Howe devoting the longest section of his chapter on the seventies to the "new generation of militant feminists" (MH, 328) whom he began to meet early in the decade. It did not take long before he deemed "the women's movement flawed, an opinion that won me few friends" (MH, 329). He did not, of course, set himself in opposition to the traditional socioeconomic demands of women's movements since the nineteenth century, but observation of the new breed of American feminists led him to declare, ruefully, that "Good causes attract poor advocates." Thus does Howe open his critique, in *Harper's Magazine* for December 1970, of "The Middle-Class Mind of Kate Millett," author of *Sexual Politics*.[3] This is one of his longest, most deeply felt essays, a fierce polemic, ostensibly against a book but ultimately against the parochialism and moral obtuseness of the women's branch of the New Left. Howe, as his colleague Michael Walzer has shrewdly observed,[4] and as the title of their magazine *Dissent* reminds us, was at his best in essays written *against* something. Yet this essay is also written in favor of something—and that something is the distinctly conservative idea of the collective wisdom of the human race, precisely that half of the truth which "original" thinkers tend to overlook.

True, the essay begins in "progressive" language. Howe alleges that the dominant economic classes and institutions prefer ideological dramatics from the feminists rather than (justified) socioeconomic demands. From the former, especially when presented as "ideologies of ultimate salvation," they even derive a kind of entertainment greatly to be valued at a time when boredom has become a dominant social fact. That is one reason why an apocalyptic ideologue like Kate Millett, who calls for abolition of the family and offers Jean Genet, celebrant of criminality and homosexuality, as moral exemplum, is made rich by the Book-of-the-Month Club and featured on the cover of *Time*. From the point of view of those who do not wish to grant the just demands of women for equality, Millett is "the ideal highbrow popularizer for the politics and culture of the New Left" (CP, 203–204).

Howe's demolition begins with a summary of the argument of *Sexual Politics*, which he calls more a cry of woe than a theory. At its center is "a nightmare vision of endless female subordination to and suffering at the hands of men." According to Millett, sexual domination has been the *raison d'etre* of the patriarchal family that has been virtually coextensive with civilization itself. This system of power, she argues, deprives women of all but the most trivial sources of dignity or self-respect. Millett resists the possibility that biological and physical differences may have determined or may still determine a sequence of secondary and social differences between the sexes, for she believes that any concession to biology must mean accepting forever the traditional patterns of male domination. "The root premise of her work . . . is that women have been kept down because men have chosen to keep them down . . . " (CP, 205, 207).

Millett, Howe charges, has no sense of history or historical change or economic or racial or religious distinctions. It also does not occur to her to ask whether the fact of being female has been more important in the social history of most women than whether they were rich or poor, black or white, Christian or Jewish. Her method (like that of so many of the leftist targets of this former Marxist), is that of "vulgar Marxism," the travesty of Marxist thought which insists that the only significant reality is economic. She flattens all history into "sexual dominion." Ignoring factors of class position—here Howe can assume the old familiar role of socialist critic—she says that the invention of labor-saving devices has had no important effect on the duration of women's drudgery. Only a Columbia Ph.D. suffering from New Left middle-class parochialism and never having known the difference between scrubbing laundry on a washboard and putting it into an electric washing machine could, Howe sneers, make such a remark.

Equally bourgeois, charges Howe, is her social outlook, which is that of an old-fashioned feminist who believes the height of satisfaction is to work in an office or a factory, rather than be burdened "with those brutes called men and those slops called children" (CP, 209–10). Few things, he says, reveal her underlying convictions more clearly than her assumption that a man's mindless labor in a factory is "distinctly human" in contrast to the "animal" activity of a woman bringing up her child.

In rebuttal of Millett's unqualified assertion of patriarchal domination, Howe argues that she has overlooked the complexities and ambiguities of the word "power" in human relationships. Even in conditions of disadvantage, he points out, women have been able to gain for themselves important powers and privileges. If, for example, women were nothing more than "chattels," why did their "masters" send themselves and their sons to die in war while trying to spare the women that fate? In arguing that relations between men and women involve a subtle chemistry not grasped by the feminist ideologues, Howe speaks less as the political than the ethical thinker, the moralist who has absorbed literature's tragic view of life: "In any relationship of caring, people gain power over one another: the power to please, the power to hurt. . . . That women have held power over men, usually in the more desirable but often enough in quite deplorable ways, is a thought with which Miss Millett will have no commerce. And it is even possible . . . that the powers we hold over one another are both the desirable and the deplorable kinds, the two fatally and forever mixed" (CP, 211–12).

If Millett is bad at theory, she is, Howe asserts, at least as bad at history. Like other New Left ideologues, she always imposes upon the past the categories of analysis and standards of judgment drawn from the present, and invariably finds the past wanting. After praising (correctly, in Howe's view) the Victorian feminist J. S. Mill, she sets up as his Victorian patriarchal foil the sexually hapless John Ruskin. (A poorer choice to represent standard masculine assertiveness could not be imagined.) But what is worse is that Millett cannot place Ruskin's praise of femininity historically, cannot understand that Ruskin attached great importance to the family home as a last resort for human beings dehumanized by the industrial system that he loathed.

Repeatedly Howe stresses the folly of Millett's onslaught upon the institution of the family. In her inane remarks upon the totalitarian regimes of Hitler and Stalin as celebrants of "motherhood," she overlooks the fact that in every totalitarian society there is, inevitably, a clash between the state and the family, which is regarded with suspicion by the authorities as a competitor for the individual's loyalty. Her ideological blinders keep her from seeing that the ostensibly "conservative" institution of the family becomes a subversive element in a totalitarian regime. Indeed, the most egregious of her fantasies, in Howe's view, is her frivolous play with the notion of abolishing the family altogether. The family may be the most conservative of human institutions; yet, he points out, it has been endlessly open to social and psychological changes. Above all, however—and here it is Howe the conservative who speaks—one must ask, with respect to an institution that "has been coextensive with human culture itself," not simply the radical's standard question, "is it true?" but also the conservative's question: "what is the meaning of it?" It is important to recall that Howe, in his autobiography, described the great intellectual transformation which he underwent during his year and a half in Alaska in the following way: "As I read without scheme or purpose, I was discovering 'what everyone knew.' 'What everyone knew' is the very substance of education, regained in each life" (MH, 96). If, as Millett herself keeps complaining, the family has doggedly persisted for thousands of years, then it "may therefore be supposed to have certain powers of endurance and to yield certain profound satisfactions to human beings other than merely satisfying the dominating impulses of the 'master group'" (CP, 222n).

Among modern thinkers about the relations between men and women, Sigmund Freud was Millett's main target. Although Howe had no stake in any particular Freudian notion, he saw Millett's unbridled attack on Freud as a form of intellectual thuggery and a repudiation of the tragic complexity of life. In passages where Freud was reflecting upon the difficulties we all have in accepting the limits of being human, Millett thought he was giving women vocational guidance. She could not understand that one might be committed to equality between the sexes and yet recognize that Freud, stressing the idea of sexual difference, was one of the great minds of the age. Millett raged against Freud and the Freudians because they persisted in seeing a distinctive nature and role for women. She wished to abolish the words "masculine" and "feminine," alleged by her to be meaningless, and replace them with the biologically "verifiable" male and female.

Here Howe invokes the anecdote about Oscar Wilde's reply to a contentious question about the differences between the sexes: "Madam, I can't conceive." He interprets this as pointing to a fundamental (and, one might add, again distinctly "conservative") truth: namely, that along with the mere prejudices and irrational customs accumulated over the centuries, "there really is something we might call the experience, even the wisdom, of the race, and it is not to be disposed of simply by fiat or will (as many revolutionists find out too late)." What this collective wisdom tells us, through the historical pattern of a sexual division of labor that is universal in form although variable in content, is that conduct and culture are shaped by nature and biology. Although Millett obsessively insists that all but rudimentary sexual differences are cultural rather than biological in origin, the history of the human race suggests otherwise. "If certain patterns of existence, such as the family, are invariable throughout the development of human culture, then it seems reasonable to suppose . . . that they satisfy requirements of our biology as these have manifested themselves through culture" (CP, 227).

Finally, Howe looks at the two worlds he has known to see if they reflect at all Millett's descriptions of the status of women in society. Among his current friends (presumably academic and literary, for the most part) he finds women who free themselves even as they recognize the limits that circumstance, sex, history, and fortune impose on them; certainly they are not "chattels" or "sexual objects." But then he thinks back to the other world he has known well, that of immigrant Jewish workers, and this remembrance of things past wells up into a moving peroration that is one of the great moments in Howe's writing and also a foreshadowing of *World of Our Fathers* (which Howe had already been working on for several years):[5]

> I recall my mother and father sharing their years in trouble and affection, meeting together the bitterness of sudden poverty during the Depression, both of them working for wretched wages in the stinking garment center, helping one another, in the shop, on the subways, at home, through dreadful years. And I believe, indeed know, that they weren't unique, there were thousands of other such families in the neighborhoods in which we lived. These people, less sophisticated than Miss Millett and her colleagues, were nevertheless animated by values of compassion, affection, and endurance. . . . They struggled . . . to make something of their lives, to make something *human* of their lives, together. And, like millions of other people in other cultures, other places, other moments, some of them succeeded.

It is an outrage to reduce them to mere categories of ideology. Was my mother a drudge in subordination to the "master group"? No more a drudge than my father who used to come home with hands and feet blistered from his job as presser. Was she a "sexual object"? I would never have thought to ask, but now, in the shadow of decades, I should like to think that at least sometimes she was. (CP, 231–32)

The Radical Assault (Once More) on Literature, 1971

During the thirties, the Stalinist exploitation of literature for narrow, partisan political ends repelled even the devoutly Marxist young Irving Howe. Then, in the late forties, when he was writing literary criticism himself, he came into conflict with radical critics of both the Stalinist and Trotskyist persuasions who believed that there was a Marxist "method" fully adequate to the analysis of literature, a distinctive radical aesthetic. *Politics and the Novel* grew partly out of this conflict, for in it Howe showed that whenever one made a foray into the so-called Marxist method, loyalty to the text required the critic, if he was honest, to move to insights distinctly outside of the Marxist field of vision. Dostoyevsky, Stendhal, Turgenev, and Conrad, Howe showed in his analyses, were moved by values apart from, and felt to be superior to, public life. "What could Marxism tell us about the values and emotions, the deepest inclinations of passion and vision in even these most political of novels? Not terribly much" ("Literary Criticism and Literary Radicals," 114). Marxism, for Howe, had proved to be inadequate in literary criticism before he fully discovered its inadequacy in politics.

But then, in the late sixties, Howe found himself forced to return yet again to the old questions, the old battles. For the same New Leftists who revived the Stalinist theory of "Social Fascism" as "liberal fascism" also revived the Stalinist conception of literature as an instrument of revolution. Here is the way Howe put it in his 1969 essay on "The New York Intellectuals":

We are confronting, then, a new phase in our culture, which in motive and spring represents a wish to shake off the bleeding heritage of modernism and reinstate one of those periods of the collective naif which seem endemic to American experience. The new sensibility is impatient with ideas. It is impatient with literary structures of complexity and coherence. . . . It wants instead works of literature—though literature may be the wrong word—that will be as absolute as the sun, as unarguable as orgasm, and as delicious as a lollipop. It schemes to throw off the weight of nuance and ambiguity, legacies of high consciousness and tired blood. It is weary of the habit of reflection, the making of distinctions, the squareness of dialectic, the tarnished gold of inherited wisdom. It cares nothing for the haunted memories of old Jews. It has no taste for the ethical nail-biting of those writers of the left who suffered defeat and could never again accept the narcotic of certainty. . . . It breathes contempt for rationality, impatience with mind, and a hostility to the artifices and decorums of high culture. It despises liberal values, liberal cautions, liberal virtues. It is bored with the past: for the past is a fink. (SW, 273)

By the seventies, Howe was convinced that American society was experiencing "a fallout, delayed but powerful, of totalitarian and authoritarian ideologies, debris from the thirties" ("Literary Criticism and Literary Radicals," 117). But now the lethal combination of Stalinism and native know-nothingism was finding a cozy reception within the universities, most especially the English departments. Indeed, the Modern Language Association of America (to its everlasting disgrace) had just installed as president one Louis Kampf, an acknowledged spokesman for "leftist" English professors. He came to provide teachers and critics who never cared much for literature in the first place a rationale for their hostility to literary studies: they were both a result and an instrument of class oppression.

It was the growing influence of such academics that led Howe to declare in 1971, in a debate between himself and Kampf at the Philadelphia meeting of the Northeast Modern Language Association, that "we are in the midst of a struggle more deep-going than any that has occurred since the period of Stalinism: a *kultur kampf* [no doubt Howe intended the pun] that racks intellectual life and the academic profession. This struggle . . . calls into question the value of literature itself, particularly when there is no utilitarian rationale for reading or studying it" ("Literary Criticism," 116).

Before directly commenting on Kampf's fantasies of revolution via the English department, Howe defines his own position in partly historical terms. He notes that Americans are engaged in the first effort in history to provide higher education to the great mass of the people. This is an effort that must be applauded by every democrat. But the commitment to democracy must be complemented by "the preservation of the cultural heritage and the idea of a serious university" ("Literary Criticism," 117). Once again, Howe writes in the spirit of the Matthew Arnold of *Culture and Anarchy*, who also had the democratic insight that a value exists to the extent that it is shared, but complemented it by the conservative recognition that what is shared must be real thought, real literature, real culture, not something watered down for "the masses."[6]

Howe's analysis of Kampf's ponderous and self-flattering imbecilities is nothing short of a devastation, but one done with humorous mockery and lethal irony. To show his contempt for conventional modes of education, Kampf reported how while teaching a seminar on Proust, his "head was getting scrambled." Boredom reigned in the class until salvation came via a student takeover of a campus building, to which liberated territory Kampf transferred his seminar. At this point, Kampf claimed, "The reading of Proust became . . . intimately tied to the goings-on in . . . the hall. . . . Proust's sensibility became politicized for us. . . . " This happened because a group of individuals had been coalesced into a body by a common struggle. About this touching saga Howe says several things: first, that a professor of literature who finds that teaching Proust scrambles his brains should consider vocational retraining; second, that Kampf's failure to describe the "politicizing" of Proust's sensibility should be considered an act of mercy; third, "the notion that a literary response can be passionate only if socketed into political action is a betrayal of literature and a small service to politics"; fourth, that it is rather extravagant to hope that for every boring seminar we can arrange the takeover of a building "as a strategy of pedagogical stimulation" ("Literary Criticism," 118).

Kampf also complained that he, like his brother radicals, became estranged from English literary tradition when he "discovered" that "many great writers of the past did not think as we should like them to, and therefore might not like him." Indeed, Kampf is certain that neither Swift nor Pope would have received him in their home. What Howe (deliciously) labels "this domiciliar theory of relevance" not only reveals the radicals' lack of any historical sense; it also offers intriguing possibilities for a new approach to the literary past: "One could consider the great writers whom one would refuse to allow into one's own home; or consider those to whom one would refuse to lend money; or consider the women writers of the nineteenth century whom one might find unsatisfactory for matrimony . . . " ("Literary Criticism," 118).

When Kampf moves slightly away from his personal problems with the great writers of the past, he enumerates his special problem with the genre of tragedy, which he finds "counterrevolutionary" in its acceptance of fate. But why single out tragedy? asks Howe. What about comedy that often leads men to reconcile themselves to their society? And how about tragicomedy, guilty of a double reconciling? Howe's point, of course, is that ultimately all literature is the enemy of "persons of Professor Kampf's political outlook," that is to say, those confident that they have a stranglehold on history, a confidence that has usually led to dictatorship and terror.

Kampf, the self-proclaimed radical, is wary of giving the "oppressed classes" access to "the cultural treasures of the West," partly because this could be "a weapon in the hands of those who rule" ("Literary Criticism," 119) and partly because the oppressed already have—multiculturalism looms on the horizon—"a culture of their own" ("Literary Criticism," 119).[7] Thus does Kampf celebrate cultural backwardness and deprivation in the name of political advance. But, says Howe, those progressives who have grasped the humane values and refining powers of literature will be the most zealous to share them. He concludes with a wonderfully apt story:

> Perhaps, in a less solemn way, I can sum up the matter with an anecdote in which I will ask my readers . . . to see the idea of culture in the guise of a cigar. In the early twenties the leader of the I. W. W., Big Bill Haywood, was going abroad and, as he left, granted an interview to the reporters. They noticed that he was smoking a twenty-five-cent cigar, very expensive for those days, and twitted him on this indulgence. 'Boys,' he answered, 'nothing is too good for the proletariat.' ("Literary Criticism," 120)

This, surely, ought to have ended the debate on radicalism and literary study. Indeed, two years later, Howe, in a discussion of the problems of teaching English, seemed to say that he had overstated the danger posed by Kampf and his English department insurgents. In "Living with Kampf and Schlaff," the latter Howe's caricature of the sleep-inducing traditionalism of the pre–New Criticism English departments, he still insisted that if forced to choose between the anti-intellectuals of struggle and the genteel exclusivists of "schlaf," he would opt for the latter. But for the moment it seemed that all the revolutionists had done was "to arrange for some disgraceful freshman anthologies and provoke among many of their colleagues a relapse into old-style academicism" ("Kampf and Schlaff," 107). But Howe relaxed his vigilance prematurely, for the threat from the literary radicals would return, in yet uglier form, a decade later.

Irving Howe and Philip Roth: Milton Appel and Nathan Zuckerman, 1972(–1983)

In the *New Republic* for 15 June 1959 Irving Howe published a most laudatory review of the first collection of stories by a young writer named Philip Roth. According to Howe, *Goodbye, Columbus* shows that young Roth has already achieved "what many writers spend a lifetime searching for—a unique voice, a secure rhythm, a distinctive subject" (C&A, 35). There are, Howe insists, no grounds for objection to Roth on either literary or nonliterary grounds, for he has absorbed the lessons of modern craftsmanship and has depicted American middle-class Jews with unerring truthfulness. Indeed, he works the theme of the moral and psychic consequences of the transformation of Jewish life from proletarian immigrant poverty to middle-class suburban comfort more successfully than any other writer.

In fact, writes Howe, it is precisely Roth's accuracy of depiction that may keep him from the higher ranges of literary achievement. So far is he from caricaturing the Patimkin family of the title story of the collection, so close does he stay to "surface realities" that there is not enough "imaginative transformation" of his raw material. As a result, the reader's interest flags about two-thirds of the way through *Goodbye, Columbus*. Indeed, this drop of interest is a threat to the effect of all Roth's stories because they use their subjects as targets and "drive openly to moral conclusions, hammered out with aggressive intent." The reason for this, Howe surmises, is that Roth cannot find within the Jewish tradition the forces needed to resist the spiritual corrosion of it in Jewish middle-class life. Howe is not censorious but analytical in dispassionately observing that Roth "is one of the first American Jewish writers who finds . . . almost no sustenance in the Jewish tradition" (C&A, 37). Unlike Delmore Schwartz or Bernard Malamud, Roth has few genuinely Jewish memories, whether from family life or Jewish tradition. As an instance, Howe notes Roth's failure either to remember or think it important that the protagonist's Aunt Gladys, who still attends Workmen's Circle "affairs," may once upon a time have been a Yiddishist firebrand or a trade union activist.

Howe's observation about the absence of Jewish memory and Jewish values in Roth is, in this review of 1959, less a critique of the young writer than an anticipation of the crisis of faith in store for American Jewry. That so intelligent and perspicacious a young writer should fail even to remember the Yiddish tradition, much less find sustenance in it, means that that tradition is nearing its end. "If so, that is a saddening thought, since it is hard to see what new sources of value are likely to replace the Yiddishist tradition and the American Jewish *milieu* at its best, against which many of us rebelled but which, by shaping the nature of our rebellion, helped to give meaning to our lives" (C&A, 37–38). It was always an axiom of the mature Howe that one of the main virtues of traditional systems is that they endow gestures of rebellion against them with tremendous potency. Yet none of these reservations, Howe concludes, should detract from Roth's achievement. "Nor," he adds (ironically, in view of what he would later write about Roth) "should [they] give an inch of encouragement to those in the 'Jewish community' who have begun to mutter against his book as an instance of 'self-hatred'" (C&A, 38).

More than thirteen years later, by which time Roth had published several novels, including the notorious *Portnoy's Complaint* in 1969, and achieved considerable reputation, Howe published in *Commentary* (December 1972) a searing attack called "Philip Roth Reconsidered."[8] In it, he is still willing to allow that the stories in *Goodbye, Columbus* possess "the lucidities of definition" but now adds that these lucidities are "harsh and grimacing in their over-focus." Moreover, despite the fact that none of the fiction Roth has published since 1959 approaches the first book in literary interest, his reputation has steadily grown, and he now stands close to the center of American culture (not, Howe is quick to add, necessarily a good thing). He is given serious attention by numerous literary critics and also "those rabbis and Jewish communal leaders who can hardly wait to repay the animus he has lavished upon them" (CP, 136). By this peculiar formulation Howe seems to suggest that Jewish spokesmen secretly relish being dragged through the mud by Roth. Although he had, upon its publication, praised *Goodbye, Columbus* for its truthfulness, Howe now charges that those stories show little talent for the objective rendering of human experience and none for "affectionate renderings of regional, class, or ethnic behavior." Carrying to extreme form a criticism he had hinted at in 1959, Howe now depicts Roth as a Jacob who can leave no doubt that he will pin his opponent: he cannot bear uncertainties, mysteries, doubts, for he lacks the discipline of patience; neither can he subdue his "clattering voice." As in the earlier essay, Howe charges that Roth's stories get tiresome because he keeps nagging, prodding, and beating the reader over the head with "the poker of his intentions" (CP, 138–39). Beyond the "point" he wishes to make, there is little autonomous life.

Withdrawing his 1959 praise of Roth's accuracy, Howe now charges that even in depiction of details of milieu and manners, Roth's will takes over and distorts the social evidence he marshals. But the far more serious accusation is that Roth lies, and lies in an obscenely defamatory way, by omitting the historical context of his characters. What in the earlier essay was a lamentable ignorance of the Jewish past for which Roth could not be held culpable has now become deception, treachery, vulgarity. The history of the Patimkins in "Goodbye, Columbus" is invoked, according to Howe, only for the purpose of condemning them, not for making them understandable as human beings. "Their vulgarity is put on blazing display but little or nothing that might locate or complicate that vulgarity is shown; little of the weight of their past . . . nothing of that fearful self-consciousness which the events of the mid-20th century thrust upon the Patimkins of this world. Ripped out of the historical context that might help to define them, the Patimkins are vivid enough, but as lampoon or caricature . . . ," which is precisely what Howe in 1959 had said they were *not*. Although he does not explicitly call Roth's caricatures antisemitic, he may be said to do so by analogy. He gives as an example of Roth's unpleasantness in the ethnic direction his snooty reference to Mrs. Patimkin's membership in Hadassah, "employed as a cue for easy laughs," Howe charges, "in the way watermelons once were used for Southern blacks[9]—it is an instance of how a thrust against vulgarity can itself become vulgar . . . " (CP, 140). Howe repeats, but much more sharply than in 1959, his objection to Roth's allusion to Aunt Gladys' Workmen's Circle connection from the past. Then it was an instance of Roth's innocence or ignorance; now it exemplifies both his cruelty and his vanity, for she must serve his egoistic fable of suburban-Jewish vulgarity ganging up against the poor but honorable protagonist, Neil Klugman, whom Howe takes to be Roth's "vapid alter ego" (CP, 141).

Howe insists that the issue is not whether newly rich suburban Jews are vulgar nor whether they are proper targets of satire; everybody is. The point is that Roth's first volume of stories does not draw upon a fresh encounter with the postwar experience of suburban Jews "but upon literary hand-me-downs of American-Jewish fiction" (CP, 141). Far from being a scrupulous observer of the social fact, Roth lacks the fullness and precision that can come only with a sense of his characters' past. It is as if Howe, in the years intervening between his first and second Roth essays, had come to look upon American Jews with a greater sympathy for their spiritual deprivation and historical shock than he could muster in 1959. Perhaps he could forgive neither Roth nor himself for having lacked in 1959 the imaginative sympathy he had slowly acquired (and which would result in *World of Our Fathers*, which he was engrossed in). By 1972, there had been a notable increase of interest in Yiddish in American universities. (Early the following year, Howe said to me: "How long will this fad continue?—three years?")

Again, Howe proclaims his receptivity to satire, including satire of Jews. But Roth is not really working in the tradition of Jewish self-criticism and satire, a tradition extending in Yiddish from Mendele Mocher Sforim to I. B. Singer, and in English from Abraham Cahan to Malamud and Saul Bellow. These writers criticize Jewish philistinism and social pretension more sharply and precisely than Roth does. But he, unlike them, finds in Jewish tradition "no sustenance, no norms or values from which to launch his attacks on middle-class complacence." Neither does he find sustenance in other cultures or traditions. But satire, Howe intimates, requires a norm; where everything is ridiculous, there is finally no comedy—and no moral standard.

In concluding his reassessment of *Goodbye, Columbus*, Howe not only declares the stories unsatisfactory because they come out of "a thin personal culture"[10] from an author who, whether because of ignorance or willfulness, no longer gains nourishment from Jewish tradition. He actually declares Roth mentally disturbed: "Unfocused hostility often derives from unexamined depression ... which I take to be the ground-note of Roth's sensibility" (CP, 147).

Moving on to discussion of Roth's novels (*Letting Go* and *When She Was Good*), Howe asks why this novelist hates his characters so. His answer is conveyed through images so scatological as to suggest some profound disorder in Roth. He refers to "a swelling nausea before the ordinariness of human existence, its seepage of spirit and rotting of flesh. . . . It starts as a fastidious hesitation before the unseemliness of our minds and unsightliness of our bodies; it ends as a vibration of horror before the sewage of the quotidian" (CP, 149). In effect, Howe charges, Roth rages at the human condition itself.

Portnoy's Complaint (1969) brings Howe once again to the vexed question of whether Roth is, if not quite guilty of, then complicit in, antisemitism. He begins his discussion of this most notorious of Roth's novels (until *Sabbath's Theatre* of 1995) by expressing confidence that Portnoy's repudiation of Jewish guilt, Jewish history, and Jewish inhibition and repression "*speaks in some sense for Roth* [my emphasis]." The book is not, as "enraged critics" had charged, antisemitic, but full of nasty contempt for Jewish life. If Howe is right about Portnoy speaking partly for Roth, then the reader may legitimately infer that it is not only Portnoy but his author who says: "stick your suffering heritage up your suffering ass." As to the charge of antisemitism brought by some of Roth's critics, Howe equivocates: the novel is not antisemitic but does contain "plenty of contempt for Jewish life." But what to Howe is most impressive (and most foolish) about the book is its yearning to escape Jewish fate. Portnoy most of all wants to be left alone, "to be released from the claims of distinctiveness and the burdens of the past, so that ... he may create himself as a 'human being.'" In this respect, Portnoy-Roth is a Jewish version of Ralph Ellison, whom Howe had criticized for trying to liberate his fiction from the exigencies of the black struggle. "Who, born a Jew in the 20th century, has been so lofty in spirit never to have shared this fantasy? But who, born a Jew in the 20th century, has been so foolish in mind as to dally with it for more than a moment?" (CP, 152–54).

The novel's cultural influence, Howe maintains, has been considerable—and all for evil. It has encouraged younger Jews, wearied with talk of their "heritage," to let go both of it and themselves. More serious has been its impact among Gentiles. The Holocaust had, for two decades following the Second World War, given antisemitism a bad name, had indeed, in America, given rise to a wave of uncritical philo-Semitism. Those literary people who had chafed against this (Truman Capote and Gore Vidal come to mind) were liberated by *Portnoy's Complaint*, which put an end to philo-Semitism in American culture: "one no longer had to listen to all that talk about Jewish morality, Jewish endurance, Jewish wisdom, Jewish families. Here was Philip Roth himself . . . confirming what had always been suspected about those immigrant Jews but had recently not been tactful to say" (CP, 155).[11]

A few months later (March 1973) *Commentary* printed two letters responding to Howe's essay. One defended Roth and accused Howe of harboring a personal animus against the novelist, a charge Howe of course denied, while claiming (not very convincingly) that he had not criticized Roth's own character, but rather his "temperament as a writer." The other was by the Zionist writer and literary critic Marie Syrkin. She thought the essay "superb," but criticized Howe for letting Roth off too lightly on the charge of antisemitism. First, she says, the line between "contempt for Jewish life" and antisemitism is shaky; in any case, Roth remains open to the heavier charge. After all concessions to artistic probity are made, "there remains in *Portnoy* a distillate of something describable only as plain unadulterated anti-Semitism." The core of antisemitic slander, she says, is that the Jew "is the defiler and destroyer of the Gentile world." In his novel, Roth gives "a classic description of what the Nazis called *rassenschande* (racial defilement)" since Portnoy says he lusts after blond *shikses* so that he can conquer America. "The scene in which he gloats at the contrast between his swarthy body and that of the fair Nordic patrician maiden he possesses is straight out of the Goebbels-Streicher script." She also cites Portnoy's relish over exposing Charles Van Doren in the TV quiz scandal to fill out the picture of Roth invoking the "two crudest and most venerable stereotypes of anti-Semitic lore—the Jew as sexual defiler and malevolent destroyer. . . . " Syrkin also argues (actually with more textual evidence than Howe had adduced) that the voice of the most offensive passages "is that of Roth not of Portnoy." To this formidable indictment of Roth, Howe barely replies except to hint that it may be excessive, and that "there should be a way of distinguishing between an anti-Semite and someone who dislikes us or between an anti-Semitic book and someone whose book 'contains plenty of contempt for Jewish life.'"[12]

The main subject of this intense speculation contributed nothing at all to the debate in 1972–73. Instead, he seems to have brooded over it incessantly, one might even say morbidly, for at least a decade. In *The Ghost Writer* (1979) Nathan Zuckerman, a Jewish writer from Newark (as was Roth himself) is accused by a Jewish community leader, Judge Leopold Wapter, of producing antisemitic caricatures that would warm the heart of Streicher and Goebbels. Here one can see Roth "responding" to the outraged Jewish community. But it was not until 1983, with the publication of *The Anatomy Lesson*, that Roth finally retaliated against the far more sophisticated critique of Irving Howe, who by now had not only published the two essays on Roth but also republished them in anthologies of his work. In the second chapter of the novel we are told that "in *Inquiry*, the Jewish cultural monthly that fifteen years earlier had published Zuckerman's first stories ["Eli, the Fanatic" appeared in *Commentary* in April 1959] Milton Appel had unleashed an attack upon Zuckerman's career that made Macduff's assault upon Macbeth look almost lackadaisical. Zuckerman should have been so lucky as to come away with decapitation. A head wasn't enough for Appel; he tore you limb from limb."[13] Although Roth takes liberties (if one may use such an expression in discussing a work of fiction) with many details—such as moving "Appel"'s original review from the *New Republic* to the *New York Times* and changing *Goodbye, Columbus* to *Higher Education*—he stays close enough to the facts of Howe's career to make the identification of Milton Appel as Irving Howe indisputable.

Roth's account, as narrator, of Appel-Howe's two essays on him, though compressed and simplified, is reasonably accurate, as is his description of Howe's career. But he does introduce at least one key invention, based on an actuality, but going well beyond it. This is "one of Appel's own early *Partisan* essays, written when he was just back from World War II" (476). According to Zuckerman, this essay became cherished reading for him and his friends. And why? Because in it Howe had written unapologetically about "the gulf between the coarse-grained Jewish fathers whose values had developed in an embattled American immigrant milieu and their bookish, nervous American sons." Indeed, whenever young Zuckerman had a falling out with his father, he would take his copy of this (to him) wonderful essay out of a file folder marked "Appel, Milton, 1918–" and reread it to gain perspective on his dilemma. Appel's essay reminded him that he, Zuckerman, "wasn't alone. . . . He was a social type. . . . His fight with his father was a tragic necessity" (476–77). Thus does Roth come close to making Howe himself responsible for his own stress on alienation from the world of his fathers, the very thing which Howe had deplored in Roth's fiction. Zuckerman believes that, by careful analysis of Appel's early essays in *Partisan* and elsewhere about his rootlessness, he can actually demonstrate "how Appel harshly denounces Zuckerman because of a distressing conflict with Poppa insufficiently settled in himself" (498). This father, according to the narrator of *The Anatomy Lesson*, was an "ignorant immigrant junkman who, if he hadn't driven young Milton even crazier than Carnovsky [Portnoy], had clearly broken his heart" (492).

The autobiographical essay in question appeared, of course, not in *Partisan Review* but in the October 1946 issue of *Commentary*. Howe calls attention to it in his intellectual autobiography, *A Margin of Hope*. It is highly unlikely that Roth read this essay in 1946, when he was thirteen years old, and it was not among the essays that Howe chose to reprint in anthologies of his work, but Roth claims (according to his friend Asher Z. Milbauer) that he was aware of it before Howe's reference to it in *Margin of Hope* in 1982. In the book, Howe recalls having written "an impressionistic piece called 'The Alienated Young Jewish Intellectual,' [in fact, the title was "The Lost Young Intellectual"] indulging a fashionable taste for Jewish self-scrutiny through talk about 'alienation' and putting down some troubling memories" (MH, 114). He dismisses the ancient piece as "badly written but with lively patches," which is a far more accurate description of it than Zuckerman's rhapsodic paraphrases. Nevertheless, the embattled Roth seems to have decided that in this youthful essay of Howe lay the ammunition for his counterattack, especially because the single anecdote that Howe revived from the essay (which contained only two references to his personal experience) was the one in which he recounts the incident, about which "half a century later, I still feel shame," in which his father embarrassed him by Yiddishizing his name into "Oivee" (MH, 114). If Roth exploited Howe's acknowledgment of shame over his father's having loudly Yiddishized his already "unloved" first name a half century earlier, Howe ought to have been grateful that Roth (apparently) knew nothing of the fact that Irving Howe had not yet been invented at the time of the incident, which involved, as we know, one Irving Horenstein.

After biding his time for over a decade, Roth, emboldened by what he now knew of Howe's own life story, struck back as hard as he could in *The Anatomy Lesson*. Zuckerman, declaring that he has never set himself up as Elie Wiesel, is shocked, outraged, and hurt by "the polemical overkill, the exhaustive reprimand that just asked for a fight" (476). Roth, to be sure, has protested that "I wouldn't write a book to win a fight. I'd rather go 15 rounds with Sonny Liston. . . . Milton Appel is not in this book because I was once demolished in print by Irving Howe."[14] But there is no doubt that Zuckerman believes himself in a fight, and conducts himself accordingly. At first, as we have observed earlier, he interprets Appel-Howe's career with sympathy for the critic's desire to discover the full range of Yiddish and admiration for his mockery of both the Jewish assimilationists and the Christian guardians of the English departments. Who can doubt that Roth, like Zuckerman, identified with the iconoclastic intention of the Yiddish anthologies? "To Appel's restless, half-formed young admirer, there was the dynamic feel of a rebellious act in the resurrection of those Yiddish writers, a rebellion all the more savory for undercutting the anthologist's own early rebellion" (481).

But soon the desire to retaliate an injury proves irresistible. It infuriates Zuckerman that "when literary Manhattan spoke of Appel, it seemed to Zuckerman that the name Milton was intoned with unusual warmth and respect. He couldn't turn up anyone who had it in for the bastard. He fished and found nothing. In Manhattan. Incredible" (482). St. Irving, in short! Despite the manifest injustice of Appel's assault on his work, *Inquiry* (that is, *Commentary*) received only one letter in his defense, and this from a young woman he'd slept with one summer at Bread Loaf. It rankles Zuckerman that the people who will derive most satisfaction from Appel's critical attack are the very same Jewish xenophobes, philistines, and chauvinists for whom Appel has less tolerance than Zuckerman himself. In fact, says Roth (as narrator), Appel still wrote "short scalding pieces . . . in the back pages of the intellectual journals" excoriating Jewish taste in entertainment, Jewish attraction to "cheap middlebrow crap." Trying to turn the tables on his attacker, Zuckerman thinks how *he* had actually been raised among these Jewish philistines, known them all his life as relatives and friends, while Appel "was arguing in his editorial office with Philip Rahv and acting the gent to John Crowe Ransom" (483–84).

The most specifically identified example of Howe's out-Rothing Roth is his evisceration of *Fiddler on the Roof*, which appeared as "Tevye on Broadway" in *Commentary* in November 1964. Roth says that "Appel's disgust for the happy millions who worship at the shrine of the delicatessen and cherish *Fiddler on the Roof* was far beyond anything in Zuckerman's nastiest pages" (484). By Appel's standards, he himself is more "antisemitic" than Zuckerman. The crux of the matter, then, is that Appel-Howe stands accused of charging Roth-Zuckerman with his own crime and castigating himself in Zuckerman. But if we take the trouble to look at Howe's review of *Fiddler*, we may well be skeptical of the critical acumen of Philip Roth, or at least of Nathan Zuckerman.

Howe does indeed attack the production, calling it a reflection of "the spiritual anemia of Broadway and of the middle-class Jewish world which by now seems firmly linked to Broadway." But the critique of middle-class American Jewry is made, as it never is in Roth, from the perspective of a defender of Sholom Aleichem, of Yiddish culture, of the

Jewish past, even of the Jewish God. "In Sholom Aleichem's stories," writes Howe, "God is a presence to whom Jews can turn in moments of need and urgency; in *Fiddler on the Roof* He ends up as Zero Mostel's straight man." Howe might even justifiably claim that his critique of American Jews for indulging themselves in unearned nostalgia is tempered, as Roth's satires are not, by an awareness of the deprivation and decline which conduced to beggarlike gratitude for such dismaying popularizations as *Fiddler*: "If a future historian of the Yiddish epoch in American Jewish life [precisely what Howe would become twelve years later] will want to know how it came to an end, we now can tell him. Yiddish culture did not decline from neglect, nor from hostility, nor from ignorance. If it should die, it will have been from love—from love and tampering."[15] Of course, the sour Zuckerman would retort that Appel's sympathy for the ghetto world of the traditional fathers after they are gone is itself feigned, that in truth people like Appel fled the ghetto as soon as they could, in order "to write about great Jews like Ralph Waldo Emerson and William Dean Howells" (504).

Roth moves the actual date of Howe's attack on his work (December 1972) ahead six months to May 1973 so as to get closer to the Yom Kippur War which the Arabs launched later that year, and which provides yet another occasion for offense by Appel against Zuckerman. Appel is depicted as so desperate in his search for allies for a beleaguered Israel that he turns to Zuckerman, "to the worst of Jewish writers for an article in support of the Jewish state" (485) that would appear on the *New York Times* op-ed page. Zuckerman is especially infuriated by Appel's asking whether Zuckerman still feels that, "as his Carnovsky [i.e., Portnoy] says, the Jews can stick their historical suffering up their ass?" Scurrying back to the text of his novel, Zuckerman is outraged that "Appel had attributed to the author the rebellious outcry of a claustrophobic fourteen-year-old boy. This was a licensed literary critic? No, no—an overwrought polemicist for endangered Jewry" (491–92).

In a series of imagined and real replies to Appel, Zuckerman wonders just what has moved him to enlist Zuckerman's aid. Is it that "you've changed your mind about me and the Jews since you distinguished for Elsa Stromberg [Syrkin] between anti-Semites like Goebbels (to whose writing she compared my own in the letters column of *Inquiry*) and those like Zuckerman who just don't like us . . . a most gracious concession"? (551) Or does Appel perhaps suspect that, deep down, Zuckerman doesn't really dislike Jews for being Jews, and is actually troubled by their troubles?

The notion of Irving Howe beseeching Philip Roth to write a *New*

York Times op-ed column on behalf of Israel back in 1973 has a quaintly anachronistic ring in a novel of 1983. By that time, the Likud government had already been in power since 1977, and left-leaning Jews like Howe were busy enlisting others (even including "Elsa Stromberg") on behalf of strident statements *against* Israel. Peace Now manifestoes emblazoned on the front page of the *Times* excoriated not the Arab states or the PLO but Israel itself as the obstacle to peace in the Middle East. The herd of independent thinkers who signed these manifestoes sometimes included Roth himself. Also anachronistic is the impression given by Zuckerman's reference to *Inquiry* as a magazine run "by the kind of people [Appel] used to attack before he began attacking people like me" (503). By 1983, of course, Howe had already returned to attacking *Commentary* (for which he wrote his last article in January 1980), for having turned conservative.

Whatever plausibility and insight that may reside in Zuckerman's attempt to interpret Appel's "bloodthirsty" (572) attack on him in light of his youthful essay about "being insufficiently Jewish for Poppa and the Jews" (573) soon fade as Roth succumbs to his sexual obsessions. Zuckerman, on a flight to Chicago (to attend medical school and join a profession more highly valued by Jews than writing) tells a fellow passenger that *he* is Milton Appel, the publisher of a pornographic magazine called *Lickety Split*. Closely involved with him in the sex business is one "Mortimer Horowitz . . . *Inquiry*'s editor in chief" (590) and (why omit anything salacious?) Mrs. Appel's lover.

In an interview given the year after *The Anatomy Lesson* appeared, Roth agreed with the interviewer's suggestion that Appel-Howe comes out of the argument in the novel better than Zuckerman-Roth: "Of course you give the other guy the best lines. Otherwise it's a mug's game." Although many readers will be skeptical of the claim that Howe's fictional representative gets "the best lines," this statement of Roth's would seem to acknowledge that he and Zuckerman are, after all, the same person. "Tilting at yourself," he adds, "is *interesting*, a lot more interesting than winning" (*Reading Myself*, 131). This recalls the moment in the novel where Zuckerman nearly succumbs to his critical adversary, recognizing his insight and his shrewdness: "What if my writing's as bad as he says? I hate his guts, and obviously the sixties have driven him batty, but that doesn't make him a fool, you know. . . . Suppose what he implies is true and I've poisoned their sense of the Jewish reality with my vulgar imagination. . . . What if twenty years of writing has just been so much helplessness before a compulsion . . . " (507–508). If Howe did not emerge victorious from this debate, he at least provoked his opponent to literarily fruitful self-examination; and the novel's representation, however skewed, of Howe's place in modern Jewish imagination remains of great value.

The Death of Lionel Trilling

The death of Lionel Trilling in 1976 afforded Howe one more opportunity to come to terms with the Columbia critic who had helped and stimulated, but also irritated and infuriated, his younger, uneasy admirer. His elegy appeared in the *New Republic* on 13 March 1976. It begins by paying tribute to Trilling as second only to Edmund Wilson in his influence upon that shadowy area between literature and morality called cultural values. Trilling's primary purpose, writes Howe, has been "to transform the dominant liberalism of the American cultivated classes into something richer, more quizzical and troubled than it had become during the years after World War II." Back in the fifties, as we have seen, Howe had been Trilling's intellectual adversary because he was convinced that Trilling's work was becoming a veiled justification for the increasingly conservative mood among American intellectuals. Now, in 1976, he confesses that the matter is more complicated than he had recognized, "and I still can't pretend to have sorted it out." If liberals really believed that all human problems can be solved through social action, then Trilling was right to criticize their narrow smugness. (That Howe himself had once believed this, as we have seen from some of his attacks on the intellectuals' "flight from politics" in the late forties, is not mentioned here.) But how many of them still do? And besides, why is it "not possible to bring together the dialectical reflectiveness and subtlety of response that Trilling's criticism encouraged with a readiness to do public combat for liberal or radical ends?" But life, Howe knows, is not logic, and principle is not practice. In America, he grants, it has always been hard to combine the two. Perhaps, indeed, it is in the nature of things that "there always has to be some disharmony between the life of the mind and the life of politics," and perhaps Trilling had provided not so much a justification for a new conservatism as "an inducement for a conservatized liberalism."[16]

Yet now, looking back upon Trilling's fully accomplished career, Howe can no longer believe that the major reason for his influence was his conservatism, real or alleged. Rather, it was what Howe calls a "radical" approach to culture. In an age that had surrendered itself to a host of determinisms and assumed that literature is essentially a "reflection" of a fixed, given external reality, "Trilling believed passionately—and taught a whole generation also to believe—in the power of literature, its power to transform, elevate and damage." In the most exact definition of Trilling's manner that anyone has ever given, Howe describes how the great critic, in his wonderful essays, "would circle a work with his fond, nervous wariness, as if in the presence of some force, some living energy . . . as if he were approaching an elemental power" (30).

In conclusion, Howe sums up the two kinds of influence which Trilling had. The hold he exercised upon his readers in general arose from their sense that he spoke for "the imperilled autonomy of our life." But the other kind of influence was that which he exerted upon colleagues, students, friends—in which last category Howe no doubt includes himself. His parting tribute to Trilling is one of the most beautifully generous moments in his work, an acknowledgment of the influence that a writer of grave elegance like Trilling might have upon his seeming opposite, a writer of polemical sharpness like Howe: "And here we come to the mystery of quietness, the power that a reflective calm may have in the passage of our life" (31).

World of Our Fathers: The Journey of the East European Jews to America and the Life They Found and Made, 1976

Who that had known the Irving Horenstein of City College or even the Irving Howe of *Labor Action* in the 1940s would have predicted, could have imagined, that his most successful book and also the book for which he would become best known among American readers in his own lifetime and afterward would be a massive history of the immigrant Jewish world of New York? Or that he would time its publication for the bicentennial celebration of American independence, as if to stress that the history of the two million East European Jews who came to the United States starting in the 1880s was a distinctly American story, a part of American history? Who among his old comrades at *Partisan Review* could have refrained from laughing at the notion that Irving Howe would produce a book that would become a standard bar-mitzvah present? (In fact, Milton Hindus claims that Philip Rahv told him, when he heard of the East Side project, that Howe was "wasting his time.")[17] Who among his literary colleagues that admired the perfection to which he had brought the essay form could have imagined that he would, in collaboration with a team of researchers, devote himself for years to poring over memoir literature in English and Yiddish, secondary scholarship dealing with the varied aspects of immigrant experience, the Yiddish press, accounts in American newspapers, journals, historical studies, personal interviews and works of fiction in order to produce a work of social and cultural history that could "[lay] claim ... to being an accurate record" (WF, xix)?

But who among Howe's friends and readers could have understood the tangle of feelings that bound him to his father and his father's world? For *World of Our Fathers*, though a masterwork of historical writing (more than of historical research in the strict sense), is also a tribute offered to his father, who had become seriously ill in 1976.[18] He had drawn closer to his father during David Horenstein's years of aging, and had belatedly come to recognize in him an embodiment of the received values and ingrained feelings of the immigrant Jewish world. "It was easy enough to see whatever was parochial in these values and feelings, but it took years to learn that they also formed the firmest moral norms I would ever encounter." At the same time that, in the early seventies, he was immersing himself in the American Yiddish poets, Howe recognized the unwavering solidarity of his father (with a son whose actions he often disapproved) as deriving from a deep sense in the immigrant milieu of what a Jew owed his son. "Reading Mani Leib's sonnets and Moishe Leib [Halpern]'s poems, I learned to value that solidarity. Reading those sonnets and poems I learned where I had come from and how I was likely to end" (MH, 269). Howe's description of his father's end, of his slow death, is the only fully recounted personal experience in his entire autobiography. Recognition of the depth of his father's loyalty was the necessary prelude to *World of Our Fathers*, in which Howe brilliantly combines a spirit of critical detachment with a sense of natural piety: "Even while still breathing [my father] had become for me a representative figure of the world from which I came, and I suppose a good part of *World of Our Fathers* is no more than an extension of what I knew about him" (MH, 339).

Although Howe is anything but sentimental in his account of the East European Jews, he is eager to show that the absence of ideological intent among the vast majority of those who left the old country does not mean they came to America for merely material motives. (Howe knows, though he does not mention, that the ideologically motivated Jews of eastern Europe were not the two million who left for America but the sixty thousand who left for Palestine.) The migration of about one-third of the East European Jews in the thirty-three years between the assassination of Czar Alexander II and the outbreak of World War I was comparable in modern Jewish history only to the exodus from Spain provoked by the Inquisition. Although he grants that some fled in the wake of pogroms out of fear for their lives, and others went in organized groups hoping to recreate Jewish life in new soil, and most went for personal reasons—to find more tolerable conditions of life—

Howe also insists that some more profound motive was at work: "... In its deepest significance, the migration of the East European Jews constituted a spontaneous and collective impulse, perhaps even decision, by a people that had come to recognize the need for new modes and possibilities of life" (WF, 26). Their departure, he argues and tries to demonstrate throughout "Toward America," the first of the book's four sections, was not just a sum of personal responses but also a collective enterprise, not just a reaction to material need but also a sign of moral yearning, "not merely . . . a consequence of despair but also . . . a token of morale" (WF, 34).

Howe's sketch of the world of the shtetl and its demise, then of the trials of departure from the old world and arrival in the new, comprises two relatively brief but scintillating chapters, and is mainly prelude to the lengthy and detailed ten chapters that comprise "The East Side," the book's second section. Here Howe shows how the Jews dealt with the three great changes brought about by migration. The first was physical uprooting from the familiar setting of small-town life in eastern Europe to "the wastes and possibilities of urban America" (WF, 115). The second was severance from and sometimes loss of the moral values and cultural supports of Jewish tradition. The last was a radical class shift, generally taking the form of sudden enforced proletarianization. Compared with other immigrant groups, the Jews had the advantage of having already experienced life as a minority group within the larger society; unlike most of the other groups, they came to the United States with two, or even more than two, cultures. Nevertheless the suffering that Jews had to bear in the new world—and Howe stresses that Jewish-quarter living conditions in late nineteenth-century New York were as bad as any in early nineteenty-century London—although it might by any "objective" standard be less onerous than what they endured in the old, was harder to bear: in the shtetl suffering was collective and therefore meaningful, whereas in America economic pressure weighed most heavily on the individual. "Jews trapped in a *shtetl* or a Polish city," Howe shrewdly observes, "could feel they were martyrs for a sacred cause, and thereby take a kind of comfort in their misery . . . " (WF, 77).

Howe presents the lower East Side as predominantly "a secular community" (WF, 95) and more than one review of the book complained of his inadequate attention to religious life (especially in comparison to the vast attention given to the politics of the labor movement).[19] Yet his view of the relation between "secularity" and religion is, as usual, more sensitive and complex than might at first appear. He describes how the anarchists and some of the social democrats made a point of holding balls and parades on the eve of Yom Kippur, the most sacred moment in the Jewish year; and then he observes that this was a display not merely of insensitivity but also of "the extent to which traditional faith dominated those who denied it" (WF, 106). Later, in a discussion of the family in the chapter called "The Way They Lived Then," he describes how, in a culture cracking apart, order and cohesion returned only on Friday nights, when the family came together to take the Sabbath meal: "Decorum reigned again, the pleasure of doing things as everyone knew they should be done. When a son failed to show up for Friday-night dinners, that was a signal of serious estrangement—not the least use of rules being that they lend clear meaning to violations" (WF, 171). That is to say, the culture of "secular Jewishness" which epitomized the East Side for thirty or forty years—and not longer—was dependent for its existence precisely on that which it denied.

"Were they believers, these masses of immigrants?" To this question, a far more immediate one to the mature Howe than his self-definition as a partial Jew might suggest, Howe gives an ambivalent answer. Although secularist ideologies flourished, few Jews among the immigrants could imagine a time when the *shul* would no longer be at the center of Jewish life. In a peculiarly Howeian formulation, we are told that "God could easily be neglected in New York, it was probably not His favorite city, yet He was not at all forgotten." Far more confident that the Jewish immigrants were not disbelievers than that they were believers, Howe settles finally for the attitude that arises from the writings of Sholom Aleichem, in which God is an indestructible presence in Jewish life, "someone to whom Jews must keep talking, and as for whether He 'exists' or not, that is a problem for philosophers" (WF, 190–91).

Although insistent that the immigrant Jewish culture was essentially secular, its vibrant institution the Yiddish theatre and not the synagogue, Howe nevertheless acknowledges that without religion American Jews would not be able to preserve a culture and inner world of their own. "Coming to America, the immigrants brought with them a historically complex and deep culture. It was by now a culture mostly in fragments, brilliant particles in disarray. It was a culture that no longer had the inner principle of order—the assumption that God had stamped a unique destiny upon the Jews—which had once kept it in severe control" (WF, 222). Once the Jews were freed from the discipline of religion, their culture was more energetic, but it lacked coherence.

It was, however, part of Howe's socialist faith that the most urgent force in Jewish tradition could survive in secular form. This force was the idea of messianism, a fervor of expectation that derived from a mixture of prophecy at its best and apocalypticism at its worst. The "false Messiahs" such as Sabbatai Zevi and Jacob Frank (to say nothing of the Christians' candidate for messiahship) had brought a good deal of misery to the Jews over the centuries. Nevertheless, Howe believed, it was this messianic fervor that informed both the socialism and the Zionism of the immigrant world. In these ideologies the figure of the Messiah was replaced by the messianic principle, the expectation of a collective upheaval.

Eager as he is to identify socialism as a secularized form of Jewishness, Howe does not blind himself to the problems involved. Some of these are, of course, matters of simple logic. If Jewishness consists of being a socialist, then one should be able to become a Jew by becoming a socialist; yet no one has ever succeeded in doing so. And if socialism was a natural outgrowth of Jewishness, why was it that the East Side was constantly the scene of conflict between socialist principles and Jewish sensibilities, a conflict so amply documented by Howe that it runs like a red thread through *World of Our Fathers.* Jewish interests rarely coincided with class divisions. The fact that the Jewish Socialist movement was unique on the East Side in "preaching . . . concern for issues transcending the ethnic group" did not endear it to Jews concerned about, for example, pogroms in Europe. Thus one Yiddish daily, the *Varheit,* asked where the Jewish Socialist leader Morris Hillquit had been during the 1903–1904 protests against the Kishinev pogrom. The answer was that the New York Socialist party, right after the pogrom, had warned its members not to be swept away by "Jewish nationalism" (WF, 314). The socialists also set themselves in opposition to Jewish interests by opposing further immigration from eastern Europe. Also in 1903, Jewish socialists of New England at a conference in Rhode Island rejected a proposal from a minority of delegates that the "Jewish question" be put on the agenda. Most of the delegates were convinced that the only solution to the Jewish question was socialism (WF, 288).

In reading *World of Our Fathers,* one senses in this narrative of the conflict between socialism and Jewishness just how immediate is the story of the book to the life of Howe himself. For the Howe who wrote for *Labor Action* in the early 1940s was not all that different from the Jewish radicals of the first decade of the century whom he mocks in his account of the internecine conflicts within Jewish labor and Jewish socialism. "Rebelling against the parochialism of traditional Jewish life, the Jewish radicals improvised a parochialism of their own—but with this difference: they called it 'universalism.'" The Jewish radicals strove to harden themselves against any sensitivity to the religious or cultural feelings that immigrant workers brought with them from Europe. "To recognize that Jewish socialists had to write and speak in Yiddish not merely because it was the only language the immigrants understood but also because there were urgent Jewish problems touching all Jews

. . . this led to insinuations of 'nationalism.' And before the charge of 'nationalism,' courageous men quailed, as their grandfathers might have quailed before charges of heresy" (WF, 291). In retrospect, writing in the seventies, Howe takes the side of the "Jewish" Jewish socialists against the "cosmopolitan" Jewish ones; but when World War II was raging, he had been among the cosmopolitans.

Yet despite his detailed enumeration of the mistakes and failures of Jewish socialism, despite his clear recognition that American society accepted the Jews but rejected their socialist programs and ideas, Howe maintains that the movement transformed the consciousness of the Jews. The same Irving Howe who, when writing about literature, was attracted again and again to the wisdom of anti-utopias or dystopias[20] praises the Jewish socialists for bringing "to unprecedented intensity the vision of a secular utopia" (WF, 323). He even praises Jewish socialism (and, in passing, Zionism) for creating a new Jewish type, who wanted to share the future of industrial society with the rest of the world.

Howe's story of the social and political movements of the East Side culminates, as does the second portion of the book, with a picture of American Jews in thrall to Franklin Delano Roosevelt at the very time that he was demonstrating his indifference to the terrible fate of European Jewry. One reason why most Jews—though not Howe—abandoned the socialist movement was that Roosevelt's proposals for social security, unemployment insurance, and pro-union legislation seemed to them at least a partial realization of their old socialist programs, even if the capitalist system as a whole remained intact. It apparently did not much matter to them that, as Howe says at the beginning of the book's lengthiest (and most uncomfortable) footnote, "with regard to the Jewish refugees in Europe, the record of the Roosevelt administration was shameful" (WF, 392n). Without perhaps fully recognizing the enormity of his admission, Howe acknowledges that the Jewish organizations concerned with rescue lacked political leverage with the Roosevelt administration because the American Jewish vote had so long and so automatically belonged to Roosevelt that they could not plausibly threaten to withdraw it from him unless he took decisive measures to save the refugees. In any case, Howe remarks, the Jewish organizations not only made few efforts to challenge Roosevelt publicly on the matter of rescue; they also did not allow the revelation, in later decades, of just how dreadful his policy on rescue had been to affect their high estimate of him. What he does not remark is that this unforgivable political obtuseness derived from their continuing adoration of "socialism," even in adulterated form.

The third part of *World of Our Fathers* deals with "The Culture of

Yiddish" and is the one part that could be lifted from the rest and published as a complete book in its own right. It touches on matters even more personal to Howe than the story of Jewish labor movements and Jewish socialism. For it was his connection to the small remaining group of Yiddish poets in New York that, along with his filial piety, led him to undertake *World of Our Fathers* in the first place. The Yiddish writers whom he came to know were all elderly, all valiantly devoting their lives to a literature approaching its historical end. They were for him heroic figures, refusing to acknowledge the bleakness of their future, the bleakness of the future of Yiddish. Despite their hopelessness, "they still felt an obligation to confront the world with a complete firmness of posture. *One of the arts of life is to know how to end.*" That is to say, it is nobler to end by resisting the inevitable than by succumbing to it. That helps to explain why Howe attached himself to these writers—Eliezer Greenberg, Jacob Glatstein, Singer, Chaim Grade, and others—as their friend, commentator, champion. "I found strength in joining their moment of weakness. I loved them, I loved their words" (MH, 264, 267).

Reading the Yiddish poets, the dead as well as the living, helped Howe to feel at ease, finally, with his own past, if not with himself. The reading opened memories and revived feelings long dormant. "The experiences of the immigrant world had long been left behind, and there was not the faintest chance of going back to them. My problem . . . was to 'come to terms' with those experiences . . . to rid myself of the double weights of nostalgia and shame, aggressiveness and denial" (MH, 267). *World of Our Fathers* as a whole was that coming to terms, and "The Culture of Yiddish" is, among other things, an excavation of Howe's buried life and of the foundations of his secular Jewishness.

American Yiddish literature, Howe argues, is unique in the modern period because it is a literature arising from an uprooted people and a broken culture, provincial in accent yet universalist in its claims. "The Culture of Yiddish" is divided into four chapters: "The Yiddish Word," "The Yiddish Theatre," "The Scholar-Intellectuals," and "The Yiddish Press." The most important of these, the first, is largely a repetition of the capsule history of American Yiddish poetry, which we discussed in the previous chapter; but it is significantly enriched and amplified by personal portraits (these are among the chief glories of *World of Our Fathers*) of key figures, such as the poet Glatstein and the fiction writer Singer. Both, it is worth recalling, espoused political positions sharply at variance with Howe's. Glatstein was an ardent Zionist and a defender of Jewish interests in a way that Howe never could be; and Singer was fiercely opposed to socialism, especially socialism in the guise of messianism. Nevertheless, both were moral and cultural exemplars for Howe, Glatstein in the way described earlier, and Singer in a different, perhaps more immediate way that reveals the governing intention of *World of Our Fathers*. Howe had first discovered Singer when Lazer Greenberg read "Gimpel the Fool" aloud to him in Yiddish: "It was a transforming moment. How often does a critic encounter a major new writer?" (MH, 262).[21]

After discussing Singer's ambivalent relation to modernism and his wish to be a writer in the Jewish rather than the Yiddish tradition (which he thought tainted by sentimentality and longings for social justice), Howe celebrates the recklessness of Singer's surrender to the claims of imagination. Singer, in his best stories and novels, "wrote about a world destroyed beyond hope of reconstruction," yet he wrote about Frampol, Bilgoray, Kreshev, "as if they were still there, as if the world of the past were still radiantly alive: the Hasidim still dancing, the rabbis still pondering, the children still studying, the poor still starving, and nothing yet in ashes." Singer thus becomes, as Robert Alter has pointed out,[22] a kind of model for Howe's own imaginative resurrection of a dead world in this book. When Howe says about Yiddish literature in general that it bore witness to the tragic fact that "the central premise of Jewish survival is a defiance of history" (WF, 458–59), he is speaking of the way in which *World of Our Fathers* itself bears witness against the crumbling of history.

The last section of *World of Our Fathers*, called "Dispersion," is, like the opening one, brief—composed of two chapters on the later generations of American Jewry and the future (if any) of American Jewish life. Noting that "cultures are slow to die," Howe asks to what extent the culture of East European Jewish immigrants was still active in second- and third-generation Jews. He claims that although "a great many" suburban Jews no longer spoke Yiddish and a growing number did not understand it or even know what it was that, as Jews, they did not know, nevertheless their deepest inclinations of conduct showed signs of immigrant shaping. The kinds of vocation toward which they urged their children, their sense of appropriate family conduct, their idea of respectability and its opposite, all, according to Howe, "showed the strains of immigrant Yiddish culture, usually blurred, sometimes buried, but still at work" (WF, 618). Jewish socialism as such nearly vanished, but took on a second, less vigorous life in the standard liberalism of suburban Jews. But the uglier impulses of Jewish radicalism, going back to the 1880s, also (as he had noted in 1970) survived in the children of the Jewish suburbanites who filled the ranks of the New Left in the sixties (and whom we met in the previous chapter): "A few of these young people . . . became enemies of Israel . . . ; they collected funds for Al Fatah, the Palestinian terrorist movement." This too, Howe candidly acknowledges, had its precedent in the immigrant world. "Was there not a line of continuity . . . between the Jewish anarchists of the 1880's who had ostentatiously held Yom Kippur balls and the Jewish New Leftists of the 1960's who aligned themselves with the Arabs? Was there not a long-standing tradition of violent dissociation, postures of self-hatred and contempt for one's fathers?" (WF, 619).

On the whole, however, Howe is inclined to be charitable toward the attempts, often pathetic, of suburban Jews to hang onto some tatters of their past. People who contemptuously dismissed "bagel and lox" Jewishness did not grasp that such things as residual attachments to certain foods, a few half-remembered customs, a garbled Yiddish phrase, might signify "not merely self-serving nostalgia but also blocked yearnings for elements of the past that seemed spiritually vital" (WF, 620). Understanding of the forces that had made the Jewish suburbs what they were might lead to some (highly desirable, in Howe's view) tolerance and affection.

Writing in 1976, Howe saw American Jewry trying to perpetuate itself in two ways now that its religious faith had been hollowed out, and the culture of the immigrant parents had dwindled into a memory: liberalism and solidarity with Israel. Surprisingly, in view of the rela-tively "late" date, he does not consider what has come to be called "Holocaust Judaism" as a third option, and writes as if the Holocaust were still a subject little spoken of by ordinary Jews.

The commitment of American Jews to liberalism was partly a residue (as in Howe himself)[23] of the once-powerful tradition of secular Jewish socialism, and partly a result of the assumption that Jewish interests and survival were best protected in an open and secular society. Howe gives no credence, it is important to note, to the claim of Jewish New Leftists of the sixties that their politics is grounded in the "prophetic tradition." He remarks, correctly, that with enough wrenching one can find ancestors in the Jewish past for virtually any political position. "If one wanted a 'Jewish justification' for liberalism or radicalism, the honest course was to provide it in terms of the present situation rather than trying to enlist prophets no longer in a position to speak for themselves" (WF, 623n).

Although lamenting that American Jewish liberalism has, in the decades following the Second World War, become more "moderate" and more conservative, Howe nevertheless insists that there are factors in Jewish life that encourage the persistence of liberalism, the main one being that it has become a kind of substitute religion among nonreli-gious Jews, especially those involved in Jewish organizational life. If their liberalism and "social idealism" were taken away from these Jews, they would suffer a severe crisis of identity. Howe thus finds himself in the peculiar position of saying, on the one hand, that there is no mandate in Jewish religion for liberalism[24]—and, on the other, that without liberalism many Jews would cease to think of themselves as Jews. In other words, Howe understands that whatever these liberal Jews may believe in, it is not Judaism; but they must go on believing it lest they face up to the truth.

He takes a very different tack with Zionism. "For non-religious Jews," Howe says, "Israel became the chief alternative to assimilation." That is to say, it is even more crucial to the chances of Jewish collective survival in a nonreligious form than liberalism. But whereas Howe's discussion of "Jewish" liberalism becomes a plea for its perpetuation, he says of Zionism that it enabled American Jews "to postpone that inner reconsideration of 'Jewishness' which the American condition required." Establishing oneself as a Jew by "working for Israel," Howe observes, and quite correctly, enabled Jews to put aside irksome spiritual and metaphysical problems that life now imposed on the nonreligious. "This was neither an unworthy nor a dishonorable evasion—first comes survival and then definition. But it left a growing mound of intellectual debts which sooner or later would have to be paid" (WF, 628–30).

Howe might have been harsher in his judgments of *all* the varieties of secular Jewishness by pointing out that none of them seemed capable of producing more Jews. The Jewishness based on liberalism, the Jewishness based on the Israeli Jewish experience of a constant burden of struggle against implacable enemies, the Jewishness based on the European Jewish experience of the Holocaust, have all been tried, and found wanting—if the epidemic proportion of intermarriage between Jews and unconverted Gentiles and the suicidally low birth rate of Jews may be taken as valid indications of a people's loss of the will to live. Howe, whose second wife was a Gentile, with whom he produced two non-Jewish children, did not look at things in this way. But in concluding, as he does in his epilogue to *World of Our Fathers,* that very little of what had held the immigrant Jews together—customs, tradition, language—was able to survive much beyond a century, he was writing an elegy not only for a vanished culture but for American Jewry. A few months after the appearance of the book, Howe wrote to me that the death of Greenberg had cut his last significant contact with the old Jewish world, that his own Jewish world had come to an end, and that he didn't much like whatever else was in sight.[25]

Howe ends his book with an impressive example of that union of natural piety with critical detachment to which he has aspired. On the one hand, he sings the praises of the immigrant Jewish milieu. Its strengths included "a rich and complicated ethic that remains embodied in the code of *menshlichkeit,* a readiness to live for ideals beyond the

clamor of self, a sense of plebeian fraternity, an ability to forge a community of moral order even while remaining subject to a society of social
disorder, and a persuasion that human existence is a deeply serious
matter for which all of us are finally accountable. . . . We cannot be our
fathers, we cannot live like our mothers, but we may look to their experience for images of rectitude and purities of devotion." But he also
grants that the worst as well as the best in Jewish life derived from the
messianic impulse of secular Jewishness. "The intense moral seriousness of Jewish life was shadowed by a streak of madness, the purity of
messianic yearning by an apocalyptic frenzy" (MH, 646). This dramatic
struggle between the good and bad angels of Jewish religious myth is
more the stuff of literature than of history as currently understood, just
as the beauty of deliquescence which Howe achieves by the end of his
book is the beauty of the storyteller, not the chronicler. "A story is the
essential unit of our life, offering the magical imperatives of 'so it began'
and 'so it came to an end.' A story encompasses us, justifies our stay,
prepares our leaving" (MH, 645–46). Not long after finishing the story
of the immigrant Jews, Howe began, at age fifty-seven, to write his own
story, an autobiography which would deal not with private life and
loves so much as with public events, public involvements, public affairs.

   World of Our Fathers was the only one of Howe's scores of books that
became a popular success. For many months it was at the top of the best-
seller list. He was immensely pleased, yet tried to conceal his satisfaction with a litany of complaints. He would say that he was not used to
the tremendous pressures that such success brought, and even told
Ruth Wisse in 1976 that he was being driven crazy by all the publicity
and the lecture invitations, becoming the itinerant *magid* (preacher) of
the Jewish community in America.[26] He especially disliked being
thought of as head of the Jewish branch of the burgeoning ethnicity
industry. In the year following the book's publication, he insisted he
had written it "in innocence of the uses to which it may be put."
Traveling around the country promoting the book, he would meet
middle-class Jewish ladies intent on discovering their ethnic roots in
family genealogies and tell them, "not very graciously, that if they were
serious they would first try to learn their people's history and then they
might see that it hardly mattered whether they came from the Goldbergs
of eastern Poland or the Goldbergs of the western Ukraine." When he
attended a pageant in an eastern city purporting to recreate the Lower
East Side—pushcarts, onion rolls, etc.—and was asked whether anything was missing, he answered, "again not very graciously, that a
touch of reality might have been added by a tubercular garment worker
spitting blood from his years of exhaustion in a sweat shop."[27]

   Howe had grave doubts about the new turn toward ethnicity, a term which he said was widely used precisely because nobody knew what it meant. He saw ethnic groups, including the Jews, searching for fragments of national identity that stirred them to the extent that, or perhaps because, it was no longer available. He suspected that ethnic groups were preserving not a rich old-world culture, but only "some scraps and debris of that culture which were brought across the ocean." Both his socialist dogma and his version of secular Jewishness kept Howe at arm's length from the ethnic revivalists. The first taught that the central problems of American society had to do not with ethnic groupings but with economic policy and class conflicts. The second was, once more, the code of *menshlichkeit,* which in Howe's view offered a higher moral vision than Jewish or black or any other ethnicity:

> But there is also another moral possibility [than ethnicity], one that we call in Yiddish being or becoming a *mensch.* The word suggests a vision of humanity or humaneness; it serves as a norm, a possibility beckoning us. You don't have to be Jewish (or non-Jewish), you don't have to be white (or black) in order to be a *mensch.* Keeping one eye upon the fading past and the other on the unclear future, enlarging ethnic into ethic, you can become a man or woman of the world, even as you remember, perhaps because you remember, the tongue your grandfather and grandmother spoke in, though in fact the words themselves are fading from memory. (19)

After the spectacular success of *World of Our Fathers,* Howe was skittish about doing another book on a Jewish subject because, he believed, he had received more praise for the book than the world, parsimonious of good wishes, is usually ready to allot. When the University of Washington Press tried to persuade him to make a book called *Jewish Voices* out of a series of lectures he had given in Seattle, he expressed fear that the political enemies he'd made in the Jewish and non-Jewish worlds would make him a sitting duck for those wanting to knock him down from his perch.[28] He complained and complained, but no one ever doubted that he enjoyed his newly won prominence and prosperity. They helped him to bear the family problems that were again besetting him. Some were dreadful: in November 1977 both his father and stepmother were in hospital and destined to enter a nursing home; by December his father, who had sunk to a miserable condition, was dead, at age 85. His third marriage, to Arien, had foundered. His children Nicholas and Nina were at turning points in their lives. The former, a graduate student in medieval literature at Yale, was trying to get a teaching job, and his father, inundated with offers, felt intensely frustrated and heartsore at not being able to turn any of them over to his son, even apprehensive that some of his "enemies" in the academy would retaliate against his son.[29] His daughter Nina had just married and was going to live with her new husband in Edmonton, Alberta, a place which to the still provincial Howe was indistinguishable from Siberia.[30]

Ashes Out of Hope: Fiction by Soviet-Yiddish Writers, 1977

Following the distinctly American work about a Jewish culture that had flourished in the center of world capitalism, Howe turned back to a Jewish culture that had been destroyed in the capital of world socialism, the Soviet Union. Ever cognizant of the importance of anthologies in Jewish tradition, Howe published in 1977 an anthology of fiction by Soviet-Yiddish writers, many of whom had been murdered by the regime in which they placed their hopes, the socialist regime which had been, in the phrase endlessly repeated by Howe and his colleagues at *Dissent*, the name of their desire (apparently a variant of Tolstoy's saying that "religion is the name of our desire"). In the course of preparing the book, Howe had become deeply involved with the terrible experiences of these Russian Jews, and told Wisse that he would like to write a whole book about them, if only he knew enough. He especially wanted publication in 1977, which was twenty-five years after the slaughter.[31] He was nervous about this anthology because its material was not "folksy" like other Yiddish writing and was therefore, he thought, likely to be neglected by American Jews. Also, he knew that this would be the last Howe-Greenberg book, for Greenberg was already eighty and in failing health.[32]

Howe had already published a modest sample of Soviet Yiddish poetry in the earlier *Treasury of Yiddish Poetry*, and some prose fiction had appeared in the first anthology, *A Treasury of Yiddish Stories*. But now he sought, in the introduction coauthored with Greenberg, to tell the story of the Soviet Yiddish writers as one of betrayal of Jewish hopes by communism, the most tragic chapter in the history of modern Yiddish literature. Elsewhere in Europe, of course, scores of Yiddish writers were destroyed by the avowed enemies of the Jews; but in the USSR an entire generation of Yiddish writers was destroyed by the regime to which they had pledged themselves. It was also the very state to which the young Howe's ideological progenitors had pledged *them*selves, until their beloved Trotsky went into exile in 1929; thereafter they continued to ask, as Howe put it in 1971, "why it was that the October Revolution, once seen as the liberating event of modern history, had ended with one of the great tyrannies of modern history" ("Literary Criticism and Literary Radicals," 113).

Howe begins his story in 1912–13, when a new group of Yiddish writers arose in Kiev, a major center of East European Jewish culture. These writers—the best known among them being David Bergelson, Der Nister (the Hidden One, a pen name of Pinhas Kahanovich), Peretz Markish, and David Hofstein—had a "European" education and, unlike Sholom Aleichem and I. L. Peretz, thought of themselves, in the usual "modernist" style (and in a manner similar to the young Glatstein), not as moral spokesmen for the Jewish community but as individual writers for whom Yiddish was a natural medium. Some were sympathetic to the Bolshevik Revolution, though only a few of the younger ones regarded themselves as doctrinal Communists. These tended to turn their backs upon the shtetl and its culture. Their euphoria for the new regime was joined to unbridled contempt for their own community. One of them, Izzi Charik, contemptuously addressed the remnants of the *shtetl*: "Each day a Bolshevik appears / And each Bolshevik is our friend. / As for us, rising out of need and woe, / Emerging from the old and quiet streets, / We will trample and forget you, / Like rotted straw."

Howe defines two main tendencies in Soviet Yiddish literature, beginning in the early 1920s. The line of Kiev supported the Bolshevik Revolution but tried to maintain an autonomous Yiddish literature of diverse voices and techniques; but the "proletarian" writers, some of them members of the Bolshevik party, sought to create a militant, propagandistic literature, positive in tone and accessible to "simple" readers. The former group, including Bergelson and Der Nister, published, starting in 1922, a journal called *Shtrom*, which was internationalist in scope and content, containing contributions from Yiddish writers in Warsaw, Berlin, and New York, as well as Moscow and Kiev. But to recognize an international Yiddish literature with themes and norms not determined by the Russian revolution or the Communist party was to invite attack and trouble. The Kiev group was soon accused of failure to engage in political work and of "shutting themselves up in their own world and in their artistic problems." By 1924 the journal was finished, the last independent Yiddish journal in the USSR. "From the mid-1920s until after the Second World War, Yiddish literature was harassed with the same dull-witted fanaticism that the Stalinist state showed toward other literatures of minority peoples" (*Ashes*, 9–10).

By 1925, the proletarian Yiddish writers and critics had triumphed over the Kiev group. In their journals (*New Earth* and *October*) they began to define the errors and sins of the Kiev group, including separation from "real life," idealized pictures of the "backward" classes, individualism and symbolism. Soon all Yiddish writers recognized that they would have to bend to Bolshevik orthodoxy if they were to continue to write, or indeed to live. The situation worsened until by the end of the thirties even the proletarian poet Charik, quoted above, was accused of Trotskyism; and the Stalinist critic Abtshuk, who had defined the sins of the Kiev group, was put to death.

With the increasing terror of the Stalin years, only the strictest proletarian writers, and eventually not even they, could escape punishment by the Yiddish commissars. These overseers of Communist orthodoxy examined Yiddish texts for evidence of nostalgia for the old world, emotional ties to the Jewish past, failure to apply the "methodology of class struggle" to the life of the *shtetl* (*Ashes*, 16). Since the life of the shtetl was so thoroughly intertwined with Yiddish, it was, of course, almost impossible to write anything in Yiddish without employing Hasidic sayings, folk proverbs, and—most offensive of all to Communists—the imagery of religious belief.

Since Yiddish contains many Hebrew and Hebraic words, it was always open to the charge of heresy. The language, Howe points out, could not be "cleansed" of Hebrew without cutting it off from its vital sources, thereby destroying both the language and the culture from which it arose. The Bolsheviks violated what had long before 1977 become a central tenet of Howe's secular Jewishness—that history cannot be undone, that religion had always been interwoven with daily speech and manners and modes of thought of ostensibly secularist Yiddish writers. Such writers knew that Yiddish was full of references to and metaphors of the faith they had abandoned. Inevitably, the Soviet campaign against Hebrew and Hebraisms crippled Yiddish language and literature. (Howe fails to mention that the brutal Soviet persecution of the Hebrew language itself during the twenties and thirties was fueled to a large extent by the anti-Zionist zeal of the Yiddishists, who probably made the persecution worse than it would otherwise have been.)[33]

Yiddish, Howe adds, aroused the suspicion and hatred of the Stalinist authorities for yet another reason: it was an international language, part of an international culture. To write in Yiddish was to be in touch with writers throughout the world—in Warsaw, Paris, Buenos Aires, New York, even Tel Aviv. However "internationalist" the Soviets might be in ideology, in practice their old Russian nationalism bridled at the threat of cultural universalism, especially if that universe included capitalist America and Jewish Palestine.

World War II, according to Howe's short history of Soviet-Yiddish literature, brought a temporary reprieve to the Yiddish writers. In response to Nazism, and because the Soviet regime now encouraged the release of national sentiments in order to rally support for the war, the Yiddish writers felt freer to express again their Jewishness. Der Nister, for example, wrote stories about victims of the Holocaust in Poland; it was easier to show traditional Jewish feelings if they were located beyond Soviet borders. A Jewish Anti-Fascist Committee was organized, and its chairman, the actor Solomon Mikhoels, toured the United States seeking support for the struggle against Hitler.

But the reprieve was brief, and the end terrible. In 1948, Mikhoels was murdered by the secret police. The regime launched a new campaign against "nationalism" and "cosmopolitanism" in literature: Yiddish managed to be guilty of both, simultaneously. Hofstein wrote a poem that included the traditional Hebrew phrase, "for learning issues from Zion," and was fiercely attacked. A writer named Kipnis was forced publicly to confess his error in having written about his pleasure in hearing Yiddish spoken in Europe. By the end of the decade, all Yiddish publications had been closed down, and the Jewish Anti-Fascist Committee dissolved. About 500 Yiddish writers were sent to concentration camps, where many of them died. Der Nister died in prison. And then, on August 12, 1952, the secret police executed a number of Yiddish writers, including Bergelson, Markish, Hofstein, Kvitko, Feffer, and Persov. "What Hitler had left undone," Howe concludes, "Stalin completed" (*Ashes*, 21). To speak of Yiddish was, once again, to preside over a funeral. But Howe's American mourning, in *World of Our Fathers*, was over death by attrition, and achieved a kind of beauty; his dirge for the Soviet-Yiddish writers was over death by oppression and shots in the back of the neck.

Leon Trotsky, 1978

In *World of Our Fathers*, Howe embraced what he had once rejected; in *Leon Trotsky*, published in 1978, he repudiated much (if not quite all) of what he had once embraced. We have seen how virtually all of Irving Horenstein's classmates remembered him as the Trotskyist *par excellence* of City College of New York in 1938–39, the college's commissar of the revolution and chief Trotskyist theoretician. Forty years later, still mindful of the horrendous errors of judgment, especially about World War II, into which Trotsky had led him, Howe sought both to exorcise the demon of Trotsky and to offer what the Soviet expert Alexander Rabinowitch described as "a carefully focused, interpretive essay [on] Trotsky's ideas and historical importance."[34] The book, written in *Dissent* style, without any source references, is not, according to Howe, a biography but a "political essay with a narrative foundation."[35] It is one of Howe's most impressive achievements, an elegant integration of history, portraiture, political analysis, moral philosophy, and literary criticism. It also achieves a rare balance between praise and detraction, admiration and tough-minded criticism of the man who became Lenin's accomplice and Stalin's foe.

Like Howe, Trotsky was a Jewish name changer. He began life as Lev Davidovich Bronstein, but as a young revolutionist adopted (in a move guaranteed to intrigue Viennese doctors) the name of his jailor in the Siberian exile from which he escaped in 1902. Also like Howe, he early acquired and never relinquished the feeling that it was not politicians but, in Trotsky's words, "authors, journalists, and artists [who] stood for a world more attractive than any other, open to the elect" (LT, 3–4). Throughout the book, Howe stresses Trotsky's literary powers and proclivities. Even during revolutions, the Bolshevik leader stressed the continuity of human culture, often taking weeks to write about literature and frequently speaking in defense of at least partial artistic autonomy. Howe describes him, especially in the last decade or so of his life, as possessed of "an authority of statement, an incisiveness of structure, a cutting sharpness of phrase, a flowing range of metaphor that demand that he be regarded as among the great writers of his time" (LT, 136). He was also a potentially great literary critic, displaying not so much system or erudition but the gift for evoking "a writer's essential quality, his voice, inflection, accent, vision" (LT, 95).

Unlike Howe, Trotsky totally abandoned Jewishness in early youth and behaved as a completely assimilated Jew throughout his life, a decision for which Howe does not criticize him. He does give Trotsky some credit for showing greater "flexibility" on the Jewish Question, perhaps even acknowledging the existence of a "Jewish nation," late in life. But Howe makes no attempt to disguise the fact that for most of his life Trotsky adhered to the orthodox Marxist line (which had also ensnared the young Howe) that socialism, the universal panacea, would end anti-semitism and solve the problems of the Jews. Likewise, despite the wisdom that Howe (too generously) ascribes to Trotsky's analysis of Nazism, he also takes account of gross failures in this realm: Trotsky clung (as would the dutiful Trotskyist Howe in 1942) to the Leninist theory of imperialist war with respect to World War II; Trotsky failed, as would Howe, to acknowledge that Nazi Germany was an evil different from, and far greater than, traditional capitalism; and Trotsky's theory of Nazism as the last brutal attempt by the German bourgeoisie to retain power was quite useless as an explanation of the murder of six million Jews.

For the Howe who moved from Trotskyism to social democracy, the great contribution of Trotsky to modern thought and politics was his sustained critique of Stalinism. "Begun in 1923 . . . this critique touched upon every area of social life. . . . Is there another instance in modern history where a powerful mind directed itself with such persistence and passion to exposing the false claims of a regime that still commanded the loyalties of millions of people throughout the world?" (LT, 121). Yet Howe is rigorously honest in pursuing the question of whether totalitarianism was inherent in Bolshevism itself, that is to say, the question of how far Trotsky himself was responsible for the debacle that eventually destroyed the revolution's idealism (and also Trotsky). Did not Trotsky's cynical argument, back in 1920, that the Bolshevik government represented the Russian workers, whose desires it in fact disregarded entirely, provide the formula that later rationalized the Stalinist plunge into totalitarianism? Had not Trotsky himself condoned acts of repression that undercut whatever remained, just three years after the revolution, of "Soviet democracy"? (Bertrand Russell, visiting the Soviet Union in the spring of 1920, said that "the country comes to resemble an immensely magnified Jesuit College" [LT, 78].)

Howe pays particular attention to Trotsky's *Terrorism and Communism* (1920), a book he describes as "breath[ing] the arrogance of the ruler lodged in power" (LT, 70). In it, the pernicious doctrine of historical necessity, the idea that the Communist party is the dutiful servant of history and therefore innocent of all crimes committed in behalf of its furtherance, is given its most brutal expression. "Finally, all that Trotsky is saying comes down to a claim that 'we' in power represent the forces of progress and therefore are justified in taking the measures that 'we' do take. The criticism of 'our' means is thus disarmed by the declaration of 'our' ends. . . . And all through this argument there is a kind of mythologized 'we,' a grand appropriation of progress and the proletariat, that constitutes the ultimate hubris of the Bolshevik outlook" (LT, 72).

This hubris had once been Irving Howe's, or at least Irving Horenstein's. A bit later in the book, Howe discusses Trotsky's decision to suppress brutally the Kronstadt sailors' rebellion of 1921. The sailors had demanded free elections to the Soviets, and freedom of speech and press for workers, peasants, anarchists, and socialist parties. But Trotsky, rejecting the option of even partial democratization of the regime, demanded unconditional surrender, and when he did not get it, he ordered the Red Army to attack. Howe roundly condemns Trotsky for his role in "one of the darkest episodes in the history of early Bolshevism" (LT, 81). But Daniel Bell recalls a very different view taken of Kronstadt by the Howe of 1938. "At City College," says Bell, "I would flash my steel at the Trotskyists and shout: What about Kronstadt? And they would reply: Where's Kronstadt? Irving knew. And he defended Trotsky's action as 'historical necessity'" ("Remembering Irving Howe," 517). Just how far Howe had come with respect to the invocation of "historical necessity" as justification for murder would become evident in his remark, in an essay of 1986, about a crucial moment in Aharon Appelfeld's Holocaust novel, *Badenheim 1939*. "A musician," says Howe, "explains deportations of Jews as if he were the very spirit of the century: it is 'Historical Necessity.'"[36] Howe's repudiation of his earlier, Trotskyist self involved repudiation of nothing less than the sinister ideological underpinnings of the two totalitarian philosophies of the twentieth century.

It is characteristic of the mature Howe that he admires Trotsky more in opposition than in government, more in defeat than in triumph, more in exile than in the homeland. In exile, Trotsky, denounced by the Stalinist regime as heretic, traitor, and accomplice of fascism, remained "faithful to his vision in both its truth and error, its insight and blindness. Even those rejecting his every word must recognize that in the last ten or twelve years of his life Trotsky offered a towering example of what a man can be" (LT, 130). In spite, or perhaps because, of being a political failure, Trotsky became a moral hero. As such, he remains valuable to Howe as a foil to the countless members of the Western liberal and radical intelligentsia who were applauding the wisdom and humanity of the Stalin dictatorship up until Khrushchev's denunciation of Stalinism in 1956. (Howe does lapse into an embarrassing provincialism when he states that "all through the 1930s Trotsky stood almost alone in pointing to the facts . . . about the Stalin regime" [LT, 134–35].)

More than such tribute, however, Howe is unwilling to pay Trotsky or his followers. Trotsky's dismissive "class analysis" of democracy as merely a guise for class domination blinded countless socialists to the fact that freedom and liberty are, far more than state ownership of the means of production, the most precious values of modern society. Trotsky was as unreliable about the particular situation of Russia as about democracy, and nearly all his prognoses for the USSR failed to be realized. Most important, Trotsky refused to rethink his intellectual premises, even though "the whole outlook of revolutionary Marxism-Leninism . . . broke down before the realities of mid-twentieth century political life" (LT, 191). In consequence, Trotskyism, which had once been the religion of Irving Howe, is now declared by him to have been "for many years without political or intellectual significance: a petrified ideology" (LT, 192). A finely balanced and rigorously honest book, *Leon Trotsky* is that rare instance in political writing—a radical telling the truth about his own past politics without announcing his conversion to conservatism. All of Bolshevism and much of Trotsky are repudiated in this book-length political essay; but the ultimate lesson Howe draws from Trotsky's debacle is not that the revolutionary impulse is inherently flawed, but that "all theories of politics tend to underestimate the role of human stupidity" (LT, 142). Perhaps the inventors of these theories avert their view from something yet more deep-seated and incurable: "So I walk along 42nd Street," wrote Howe in the spring 1978 issue of *Dissent*, "and seeing what one sees, I remember Trotsky's expectations at the end of his book, *Literature and Revolution*, that mankind would yet rise to the levels of Goethe . . . and Marx . . . but . . . the sheer moral ugliness of the porn scene . . . —how can that be reconciled with social hopes? I find 42nd Street more destructive of my morale as a socialist than all the neoconservative polemics of the last 30 years."[37]

What Howe saw on 42nd Street was but one aspect of the urban degradation that now evoked from him cries of despair. In 1977, for example, he offered to escort the new president of the United States on a half-hour walk through Detroit (where Howe had been a visiting professor at Wayne State University) "so that [Carter] might grasp what the 'crisis of the cities' really signifies." What it signified, in Howe's view, was a new version of *apartheid*, "with the rotting core cities abandoned to the blacks, where they can elect officials and have 'power' over nothing worth having, while the whites move out"—and, Howe added, it was foolish for black leaders to blink the fact that whites were moving out largely because of their fear of black crime.[38] Of course, Howe blamed urban decay and other burgeoning social diseases on the rightward lurch of American social and political thought, even as he granted that one main reason for that rightward turn was the blasting of the hopes of the early 1960s for an era of good feeling between the races. Other reasons were the (justifiable) reaction against Stalinism and the failures of Social Democracy, the excesses of the New Left, and the difficulties of, and attack against, the welfare state. This attack was led by "sophisticated chaps like Irving Kristol" (whom Howe had recruited into the Young People's Socialist League forty years earlier) in league with increasingly sophisticated corporations. Conservatism of the worst kind, in Howe's estimation, was now in the ascendancy: "There is conservative thought that is traditional, serious and worthy of consideration. But what is happening in America now . . . is something else again. It is the start of a crude, mean-spirited, demagogic attack on the welfare state, a kind of class struggle by some of the haves against many of the have-nots."[39] (Howe never subjected the welfare state to sustained critical analysis, always accepting it as an unqualified good.)

Aggravating Howe's gloom over the social-political scene as the decade came to an end was a feeling that he was being overwhelmed by all the accumulated clutter of literary life, especially in the wake of the great success of *World of Our Fathers*. Late in November of 1979 he told me that he was in danger of becoming an institution, endlessly beseeched to write recommendations, read manuscripts, give testimonials. You couldn't complain about it—he complained—because then people suspected you of boasting. Teaching, which he did very well, had nevertheless become a "drag" for him, and he hoped some kindly millionaire would rescue him from it. Meanwhile, he plugged away at what he was now tentatively calling *A Chronicle of Our Times* (eventually *A Margin of Hope*) and brooding over the fact that he was just half a year away from his sixtieth birthday.[40]

EIGHT

The Final Reckoning: Socialism, Jewishness, Literary Study

We must veer and tack, stressing at one moment the traditionalist and at another the populist option. But how shall we know which to favor at any given point? Here we ought to trust our instincts, which will tell us soon enough who is getting to be an overbearing nuisance, who is displaying the "insolence of office." I would propose a rule of thumb: criticize whichever outlook is dominant at the moment, whether in the sphere of cultural opinion or public decision. No one has ever gone very wrong by jabbing at established power. ("Toward an Open Culture," 29)

Socialism and America, 1981, 1985

In 1981, Isaac Bashevis Singer said to me: "A wonderful man, Irving Howe. He's done so much for Yiddish literature and for me. But he's not a youngster anymore, and still, still with this socialist *meshugas!*" Howe's commitment to socialism never wavered. Neither was it exclusively in the realm of ideas. In his youth, he had fancied himself a union organizer (though it is hard to find any of his Trotskyist colleagues who give him high marks in this area); and as late as 1977 he delivered the keynote speech at the Democratic Socialist Organizing Committee convention in Chicago.[1] In the very year that Singer expressed his distress over Howe's socialism, his friend delivered three lectures at the University of Michigan Law School on the subject of why socialism had thrived at a few moments in twentieth-century America and failed at most other times. In revised and enlarged form, the lectures became a book of 1985 entitled *Socialism and America*, whose ideas Howe encapsulated in an interview with Herbert Mitgang: "I remain a liberal Socialist or democratic Socialist. That is to say, Socialism as an extension of democratic processes. I don't consider myself a Marxist."[2]

Howe was by no means the only ex-Marxist reevaluating the socialist enterprise in the eighties. Here, for example, is Eugene Genovese at the end of the decade (in a *Commentary* symposium called "The American 80's: Disaster or Triumph"):

> [S]urely, the 80's will be remembered as the decade in which socialism met its Waterloo. No amount of blather about the collapse of Communism's having opened the way to "real" and "democratic" socialism will serve. The Communists, for better or worse, introduced the only socialism we have had, whereas the social democrats have everywhere settled for one or another form of state-regulated capitalism. Many things went into the making of the collapse of the Communist regimes, but, as every honest Communist from Gorbachev on admits, the immediate cause has been exposed as state ownership of the means of production—and for reasons that, alas, Ludwig von Mises, among other right-wingers, long ago identified.[3]

Howe's book was in part, like Genovese's mordant reflection, a postmortem for the socialist movement, one of Howe's "lost causes," but in part too, in sharp contrast to Genovese, an affirmation of his continuing faith in the socialist idea, and, albeit not consciously, an explanation of the earlier shift in his career from politics to literature. The book is admirably honest in its criticism of the failures of socialism and also the failures of Irving Howe; yet finally it forces us to ask whether, in this instance, Howe did not misconstrue his own stern precept: "One of the arts of life is to know how to end" (MH, 264). For he always takes for granted what for many people is precisely at issue: he always asks why socialism did not triumph, never whether it should have triumphed, whether it might simply be a wrong and a bad system.

Socialism and America is not a full account of "the whole sad history of the American left"[4] but a stringent analysis of its historical crossroads, primary figures, and continuing political quandaries. Howe begins in the year 1912, one of the few good years for American socialism, when it was under the leadership of Eugene V. Debs. Debs, "an orator able to establish a rapport with the American people such as no other radical in this country has ever had" (5), endowed radical slogans with so much truth, beauty, and hope that he brought the party to its all-time peak membership of 118,000, with 879,000 people voting the Socialist ticket in the 1912 elections. Nevertheless, within six or seven years, the party was in shambles, and Howe seeks to discover the reasons why.

Two recalcitrant problems were racism and unionism. The racism characterizing American society as a whole was by no means absent from socialism, including left-wing socialists like Jack London. Debs, despite his generous readiness to offer solidarity to the oppressed— striking workers, desperate farmers, isolated miners, hungry share- croppers—was obtuse on the racial question. He insisted that there was no "Negro problem" apart from the general labor problem, that the party had nothing specific to offer the Negro, and would therefore make no special appeal to a particular race. A more crucial problem was what attitude the socialist movement should take toward the labor unions, especially the AFL and its moderate, even conservative leaders. Social- ists often found themselves in opposition to the labor movement, which included strongly antisocialist "ethnic" elements, especially among Catholics.

Underlying these specific problems, Howe points out, was the larger one of simpleminded dogmatism, which prevented the Debsians from seriously examining socioeconomic arrangements that fell somewhere between capitalism and socialism. Debsian socialism had already been invaded by the "dybbuk of sectarianism" (31) that would damage American socialism even in its best years. This political version of Protestant evangelical fundamentalism held doggedly to "the notion that there were two, and only two, choices facing mankind: capitalism (the devil's spawn) and socialism (the angelic promise)" (32). Howe criticizes the Debsian refusal (or inability) to recognize the growing complication and sophistication of capitalism, and Debs's "almost reli- gious belief" (33) that a true socialist should never vote for any candi- date, however liberal, who ran on one of the old-party tickets. Lest Howe's anger at Debsian rigidity should seem self-righteous, he can- didly admits in a footnote that his anger is also directed at his former self: "I can testify to the power this belief held over people on the left even in later years. To vote for Norman Thomas [Socialist party candi- date for president from 1928 to 1948], during the years of my socialist youth [i.e., the 1930s and 1940s], seemed akin to being flooded with grace—or at least sprinkled. Even after many of us had decided that running socialist candidates once there was barely a socialist move- ment had become a humiliating ritual, and that it was necessary to vote for 'the lesser of two evils' when there was one—even then it was still emotionally hard to go to the polls and pull down an old-party lever. The first time I did that, voting in 1952 for Adlai Stevenson, I came out of the voting booth feeling almost physically sick" (33n).[5] This means, of course, that Howe did not cast a vote in 1944 for Franklin Delano Roosevelt, who was in fact his constant target during the 1940s.

The high point of American left-wing strength came in the 1917 local elections. But by 1919 "the golden age of American socialism . . . was over" (48). Socialist infatuation with communism (the Socialist party applied for membership in the Communist International—and was refused), political competition from the Progressives, wartime repression, inability to overcome its ignorance of American life and society or its sectarianism—all contributed to the decline.

By the late 1930s, after a few good years (1931–35) under the leadership of Thomas, the Socialist party's endemic sectarianism had become suicidal. Apart from, although of course aggravating this little imperfection, was a host of problems that would eventually overwhelm American socialists. These were, according to Howe: (1) the Soviet Union, the Communists, and the United Front; (2) third parties, coalitions, and splendid isolation; (3) Hitler's triumph; (4) the New Deal.

As for the Soviet Union, Howe contends, as he did for most of his career, that socialists, even left-wing socialists, were more clear minded about the horrors of Stalinism than American liberals were. The problem of the United Front was a more difficult one. This tactic of the Communists grew out of Stalin's dogma that "objectively, Social Democracy is the moderate wing of fascism," a dogma that spawned the theory of "social fascism," which saw social democracy and fascism as twins. The doctrine played an important role in bringing Hitler to power in Germany because it prevented the Communists and social democrats from joining in opposition to the Nazis. In America it led to an appeal by the Communists to Socialist party members for "a united front from below," that is, for unity with the Communists against their own socialist leaders (59). Although Howe maintains that the tactic drew off only some left-leaning socialists in the early thirties, it gained strength in 1934 and 1935, partly because Howe's (belatedly adopted) hero Thomas was too open-minded and democratic to deal with it effectively. His very virtues proved political liabilities: "Complexity of vision, intellectual doubt, humane tolerance are often a handicap in politics" (63).

A second major problem for the socialists of the thirties, according to Howe, was whether to join with new radical but non-Marxist parties or remain separate and distinct, still more whether to support one of the "rotten" old parties, which in practice usually meant the Democratic one. When the novelist Upton Sinclair, who had several times run as a socialist candidate in California, entered and won the Democratic primary for governor in 1934, the socialists refused to support him, preferring to run their own candidate. "What Sinclair kept asking, and the socialists never found an adequate way of answering, was simply this: why was it worthy to push certain ideas outside the rim of the old-party structures and heresy to push the same ideas within it?" (66). As so often in this book, the fundamentalist socialist line that the sixty-five-year-old Howe castigates for its rigid and destructive self-righteousness had been the cherished article of faith of the young Howe (and of Horenstein before him): "I remember making speeches on the theme that 'it's better to vote for what you want and not get it than to vote for what you don't want and get it'" (67). In retrospect, he says this was "a nice slogan," but hardly answered to the American situation, in which flexibility in the voting booth might gain important advantages.

Perhaps the greatest error of perception of the socialists of the 1930s, Howe suggests, was the supposition that the apocalyptic events of the times portended the final breakdown of world capitalism, when in fact what they portended was the collapse of European civilization itself. The socialists were unnerved by the fact that a thuggish lunatic like Hitler had been able to destroy all opposition in Germany without meeting resistance either from the social democrats, with their seven million votes, or the Communists, with their five million. Nevertheless, much of the energy of the American socialists, especially the party's militants, was devoted to mobilizing resistance to American entry into war and attacking the "bogus democracy of capitalist parliamentarianism" (72)—this at a time when the United States, under Roosevelt, was engaged in a major program of social reform. Howe's own political development, we might recall, consisted in large part of his growing recognition of just how tragic had been the historic split between socialism and the liberal democratic tradition.[6]

Roosevelt's reformist program would itself constitute a major problem for American socialism. "What cut the ground out pretty completely from under us was," lamented Thomas, "Roosevelt in a word." Howe grants this interpretation a measure of truth, but discounts it as a sufficient explanation. Once again, he lays the blame for socialist failure upon the socialists themselves. The Roosevelt administration had modulated the "heartlessness" of rugged individualism; it had created a tension between government and economy, state and society, a welfare state that had saved capitalism from its own self-destructive excesses. The socialists, as usual, failed to recognize that capitalism was a developing, not a fixed, system. They insisted upon running their own candidates in the 1936 election, even though most of the working class and the unions favored Roosevelt. "Electoral opposition to all capitalist candidates had become a kind of religion, or at least ritual" (82–83). Howe knew whereof he spoke: he had believed in this religion. That may help to explain the sympathy with which he still, in 1985, speaks of the intransigence that led to socialist catastrophe at the polls in 1936 and to decimation of its ranks by 1938. "There are times when a confluence of pressures comes down upon us with a force that neither strength of character nor clenching of will can finally resist" (83).

In retrospect, Howe criticizes Thomas and his comrades for using a leftist rhetoric that brought them moral pleasure but no political gain. "Had they only bent a little more, they might not have broken." But this too becomes a self-indictment: "At the time, all of us on the party's 'left' would have regarded such an approach [continuing to criticize capitalism, yet allowing supporters to participate in the movement of Roosevelt reform] as rank betrayal" (85). Nor is Howe talking merely about the socialists of the 1930s. The problem of how to reconcile the vision of a new world with day-to-day issues "was for the socialists a seemingly insoluble problem. Perhaps it still is" (86).[7] As for the collapse of American socialism in the decades since 1933, Howe concludes in the second chapter of his book, it had deeper historical reasons than anything the party did or did not do. Writing in the decade when the Marxist regimes of Europe were collapsing in ruin or being thrown off by (working-class) rebellion, Howe cannot but acknowledge that "a whole generation was haunted and destroyed by the terrifying rise of Stalinism, which led to a perhaps fatal besmirching of the socialist idea" (86).

The concluding chapter of *Socialism and America* in its original form (Howe subsequently added two essays from *Dissent*) undertakes to minimize, though not dismiss, the numerous explanations that have been offered by thinkers (socialist and other) for the failure of socialism in America, and to argue that the explanation should be sought in cultural, subjective causes far more than objective economic and material ones. That is to say, "American exceptionalism," the idea that historical conditions in the United States differ crucially from those laid down by the Marxist model for the development of capitalism, may be true, but not in the sense usually accepted.

Werner Sombart had asserted, in a pithy and vivid observation, that America was "the promised land of capitalism," where "on the reefs of roast beef and apple pie socialist Utopias . . . are sent to their doom." Howe insists that, although material comfort among some segments of American workers has limited the growth of socialism, there is more truth to be found in Nathaniel Hawthorne's statement that "in this republican country, amid the fluctuating waves of our social life, somebody is always at the drowning-point" (117). He painstakingly demonstrates that the history of American workers affords evidence not that an abundance of good things led to passive satisfaction, but only that the numerous outbursts of labor militancy—at least on a par with anything in Europe—rarely ended in socialist politics. His crucial point is that social mobility in America has been *perceived* differently from the way it was in Europe. Here Howe the literary critic comes to the aid of Howe the political thinker. "The myth of opportunity for energetic individuals rests on a measure of historical actuality but also has taken on a power independent of, *even when in conflict with,* the social actuality. . . . Here we enter the realm of national psychology and cultural values, which is indeed what we will increasingly have to do . . . " (122).

Another element of the "American exceptionalism" explanation of socialism's failure that Howe calls largely mythological is that in America, unlike Europe, people could escape from bad working conditions (in the East) to free land (in the West). In the 1960s, he observes, for every industrial worker who became a farmer, twenty farmers became city dwellers. Nevertheless, if the dream of free land was rarely realized, neither was it dismissed. The frontier and the wilderness remained powerful *symbolic* forces that enabled Americans to console themselves with the dream of escape, even if they never acted upon it. Here again Howe's argument veers away from economic, material conditions toward cultural ones as well as the problems of American socialists that were (and are) open to solution by the application of will and intelligence, such as the immigrant problem and the distinctive American political structure.

Showing a candor that would have saved him from some egregious errors (especially about the Jews) back in the 1940s, Howe grants that Marxist dogma prevented socialist recognition that ethnic divisions are often felt far more strongly than any (supposed) class consciousness. Neither did socialists recognize the element of social conformism working against them: "it was hard enough to be a Slav in Pittsburgh or a Pole in Chicago without the additional stigma of anti-Americanism with which the socialists were often tainted" (127). The unions that tried to organize plants in which the workforce spoke twenty different languages faced the problem of ethnic and linguistic fragmentation. Nevertheless, Howe maintains that the divisive effects of immigration also fail to explain the difficulties of American socialism for the simple reason that the socialists (unlike the unions) had not been successful among native-born Americans and never really had a chance to reach many of the new immigrants.

A more serious problem for American socialism lay in the distinctive character of the American political system, one "objective" factor in socialism's failure to which Howe does assign substantial importance.

The American system, he argues, "tends to give the political center an overwhelming preponderance, and makes it tremendously difficult for insurgent constituencies to achieve political strength unless they submit to the limits of one of the major parties" (130). Howe takes the opportunity to recall his "most wearying memories" (131)—and we tend to forget that Howe was once a political organizer—those of efforts he made on behalf of various socialist groups merely to get on the ballot. He recalls, with equal chagrin, the frequency with which people sympathetic to socialist candidates, especially Thomas, would come up to them and say that although they agreed with socialist views they would vote for "the lesser evil" rather than "throw away" their vote. Thomas, Howe concludes, was right to argue that if America had had a parliamentary rather than a presidential system, the country would have had a moderately strong socialist party (132).

Apart from this one instance, Howe discounts (though he does not dismiss) the customary "objective factors" usually invoked to explain the failure of American socialism. "American exceptionalism" exists, but in ideological or mythic form, especially "the idea that this country could be exempt from the historical burdens that overwhelmed Europe" (133). According to Howe, the American myth is the belief that the country and its people have been shaped by Providential covenant, that they represent "humanity's second chance" (134). America, from this perspective, does not need a revolution either because (in the view of native-born Americans) it already had one, led by George Washington, or (in the view of the millions of immigrants who came here in the last 150 years) because the act of coming itself constituted a kind of revolution. Howe does add that Americans can hold this myth and at the same time attack almost everything in America, with considerable stridency and bitterness. This is a "contradiction" from which American collective existence has been formed.

For this complex of myth and ideology, this belief that the new American would create himself instead of accepting the European view that people are defined socially, Howe uses the label "Emersonianism."[8] Contrary to the Marxists, American exceptionalism is rooted in the mythic depths of American imagination, which Howe was shortly to explore in his Harvard lectures on Emerson and the American newness. Therefore, "if socialism is ever to become a major force in America it must either enter deadly combat with and destroy the covenant myth or must look for some way of making its vision of the good society seem a fulfillment of that myth. Both are difficult propositions, but I need hardly say which is the less so" (139). This statement of the future task of socialism is not only an explanation of its past failures but of Howe's own past. At a certain point in his career, he saw that Marxism was really a comfortable retreat into claims of universal applicability and certain fulfillment, when what was wanted for the socialist renovation of American society was an understanding of its culture, not of its industrial structures, production levels, or standards of living. He did not so much turn from politics to literature as come to recognize that political and material explanations were partial, if not rigid and barren, without the cultural understanding that only literature could provide. That recognition underlay the complex unity of his thought.

Most of the analyses and speculations in *Socialism and America* applied to the years prior to World War II. But in conclusion Howe again stresses that the troubles of all, not just American, socialism since the thirties must be located in the triumphs of Hitlerism and Stalinism. The former called into question "a good many traditional assumptions of progress and schemes for human self-determination—called into question the very enterprise of mankind." The latter, which he calls, in literary parlance, "a kind of grotesque 'double' of the socialist hope," led to "the destruction of entire generations, the disillusionment of hundreds of thousands of committed people, the besmirching of the socialist idea itself." Together, these catastrophes caused an inner crisis of belief and a disintegration of socialist thought, perhaps more so than any specifically American factors. Nevertheless, Howe restates with admirable firmness his conviction that "the American socialist movement must take upon itself a considerable portion of the responsibility for its failures" (141–42).

The overall impression left by *Socialism and America* was pungently described by Howe's longtime friend Dennis Wrong in a lengthy review in the *New Republic*: "Irving Howe has in the past written powerful and moving requiems: for the Jewish immigrants to America in *World of Our Fathers*, for Yiddish literature in essays and introductions to anthologies, for the New York intellectuals . . . in the best full-length treatment of them as a group. He may not have intended *Socialism and America* as another requiem, but it is one all the same."[9]

Socialism and Israel

If socialism perpetually failed in America, could it perhaps survive and flourish elsewhere? To put the question more personally (and accusatorily), did Howe attempt to resurrect or realize his socialism as a form of secular Jewishness, not in America but in Israel? Back in 1971, as we have already seen, he praised Israel as the best available model for the democratic socialist hope of combining radical social change with political freedom. But after the defeat of the Israeli Labor party in 1977,

Howe began to sour on Israel as a bastion of socialist dedication. In August of that year he paid a visit of several weeks to Israel, where, riding the crest of the success of *World of Our Fathers,* he and Ilana Wiener (whom he was now calling his Israeli "lady friend") stayed at the elegant guest house Mishkenot Sha'ananim as guests of the Jerusalem Municipality. He recorded his impressions in "Israel: A Visitor's Notes," in the Fall 1977 issue of *Dissent.* They are a grave disappointment, and not so much because they lament the ascendance of Likud and Menachem Begin to power for the first time—nobody familiar with Howe's life work could have expected otherwise[10]—as because they contain no fresh, firsthand impressions, and are little more than a regurgitation of the self-interested interpretations of their defeat by some of the most tired apologists for the Israeli Labor party. In his weeks in Israel, Howe does not seem to have exchanged a single word with people connected with, or supportive of, the new government. Instead, we get a report of what such Labor party functionaries as "the respected Israeli political scientist" Shlomo Avineri or the "highly qualified . . . non-Marxist economist"[11] Haim Barkai had to say about why, after twenty-nine years, the Labor party had lost control of a government it had come to consider its exclusive property.

Avineri told Howe that the election results could in part be explained by the fact that the children of Ashkenazi Labor Zionist pioneers now went to universities, and so their values and ideas were no longer proletarian. He appears not to have told Howe that these newly bourgeoisified Israelis voted Labor quite as automatically as their parents did. Howe was also told, accurately enough, that Begin received much of his support from the "Oriental" Jews; and, much less accurately, that these Jews did not respond to Zionist symbols, and were intellectually and culturally inferior to the Ashkenazi socialists. This inferiority made them "ripe for Begin's chauvinist appeals" and incapable of understanding the complexities of Middle Eastern politics except through "the nationalist slogans of the Likud." These benighted Orientals could not grasp "the universalist subtleties of the Israeli left" (360)—a remark which simultaneously brings laughter to the throat and tears to the eyes.

Howe does, however, seem to understand that the defeat of Labor was due as much to Labor Zionism's intellectual and spiritual decline as to Begin's wiles practiced upon simpletons. "There appears to be a considerable disillusionment—a weariness, a boredom—with socialist values, and even if Labor were to return to office it would probably be less as a result of a socialist renewal than out of a fear . . . that Begin will precipitate a new war" (361).[12] But if Labor Zionism has been weakened as a political and moral force in Israel, what is to replace it? However much beguiled by his Labor party cronies, Howe was shrewd enough to understand one cardinal point: ". . . this country, because of its traditions and circumstances, needs belief—its very oxygen of survival." But what if that belief should be what Howe could not tolerate? He observes that "there occurs a growth . . . of a nationalist-clerical outlook in which the symbols of religion matter both in their own right and as political tokens to be manipulated by Begin and his allies" (361–62). This, needless to say, he finds unacceptable. We already see here the seeds of the Peace Now philosophy that would soon take hold among certain American Jews: namely, that unless Israel were virtuously and commendably socialist, it might not command the support of Diaspora Jewry, especially if it pursued a foreign policy unacceptable to the devotees of a Palestinian Arab state in the disputed territories of Judea and Samaria.

Precisely foreign policy was Howe's ultimate reason for dismay over the victory of Begin. For Begin not only insisted on keeping "the West Bank" (as Judea and Samaria had been renamed by Jordan's King Abdullah after his country occupied them in 1948); he insisted on doing so for reasons of right rather than security (the Labor party rationale). This, in Howe's mind, raises the ugly spectre not only of religion—which he assumes to be the exclusive domain of Muslim Arabs in that part of the world—but of intransigence, permanent rule over the Arabs who constitute the vast majority of the population in the disputed territories. At no point does Howe ask why the Arabs, during the nineteen years (1948–67) they had been in possession of these territories, neglected to set up the Palestinian state they now demanded so vociferously, and never ceased to attack the sliver of mandatory Palestine that was now called Israel.

Although Howe softened what he called in 1982 the "blind hostility to the Zionist movement" ("Range," 276) of his socialist youth, he never took it seriously as a system of values and beliefs, or bothered to learn Hebrew[13] despite the fact that his fourth wife, Ilana Wiener, was an (expatriate) Israeli. In a fine essay of 1979 about *Daniel Deronda*, he stressed George Eliot's "heroic" attempt to create a counter-myth in English literary culture to that of Fagin, the satanic Jewish villain,[14] but barely mentioned the religiously Zionist thrust of the novel, which was strong enough to inspire Eliezer Ben-Yehudah (the man credited with reviving Hebrew as a living language) and to earn the novelist a street named after her in each of the three major cities of modern Israel. As late as 1982, he said in an interview: "I still don't think of myself as a Zionist—I'm not a Zionist . . . " ("Range," 287). Although he sensed the desiccation of Labor Zionism and instinctively knew that Israel needed "belief," Howe readily adopted the view of his socialist friends in Israel that traditional Jews must have no part in reviving Zionist belief—rather a presumptuous position to be taken by somebody not a Zionist himself.

In April 1978 Howe's name began to appear in ads placed by a group called American Friends of Peace Now urging Prime Minister Begin to show "greater flexibility" on issues of peace with the Arabs. The position of this organization with respect to what it chose to call "the Arab-Israeli conflict" rather than "the Arab war against Israel" may be readily inferred from an episode of 1980. On May 31 of that year, Al Fatah, largest faction of the PLO, headed by Yasir Arafat, formally recommitted itself to the obliteration of Israel, vowing to continue its struggle "until the Zionist entity is liquidated and Palestine is liberated." On June 13, the European Economic Community, fully aware of the PLO's 31 May declaration, called for its inclusion in the Middle East negotiating process. Meanwhile, Saudi Arabia, recently the recipient of F-15 fighter bombers from the United States, strenuously denied reports that it was considering an opening to Anwar Sadat, for he had committed the crime of making peace with Israel. "This," wrote Ruth Wisse, "was the moment chosen by a new coalition of American Jews to find its voice and issue a call for action—not against the genocidal intentions of the PLO, or against the cynicism of countries held in the thrall of the oil cartel, or against the implacable enmity of the Arab states, but against the government of Israel for proving a stumbling block to peace."[15]

In subsequent years, Howe would be a prominent tribune of Peace Now. In September 1982, for example, he wrote an op-ed piece for the *New York Times* reporting that he had "been thrown into emotional turmoil by the revelations about the Beirut massacre" [of Palestinian Arabs in the camps of Sabra and Shatila by Christian militiamen]. He wrote in terms of "we" and "they." "We" were the opponents of Begin-Sharon, as Howe called them, the righteous American Jews who thought it a political and moral disaster for Israel to retain the "West Bank." "We" were experiencing a "conflict between the values of democratic conciliation and the goal of imperial domination." Above all, "we" were warm friends of Israel, but open critics of Begin-Sharon, critics for whom, "after Beirut, silence is impossible."[16] Criticism of Israel for indirect responsibility for Sabra and Shatila seemed reasonable enough, given the fact that the Israelis were in temporary military control of the area where the massacre was perpetrated. But once the government of Israel began an investigation of its failure to prevent the massacres, Howe and the other Jewish critics of Israel lost interest in the matter. Once again Wisse is incisive: "Whatever happened to the killers? . . . If the outrage was so great and the crime so brutal, where was the call for justice? In truth, there was no moral outrage and no desire for retribution. The massacre was morally interesting only as a moment of reckoning with the Jews. . . . "[17]

Nor was it only "right-wing" Jews who were censorious of Howe's selective morality with respect to Israel. In February 1983 he received a stinging rebuke from his old friend and socialist colleague Albert Glotzer (the same Albert Gates of *Labor Action* and *New International* who had been a strident anti-Zionist back in the early forties):

> I remind you that we are both members of SI [Socialist International] through SD [Social Democrats] and SDA [Democratic Socialists of America]. I know there are many political tendencies in that body, but one which predominated for a long time was the anti-Israel attitude of several leading parties in Europe and a number of leaders of the Buro. This attitude toward Israel preceded the stewardship of Begin and his coalition, because it was so when the Labor party was the leader of the nation. It also preceded the Lebanese invasion. . . . It was part of a world-wide antipathy that flowed out of the reactionary UN Russian-Arab-3rd World alliance. . . . Herr Kreisky paraded up and down the Continent with Yasir Arafat in tow, and with the connivance of Brandt, invited him to address the Buro (without his machine gun). . . . The SD protested, but not your SDA. And now, your SDA demands . . . the end of all military aid to Israel unless and until it withdraws all its forces from Lebanon, as though this was a very simple matter of turning around and walking away. Is it predicated on the simultaneous withdrawal of Syria and the PLO? No. Always the demands are made of Israel.[18]

For the rest of his life, Howe persisted in attacking the Israeli government of the Likud as the main impediment to peace in the region. His attacks became more and more strident, especially after the *intifada* broke out at the end of 1987. In January of 1988, he joined with Michael Walzer, Henry Rosovsky, and Arthur Hertzberg (who in the previous year had expressed regret that the Six-Day War had not ended in "a draw") in decrying Israel's "strong-arm methods" and warning that they would lead to "a harvest of hate."[19] Apparently Howe and his epistolary colleagues had forgotten that it was the hatred expressed in the Arab aggression of 1967 that had led to the "occupation" in the first place, and not the occupation that had led to the hatred.

In summer 1988 Howe paid another visit to Israel, where he and his wife once again stayed, in style, at Mishkenot Sha'ananim. Upon his return to America, he lost no time in biting the hand that had fed him by publishing an account of his visit in the pages of the *New York Review of Books*, a consistently virulent critic of Israel ever since 1967. Howe provided the journal's readers (who found in the same issue a piece by the anti-Israel Arab Israeli writer Anton Shammas) with precisely what they wanted on this subject. He linked the Israeli response to the organized violence of the *intifada* with the Nazi and Stalinist terror of fifty years earlier, stopping just an inch short of the Israeli-Nazi equation that had long been a commonplace among anti-Israel propagandists. He also indulged in the typical inversion of Arab propaganda by making the Arabs into "Zionists," in whose riots against Israeli authority he saw "a sustained venture in nation-building."[20] Apparently Howe was not aware or chose to forget that the Jews had been able to lay claim to a state in Palestine not because they threw rocks, burned buildings, and blew up passenger-filled buses, but because they worked diligently to extend Hebrew culture, in the most comprehensive sense of that term, to whatever land they were able to acquire under the British Mandate. He failed too to recognize that Arab nationalism was very nearly the opposite of Jewish, rather than a repetition. The Jewish people of the Diaspora had supported the Jews of Palestine through the United Palestine–United Israel Appeal, a continuation of the tradition of communal self-help; that was how money was raised to resettle Jewish refugees in the land of Israel. The Arabs, on the contrary, showed not the slightest interest in helping their brethren in Palestine through philanthropy in the Arab "diaspora." Instead, they invested their money in propaganda to blacken the image of Israel and to insure that Arab refugees remained refugees and thus politically valuable.

But Howe had been duped less by the Arabs than by his friends in Israel, whom he describes, with no embarrassment or unease, as without exception "doves of various kinds." Now, as in his visit of 1977, he reports speaking to nobody except Jewish doves and Arab militants. The former told him that "the sole hope . . . was that the Big Powers would impose a solution of sorts in the Middle East" (13). The Arab militants, at a forum arranged by the Peace Now organization, assumed a smooth, conciliatory manner that was enough to make Howe overlook the fact that he was talking to none other than Arafat's proxies in Jerusalem, most prominent among them Faisal Husseini. If the leaders of the Israeli government were assumed by Howe to be beyond the pale, then the few advocates of "transfer" of the Arabs from the disputed territories were nothing less than "fascist." Fortunately, Howe did not live long enough to see the policy of transfer advocated, after 1993, by his own friends in the Labor party—not for Arabs, of course, but for Jews.

The parochial dogmatism of Howe's writings on Israel from 1977 onward is disheartening; and the contrast between their purblind conformism and the clear-sighted independent intelligence of his literary criticism of the same period is mind-boggling. In some ways, his polemics against Israel are a throwback to his dismal blindness of the forties, when he could see no important difference between the Allies and the Axis powers; for to refer to the long Arab war against Israel as "the Arab-Israeli conflict" is tantamount to referring to Hitler's war against the Jews and the Allies as a conflict between two capitalist powers. At first, the problem seems to arise from his disappointment at Israel's apparent turning away from socialism with the election of Begin in 1977. But he did not really expect that the socialism which had failed in America would (with massive infusions of aid from American capitalism, in "land for peace" deals which were actually "land for socialism" arrangements) survive in Israel.[21] Rather, his involvement in what must be called anti-Israel American Jewish politics (involvement of a kind that has sustained many an American-Jewish "identity") was a refusal to accept the consequences of being a "partial Jew" and a desperate attempt to turn a lost cause—secular Jewishness—into a thriving one. In his autobiography of 1982, Howe had admitted that in the long struggle between Zionism and Yiddishism for the loyalty of secular Jews, Zionism had triumphed: "When the writer Hillel Halkin sent from Israel [in 1977] a powerful book [*Letters to an American Jewish Friend*] arguing that the Jews in the West now had only two long-range choices if they wished to remain Jews—religion and Israel, faith and nationhood—I searched for arguments with which to answer him. But finally I gave it up, since it seemed clear that the perspective from which I lived as 'a partial Jew' had reached a historical end and there, at ease or not, I would have to remain" (MH, 281). But it is dangerous to publish one's autobiography at the age of sixty-two. In the same book, as we have already noted, Howe had said that one of the arts of life is knowing how to end; but he could not quite achieve the perfection of his own ideal and accept the limitations of being a partial Jew or the implications of the demise of the culture of Yiddish socialism. By contrast, Lucy Dawidowicz said in 1990 that "I had to come to terms with the idea that I had reached the end of the line of the Yiddish world. I grew to realize that Judaism . . . was where the strength of Jewish survival lay. This was something that people gave their lives for. It was, and still is, a transcendental idea. Reading Sholom Aleichem is not. Nobody is going to die for Sholom Aleichem or for the right to read him."[22]

One sees Howe succumbing to the temptation to revive the spirit if not the substance of "Jewish" leftism in the language he used in a speech he gave in December 1988 on "American Jews and Israel" at a conference in New York sponsored by *Tikkun* magazine. (Howe's willingness to cooperate with the buffoonish apostle of "the politics of meaning," Michael Lerner, a classic instance of the "do-gooder" who confuses doing good with feeling good about what he is doing, stands in sharp contrast to his uncompromising condemnation of the anti-

Israel politics of the New Leftists of the sixties.) On the surface, Howe appears ready to acknowledge the demise of the old faith and to admit that "few of us in America can claim to be more than partial Jews." He includes Jewish socialism in the list of dead faiths, along with religion ("the privilege of a small minority"), Yiddish,[23] Zionism, and liberalism. For most American Jews, he observes, "Israel represents *the last Jewish hope*," which is a main reason why American Jews, apart from the righteous minority to which Howe belongs, refrain from sharp, open criticism of Israeli policies: "*they simply could not bear it; they would feel there is nothing left.*" He is prescient in his warning that "if Israel were secure and prosperous, and therefore no longer in need of its immobile brothers across the Atlantic, they . . . would be left empty-handed and might have no option but to ask: Why do we exist? What makes us Jews?" ("American Jews and Israel," 72–73).

Howe mischievously repudiates the central premise of the *Tikkun* conference at which he is speaking by remarking that "there is no unquestionable sanction in Jewish tradition or thought for political liberalism. . . . [T]o claim that a liberal politics is somehow sanctioned by Judaism leads to parochial sentimentality or ethnic vanity" (74). So far, so good; and yet he comes back in the end to the outrageous and demeaning claim that the chief task of American Jewish life is to espouse national rights for the Palestinian Arabs, or, in less euphemistic terms, an irredentist PLO state next to Israel. The whole of the Jewish heritage in its American incarnation is to center upon this (ill-conceived) political campaign! "The central issue of Jewish life today," according to Howe in 1988, is not the failure of Jews to reproduce themselves, or to keep within the fold the few offspring they do produce, or to impart to these offspring a measure of Jewish literacy and faith, but to pressure the sovereign state of Israel to bring about an independent state for Arafat and his followers, who just happen to be committed to the elimination of Israel. Howe, who for much of his life saw not the slightest need for an independent Jewish state and in old age reverted to defining himself as a non-Zionist, now decided that a second Palestinian Arab state was the *sine qua non* of Jewish existence. In other words, Howe behaved with respect to Israel in the very way that the assimilationist Jews he scorned had always behaved with respect to Jewish nationhood: they are passionate for the rights of every national group—except the Jews. But Howe's position was even worse, for the group he now championed defined itself as an anti-nation, whose whole meaning and existence derived from its desire to pull down and replace a living Jewish nation. Of course, Howe adds that the creation of the Palestinian Arab state should be done "with all due precautions," a nod in the direction of the (public) Peace Now position that the PLO state should be demilitarized.[24] But even if creating a PLO state were a worthy political aim, it is hard to see how the whole Jewish tradition could be said to devolve upon this singular goal.

On one matter, however, Howe was right. He predicted that "in the next few years there is probably going to be a 'war among the Jews'— an intellectual, political 'war'—concerning the Israeli-Palestinian conflict" (74). What he did not foresee was that within five years of this speech of December 1988, the Israeli government would be in the hands of his ideological comrades. Several of the ministers of the Rabin-Peres government called themselves "post-Zionists" and had, like Howe, a far stronger commitment to a PLO state than they did to a Jewish one. From 1993 until their defeat by Benjamin Netanyahu in 1996 they would embrace the PLO and even subcontract Israel's security to this terrorist band, while the American Jews openly critical of Israeli policies would be the spiritual descendants of Begin and Yitzhak Shamir. One wonders what Howe, had he been alive, would have said then about the moral necessity of American Jewish dissent from the policies of the Israel government.

The American Newness: Culture and Politics in the Age of Emerson, 1986

Like *Socialism and America, The American Newness* began as a series of lectures that Howe, by now an éminence grise, was invited to present, this time at Harvard in 1985. Modestly disavowing any claim to add even a mite of scholarship to the study of nineteenth-century American culture, Howe begins by saying that his aim is "merely to understand: What were they up to, Emerson and his disciples? What drove them, what blinded them? And . . . what can they still mean to us?"[25] Although he does not say so explicitly, he is also continuing the search, begun in *Socialism and America*, for explanation of the resistance of the American psyche to socialism. His special interest is in the decades of the 1830s and 1840s, when ideas of the American "newness" began to emerge.

The first lecture deals with Emerson and Hawthorne as linked opposites, each retaining jagged, often incoherent bits of Puritanism. Hawthorne especially sensed—and here the language of Howe is typical of the conservative sensibility of his maturity—"how strongly all of us, even spiritual rebels, like the young Emerson, remain in the grip of the past." Repeating his customary complaint, once shocking to those who had known him as the ideologically rigid Trotskyist but by now quite routine, that America is a country "which makes the refusal of history into a first principle," Howe remarks upon the paradox that the country's first major writer of fiction "should have grappled with his provincial history as if it held the weight of the ages" (3–4).

Both Emerson and Hawthorne, according to Howe, responded to the Puritan tradition in its decline. Hawthorne made of Puritan New England a place not of moral grandeur but of moral disorder, and could realize his values only through images of violation. But whereas Hawthorne "stood still in confronting his religious crisis . . . Emerson chose to shake off . . . his received terms of belief." Emerson granted that the Puritans had once served useful purposes, but now their day was done. He, at any rate, would set off on his own. Both writers, Howe observes, struggled with spiritual isolation. Despite obvious contrasts between them, they are linked by a devotion to *"inwardness,* a risky, powerful mode of personal existence that . . . is just starting to undergo historical test" (7). Despite the symmetrical title, "Emerson and Hawthorne," it is Emerson's quest that primarily concerns Howe in the first section. In the 1830s Emerson propelled himself "onto a journey free of mere destination, a perpetual motion of spirit" (8). He came to believe that primal intuitions had no history, but came straight from the heart and were therefore infallible.

Without actually aligning himself with Emerson's conservative critics at this point, Howe nevertheless states their skeptical view very sympathetically: an external source "transmit[s] the accumulated experience and wisdom of the race, for we do not always begin from the beginning; while an inner voice . . . must always begin anew, unprotected in its innocence." Howe's own objection to Emerson's reliance on the inner light is phrased differently: "for those of us who are cool to revelation there remains a serious difficulty in [Emerson's] treatment of the relation between authenticity and truth" (10). Nevertheless, Howe stresses (and this in language that reflects his own growing sense of mortality) that even though he was awaiting encounters with sublimity, Emerson showed "tough-minded awareness of the sheer drag and waste of daily life, the wearing down of hope by time" (12).

Howe seems ambivalent in his treatment of Emerson's attempt to reconstitute religious faith in secular form. On the one hand, he says that Emerson's recombination of the fragments of the old faith was a notable intellectual maneuver: "He collapsed the distinction between religious and secular, so that the exultations of the one might be summoned for the needs of the other." On the other hand, Howe observes (as he would often do about the secularized version of Judaism called "Jewishness") that Emerson's faith was amorphous: "Everything grows more slippery and insubstantial . . . " (12).

But Emerson's centrality for American culture—and Howe reminds his audience that he writes from a "non-Emersonian angle of vision"

(15)—cannot be understood merely from a scrutiny of his inner spiritual development. Rather, it was his project, begun at about the time he resigned his ministry, to elaborate the myth of what later came to be called American exceptionalism, the phenomenon Howe had just examined in his book on socialism in America. Here too, as in the previous book, he confirms the death of his earlier Marxism by roundly asserting that "myth is itself a reality, and American myth an American reality, the most powerful and enduring that we have" (16). What Emerson now tried to do was to overreach the founding fathers. Unlike all the other reformers, crusaders, utopians, and cranks of his time, "he improvises a strategy for engaging the consciousness of the nation as a whole. . . . He starts from where people actually are—slipping away from but still held by religious faith—and helps them move to where, roughly, they want to go: an enlightened commonality of vision justifying pride in the republic, a vision akin to, yet distinct from, religious faith." Thus did Emerson attempt to make the remains of religious sentiment the grounding for a high public culture, "to make new the new republic" (20). Very far from being a revolutionist in the ordinary sense, Emerson spoke for a permanent revolution of the spirit.

Casting aside, at least temporarily, his old socialist censoriousness, Howe says that Emerson recognized the flaws of his society, but did not think them serious enough to block that reformation of being which was the imperative of the moment. All traditional authorities, customary manners, oppressive castes, would be thrust aside to make way for man himself in his natural perfection. Emerson did not, contrary to popular supposition, propose withdrawal from public life or ignore social conditions; rather, this nonpolitical man was really, in his own way (which had rarely been Howe's), the most political of Americans, one who called for that revolution of spirit "which encompasses and dwarfs all other revolutions." In doing so, he set the agenda for generations to come, and not only in America—Howe quotes Trotsky and David Ben-Gurion as examples of exported Emersonianism in modern political leaders. Emerson's project failed because he did not adequately reckon with the circumstances of his moment. But then, it is to be remembered, "all such projects fail" (26), and Emerson's great failure counts for more than many a mean success.

By Part II of The American Newness, "Disciples and Critics," it is clear that Howe has undertaken to view American literature itself in relation to Emersonianism, which may serve as influence or foil. He begins with two of Emerson's disciples, Thoreau and Whitman. Although Thoreau grasped better even than Emerson himself the "immediate guise of the alienation they both deplored" in the fact that the laboring man lacked the leisure for a life of integrity, he coarsened, Howe charges, the texture of Emersonian thought. He was too eager to offer "answers" to the problems of life, answers that turned out to be merely literary. That Emerson recognized this, says Howe, is evident from his cutting note: "My dear Henry, A frog was made to live in a swamp, but a man was not made to live in a swamp" (34). Howe also accuses Thoreau of adopting a view of freedom too absolute, not sufficiently dependent, as Emerson's was, on communal experience. Not surprisingly, Howe chastises Thoreau for the political implications of his saying that "a man more right than his neighbors constitutes a majority of one already" (35). How does one establish that rightness or deal with competing claims of rightness? Howe sees in Thoreau's absolutist vision the germ of both the "conservative bullying and radical posturing" (35) that would undercut American democracy in the decades to come. Candidly, he grants that "if I have been unfair to Thoreau, it is because I have meant to be unfair. . . . His intellectual style seems to me troubling, sometimes repellent" (36).

Whitman, by contrast, broadened the Emersonian vision while remaining true to its core. Howe sees him as both enchanting and alarming Emerson, for whom Whitman's poetry took the vision of democratic sublimity to places he could hardly imagine, much less approach: "to alleyways and cellars, boardinghouses and military hospitals." True, democratizing the sublime meant risking the loss of an aspect of sublimity. Whitman aspired to satisfy Emerson's prescription that the American poet evoke the new democratic man, but he did so less through exaltation than through variety and possibility.

Even with two such disciples of genius, Howe argues, the Emersonian vision was flitting and elusive, partly because it may be delusive to assume that a new country must give rise to a new mankind, partly because the favorable American setting that Emerson took for granted was already being overtaken by history, and partly "because a project of this kind . . . is never to be completed" (38). At a lower level of discourse than Thoreau and Whitman (and the [mainly] adversary Hawthorne), Howe notes (probably with a backward glance at his own youthful rigidities) that "a time of reforming zeal brings a clutter of cranks, fanatics, and bores. In the years of 'the newness' there were fanatics, despots of conscience, for whom any political compromise seemed the work of the devil. There were cranks who thought converse with the ordinary world a stain of corruption" (39).

But what exactly, from the point of view of the world's practical men, was Emerson's message? So asked, Howe candidly acknowledges, the question cannot be answered. What of the linked suspicion that Emerson makes consciousness both the beginning and the end of existence, assimilating everything, and all in order "to serve as a light not upon experience but upon itself" (40)? Did T. S. Eliot have this imperial consciousness in mind when he made his sardonic remark that New England was "refined beyond the point of civilization"? What, then, did Emerson really propose? What did he want?

Howe's reply to these urgent inquiries is revealing in its very ambivalence. He confesses to frustration even with Emerson's key terms, such as power, self-union, the sublime, self-reliance. The last, especially, leads to a central difficulty in Emersonian thought: namely, "a tragic sundering between democratic sentiment and individualist aggrandizement." Emerson seems to propose almost nothing yet to want almost everything. Isn't there, Howe aggressively asks, something unsatisfying in this stress on nearly absolute self-sufficiency and self-reliance, something impoverished in the related view "that contents itself with individualism as ideology" (42)? Doesn't this suppress life's complexities, possibilities, dangers, necessary entanglements? Howe maintains that the "individual" is itself a historical development, a social construct, neither fixed nor separate from time and circumstance.

But now, having played the devil's advocate, Howe comes again to Emerson's defense. If the Emersonian anthropology can be shaken by historical criticism, so can that criticism itself. Twentieth-century experience shows the inadequacies not only of absolutist individualism but also of too sweeping an attack upon it. Perhaps, he concludes, there is no perfect balance between these rival claims. Experience indubitably feels both, even as thought hungers to make them one. Argument, so far as Howe is concerned, must here yield to anecdotes, of which he supplies one from Rashi's Commentaries on the Pentateuch (one of his rare allusions to classical Jewish texts) and one from his old favorite, Silone. Both evoke "a sharing of travail that . . . the cult of self-reliance is ill-equipped to grasp." He then returns to American literature to find critiques of cunning individualism in Hawthorne's "My Kinsman, Major Molineaux" and of aggrandizing individualism in Melville's *Moby Dick.*

Within a few years, by the 1840s, Howe argues, the sanguine Emersonian project was overwhelmed by the rapid pace of American social change: slavery, the vulgarization of democratic politics, the new industrialism. Slavery had broken into Emerson's calm, forcing him "into the commonplace world of politics, reform, compromise." Worse, perhaps, he was experiencing the rise of politics as mass culture, "a phenomenon we have lived to see in its full beauty." Finally, there was the new economy, with robber barons, multimillionaires, corporations, strikes, lockouts, hordes of what Emerson called "immigrants speaking scores of tongues" (51). (With respect to the last, Howe sharply criticizes Emerson for pleading against the growing concern with "the masses," since Emerson could not understand that in the new industrial world conditions of life made collective action necessary if these "rude" masses were ever to reach individual definition.)

The more Howe writes about Emerson's difficulty in accommodating his vision of a newness rooted in individual consciousness to new social and political pressures, the more personal does his tone become. He reflects, for example, on Emerson's turning down the invitation to join the Brook Farm colony: "He might have said, what was true, that he was quite unsuited for such a place—just as today there are socialists, among whom I number, who would have to be driven by gunpoint before they would enter a commune, their hopes for a better world stopping short of the claustrophobic littleness of such colonies" (57). The vision of Howe on a commune is droll enough; but it may call to mind, disturbingly, the Marxist condemnation of small-scale experiments in socialism as "utopian" because they do not impose their vision on all of society without first testing it on themselves.

Of the three impediments that arose in the forties to Emerson's vision, the one that Howe stresses most is the slavery question. Emerson "kept rationalizing and equivocating" (59) about the Abolitionist cause. Howe cites as evidence of this vacillation two contrasting passages from the early 1850s, one a fierce denunciation of the "filthy" Fugitive Slave law, the other a "notorious" passage in which Emerson at first blames himself for not getting involved in the struggle against slavery, but then decides that "God must govern his own world . . . without my desertion of my post which has none to guard it but me. I have quite other slaves to free than those negroes, to wit, imprisoned spirits, imprisoned thoughts, far back in the brain of man." Howe, who had sharpened his critical eye for such licentious equations in writing about Sylvia Plath's appropriation of the Holocaust to magnify her personal problems, rejects the admiring reading of this passage as being merely about the old conflict between personal interest and social conscience. Instead, he upbraids Emerson for "something sadly disingenuous . . . when he uses language to suggest an equivalence or even similarity, between 'slave' meaning shackled men and women and 'slave' referring to undeveloped thoughts and spirits" (59–60).[26]

Seeing in Emerson's debate with the abolitionists a foreshadowing of twentieth-century disputes he had experienced, Howe notes that a year later Emerson subjected the abolitionist Wendell Phillips to "a kind of criticism which in our time would be made familiar by Lionel Trilling in his writings about 'the liberal imagination.'" Emerson had said of social activists like Phillips that "in a lonely world . . . these would find nothing to do. . . . [Phillips] had only a *platform*-existence, & no personality." Howe instinctively knows Emerson is wrong here because the very same thing might have been said about Thomas: ". . . in this world of wretchedness, where men like Phillips and Thomas are always in short supply, is Emerson's charge really so damning? When Phillips stood up against a lynch mob, didn't he show as much self-reliance as Thoreau subsisting on several and a half pennies in his hut?" (60). As so often, Howe's criticism is enriched by a passion arising from deep personal involvement. He too had experienced the conflict between public and private, political and literary life. Emerson had come down a bit too strongly, too confidently, on the side that Howe himself, really, had chosen; and for this he deserved a reprimand. "Emerson does not confront the possibility that the self may achieve a variety of fulfillments, including some beyond the reach of Concord. Why should he have supposed that the true self is to be cultivated best or only in the woods or, failing that, in the study? That it must be private, insulated, unspotted?" (60–61).

In the final section of *The American Newness*, "The Literary Legacy," Howe tries to measure the influence of "the newness" on nineteenth-century American literature by viewing it in relation to the Emersonian vision. This is the most leisurely and expansive section of the book, given over to relatively lengthy analyses of particular literary works. Howe proposes a tripartite division: the literature of work; the literature of anarchic bliss; and the literature of loss, announcing and mourning the end of "the newness." The first is close in subject and spirit to Emerson's vision; the second is more distant from, and sometimes hostile to, it; the third is a bitter reaction against the hopes of "the newness."

The first category is illustrated in such celebrations of the satisfactions of craft and the wholeness of independent work as Twain's *Life on the Mississippi* and parts of *Moby Dick*, as well as in early Melville. This thin but precious strand of American writing is a truly democratic literature, and in that sense satisfies Emerson's prescription; "but insofar as it rests mainly with a social or outer mode of existence and a secular view of man's destiny, it cannot finally respond to Emerson's call" (70). Perhaps it is only in Whitman, another celebrant of work, that the publicly democratic and the personally sublime are successfully fused.

The second, and for Howe richer, tradition has little relation to Emerson, for it is anarchistic, pacific, and utopian. It is informed by the assumption that "because of our blessed locale we could find space . . . in which to return, backward and free, to a stateless fraternity . . . " (71). This body of writing is embodied by James Fenimore Cooper's anarchist idyll, *Leatherstocking Tales*, and *Huckleberry Finn*, in which anarchic bliss resides on a river. Howe's remarks about this classic remind us of his deeply ingrained love of fraternity, going back to the Faulkner book, where he had described it as finer even than equality. He describes Huck's decision to help Jim even if it means going to hell as a triumph of "anarchic fraternity over registered authority. In this state of friendliness men do not need society—at least so we learn in nineteenth-century American fiction" (73). Howe also discusses variants of the theme of anarchic fraternity in early Melville, in Thoreau, even in Hawthorne. This body of writing, unlike the literature that celebrated autonomous work, lacked a basis in experience. Rather, "the enchanting mirage of unconditioned freedom speaks for some deep compulsion in the American spirit, perhaps a regret over its own existence. . . . [our writers] lapsed, with a mixture of pleasure and sadness, into that mythic quest for bliss they knew to be a chimera" (74).

The "newness" began to wane in the 1850s, when, Howe observes sourly, "a good many writers lapse into a weariness that sometimes is called realism, as if to admit the futility of great expectations" (75). Indeed, Emerson himself, as early as 1841, began to sound a note of uneasiness and self-doubt, as he wavered "between public engagement and a self-contained integrity." Once more, Howe is drawn back, almost compulsively it seems, to Emerson's crisis of 1851 when, raging against the Fugitive Slave law, he found it intolerable that "this filthy enactment was made in the 19th century by people who could read and write" and vows that he will not obey it. Having defined, in rather an exalted way, "the newness" of the thirties and forties, Howe now appears to turn upon himself and Emerson as well, and conclude that the newness fades as Emerson begins to yield to his social conscience, and is forced by it to become "a little more active in the movement against slavery" (76).

Here, once again, Howe's personal involvement with conflicting forces within American culture comes to the fore. But whereas in "Strangers," the essay of a decade earlier, Howe had examined the divide between American literature and its Jewish immigrant readers, he now writes as if from inside the tradition (and this in a way that might have amused Ralph Ellison). "Had I been alive at the time, I would probably have been on Phillips's side, raising hell in fine Abolitionist style and scoffing at Emerson's fastidious refusal to join the good fight. It now seems to me that I would have been partly wrong, failing to recognize that if the urgencies of the moment were finally prodding Emerson toward the Abolitionists, that also meant he was being driven to abandon or compromise his true vocation. It was a vocation that committed reformers, then and now, could not always acknowledge" (76).

To become a reformer of society, "*then and now*," meant to surrender the ideals of individuality and consciousness. Thus does Howe come down on the other, the nonreformist, side of the conundrum, as if to acknowledge what is lost by public engagement. Once again, his tone is intensely personal: "Once Emerson was forced to think in time, and pay closer attention to his own times, his great moment came to an end. *Anyone who has ever had to struggle with the conflict between public obligation and personal desire can only sympathize with his hesitations and uncertainties*" [emphasis added] (77). Howe, already sixty-five and mindful of how much of his life had been devoted to lost causes such as socialism and secular Jewishness[27] and humanistic literary criticism, pleads for understanding of the "older Emerson" (at that time forty-three was "older"), trapped, "like the rest of us," in circumstance, loss, depletion (78). "Whoever has known the collapse of a large ideal will share Emerson's pain" (79). So strong does Howe's identification with Emerson grow toward the end of this book that he actually tries to imitate Emerson's style and feelings by writing a faked entry from Emerson's journal of the middle 1850s reacting to Melville's *Bartleby, the Scrivener,* a work that Howe reads as an attack on Emerson's way of thought.

In conclusion, Howe asserts that, despite growing limp as a social creed and declining in the Gilded Age, Emersonianism has "remained sharp, strong, and critical in our culture" and is everywhere visible both in writers who align themselves with its claims and in those who reject them. He expresses confidence that "the newness" will come again because it is intrinsic to American life. His own hope—no surprises here—is that it will take the form of "a difficult mixture of social liberalism and a reaffirmed and critical sense of self." He ends by quoting Emerson's call for patience until a nation of men will arise for the first time. "Patience?" asks the once very impatient Howe, now assuming the mask of Emerson. "After all these bitter years? Darkened with the knowledge of loss, [Emerson] speaks again: 'Never mind the ridicule, never mind the defeat; up again, old heart!—it seems to say—there is victory yet for all justice'" (88–89). The critic and his subject having become one, the book closes.

The intensely personal note of the conclusion of *The American Newness* almost certainly arises from the crisis of confidence that Howe himself was feeling at this time. In a letter of August 1986 to his collaborator and friend Ruth Wisse, Howe wrote that, having reached sixty-five, he was at a transitional point in his life. This was not only because of his retirement from teaching at CUNY but because sixty-five symbolized entering the last lap, whether long or short. He thought he was writing better than ever before (which is true) but was uncertain of his direction. He could easily continue with "shtiklakh" [morsels or pieces] but that was just what he wanted to avoid. He felt himself—amazing revelation from someone who continually astounds us by the depth and breadth of his knowledge—to be ignorant, a jack of all trades and master of none. He was too old to be able to afford the risk of a wrong turn into something sterile or unsuitable. He wanted to return more fully to literary criticism but felt his eyes glaze over when he read deconstructionism.[28] In the event, as we shall see, Howe overcame this crisis and recognized that the sick ophthalmia of the new literary age lay in the deconstructionists and not in himself.

Rescuing Literature and Democratic Culture from the Theorists, 1986–92

During the forties and again during the sixties and early seventies, Howe had gone into combat against literary radicals who saw little intrinsic value in literature and sought to use it mainly as an instrument of their political ambitions. In the middle to late eighties, he came to the sombre recognition that this was a battle that could never be won decisively, yet had to be entered again and again. The newest wave of literary utilitarians came not in the guise of Stalinists or Marxists (although many of them were) but of "theorists," sometimes deconstructionists, sometimes sociologists manqués, often people who professed literature, but didn't much care for it. In the last years of his life, Howe found himself more and more at odds with the dominant tendencies of literary criticism. Like his mentor Matthew Arnold, he had always believed that although criticism might, at certain historical junctures, be a more pressing task than creation, creation always remained, in an absolute sense and in the long run, the higher activity. Of literary theory, as distinct from practical criticism, he had always been suspicious. But now he found that critical theoreticians sought not only to establish their equality with (if not superiority to) literary creators, but to call into question the integrity of literary creation itself. His response, in some sense heroic, came in a series of essays that sought to reaffirm the value of literature in its own right as well as its ability to confront, if not master, even the horror and incoherence of this most terrible of centuries, now approaching its end.

The first of these essays, and the only one that tries to integrate Howe's Jewish commitments with his literary concerns, is "Writing and the Holocaust," one of the most astute discussions that exists of "how literature has (and has not) met its greatest challenge" ("Writing and the Holocaust," 27). For many years, Howe had been skeptical of the very idea of a "Holocaust literature" and deeply troubled by the critical approaches taken to it by George Steiner and Lawrence Langer. At least once, and probably twice, he recommended against publication of Langer's manuscript on the Holocaust and the literary imagination when a press sent it for his review. He detested the "phenomenological" treatment, still more what he considered Langer's high-toned existentialist spirituality about six million corpses.[29] But from late 1979 through 1982 he worked sporadically on editing a collection of short novels dealing with the Holocaust, intending to include Pierre Gascar's *Beasts and Men*, Aharon Appelfeld's *Badenheim 1939*, and a work by Primo Levi. (Although in September 1982 he referred to the book as due out in late October, it never appeared.)

The essay begins with a startling confession of incapacity: "we may read the Holocaust as the central event of this century; we may register the pain of its unhealed wounds; but finally we must acknowledge that it leaves us intellectually disarmed, staring helplessly at the reality or, if you prefer, the mystery of mass extermination" (27). No rational structure of explanation for the Holocaust is ever likely to be found, for it forms a sequence of events without historical or moral precedent. Likewise, no aesthetic can prepare us for the multitudinous problems involved in the literary imagination's "use" of the Holocaust.

But if the Holocaust is a unique historical event, it must not, Howe warns, be viewed as an occurrence outside of history. To do so would be to absolve the perpetrators of the Holocaust of their responsibility.[30] Those perpetrators were ruled by an idea which Howe describes as "an abstract rage, the most terrible of all rages" (27). So far from presenting the Holocaust as a ghastly irruption of nightmare into history, Howe presents the Nazi idea as a "low parody" of two impulses that had touched even him. He follows Singer in seeing Nazism as a travesty of the "messianism that declared that once mankind offered a warrant of faith and conduct, deliverance would come to earth in the shape of a savior bringing the good days—a notion corrupted by false messiahs into a 'forcing of days' and by totalitarian movements into the physical elimination of 'contaminating' races *and classes* [emphasis added]" (27). Just how far Howe had come in his understanding of Nazism from the jejune notion of his Trotskyist days that it was just another form of the dying capitalist system is evident in his identifying in Nazi ideology also a debased version of "that yearning or mania for 'completely' remaking societies and cultures that has marked modern political life" (27). Thus Nazism is linked, albeit as travesty, with both the messianic and utopian impulses that had touched Howe himself.

Following his introductory remarks, Howe cites several powerful statements of opposition to making the Holocaust into literary material. The critic Adorno, the poet Zeitlin, and the novelist Rawicz all expressed the view that the literary manner applied to the Holocaust is an obscenity, in Rawicz's words "the art, occasionally remunerative, of rummaging in vomit." Nevertheless, they all proceeded to do what they had inveighed against. But all, Howe points out, wished to stress the literary risk, the moral peril, of dealing with the Holocaust in literature. Given the improbability of coming up with images and symbols that might serve as "objective correlatives" for events the imagination can hardly take in, writers—these writers warned—might be wise to be silent. Perhaps they also feared that representing a horrible event in art serves to domesticate it, make it familiar and tolerable; or, worse yet, that one might gain the pleasure of "catharsis" from the aesthetic experience of a representation or evocation of the Holocaust.

Of course, the corruptions of the mass media led most writers to ignore these cautionary words. To illustrate his point, Howe invents a savage anecdote about the popular novelist Gerald Green: "I think here of a story that I have on the highest authority. The producers of the television serial called 'Holocaust' first approached Leo Tolstoy with a tempting offer to write the script, for they had heard he was the author of some good books. After listening to them politely, the Russian writer turned pale and mumbled: 'No, no, there are some things that even I cannot do. For what you want, you should turn to Gerald Green'" (29). Howe, in certain respects the inveterate secularist, here identifies with the old-fashioned religious feeling that there are some things that are too terrible to be looked at or into directly: "Perseus would turn to stone if he were to look directly at the serpent-headed Medusa, though he would be safe if he looked at her only through a reflection in a mirror or a shield . . . " (29). Eventually, Howe will argue that the shrewder writers have adopted precisely this strategy of indirection in dealing with the Holocaust, and wonders whether Adorno wanted to suggest that the Holocaust was a secular equivalent of that which in the ancient myths could not be gazed at or named directly.

Howe then moves to memoirs and diaries of the Holocaust. Memoirs have especially high value because Holocaust writings "often reveal the helplessness of the mind before an evil that cannot quite be imagined, or the helplessness of the imagination before an evil that cannot quite be understood." In the memoir, the author's sole obligation is to tell, accurately and soberly, what he experienced and witnessed. The respect given to memoirs may be due to our conviction that human experience is not to be judged primarily by an aesthetic standard and that—here is an old subject for Howe, one to which he brought a ripened wisdom—"there can be, indeed often enough have been, situations in which aesthetic and moral standards come into conflict" (30). The memoirs of Holocaust witnesses, in telling us of unbearable and therefore unforgettable human experiences, summon a past without which we cannot know the time we have lived in or where we have come from. They remind us of the need to keep the Holocaust in the realm of history, so that it is neither "universalized" in the manner of William Styron nor diminished into the legend of a small and insignificant people. They also—and Howe cites as example of what he means Elie Wiesel's expression of guilty relief, in *Night*, at the death of his father—help to dissolve the impulse to judge what the victims did or did not do, "since there are situations so extreme that it seems immoral to make judgments about those who must endure them" (30), a point Howe had stressed in the long-ago debate over Hannah Arendt's book.

But what about making critical judgments of the memoirs themselves? The "skeptical voice" that Howe tends to invent in so many of his last essays as a kind of devil's advocate asks whether it is not naive to make grand claims for Holocaust memoirs. This imagined skeptic notes that memory can be treacherous, especially in people who have suffered greatly and may even feel guilt at still being alive. In reply, Howe argues that our respect for the sufferer need not prevent us from making critical distinctions among memoirs, discriminations of value, tone, authority. These can be made through the usual historical tests and also through that "indispensable organ, the reader's ear, bending toward credence or doubt" (31). Howe then offers a cogent and sensitive method for reading and evaluating Holocaust memoirs. A tactful reader will respond not only to accounts of what happened, but to qualities of being, tremors of sensibility, modesty or boastfulness, self-effacement or self-promotion, above all to the quality that, we may recall, Howe had located over three decades earlier in Yiddish literature: "*moral poise*, by which I mean a readiness to engage in a complete reckoning with the past, insofar as there can be one—a strength of remembrance that leads the writer into despair and then perhaps a little beyond it, so that he does not flinch from anything . . . yet refuses to indulge in those outbursts of self-pity, sometimes sliding into self-aggrandizement, that understandably mar a fair number of Holocaust memoirs" [emphasis added] (31–32).[31]

Still, Howe is somewhat uneasy about introducing aesthetic considerations into the discussion of testimonies by survivors; indeed, his ready acknowledgment of uneasiness, uncertainty, and incapacity in these late literary essays is part of their greatness. Much as he would like to yield his heart entirely to the demands of memory and evidence, he cannot, as a reader, ever forget that "the diarist was a person formed before and the memoirist a person formed after the Holocaust." Hence tests of authenticity become unavoidable; and Howe refers, but without naming names, to memoirists who fail this test because they have been ensnared by ideology or self-aggrandizement. His positive examples are Chaim Kaplan (*Warsaw Diary*), Filip Mueller (*Eyewitness Auschwitz*), and Levi (*Survival in Auschwitz*). There is, finally, no escape from the obligation to distinguish and discriminate: "Our desire to see the Holocaust in weightier terms than the merely aesthetic lures us into a shy recognition of the moral reverberations of the aesthetic" (32).

Precisely what, then, can the literary imagination add to the materials of Holocaust memory? "What could be the organizing categories, the implicit premises of perception and comprehension, through which the literary imagination might be able to render intelligible the gassing of 12,000 people a day at Auschwitz?" How can the novelist go beyond the documentation of such memoirists as Kaplan, Mueller, David Rousset (*Univers Concentrationnaire*), and Levi? The novelist may have studied and tried to make sense of the facts accumulated in memoirs and histories, but he needs something more, which usually comes unbidden in fictions about ordinary themes: "namely, a structuring set of ethical premises, to which are subordinately linked aesthetic biases, through which he can form, that is, integrate his materials." But in this case—when a writer broods over an infinity of murder and torture—such ethical premises and aesthetic biases are lacking. Writers who see the futility of realism in representing the Holocaust also encounter difficulties, for there are very few myths and metaphors that will work as recognizable analogues for the Holocaust experience. "Before *this* reality, the imagination comes to seem intimidated, overwhelmed, helpless . . . it can describe happenings, but not endow them with the autonomy and freedom of a complex fiction . . . " (33).

The novelist, unlike the memoirist, must, to tell a story, make sense of his materials. But, Howe argues, there are several objective reasons why he rarely succeeds. First, the Holocaust is not a dramatic subject. The mass murders of dazed and broken people, barely capable of responding to their fate, have little of drama in them. Drama requires a conflict of wills, inner clashes of belief, both rarities in the killing centers. Likewise, the death camps and killing centers gave little space for the tragic: "In classical tragedy man is defeated; in the Holocaust man is destroyed." For the vast majority of Jews, death involved no choice, and therefore no martyrdom. "They died . . . not because they chose at all costs to remain Jews, but because the Nazis chose to believe that being Jewish was an unchangeable, irredeemable condition. . . . All of this does not make their death less terrible; it makes their death more terrible" (34). In the past even writers who were determinists or naturalists intuitively sensed that to animate their narratives they had to give their fictional characters at least a touch of freedom; and this is exactly what the Holocaust writer, if he is honest, cannot do.

After discussing the Holocaust fiction of the non-Jewish Polish writer Tadeusz Borowski and the Ukrainian Jew Rawicz, Howe rounds off his essay by suggesting a simple division of Holocaust writers into those who write of the time before, those who write of the time during, and those who write of the time after, the Holocaust. His chief example of the first is the Israeli writer Appelfeld. Better than anyone else, Appelfeld understood the need to approach his subject indirectly. He told Howe, *"m'ken nisht"* (Yiddish for "one cannot") (36), to explain why his novels about the Holocaust did not represent it directly, but ended before or started after the killings. His novel *Badenheim 1939* neither spoke of nor showed what was to follow; wisely, it never named the unspeakable. For Holocaust fiction that conveys, but again obliquely, the "during," Howe recommends Gascar's long story "The Seasons of the Dead"; and for "after" another long story, "A Plaque on Via Mazzini," by Giorgio Bassani. For a profound consideration of the "aftermath" he proposes the great story by the Yiddish writer Chaim Grade called "My Quarrel with Hersh Rasseyner."

Although an essay of enormous power and insight, "Writing and the Holocaust" ends on no consolatory, transcendent, or redemptive note. On the contrary, Howe insists that reaching for such notes is a main source of the falsity that infects many accounts of the Holocaust, whether memoir or fiction, as well as the language of eloquence-prone commentators, guilty of what Eliot called the natural sin of language. This is a realm in which literature can succeed only by failing. The human imagination, he concludes, cannot encompass or transfigure the crimes of Auschwitz: "Some losses cannot be made up, neither in time nor eternity. They can only be mourned" (39).

"Writing and the Holocaust," in which Howe probed deeply the relations between the aesthetic and the moral, the imaginative and the historical, as they have been formed (and malformed) by modern history, may be said to have defined, by example, the condition to which literary criticism should now aspire. Subsequently, he published (also in the *New Republic*) a series of essays, intended as parts of a book about the novel tentatively entitled *Selected Short Subjects*,[32] in which he analyzed the maladies of literary criticism as it was currently being practiced, sharply challenging the claims (and mockingly revealing the absurdities) of the new literary imperialists.

In "The Human Factor" (May 1989) Howe took issue with the newly fashionable critical idea that we must never suppose that literary characters in any way resemble actual persons. A critic whose name Howe does not deign to mention argues, for example, that "Emma Woodhouse is not a woman nor need be described as if it were." Upon this feeble witticism Howe acidly comments that "a large gain in critical perception is evidently registered by calling Emma an 'it.'"[33] Such critics insist that readers repress the natural impulse to describe the conduct and motives of characters in the language ordinarily available to them and instead see the characters only as elements or functions in the operation of the narrative. "And," adds Howe, again with marked acerbity, "we are to repress our knowledge . . . that the great novelists strove with all their powers to make characters who would indeed *seem* like actual persons. Taking that into account might be to share the ignorance of genius" (30).

Howe singles out one of the new theorists, the "barely readable" Hélène Cixous, for having carried an already foolish theory to its most extreme form with the help of what he views as leftism gone mad. She argues that a novel with mimetic characters is a machine of bourgeois repression because it presents a historical fact or situation as if it were absolute and eternal. Roland Barthes has supplied a variant of this "idea" in his argument that use of the preterite tense is a bourgeois justification of the status quo. Such bizarre notions of fictional characterization, Howe observes, arise from a confusion between narrative conventions and social categories. Besides, he contentiously asks, "where . . . have our strongest visions of possibility, as also our most telling social criticisms, come from, if not the great novelists?" (30). Moreover, the critical visions of those novelists have survived while the ideological formulas of the social theorists "have all too often been ripped apart by historical change" (31).

In what sense, then, asks Howe, do literary characters "exist"? The answer is twofold. The shape of a novel, including such formal elements as the arrangement and proportion of its parts, helps to determine the nature of its characters. But the novel is also "a mimesis, an imitation drawing upon the writer's observations, intuition, and imaginings—a mixture of his own experience and his relations to other writers dead and alive." Where but from his own experience does a writer draw the moral and psychological traits of his characters? Theoretical critics may be partly correct in replying: from past writers. But surely, says Howe, "*somewhere* a writer must have engaged in direct observation on his own" (31). Literature (unike criticism) cannot feed off itself forever. Although he does not cite Proust, Howe is in effect reiterating the Frenchman's attack on "the fatal progress of aestheticism which ends by eating its own tail." If the theorists are also partly correct in saying that the writer draws upon his imagination, it is at least as important to add that imagination is not hermetically sealed against reality but is a way of engaging reality. The novel is both mirror and lamp. To function as elements of narrative, characters must in some way resemble actual persons. "Who'd even look at Emma Woodhouse if she were just an 'it'?" As a *reductio ad absurdum* for the arguments of those who would eliminate the human factor from literary characterization, Howe offers the apparently rhetorical question of William Gass about Henry James's Mr. Cashmore in *The Awkward Age*. By way of showing how little this character is conceived of as imitating anyone, Gass asks just what we really know about him: do we even know whether he has a nose? To which unintentionally comic query Howe replies "very likely; if he didn't, James would have been the first to notice" (33).

Howe concludes with his own question, but one to which he offers no firm answer. "Why should there be, in the academy, this humorless and pleasure-denying attack upon the mimetic view of character?" If this is a time when genuine individuality keeps withering, one would suppose that literary people "would see the value of such terms as self, individual, personality, character" (33). These may be frail defenses for a humane or humanist view of literature and humanity, but this should make them all the more valuable. Once again, as in the essay on Holocaust literature, Howe balances and integrates the aesthetic and the moral to affirm his lifelong belief in literature as an art meant to encourage moral awareness and humane understanding.

A month later, Howe published another attack upon "the treason of the critics" in relation to their role as mediators between literature and a democratic audience. What, he asks, has happened to the idea of the "common reader," that figure famously defined by Dr. Johnson in his life of Thomas Gray. "I rejoice," Johnson had written, "to concur with the common reader: for by the common sense of readers, uncorrupted by literary prejudices, after all the refinements of subtlety and the dogmatism of learning, must finally be decided all claims to literary honors." Although the exact meaning of Johnson's term might be in dispute, it is clear, says Howe, that the common reader was not a professional or a university man (and probably lacked Latin). When Virginia Woolf picked up the term in the twentieth century, she and her Bloomsbury friends had begun to suspect that the common reader, like the man of letters, was vanishing as literary life became increasingly professionalized after the First World War. At that time, advanced literary circles began to take the view that the genteel amateurism of both the common reader and the man of letters had brought about the decline of genuine literary criticism into impressionist chatter.

Of course, Howe knew from experience that this version of literary history was not the whole truth. Had he not himself begun as an imitator of such men of letters as Matthew Arnold, George Orwell, and Edmund Wilson? Did not the *Partisan Review* and *Kenyon Review* critics address themselves to a modified version of the common reader in the small audience of nonspecialists? Did they not write as if they had in their conjectural audience readers besides other critics? So far from being enamored of the "dogmatism of learning," the critics who flourished in the forties and fifties even, as we have seen, harbored a prejudice against the universities and their scholarly specialists. Although the prominent critics of those years did not shy away from difficulty, they did strive for clarity. "Almost every critic," says Howe, "would have agreed with Allen Tate's remark that 'critical style ought to be as plain as the nose on one's face.'"[34] But in the early 1950s many of these critics (like Tate and Howe himself, of course) migrated to the universities, a move which was a practical advantage but an ominous development.

Between the two world wars, Howe argues, there was a proliferation of literary publics, among them several kinds of common readers. One distinction of importance was between the literary quarterlies and political weeklies that involved their readers in intellectual exchange and debate, and a magazine like the *New Yorker* which (most notoriously, as we have seen, in its publication of Arendt's *Eichmann in Jerusalem*) presented the work of its contributors as the authoritative final word, not to be challenged by its passively receptive consumers.

Whether the idea of the common reader was an actuality or a hypothesis, it served, in Howe's view, the highly useful purpose—at least during the decade or two following the Second World War—of encouraging critics to address themselves to somebody outside the profession, outside the academy. But all this changed radically in later decades. "There now flourishes an academic community of younger, accomplished, and . . . self-assured professors of literature for whom the idea of the common reader seems to be of small interest. . . . Today most of the ambitious and talented young people within the literary academy publish only in journals read by their colleagues, and they seem to find this an acceptable . . . condition" (30). These people, ostensibly professors of literature, actually prefer the most purely "theoretical" kind of literary theory. They show little interest not only in the common reader but in literature itself. They find more sustenance in the aforementioned Cixous than in leading novelists. They produce students who are better acquainted with the works of Jacques Derrida than with the novels of Dickens or George Eliot, and are contemptuous of classmates who prefer reading novels and poems to reading modern critical theory. Moreover, they are content to address themselves exclusively to other theorists.

But if literary culture is to be confined to the academy, what happens, Howe asks, to the idea of a democratic culture that has been cherished and advocated by nearly every major American critic since Emerson and Whitman? The decline in both the presence and the idea of the common reader is not the fault of the university literature departments alone, of course. It has also been caused by "the spreading blight of television, the slippage of the magazines, the disasters of our school system, the native tradition of anti-intellectualism, the cultivation of ignorance by portions of the counterculture, the breakdown of coherent political and cultural publics, the loss of firm convictions within the educated classes . . . " (30). But, warns Howe, a democratic politics cannot thrive without a democratic culture. The relative absence of a reactionary politics among the inwardly directed literary academics is not enough to offset the effect of their professional elitism. Nor is their comical version of Marxism any cause for satisfaction. In a moment of nostalgia for his now discarded Marxism, Howe observes that "whatever Marxism may have been, it always saw itself attached to, or in search of, a mass movement of the working class. It was not merely a 'method' for literary criticism. But Marxism has gone to the universities to die in comfort" (31).

In conclusion, Howe insists that a truly democratic culture requires a vital bond between writers and "an active, autonomous public, neither academic nor professionally literary, perhaps small, but providing writers with a flow of sentiment and response." (Without mentioning it, Howe must surely here have in mind Yiddish literature, which took for granted a living, responding culture, in which the writers lived "next door" to their readers.) And he concludes with a piece of practical advice for the increasingly opaque contemporary practitioners of literary theory: namely, that they "speak in English, a language that for some time served criticism well" (31).

A far less combative and much more tentative segment of his projected book about the novel appeared in the New Republic for 3 September 1990. "History and the Novel" seems to start in medias res with the observation that most of the heroes and heroines of novels, unlike their predecessors in literature from the Aeneid through Faust, must find a way to support themselves. That is a way of saying that they are constrained by the commonplace necessities that press upon the rest of us. The reason why is that novels are time-bound, historically conditioned: "an illusion of historical stoppage is essential for that 'thickness' of specification at which many novels aim."[35]

Howe argues that Deism made the genre of the novel possible. Deism asserted that God started the world and then went to sleep, allowing its inhabitants to fend for themselves. In this way, it freed men from endlessly puzzling over origins and cleared the way for historical consciousness and the uncontested rule of natural law. Free from the dualisms of Christianity, modern novelists devised historical dualisms of their own. To the gloom of being distanced from heaven was now added the pain of feeling estranged from a society that appeared as indifferent to human beings as the universe was. Deism's putting God to sleep also, Howe believes, led to the assumption that there is a psychic presence called the self, an assumption premised on a separation of inner being from outer behavior, i.e., yet another dualism.

What, Howe asks, do we mean by the historicity of the novel? In *Middlemarch* Dorothea Brooke aspires to a heroic surmounting of circumstance, but this same circumstance limits not only her choice of vocation (unlike the novel's male characters, she can have none) but also her idea of what a heroic aspiration should be. Characters in novels emerge in part out of the writer's historical awareness. The novel is a genre resting on the assumption that it is not an unalterable human nature, but a sequence of human activities that forms man. "Man has no unchanging nature; what his nature does have is . . . a history" (30). Even novelists, like Fielding, who believe in immutable human characteristics, are touched by history in their work, albeit at times without knowing it.

History, Howe continues, makes itself felt in the best novels not as a mere reproduction of the familiar world; after all, even journalists can claim to provide accurate representation. Rather, the novel is expected—especially since the late nineteenth century—to be an agency of moral criticism, even a creator of values. History enters the novel not merely as depictions of how we live "now," but in the form of critical thought, popular sentiment, even ideologies of revolt. "Once past the sorts of novels written for amusement or shock, a representation of life can rarely be separated from a criticism of values" (30). The notion of the novel as providing a "slice of life" is brittle, for all representation implies perspective and selection, which entail criticism.

Novels with a strong political-historical slant, as Howe had discovered more than four decades earlier, make disinterested literary judgment difficult; social rhetoric and imaginative representation often conflict. Verisimilitude for Howe remains an important factor in the criticism of the novel, so that a novelist's rendering of historical events weighs heavily in estimating his aesthetic achievement. But readers with strong political opinions (of whom Howe is, of course, one) will always find great difficulty in separating ideological sentiments from literary judgments. Howe offers as an instance the problem of dealing with Dostoyevsky's *The Possessed*. "How can you say that *The Possessed* is both a great work of literature and also a work that offers a distorted, even malicious treatment of its subject?" (32). Perhaps, he acknowledges, there is no answer to this question, except to admit that the imperatives of literature and history may well conflict.

At this point, Howe—following his by now standard rhetorical practice—invents a devil's advocate to challenge his emphasis upon history as it impinges upon the novel. "History, yes," says the skeptic, "but what about the eternal themes, those recurrent human experiences . . . that . . . tell readers 'the secrets of their own hearts,' themes like love and death, innocence and experience, goodness and evil . . . ? Are not these the abiding concerns of literature, reducing to a quite secondary level all reflected changes of historical circumstances? . . . And what about the archetypal characters through whom the abiding myths are dramatized, do they not survive—Oedipus and Quixote, Clarissa Harlowe and Tess—even into the age of the computer?" (32). To this imagined devotee of the absolute and eternal themes, a descendant of Arnold perhaps, Howe responds with a "yes, but." The eternal themes, if they are stripped down to bare essentials, may come to seem commonplace or even boring. To affect readers, they must "take on flesh that will decay, be located in houses that will crumble. Eternity lodges in the temporal" (32). Even the most powerful archetypes may get worn down by time. If Oedipus, Hamlet, and Faust continue to flourish, what about Tristan or Clarissa? Do they still have the imaginative hold and authority they once did? And who now remembers such archetypes of the second rank as Sinclair Lewis's Babbitt?

Having demonstrated, to his own satisfaction, that the novel is never free from the shaping pressures of history, Howe goes on to discuss a few novels in which history is not just a felt presence but a completely dominant force. Among these are Stendhal's *The Red and the Black* and *The Charterhouse of Parma,* and Tolstoy's *War and Peace.* But Tolstoy also embodied the stunning paradox of someone who believed that history was at once everything (the whole sequence of human experience) and nothing (for it could not order or explain or justify human actions or characters by their roots in the past). This paradox was realized in *War and Peace,* where "the theorist of antihistory becomes the great portraitist of historical shaping" (33).

Howe brings this remarkable, magisterial essay to a conclusion by showing how "history may be the rock on which the novel rests, but time crumbles that rock into grains of sand" (33). He offers as an instance of how history may undo what history has helped to create the character of Sir Thomas Bertram in Jane Austen's *Mansfield Park* (1814). The head of the family that is at the center of the novel, Sir Thomas makes a business visit during the novel to the West Indies, and this at a time when slavery dominated those islands. This means, Howe observes, that he is almost certainly an owner of slaves himself. This fact does not seem to have disturbed Austen or, for that matter, most of the novel's critics (including Trilling in his famous essay on the novel). Howe himself, during his teaching years, used to "defend" Austen by telling students that the working of the West Indian estate is not central to the novel's action, and that we have to allow for the different standards of an earlier time, just as we hope a later age will make allowances for ours. But now, in 1990, he feels uneasy with this defense. Austen, to fulfill the plot requirement of getting Sir Thomas out of the way while his children and their friends plan an amateur theatrical, could have sent him to many other places. No—there is no evading the fact that Sir Thomas profits from the exploitation of black slavery and is yet accepted as a morally upright figure. Unlike Edward Said, who in his book *Culture and Imperialism* (1993), took *Mansfield Park* as sufficient evidence of its author's political wickedness, Howe does not leap to the conclusion that Austen approved of slavery. But he does recognize a problem in the fact that she could assign the patriarchal Sir Thomas a plantation in Antigua without feeling any uneasiness about his moral character.

It is, moreover, a problem to be found in many other novels as well. Howe admits he does not know exactly what is to be done about it. With some reluctance, he comes down on the side of the historical imagination which enables a reader to enter unfamiliar settings and recognize the integrity of other moralities. "It's a splendid thing, this historical imagination, and everyone needs a supply of it, but the mere fact that we need to invoke it testifies to difficulties" (34).

History does not only alter our estimate of the moral vision of novels of the past: it also drains many novels of their original power. One striking instance of this for Howe is *The Sun Also Rises*, a novel that history had pressed against people's hearts but that had by the 1970s fallen victim to history and the gap between generations. Some novels which flourished because of the power with which they addressed their historical moment will soon require explanatory notes to be understood. How many now know of the Moscow trials that are central in Arthur Koestler's *Darkness at Noon*? How many now remember fascism, central in Ignazio Silone's novels? "And isn't it wonderful that we have survived all these catastrophes? Yes, it's wonderful, but one's heart also sinks before the ravages of time, before the sheer sadness of the costs" (34). Having reached the "biblical" age of threescore and ten, Howe more and more registers the passing of the years, sounds the elegiac note. Earlier in the year, anticipating his seventieth birthday— "how could this happen to me, of all people?" he liked to ask—he had observed that, although in fairly good health, he found getting old wasn't easy, not only because one tired more easily and took longer to recuperate from illnesses, but because he had the feeling, when he read contemporary literary theory, of being passed by.[36]

Still, his fear of obsolescence is belied by what he wrote about the premises and claims of the (ostensibly) new schools of theory. As a veteran of disputes over literature and politics going back at least to 1946 and as the first and most formidable critic of the anti-western bias of the sixties New Leftists, Howe was uniquely well prepared to do battle in the eighties and nineties with the professorial antagonists of "Eurocentrism" who advocated "multiculturalism." In the *New Republic* of February 1991 he published a mournful yet relaxed and quietly authoritative piece[37] called "The Value of the Canon," in which he systematically demolished the premises and arguments of the mixture of feminists, black activists, Marxists, and deconstructionists who had banded together to lead the charge against traditional survey courses of world and English literature, and also of social thought, at colleges and universities. Given his own long experience of university administrators faced down by aggressive insurgents, he understood how dangerous was the typical campus confrontation: barbarism on the one side, pusillanimity on the other.

Howe had earned his right to defend the canon because so much of his career had been devoted to a critique of it (a critic need not necessarily be an enemy), and he had strong credentials as a literary critic who had found a legitimate way to combine criticism with political insurgency. In fact, "The Value of the Canon" cannot be fully appreciated without a glance back at a 1984 essay by Howe (briefly alluded to in Chapter Five) called "Toward an Open Culture," which defines both the use and abuse of "excellence" as a literary standard. Aligning himself with Howells, Emerson, and Whitman, Howe insists on the need for democratic culture to be open to "conflict, improvisation, uncertainty, and waste." Though careful to say that there is no inevitable upward progression in cultural any more than in political life, indeed that there may be "an inverse relationship between cultural and political progress," he asserts that the price of change, of welcoming cultural incursions from newer regions of the country, as well as from new immigrant communities and oppressed social classes, "was usually worth paying." The complex problem of American culture has always been to maintain a cultivated tradition by staying in vital relation to the classical culture of Europe while also extending a hand of welcome to "plebeian newcomers" (25–26).

This essay (originally a lecture) of 1984 fluctuates, almost from paragraph to paragraph, between endorsement of cultural insurgency and defense of conservatism. Howe does not want to claim that "the pattern of cultural incursion and assimilation that I've sketched here has always worked out well. It hasn't" (27). Moreover, the cultural vision of the conservatives who insist on an enduring hierarchy of value based upon a line of commanding classics "is by no means an unworthy vision," particularly in a country like the United States, which suffers from "terminal amnesia and oppressive faddism." Are Americans doomed to live in a permanent tension between the cultural outlook that dismisses the past as irrelevant and the one that exalts the supremacy of the past? "Neither alone is very satisfactory, though if forced at gunpoint to choose, I would of course prefer exaltation of the past" (28). His solution is to ask which stress is required at a particular historical juncture. "Some insurgencies grow so coarse, as a segment of the 1960s 'counterculture' did, that serious people have no choice but to oppose its anti-intellectualism, its dismissal of the past, its contempt for anything not conforming to the most recent improvisations. But by the same token, there are also times when invoking 'excellence' and 'standards' seems to be at the service of a narrow-spirited cultural exclusiveness. . . . " The year 1984, Howe decided, albeit reluctantly, was such a time; and so he took the side of the insurgents, defining it in his long-favored image as "the tradition of fraternity and embrace" (29).

By 1991, he has not so much changed his mind as recognized that the insurgents, living corpses of the sixties, are once again the dominant power and therefore need to be opposed. In "The Value of the Canon," he remarks, with dismay and disdain, that the anti-traditionalist insurgents usually think of themselves as leftists. "But this is a comic misunderstanding, occasionally based on ignorance."[38] Standing up for the honor of his former comrades, Howe asserts that the socialist and Marxist traditions were in fact close to traditionalist views of culture. As examples, he cites Georg Lukacs, who claimed that the major representatives of Marxism respected "the classical heritage of mankind" (41), Trotsky, who argued in *Literature and Revolution* that art must be judged by its own laws, and Antonio Gramsci, the Italian Marxist whose insistence upon the centrality of Greek and Latin approached Arnold's. Hence, the claims of many academic insurgents to be speaking from a left or Marxist point of view are bogus.

According to Howe's analysis, it is not leftism that animates the devotees of political correctness with respect to literature, but "a strange mixture of American populist sentiment and French critical theorizing. . . . The populism releases anti-elitist rhetoric, the theorizing releases highly elitist language" (42). The former may be traced to the counterculture of the sixties; the latter, encased in "a stupefying verbal opacity," arises from and further engenders a nihilism that calls into question distinctions of value and also the value of distinctions. "If you can find projections of racial, class, and gender bias in both a Western by Louis L'Amour and a classical Greek play, and if you have decided to reject the 'elitism' said to be at the core of literary distinctions, then you might as well teach the Western as the Greek play. You can make the same political points, and more easily, in 'studying' the Western" (42).

The strength of Howe's feeling on this issue arises to a considerable degree from his poor, working-class background. Countless people from such backgrounds had aspired to make the classical heritage of mankind, so long denied to them, their own. Indeed, a main task of political consciousness had been to enable the masses to share in, and actively respond to, the literature, art, music, and thought of the past. "Knowledge of the past, we felt, could humanize by promoting distance from ourselves and our narrow habits, and this could promote critical thought. . . . It would create a kinship with those who had come before us, hoping and suffering as we have . . . " (42). Although this educational vision might at times have overlooked the fact that aesthetic sensibility is no guarantee of ethical value, it was an essential part of the democratic idea. It arose from within Western traditions spanning the period from the Renaissance to the Enlightenment. It espoused such liberal values as individuality, tolerance, the rights of oppressed national and racial groups, and eventually the claims of women. Of course, such values were often violated in the West (as elsewhere), but—as Howe had argued back in the sixties—the criticism of such violations was almost invariably made in the vocabulary of Western values. Who but a cultural illiterate could suppose that most of the great works of Western literature are retrograde in outlook?

In the eighties and nineties as in the sixties, the academic insurgents clamored for "relevance," a slogan which, according to Howe, not only proceeds from an impoverished view of political life but is usually "ephemeral in its excitements and transient in its impact." He recalls seeing at Stanford's bookstore in the late 1960s large stacks of Eldridge Cleaver's *Soul on Ice,* hailed as the *ne plus ultra* in relevance—and now, a mere two decades later, virtually forgotten. American culture, Howe observes, notoriously suffers from—he has not lost his gift for phrasemaking—"the provincialism of the contemporary" (43). Americans too readily forget that the past is the substance out of which the present is formed, and that to lose touch with it is to thin out contemporary culture. Of course, serious education in a democratic society should assume a critical stance toward the very culture that sustains it. But a criticism that loses touch with the heritage of the past becomes frivolous, a litany of momentary complaints.

Howe then takes up, one by one, the objections of his (potential) adversaries to such a defense of traditional humanistic education as he has been making. The first is that by requiring students to read the classics, the university imposes upon them, in a grossly "elitist" act, a certain worldview. "In its extreme version," says Howe, "this idea is not very interesting, since it is not clear how the human race could survive if there were not some 'imposition' from one generation to the next" (44). But in a more moderate version it might be an idea that at least touches some genuine problems. Much, perhaps everything, depends on the spirit in which the individual teacher approaches a dialogue of Plato or an essay by Mill or a novel by Lawrence. They can be taught as sacred texts, instruments of indoctrination, or they can be taught in a spirit of openness, which encourages students to read carefully, think independently, and ask questions. The teacher is rightly endowed with a certain authority, but the student should be able to confront and criticize that authority. For a university to propose a few required courses so that ill-read students, survivors of America's miserable high schools, may examine what they do not know, isn't necessarily elitist. "The university is saying to its incoming students: 'Here are some sources of wisdom and beauty that have survived the centuries. In time you may choose to abandon them, but first learn something about them'" (44).

The second argument of the academic insurgents is that the list of classics includes only dead, white males, linked to the values of Western hegemony. The first part of Howe's reply is a reminder that any such lists that go past the middle of the eighteenth century will include numerous "women" writers; but he insinuates some doubt as to whether his having taught and also written about such writers made him a better teacher or person. The absence of women from the literature of earlier centuries is of course a result of historical inequities that have only recently been remedied. But, he concludes, even if the circumstances in which the achievement of "dead, white males" occurred were execrable, the achievements themselves remain precious.

The third objection to Howe's traditionalist position is that to isolate any group of texts as "the canon" is to establish a hierarchy of bias, in behalf of which there can never be certainty of judgment. In a particularly spirited response, Howe identifies a confusion or conflation of social and intellectual uses in the insurgents' use of the term "hierarchy." It is perfectly reasonable to criticize a social hierarchy that entails maldistribution of income and power. But a literary "hierarchy" merely signifies a judgment, usually based on the sound principle that time is the only reliable literary critic, that some works are of great and abiding value, others of lesser value, still others without value at all. "To prefer Elizabeth Bishop to Judith Krantz is not of the same order as sanctioning the inequality of wealth in the United States. To prefer Shakespeare to Sidney Sheldon is not of the same order as approving the hierarchy of the nomenklatura in Communist dictatorships" (46). Beyond this, the making of judgments, however provisional and historically conditioned, is inescapable in the life of culture. People who cannot make judgments or defend them should not be teaching literature.

The fourth objection to the principle of disinterested teaching and scholarship is that all texts have a social and political bias, and those who teach them should admit that politics and ideology pervade every-thing. Well, of course, says Howe, if you "look hard (or foolishly) enough," you can find social and political traces everywhere, just as you could also find religion everywhere. But although politics may be "in" everything, not everything is politics: "To see politics everywhere is to diminish the weight of politics" (46).

The fifth and final objection that has been made to conserving the traditional curriculum that Howe is defending is that the traditional canon was based on elitist ideologies, the values of Western imperial-ism, racism, sexism, etc. It is now necessary, say the insurgents, to introduce non-Western voices so that minority students may gain in self-esteem by learning about their origins. Howe begins his reply to this most-favored doctrine of the multiculturalists by pointing out how badly overdrawn is their portrait of the existing situation. He recalls from his own experience how many of his high school and college teachers, so far from upholding Western imperialism or white su-premacy, were sharp critics of American society. He had, for example, been introduced to *Jude the Obscure* by a teacher who wanted him to see how cruel society is to rebels. Proposals to enlarge the curriculum to include non-Western writings are in principle worthy of respect, but they cannot alter the fact that courses in general education must still focus primarily on the traditions of Western society. "That, like it or not, is where we come from and that is where we are" (46). The argument that minority students will gain in self-esteem by reading about them-selves (or their ancestors) is not only difficult to prove; it is also grossly patronizing in suggesting that variety and multiplicity are suitable for middle-class white students, but not for minority students, whose liter-ary regimen must be racially determined. Howe asks whether the devo-tees of multiculturalism are sure that arranging the curriculum by racial criteria will not undermine rather than encourage the self-esteem of ethnic minorities. And since when was the function of the humanities to inculcate self-esteem?

At last, Howe conjures up a critic of his essay who invokes the word most likely to strike terror into the hearts of American university profes-sors: "*What you have been saying is pretty much the same as what conserva-tives say. Doesn't that make you feel uncomfortable?*" To this kind of bully-ing Howe (not for the first time in his career) shows himself admirably immune: "No," he replies, "it doesn't" (47). There are conservatives, just as there are leftists and liberals, who are sectarian ideologues. "But there are also conservatives who make the necessary discriminations between using culture . . . as a kind of social therapy and seeing culture as a realm with its own values and rewards" (47). To exemplify his meaning, Howe even invokes (just as Arnold had done in fighting the same battle in "The Function of Criticism at the Present Time" in 1865) the great conservative figure of Edmund Burke, whose conservatism refused to lend itself to polemical ideological coarseness. Of course, Howe does not wish to cross the aisle from university followers of the democratic left to their conservative adversaries, but he cannot help being aware that, once again, he has come down on what most observers viewed as the "conservative" side of a major cultural debate.

Howe's commitment to the traditional culture in preference to leftist dogmatism is evident in his growing attachment (not fully reciprocated) to Sidney Hook, his adversary of the forties and fifties, with whom he was now glad to align himself in the culture wars. Indeed, already in 1975 Howe told Hook that although they might disagree a good deal on current political matters, their basic views were all but identical, and Howe subscribed to nearly everything Hook had written in the more fundamental essays of his book on *Revolution, Reform, and Social Justice*. In November 1982, congratulating Hook on his eightieth birthday, Howe wrote that he had learned much from him, and despite disagreements had been glad to be his near-contemporary and almost-friend. Hook, in reply, was, as usual, less accommodating: "As for your disagreements—I sometimes have thought that they were more substantial than those you expressed. And as for the latter, I felt on at least two occasions you did not state my position accurately.... Your literary criticism has always seemed to me to be more nuanced than your political criticisms and therefore fairer to those with whom you disagree."

By 1988–89 Howe threw himself completely behind Hook in defense of the traditional university curriculum, which had come under particularly sharp attack at Stanford, where Hook was ensconced in the Hoover Institution. Howe wrote that he shared Hook's anger and was eager to join him in the fight over the way in which young Americans, already shortchanged by their wretched high school educations, were now being deprived of the chance to read a play by Sophocles, a few pages of Hume, a poem by Keats, indeed anything that had survived through power of mind and language, by colleagues who tell them that Sophocles and Freud and Balzac are imperialist or racist or sexist. As a socialist, he wrote to Hook, he had always said that he wanted a better society so that the poor could get a chance at the culture previously the exclusive preserve of the rich; and now that America had provided an opportunity for this, "radicals" preferred to teach about the Trobriand Islands or assign Alice Walker (whom Howe considered an atrocious writer).[39]

That the canon was not something absolute and fixed was a truth of which Howe also reminded readers, even as he was defending the principle itself. In June of 1990 he tried to restore to the canon, or at least to provide a modicum of justice for, Arnold Bennett. Bennett had been knocked out of the canon by Woolf's 1924 essay, "Mr. Bennett and Mrs. Brown," as well as by the intolerance of literary modernism for an Edwardian novelist who believed that human nature could be revealed by depicting conduct and circumstance, i.e., from the outside.[40] In August of 1992, Howe considered several explanations of why Walter Scott's novels had also "fallen out of the canon." Ultimately he settled on what might at first seem a narrowly literary reason, but was actually rooted in a profound historical change. This was that Scott wrote "as if not only he, but all his readers, enjoyed world enough and time." The problem was not length but pacing. "Scott did not know the tempo of the city." Between readers who a century ago adored Scott and those brought up on the modernists there are profound differences, including those that "reveal themselves in the varying speeds with which the eye follows a line of type and the mind takes in its matter" ("Falling Out of the Canon," 36–37). But it is hard to resist the feeling that, in these last essays, Howe is a man who himself feels that he is running out of time. In the apologia for Bennett, for example, he writes that "growing older, I have come to recognize that 'once and for all' often means no more than a few decades" and also that "the years pass" (28), a phrase which would be a constant refrain in his very last personal letters.

The Road Leads Far Away, 1992–93

In the early months of 1992, Howe underwent three operations in sequence: heart bypass surgery, then surgery for an abdominal aneurysm, then prostate surgery. He spent most of the first four months of the year in hospital; when he was discharged, he fell into a deep depression. This lasted for several months, but he made what seemed to be a strong recovery, both physically and mentally. Still, he had been starkly reminded of what he once wrote, apropos of Tolstoy's "The Death of Ivan Ilych": "Disease . . . shocks us into awareness: we can no longer live as if we have an indefinite number of days before us. . . . Disease shatters the non-life of our customary existence and thereby restores us to a condition of freedom: for we must now struggle to assert our humanity over the torment of physical pain. But at the same time disease destroys our freedom, no man can finally stop the decay of his own body" (*Classics of Modern Fiction*, 119). Sensing that the end might be near, Howe was even willing to try the consolations of religion. His CUNY colleague Morris Dickstein recalls how "when I saw him in synagogue at the end of Yom Kippur, just before the gates of judgment were said to swing shut, I knew I was witnessing the death of socialism, or at least of socialism as a self-sufficient secular faith."[41]

The last letter I received from Irving Howe was written on April 30, 1993, five days before he died of cardiovascular disease. In it he reported how 1992 had been a terrible year for him, with the three operations following one after the other, but that he was now feeling better. Nevertheless, what he mainly wanted to tell me was that he had lived for the previous four months with the wonderful young people who had led the Warsaw Uprising. He was referring to his reading and writing about the then recently published 700-page book of memoirs by Yitzhak Zuckerman, a leader of the Warsaw Ghetto uprising in April 1943, exactly fifty years earlier.

Howe's lengthy review-essay, "The Road Leads Far Away," appearing in the May 3 issue of the *New Republic,* turned out to be the last essay published before his death on May 5. This fact lends it a particularly haunting quality, for (without ever saying so directly) it reaches back far into his own history. Decades earlier, in a letter of November 1944 to Glotzer written en route to Alaska, he mentioned having read a grisly article in the *American Mercury* about the Warsaw Ghetto which made him ill for two days. He had been shocked by the account both of the Germans' butchery and of how—for once—the Jews had nobly and heroically taken up arms. He also complained to Glotzer that the American press had neglected the events in Warsaw, and wondered if it would still be worthwhile for someone (perhaps himself) to write about it. But soon Howe was in Alaska, complaining about the fierce cold and the knee-deep snow.[42]

Now, almost half a century later, he returned to the Warsaw Ghetto and wrote that long-postponed essay. It is for the most part a very detailed recounting of the story of the uprising, as told by Zuckerman[43] and supplemented by Yisrael Gutman's book, *The Jews of Warsaw, 1939–1943,*[44] laying heavy stress on "what it meant to live and to die in the totalitarian age." It also expresses some of Howe's accustomed themes: "What held these movements together was not merely, or even mainly, their Zionist and socialist convictions: it was the systematic cultivation of fraternal ties. Friendship sustained morale and enabled these young people to take extraordinary risks."[45]

The essay is striking partly because it shows how greatly Howe had changed in his relation to Jewish history and destiny since the Second World War and even since the publication of his first Yiddish anthology. Once upon a time Howe had opposed the war against Hitler as merely a contest between two capitalist competitors and had disparaged Jewish nationalism in Palestine because it interfered with working-class solidarity with Arabs. But now, in 1993, he writes as follows of the Jewish socialist Bundists in Poland who rejected the idea of "Jewish unity" against the Nazis because major class divisions still existed within the Jewish community and because socialist etiquette required Jews to wait for the Polish proletariat to rise up before they could fight: "The Bund statement could almost have been made in 1935; it ignored the fact that what was now at stake was not politics within the Jewish community but the very survival of the Jews as a people" (34). Moreover, the Howe who had in the early fifties committed himself to the rescue of Yiddish literature partly because its great themes were "the virtue of powerlessness, the power of helplessness," was now, in the last months of his life, imaginatively immersed in the heroic armed defense, mainly by Zionist socialists, of the Warsaw Ghetto.

But the essay also reveals that, in one crucial respect, Howe could not free himself of the fetters of his "non-Zionist" principles. True, he does not besmirch himself in the anti-Zionist polemics of Israeli "revisionists" like the journalist turned popular historian Tom Segev, who blame the Jews of the *yishuv* for not having rescued the Jews of Europe during the Holocaust.[46] On the contrary, he subscribes to the view that the leaders of the Jewish community in Palestine "were genuinely concerned about the fate of Europe's Jews, and undertook a range of projects to help and perhaps rescue them" (32), but were stymied by lack of resources and by the indifference, or worse, of the European states, America, and Britain. He also makes clear that Zuckerman himself settled in Israel after the war and became a member of the Ghetto Fighters (Lohamei Hagettaot) kibbutz in the Galilee. But when he comes to assess the ultimate significance of the uprising, something is missing. "From a military point of view," says Howe, "the Warsaw Ghetto uprising was of slight significance. From what I venture to call a human point of view, its significance is beyond calculation" (36). But is it really? Has not the great Jewish philosopher Emil Fackenheim calculated its significance with exactitude?

> Mordecai Anielewicz [another leader of the Warsaw uprising] died in May 1943. Named after him, Kibbutz Yad Mordekhai was founded in the same year. Five years after Mordecai's death, almost to the day, a small band of members of the kibbutz bearing his name held off a well-equipped Egyptian army for five long days—days in which the defense of Tel Aviv could be prepared, days crucial for the survival of the Jewish state. . . . The battle for Yad Mordekhai began in the streets of Warsaw. (Fackenheim, 285)

Instinctively, Howe's moral intelligence told him that what had seemed in 1943 the desperately quixotic Jewish resistance in the Warsaw Ghetto had tremendous human significance, but he could not bring himself to say that it was indeed a *calculable* significance: precisely the events in the Land of Israel in 1948 proved that, in the long run, nothing that is done for the sake of justice is practically useless.

On 4 May 1993, Howe again expressed optimism about his health and confidence that he was wholly mended. Nevertheless, he ruefully quoted Robert Frost's lines: "No memory of having starred, / Atones for later disregard / Or keeps the end from being hard."[47] On the next day, he died of a burst aorta, a month short of his 73rd birthday.

Reflections

The life of Howe is the story of one of the most fully achieved careers in American letters. Unlike so many writers in the last two centuries who "turned" from literature to social and political criticism—Carlyle and Ruskin and Arnold come to mind—Howe remained simultaneously and permanently loyal to his three great commitments: politics, literature, and Jewishness. To all of them he brought both affection and critical intelligence, even if he could not, despite heroic effort, always reconcile the two.

He began in the socialist movement as a fervent anti-Stalinist and a passionate believer in the capacity of socialism to end war and injustice, and of Marxism to explain everything according to a single set of principles. But by the sixties he was no longer a Marxist, his socialism was hard to distinguish from liberalism, and he eventually was forced to acknowledge the universal failure of socialism as a political movement. Nevertheless, he proceeded to transform socialism into a myth of considerable power as an ethical instrument of social and political criticism.

Stirred belatedly into Jewishness (a term he carefully distinguished from Judaism) by the Holocaust, he undertook a heroic effort to save a language and a literature that had been consigned to destruction by Nazism. In the course of his labors as translator and editor of Yiddish texts and historian of the immigrant Jewish world, he endowed the idea of secular Jewishness with a special twilight beauty, but he could not rescue it from its inevitable demise; and, while remaining faithful to it, he ceased to believe in its future long before he died.

Literature was to prove his most powerful and compelling object of desire. Even at the outset of his career, when he chastised literary intellectuals for their "flight" from politics, he sought to shield the integrity of literature from political manipulation. A devoted modernist, he was forced to recognize the limitations of modernism by the Ezra Pound controversy and by appreciation of the special virtues of Sholom Aleichem. In the forties, he defended the autonomy of literature against the onslaughts not only of Stalinists but of his fellow Trotskyists; in the sixties, his defense of literature's integrity brought him into (fruitful) conflict with the New Left and helped him to see the need to conserve the very iden of the university from the political designs of those he called "guerrillas with tenure"; in the eighties, he took up arms on behalf of literature against the depredations visited upon it by a new gaggle of pedants and theorists who professed literature but were jealous of, or even hated, it, and who—in marked contrast to the always vivid, articulate, and witty Howe—could not write English.

In the course of this last struggle, Howe became acutely aware of his isolation in the academic world. He lamented to Hook that even in the *Dissent* circle of Marxists, socialists, and liberals, where he might expect to find supporters, only David Bromwich really took his side in the (losing) battle over the curriculum.[48] His discouragement arose not only from weariness over having to fight the old struggles over and over again in a country where memory is always in short supply, but from suspicion that he had become a brilliant anomaly, who had emerged from a life history and cultural background that not even his professed disciples at *Dissent* (to say nothing of the *New Republic* and *Partisan Review*) could replicate.

What then is his legacy to us? In retrospect, as we have seen, Howe viewed all three of his loves as "lost causes." Two of them, socialism and secular Jewishness, really were; the third, humane literary study, may yet prove to be so. But to chronicle a devotion to lost causes, forsaken beliefs, and impossible loyalties is also to chronicle a kind of heroism. Howe, as we have seen, liked to say that "one of the arts of life is to know how to end." Taken out of context, this might seem a counsel of stoical resignation to the inevitable. In fact, it was just the opposite. He said it when writing about the American Yiddish poets who refused, out of a sense of honor and a strength of will, to admit the bleakness of their future. However desperate, they would confront the world with firmness—and that quixotic utopianism is what Howe meant by knowing how to end. If the world of American letters cannot emulate his intellectual heroism and tenacious idealism, it should at least remember them.

NOTES

Preface

1. Al Glotzer, "On Irving Howe," *Social Democrats Notes* (May 1993), 3.

1. A Lost Paradise

1. "Immigrant Chic," *New York Magazine,* 12 May 1986, 76. Subsequent references to this work will be cited in text.

2. *A Margin of Hope: An Intellectual Autobiography* (New York: Harcourt Brace Jovanovich, 1982), 3–4. Subsequent references to this work will be cited in text as MH.

3. "Imagining Labor," *New Republic,* 11 April 1981, 33. Subsequent references to this work will be cited in text. Late in his life, though, Howe was forced to acknowledge that "the image of labor as the central agent of social reform—so strong in the years of my youth—has faded among young people."—"From Rebel to Bureaucrat," *New York Review of Books,* 24 October 1991, 55.

4. "A Memoir of the Thirties," *Steady Work: Essays in the Politics of Democratic Radicalism, 1953–1966* (New York: Harcourt, Brace & World, 1966), 356–57. Subsequent references to this work will be cited in text as *Steady Work.*

5. "The Range of the New York Intellectuals," in *Creators and Disturbers: Reminiscences by Jewish Intellectuals of New York,* ed. Bernard Rosenberg and Ernest Goldstein (New York: Columbia University Press, 1982), 270. Subsequent references to this work will be cited in text as "Range."

6. Daniel Bell, "Remembering Irving Howe," *Dissent,* 40 (Fall 1993): 517. Bell's is one of a large number of contributions under this rubric in a special issue of *Dissent.* Subsequent references to this special issue will be cited in text.

7. See, on the subject of Howe's name changing, Werner Cohn, "The Name Changers," *Forum,* 50 (Winter 1983–84): 67. Cohn asked Howe, in a letter of 8 January 1984, why his autobiographical sketch for *Who's Who* lists his parents as "David and Nettie (Goldman) H." "In the context of *Who's Who* conventions, 'H' can only mean 'Howe.' But if you were Horenstein in 1940 weren't they

similarly Horenstein? Or did they change their names also?" Howe never replied to Cohn's letter.

8. Despite being an English major, Howe received a Bachelor of Social Science degree because, according to Jacob Korg (a student at CCNY at the time), Latin was required for the BA degree in those days, and English majors could evade that requirement by taking the BSS degree instead. Foreign languages were not among Howe's numerous intellectual achievements; he appears to have been able to read only in English and Yiddish, and for the Yiddish anthologies he relied heavily on the help first of Eliezer Greenberg, then of Ruth R. Wisse.

9. *Reflections of a Neoconservative* (New York: Basic, 1983), 9.

10. Jeremy Larner cites Milton Sachs (a powerful influence on the young Howe) as the source for this story in "Remembering Irving Howe," 540.

11. Irving Howe and Lewis Coser, *The American Communist Party: A Critical History (1919–1957)* (Boston: Beacon, 1957). Subsequent references to this work will be cited in text as ACP.

12. Although Howe got no closer to the battlefields than Alaska, Kristol saw action in Alsace.

2. Labor Action

1. Letter from Phyllis Jacobson to Alan Wald, 8 September 1983.

2. "The Frauds of Louis Fischer," *New International,* 7 (October 1941): 240, 244.

3. Letter (undated) from IH to Dwight Macdonald, Dwight Macdonald Papers, Manuscripts and Archives, Yale University Library.

4. If Howe did not acknowledge this unpleasant truth in 1942, he certainly did so by 1949 when he published, with B. J. Widick, his book on *The UAW and Walter Reuther* (New York: Random House, 1949). Early in the book (14) we are told about how the attitude of workers in a UAW plant toward a Jewish union member with a racially "neutral" name changes for the worse when it is revealed that he is a Jew.

5. "Indicting American Jews," *Commentary,* 75 (June 1983): 43.

6. For Howe's letter and Dawidowicz's reply to him and her other critics, see "Exchange: American Jews and the Holocaust," *Commentary,* 76 (September 1983): 4–6, 24–28.

7. Quoted in Lucy Dawidowicz, *The War against the Jews: 1933–1945* (New York: Holt Rinehart Winston, 1975), 110.

8. It is not far-fetched to find in Howe and in his paper even an element of pro-German (though not, of course, pro-Hitler) sympathy. In the October 1941 issue of *New International,* Howe, in the course of a nasty attack upon a new "bourgeois democratic" magazine called *Free World,* spits venom at the exiled president of Czechoslovakia, Eduard Benes, whose country had been dismembered by the Munich Pact of 1938, for thinly concealing "his real program: the

dismemberment of Germany." Some unsigned articles in *Labor Action* severely criticize "so-called liberals" for making negative generalizations about the German people. One, on 22 June 1942, called "The Myth of Superior Races," actually cites a study by one Curt Reiss as conclusively demonstrating that the German working classes entirely dismiss Hitler's theory of superior races and "treat like brothers the enslaved workers imported from subjugated Europe." Out of such absurdities was the Trotskyist analysis of Hitler's Europe made.

9. Garrett was eventually drafted too, in 1943, and replaced by Albert Gates (i.e., Albert Glotzer). It is not clear why Howe favored the pseudonym of Fahan. Micael Vaughan, the Celtic scholar, has suggested to me that Howe might have known that in Anglo-Saxon a "how" is a mound, and that "fahan" is similar to the Celtic word for a gravesite. Some of his surviving colleagues at *Labor Action* claim it was invented as a cryptic allusion to his old nickname "Fangs," a reference to his two prominent eyeteeth. Perhaps it was for the cosmetic surgery on them that he told Dwight Macdonald in August 1946 that he was rolling up huge dentist bills and would therefore be grateful if Macdonald paid what he owed Howe for a batch of pieces he had written for *Politics*.—Letter of 30 August 1946 from IH to Dwight Macdonald, Dwight Macdonald Papers, Manuscripts and Archives, Yale University Library.

10. Almost forty years later, the mellowed Irving Howe would write, in partial defense of Kipling, that "what has replaced imperialism has often been something much worse, the totalitarian blight of fascism or Communism. . . . "—"The Burden of Civilization," *New Republic*, 10 February 1982, 30.

11. Howe was justifiably outraged when, decades later, Alexander Solzhenitsyn alleged that all Western intellectuals had been subservient apologists for the Soviet Union. "Long before you," he declared in an open letter to the Russian writer, "there were in the West intellectuals of the left who not only were 'outraged by individual executions anywhere else' but also spoke vehemently 'when Stalin shot hundreds of thousands.'"—"An Open Letter," *New Republic*, 3 May 1980, 18.

12. *Writers at Work: The Paris Review Interviews, Second Series* (New York: Viking, 1963), 298–99.

13. Sidney Hook is justifiably severe with Howe on this matter. He calls *Margin of Hope* "replete with barefaced inventions about *his* past . . . " and also says: "It seems somewhat bizarre for those to whom all the evils of human history were dwarfed by the enormities of the Holocaust to evade the question of their own moral irresponsibility in opposing any involvement in the war against Fascism."—*Out of Step* (New York: Harper & Row, 1987), 157. Only a highly charitable (or imaginative) reader could come away from reading *Labor Action* or *New International* from 1940 to 1944 with the impression that they supported the war against Hitler, even if only implicitly.

14. "The Dilemma of Partisan Review," *New International*, 8 (February 1942): 22–24.

15. The question of just what Howe's Trotskyist "third camp" position with respect to the war meant was fought out in the letters columns of *Commentary* following Midge Decter's review of *A Margin of Hope* in the December 1982 issue. See especially the letters by Irving Panken and Dennis Wrong, and

Decter's reply to them in *Commentary*, 75 (February 1983). Just how sensitive Howe was on the subject is evident from the fact that he upbraided Panken— in what the latter called "a paranoid letter"—for betraying both socialist and personal solidarity by conceding that Decter, although mistaken in her main charges against Howe, had written "a perceptive article." In his 1 February 1983 letter to Panken, Howe described Decter's review as a viciously reactionary and philistine demolition of him as well as his politics. Even the slightest concession to her was, in Howe's view, a betrayal by Panken of their forty-five-year connection.—Interview with Irving Panken, 11 September 1996, and letter by Howe to Panken in Albert Glotzer Collection, Box 40, Howe Folder, Hoover Institution Archives.

16. Letter of 7 March 1985 from IH to Albert Glotzer, Albert Glotzer Collection, Box 40, Howe Folder, Hoover Institution Archives.

3. Marxism and Modernism at the *Partisan Review*

1. See letter of 2 July 1946 from IH to Dwight Macdonald, Dwight Macdonald Papers, Manuscripts and Archives, Yale University Library. Macdonald disapproved of Howe's connection to *Commentary*, saying "I don't agree that the journal is worth calling attention to."—Letter of 13 August 1946 from Macdonald to IH, Dwight Macdonald Papers, Yale University Library. Between August 1946 and January 1980, Howe published in *Commentary* thirty-five articles and reviews. This did not prevent him from frequently attacking the magazine and also people who, in his view, tainted themselves by contributing to it.

2. Letter of 13 September 1945 from IH to Albert Glotzer, Albert Glotzer Collection, Box 12, Howe Folder, Hoover Institution Archives.

3. "The Significance of Koestler: An Exchange between Irving Howe and Neil Weiss," *New International*, 12 (October 1946): 251. Subsequent references to this work will be cited in text.

4. "On the Significance of Koestler: A Reply by Irving Howe," *New International*, 13 (July 1947): 158. Subsequent references to this work will be cited in text.

5. "Periodicals," *Politics* (January 1947): 31. Howe wrote only one article in *Politics* as Irving Howe; it was called "The 13th Disciple," published in October 1946. The rest were signed by Theodore Dryden. In November 1948, Howe, finding himself overburdened by work, resigned from the board of editors of the magazine.—Letter of 15 November 1948 from IH to Macdonald, Dwight Macdonald Papers, Manuscripts and Archives, Yale University Library. *Politics* ran out of money and folded in 1949.

6. "The Intellectuals' Flight from Politics," *New International*, 13 (October 1947): 242. Subsequent references to this work will be cited in text.

7. Letter of 19 December 1948 from Macdonald to IH, Dwight Macdonald Papers, Manuscripts and Archives, Yale University Library. Howe, surprisingly, thanked Macdonald for his frank and useful stylistic criticism, promising

to be on the lookout in future for the defects Macdonald had identified.—Letter of 26 December 1948 from IH to Macdonald, Dwight Macdonald Papers, Manuscripts and Archives, Yale University Library.

8. Alexander Bloom, *The New York Intellectuals and Their World* (New York: Oxford University Press, 1986), 286.

9. *Partisan Review,* 4 (December 1937): 4.

10. *Selected Writings: 1950–1990* (New York: Harcourt Brace Jovanovich, 1990), 247. Subsequent references to this work will be cited in text as SW.

11. Almost twenty years later, Howe would say, at a conference of Jewish radicals, that "listening to participants in this conference, I sometimes had a sense that, beneath the assertiveness of language, there was an even stronger feeling of 'lateness' than that felt by my own generation. . . . And from lateness to lostness is only a short distance."—"American Jews and Israel," *Tikkun,* 4 (December 1988): 73. Subsequent references to this work will be cited in text.

12. See, on this subject, both Manuel, *A Requiem for Karl Marx* (Cambridge: Harvard University Press, 1996), and Sander L. Gilman, *Jewish Self-Hatred* (Baltimore: Johns Hopkins University Press, 1986), 206.

13. Quoted by G. Himmelfarb, "The National Prospect: A Symposium," *Commentary,* 100 (November 1995): 66.

14. "The Sentimental Fellow-Traveling of F. O. Matthiessen," *Partisan Review,* 15 (October 1948): 1125–26. Subsequent references to this work will be cited in text.

15. Wallace, vice president of the United States from 1941 to 1945, in 1948 launched the Progressive party, which charged the Truman administration with primary responsibility for the cold war. Howe's loathing of Wallace is on display in his excoriation of the *New Republic* (which Wallace edited from 1946 to 1948) as the epitome of what is bad in liberal journalism at this time: "Wallace seems to me the most boring and humorless egomaniac on the American political scene since William Jennings Bryan."—"Periodicals," *Politics* (March-April 1947): 63.

16. Ruth R. Wisse, "The New York (Jewish) Intellectuals," *Commentary,* 84 (November 1987): 34. Subsequent references to this work will be cited in text.

17. *Classics of Modern Fiction: Eight Short Novels* (New York: Harcourt, Brace & World, 1968), 5–6. Subsequent references to this work will be cited in text.

18. Howe liked to quote Joyce's remark: "I am afraid poor Mr. Hitler will soon have few friends in Europe apart from my nephews, Masters W. Lewis and E. Pound" (SW, 228).

19. "An Exercise in Memory," *New Republic,* 11 March 1991, 31. Subsequent references to this work will be cited in text.

20. *After Strange Gods: A Primer of Modern Heresy* (New York: Harcourt, Brace, 1934), 20.

21. This thesis has been effectively presented by Anthony Julius in *T. S. Eliot, Anti-Semitism and Literary Form* (Cambridge: Cambridge University Press, 1996).

22. Howe quotes a snatch: "ikh ver alt, ikh ver alt, un mayn pupik vert mir kalt." (I grow old, I grow old, and my bellybutton grows cold.)—MH, 133.

23. *Commentary,* 8 (October 1949): 363.

4. The Reconquest of Jewishness

1. Howe did not know the "bars of soap" story was an exploded fiction.

2. The other editor of *Partisan*, William Phillips, contributes a revealing portrait of the young Howe in 1948: "He came to the [*Partisan Review*] office . . . and we sat for a couple of hours going over his piece. He was still a Trotskyite but was at the beginning of his dual career as literary critic and political writer. . . . [He] had the drive and sense of purpose that became even more marked later, but unlike the young authors who worked on their egos as much as their writing, he also seemed modest, flexible, and reasonable. He had a quick and responsive intelligence, but it was distinguished from that of many other writers by the fact that it was not morose or brooding."—William Phillips, *A Partisan View* (New York: Stein and Day, 1983), 114. Subsequent references to this work will be cited in text.

3. "How *Partisan Review* Goes to War: Stalinophobia on the Cultural Front," *New International*, 13 (April 1947): 109. Subsequent references to this title will be cited in text.

4. Early in the decade, he had begun to deride Hook for social patriotism, intellectual dishonesty, and pretentiousness, even urging Dwight Macdonald to demolish Hook's book *Reason, Social Myths, and Democracy.* Undated letter (probably early forties) from IH to Dwight Macdonald, Dwight Macdonald Papers, Manuscripts and Archives, Yale University Library.

5. "Intellectual Freedom and Stalinists: Shall CP Teachers Be Prohibited from Teaching?" *New International*, 15 (December 1949): 231, 236.

6. Letter of 27 August 1948 from IH to Dwight Macdonald, Dwight Macdonald Papers, Manuscripts and Archives, Yale University Library.

7. In autumn 1996 the Jewish neoconservative Gertrude Himmelfarb resigned from the editorial board of *First Things* in protest of publication by the magazine of a symposium called "The End of Democracy?" and especially of the editorial introduction to it, which likened the United States to Nazi Germany and expressed sympathy for revolution against a judicial tyranny which flouted the Catholic principle that civil law must conform to moral truth and "natural law." *First Things'* editor, Richard Neuhaus, and two of the five symposiasts were Catholics. Himmelfarb's protest was publicly supported by such prominent Jewish neoconservatives as Midge Decter and Norman Podhoretz.—See Jacob Heilbrunn, "Neocon v. Theocon," *New Republic*, 30 December 1996, 20–24, and also "Neocon v. Theocon: An Exchange," *New Republic*, 3 February 1997, 28–29.

8. Letters from IH to Sidney Hook of 30 March, 2 April, and 5 April 1949; letter from Sidney Hook to IH of 4 April 1949. Sidney Hook Collection, Box 15, Folder 39 (Howe), Hoover Institution Archives. In the 11 April 1949 issue of *Labor Action* Howe complied with Hook's request in the letter of 4 April that he voice his apology to the paper's readers as well as to Hook: "I did not make clear that what Hook was writing about was the problem of political relationships to the church, and thus might have given the impression that he proposed some sort of intellectual alliance with Catholicism. That is not true. Secondly, I

wrote with unnecessary nastiness of tone, a manner of writing that is always to be deplored. Precisely because I think the political point of the article was essentially valid do I regret these two lapses."

9. Midge Decter, "Socialism and Its Irresponsibilities: The Case of Irving Howe," *Commentary*, 74 (December 1982): 27.

10. William Phillips, "A Skeptic and a Believer," *Forward*, 14 May 1993. See letter of 27 July 1979 from IH to Albert Glotzer, Albert Glotzer Collection, Box 34, Howe Folder, Hoover Institution Archives.

11. By 1947, however, Howe would adopt the orthodox Labor Zionist view of the Irgun and its deeds. See his comments on Ben Halpern's essay on "Haganah and the Terrorists" in "Periodicals," *Politics* (May-June 1947): 125.

12. Letter of 15 August 1946 to Dwight Macdonald, Dwight Macdonald Papers, Manuscripts and Archives, Yale University Library.

13. In spring of 1947 Howe was playing with the idea of writing a book about Roosevelt.—Letter of 15 April 1947 from IH to Dwight Macdonald, Dwight Macdonald Papers, Manuscripts and Archives, Yale University Library.

14. See Howe and Widick, *The UAW and Walter Reuther*, 13.

15. "The Concentrationary Universe," *New International*, 13 (September 1947): 220–21.

16. At about this time, Howe also made good on the decision, already taken while he was still in the army, to divorce Anna, who had been deeply disturbed by his absence. He was subsequently introduced by Albert Glotzer to Thalia Filias, an archaeologist from a distinctly "right-wing" Greek family, but active in the Trotskyist movement in Buffalo, New York. They were married in 1947, and subsequently had two children, Nina and Nicholas.

17. "Of Fathers and Sons," *Commentary*, 2 (August 1946): 190. Subsequent references to this work will be cited in text.

18. "The Lost Young Intellectual," *Commentary*, 2 (October 1946): 361. Subsequent references to this work will be cited in text.

19. In February of 1945 Howe had written to Al Glotzer of his great disappointment in a Youngstown Workers party functionary named Hess because he was completely involved in petty-bourgeois Jewish existence and even working with Zionist youth groups.—Letter from IH to Albert Glotzer, Albert Glotzer Collection, Box 12, Howe Folder, Hoover Institution Archives. A few years later, in a *Partisan Review* piece of April 1949, Howe derided Leslie Fiedler, Harold Rosenberg, and other "secular theologians in *Commentary*" for their attempts to "return" to Hasidism.—"Magazine Chronicle," *Partisan Review*, 16 (April 1949): 426. Howe's more considered (and accurate) estimate of Fiedler may be found in a review-essay of 1960 called "Literature on the Couch" where he accuses him of "a corrosive knowingness, a void of nihilism."—*New Republic*, 5 December 1960, 19. There was little love lost between the two. Fiedler is reported to have said of Howe that "he entered literature via the backdoor" (Bloom, *Prodigal Sons*, 286). Larry Husten, formerly a graduate student at SUNY-Buffalo, reports that when, at his oral examination in 1980, he named Howe among the critics he most admired, he was sharply rebuked by Fiedler, who said that Howe didn't belong in the company of people like

Wilson and Trilling, and that his book on Faulkner was hateful.—Letter from Larry Husten to EA, 11 September 1995.

20. "Strangers," *Yale Review,* 66 (June 1977): 486, 488, 493. Subsequent references to this work will be cited in text.

21. "The Stranger and the Victim: The Two Stereotypes of American Fiction," *Commentary,* 8 (August 1949): 147. Subsequent references to this work will be cited in text.

22. "Periodicals," *Politics* (January 1947): 31.

23. Quoted by Howe in "The Case of Ezra Pound," *The Critical Point* (New York: Delta, 1973), 113. Subsequent references to this work will be cited in text as CP.

24. Quoted in Joseph Epstein, *Pertinent Players* (New York: Norton, 1993), 261.

25. When, in late 1973, Professor Alvin Rosenfeld called this statement by Stevens to Howe's attention, he expressed regret that he had not known it when he wrote his 1972 essay on Pound.—Letter from IH to Alvin Rosenfeld, undated, but probably early 1974.

26. Preface to *The Picture of Dorian Gray* (1891).

27. Of course, there were exceptions. The non-Jewish "New York" critic, Dwight Macdonald, was resentful of the Jews who opposed the award. Indeed, he outdid the Southerners by declaring that the judges' decision was "the best political statement made in this country for some time . . . the brightest political act in a dark period."—quoted in Michael Wreszin, *A Rebel in Defense of Tradition: The Life and Politics of Dwight Macdonald* (New York: Basic, 1994), 227. He told Howe himself that "I'm really floored by the attitude taken by many of my friends, including yourself, on the Pound award. . . . I am not convinced by the arguments of your side, which seem to me illiberal and specious."—Letter of 21 May 1949 to IH, Dwight Macdonald Papers, Manuscripts and Archives, Yale University Library.

28. "The Question of the Pound Award," *Partisan Review,* 16 (May 1949): 517.

29. "The Jewish Writer and the English Literary Tradition," *Commentary,* 8 (October 1949): 364–65.

30. *Celebrations and Attacks* (New York: Harcourt Brace Jovanovich, 1979), 70–71. Subsequent references to this work will be cited in text as C&A.

31. "The Burden of Civilization," *New Republic,* 10 February 1982, 31.

32. See, for example, "This Age of Conformity," the essay of 1954 in which Howe complains about the "high prestige" of Original Sin in the literary world (SW, 40–42).

33. "Does the Jew Exist? Sartre's Morality Play about Anti-Semitism," *Commentary,* 7 (January 1949): 9. Subsequent references to this work will be cited in text.

34. Simon Rawidowicz, "Israel the Ever-Dying People," in *Modern Jewish Thought,* ed. Nahum N. Glatzer (New York: Schocken, 1977), 142.

35. See, e.g., Haim Hazaz's story of 1942, "The Sermon," and Emil L. Fackenheim's *The Jewish Return into History* (New York: Schocken, 1978).

36. Letter of 14 February 1949 from IH to Dwight Macdonald, Dwight Macdonald Papers, Manuscripts and Archives, Yale University Library.

37. House of Commons speech. 26 January 1949. Winston S. Churchill, *His Complete Speeches: 1897–1963*, 8 vols. (New York: Chelsea House, 1974), VII: 7777.

38. Howe had a terrific dispute with Dwight Macdonald over this article. Macdonald described Howe's criticism of *PR* as a "mumbled aside" and accused him of being "cowardly" in not specifying *Politics* as the desirable political-cultural alternative among radical magazines.—Letters of 5 April, 21 April, 21 May 1949 from Macdonald to IH and of [?] April and 8 May 1949 from IH to Macdonald, Dwight Macdonald Papers, Manuscripts and Archives, Yale University Library.

39. *The 'Other' New York Jewish Intellectuals* (New York: New York University Press, 1994), 9–10.

40. Letter of 16 July [1979] from IH to Albert Glotzer, Albert Glotzer Collection, Box 34, Howe Folder, Hoover Institution Archives.

41. Niger was commenting, in *Der Tog*, on an article in the *Saturday Review*. See *Contemporary Jewish Record* (June 1945).

5. The Fifties

1. "Periodicals," *Politics* (March-April 1947): 63.

2. "The Value of Taste," *Partisan Review*, 18 (January-February 1951): 124–26. See also "A Man of Letters," C&A, 221–24.

3. "Literary Criticism and Literary Radicals," *The American Scholar*, 41 (Winter 1971–72): 116. Subsequent references to this work will be cited in text.

4. "Toward an Open Culture," *New Republic*, 5 March 1984, 28. Subsequent references to this work will be cited in text.

5. *Sherwood Anderson: A Biographical and Critical Study* (New York: William Sloane, 1951). This first citation is from p. viii of the Author's Note to the 1966 Stanford University Press reissue of the original book. After the Author's Note the pagination is identical in both editions. Subsequent references to this work will be cited in text as SA.

6. Susanne Klingenstein, *Jews in the American Academy: 1900–1940* (New Haven: Yale University Press, 1991), 97.

7. "Lionel Trilling, A Jew at Columbia," *Commentary*, 66 (March 1979): 44. Subsequent references to this work will be cited in text. Mrs. Trilling amplified this account in *The Beginning of the Journey* (New York: Harcourt Brace, 1993), 268–81.

8. *World of Our Fathers* (New York: Harcourt Brace Jovanovich, 1976), 412. Subsequent references to this work will be cited in text as WF.

9. Alfred Kazin, recalling that he and Howe were essentially autodidacts who could never quite fit into the university ambience, claims that even now there are strong pockets of resistance to the Jewish presence in English departments: "Harold Bloom . . . infuriated the high priests at Yale to the point where one professor's wife told me that her husband was in church, on his knees, 'praying for the death of Harold Bloom'" ("Remembering Irving Howe," 536).

10. Many years later, however, Howe decided that Trilling's lecture had been a remarkable performance, an elegant affront to the genteel antisemitism of Princeton.—Letter from IH to EA, 2 June 1983.

11. Letter from IH to EA of 2 June 1983; see also MH, 265.

12. Preface to *The Liberal Imagination* (New York: Viking, 1950), x.

13. Abram Sachar, *A Host at Last* (Boston: Atlantic-Little Brown, 1976), 216.

14. Lecture of 15 April 1994 at City University of New York Graduate Center's "Irving Howe and His World" Memorial Conference.

15. Letter of 14 September 1995 from Rhoda Rome to EA.

16. "Irving Howe: A Triple Perspective," *New Leader*, 21 May 1979, 19.

17. See "Magazine Chronicle," *Partisan Review*, 16 (April 1949): 426.

18. Robert Alter, "The Jewish Voice," *Commentary*, 100 (October 1995): 43; David Roskies, Lecture of 15 April 1994 at "Irving Howe and His World" Memorial Conference, CUNY.

19. "Envy; or, Yiddish in America," *Commentary*, 48 (November 1969): 44.

20. *Ashes Out of Hope: Fiction by Soviet-Yiddish Writers*, ed. Irving Howe and Eliezer Greenberg (New York: Schocken, 1977), 1. Subsequent references to this work will be cited in text as *Ashes*.

21. *Voices from the Yiddish: Essays, Memoirs, Diaries*, ed. Irving Howe and Eliezer Greenberg (Ann Arbor: University of Michigan Press, 1972), 2. Subsequent references to this work will be cited in text as VY.

22. Joel Blocker and Richard Elman, "An Interview with Isaac Bashevis Singer," *Commentary*, 36 (November 1963): 368.

23. "In a Ghetto," *Selected Poems of Jacob Glatstein*, trans. Ruth Whitman (New York: October House, 1972), 110.

24. *A Treasury of Yiddish Stories* (New York: Viking, 1954), 21, 28. Subsequent references to this work will be cited in text as TYS.

25. *Letters to an American Jewish Friend: A Zionist's Polemic* (Philadelphia: Jewish Publication Society, 1977), 94.

26. Quoted in Charles Madison, *Yiddish Literature: Its Scope and Major Writers* (New York: Schocken, 1971), 107–108.

27. *Prince of the Ghetto* (New York: Meridian, 1948), 178–79.

28. *Selected Stories: I. L. Peretz*, ed. Irving Howe and Eliezer Greenberg (New York: Schocken, 1974), 10.

29. *A Treasury of Yiddish Poetry*, ed. Irving Howe and Eliezer Greenberg (New York: Holt, Rinehart and Winston, 1969), 10. Subsequent references to this work will be cited in text as TYP.

30. To some extent, Christians had already experimented with the idea of literature as a substitute for religion. As early as 1841, John Henry Newman, in *The Tamworth Reading Room*, wrote derisively that "a literary religion is . . . little to be depended upon; it looks well in fair weather, but its doctrines are opinions, and, when called to suffer for them, it slips them between its folios, or burns them at its hearth." Nevertheless, Matthew Arnold, almost forty years later in "The Study of Poetry," insisted that "The strongest part of our religion today is its unconscious poetry."

31. David Roskies has pointed out that one result of Howe's anthologies that their compiler did not anticipate and would have been surprised to see was that a group of third- and fourth-generation American-Jewish writers who

knew little of the shtetl apart from what they had picked up from the Howe-Greenberg *Treasuries* would "reclaim that same *shtetl* for their own fictional purposes."—"Beyond the Pale," *Commentary*, 102 (December 1996): 65.

32. *The Anatomy Lesson*, in *Zuckerman Bound* (New York: Farrar Straus Giroux, 1983), 480–81. Subsequent references to this work will be cited in text.

33. "Philip Rahv: A Memoir," *The American Scholar*, 48 (Autumn 1979): 490. Howe resented the fact that Rahv pushed him into battle while avoiding the return fire himself. "The opinions I expressed were my own, but the enemies I made should have been Rahv's too" (490). Subsequent references to this work will be cited in text.

34. Symposium on "Our Country and Our Culture," *Partisan Review*, 19 (September-October 1952): 577.

35. "My 1950's," *Commentary*, 96 (September 1993): 38. See also Norman Podhoretz's discussion of Howe's essay in *Breaking Ranks* (New York: Harper & Row, 1979), 66–67.

36. Needless to say, Howe's critics have not hesitated to level the charge of hypocrisy against him for accusing intellectuals of selling out to middlebrow culture or taking jobs in the universities when he himself had done precisely both. (Very few of his critics knew that he had also earned money by some writing for Paramount Studios.) In a lengthy and bitingly satirical letter to *Partisan Review* in spring 1954 about Howe's attack on conformity, Robert Warshow pointed out that "Professor Howe" (this with hammering repetition) made hostile references to a whole host of magazines but not to the Luce publications, for which he worked. Warshow also related the following anecdote about Howe's early days at *Time*: "The story is told that during the years when Professor (then Mr.) Irving Howe worked as a writer for *Time*—on a part-time basis—he met one day in the corridors of the Time-Life Building an acquaintance whom he had known only in the less commercialized world. 'My God,' said Mr. Howe, immediately taking the offensive, 'what are *you* doing here?' 'Why, I'm working here,' said his acquaintance. 'Full time?' said Mr. Howe."—Robert Warshow, "This Age of Conformity," *Partisan Review*, 21 (March-April 1954): 235. See also Hilton Kramer, "Irving Howe at Seventy," *New Criterion*, 9 (October 1990): 6–9.

37. Quoted in Dennis Wrong, "Heretic, Yes," in *New Republic*, 13 November 1995, 46.

38. Only much later did Howe acknowledge that "in the fifties we were a little slow in noticing that 'orthodox' is . . . not a literary term at all, or that 'original sin' is a category of but one theology" (MH, 178).

39. "A Mind's Turnings," *Dissent*, 7 (Winter 1960): 31.

40. "The help and encouragement I have received from Lionel Trilling form only one of my debts to him."—Preface to SA, xiii.

41. *Dissent*, 3 (Fall 1956): 437.

42. *The Beginning of a Journey: The Marriage of Diana and Lionel Trilling* (New York: Harcourt Brace, 1993), 420.

43. Mark Krupnick offers the following description of the changing attitude of Howe to Trilling over the decades: "Irving Howe . . . started out in the late forties defending him against 'calcified' critics on the left like James T. Farrell. But in the mid-fifties, Howe himself was criticizing Trilling from the left. Then

in the late sixties, under pressure from 'the adversary culture,' Howe swung back to become Trilling's most ardent and articulate champion."—*Lionel Trilling and the Fate of Cultural Criticism* (Evanston: Northwestern University Press, 1986), 129n.

44. *Dissent*, 1 (Winter 1954): 3. Subsequent references to this work will be cited in text.

45. *Breaking Ranks*, 65.

46. "Does It Hurt When You Laugh?" *Dissent*, 1 (January 1954): 5. Subsequent references to this work will be cited in text.

47. Decades later, *Dissent* published as "A Special Feature" a narrowly polemical piece by the pugnacious Bernard Avishai lambasting *Commentary*, and then aggressively distributed the article in pamphlet form.—See "Breaking Faith: *Commentary* and the American Jews," *Dissent*, 28 (Spring 1981): 236–56. Avishai, in turn, got his comeuppance in Edward Alexander's "Liberalism and Zionism," *Commentary*, 81 (February 1986): 28–33.

48. "Philistine Leftism," *Commentary*, 17 (February 1954): 201. Subsequent references to this work will be cited in text.

49. Howe, who served well over three years in the army, disavowed the pacifist label, but would sometimes support pacifist groups. In 1973, for example, he accepted Dwight Macdonald's invitation to join a committee to celebrate the fiftieth anniversary of the War Resisters League.

50. In the April issue of *Commentary*, C. Wright Mills and Harold Orlans replied on behalf of *Dissent* to Glazer's attack.

51. H[al] D[raper]. "A New Magazine Presents Itself to the Socialist Public," *Labor Action*, 22 February 1954. See Alan M. Wald, *The New York Intellectuals* (Chapel Hill: University of North Carolina Press, 1987), 323.

52. Letter of 15 November 1958 to Dwight Macdonald, Dwight Macdonald Papers, Manuscripts and Archives, Yale University Library.

53. "The White Negro: Superficial Reflections on the Hipster," *Dissent*, 4 (Summer 1957): 276–93. In retrospect, Howe did admit that it was "unprincipled" to accept Mailer's essay. He grieved especially over the sentence in which Mailer wonders about the propriety or good of "beat[ing] in the brains" of a fifty-year-old storekeeper as a way of articulating selfhood.—MH, 240. His coeditor, Lewis Coser, recalls no debate among the editors of *Dissent* (Mailer was then on the *Dissent* board) about the wisdom of publishing the piece. "Only later did some of us feel that we had made a huge mistake."—Letter from Coser to EA, 25 June 1996.

54. "A Revival of Radicalism?" *Dissent*, 10 (Spring 1963): 110. See also "The First Ten Years," *Dissent*, 11 (Spring 1964): 150–52.

55. Introduction to *Jewish-American Stories* (New York: New American Library, 1977), 2–3. Subsequent references to this work will be cited in text as J-A.

56. Letter of 21 March 1991 from IH to Robert B. Heilman. Heilman also reports the following remark made by Howe in that long-ago summer of 1952: "In this department I feel more at home with the critics and writers than I do with those department members of whom I am supposed to be a socio-political ally."—Letter of 8 August 1995 from Heilman to EA.

57. *William Faulkner: A Critical Study* (Chicago: Ivan R. Dee, 1991), 7. Subsequent references to this work will be cited in text.

58. For example, in an essay of 1967 called "Anarchy and Authority in American Literature," Howe writes: "In my capsule description of this anarchist vision, the key word is 'fraternal'—the notion of a society in which the sense of brotherhood replaces the rule of law. . . . "—SW, 108. In an essay "How Are Characters Conceived?" written near the end of his life, Howe writes of the relationship between Huck and Jim that "for an exquisite moment something even better than formal equality—a fraternity of companions—is established."—*A Critic's Notebook*, ed. Nicholas Howe (New York: Harcourt Brace, 1994), 69.

59. This is stressed by John Hollander, who was Howe's student that summer in a seminar on the political novel. See Hollander's Memorial Conference lecture of April 1994, mentioned above.

60. "'1984'—Utopia Reversed: Orwell's Penetrating Examination of Totalitarian Society," *New International*, 16 (November-December 1950): 360–68.

61. *Politics and the Novel* (New York: Horizon, 1957), 22. Subsequent references to this work will be cited in text.

62. Someone familiar with George Eliot's essays as well as her novels will be struck by a contrast between them similar to that in Howe between his polemically socialist writings and his literary criticism. In writing of evangelicalism, for example, in her *Westminster Review* essays, she is a fierce antagonist, resorting to every *ad hominem* device for blackening her opponents; but when she deals with evangelicalism in the novels, she has on full display her powers of imaginative sympathy.

63. Some think a Jewish friend had told Orwell that the Jewish year *tashmad* (meaning destruction) would fall in 1984, and that is why he chose the title he did.

64. "Why I Write," in *The Orwell Reader*, ed. Richard Rovere (New York: Harcourt, Brace & World, 1956), 394.

65. "Again: Orwell and the Neoconservatives," *Dissent*, 31 (Spring 1984): 236. Nevertheless, Howe would be sharply criticized by conservatives for scanting conservative interpretations of *1984*. See, e.g., "Becoming a Non-Person," *National Review*, 28 October 1983, 1324.

6. The Sixties, Decade of Controversy

1. "Historical Memory, Political Vision," *New Republic*, 9 November 1974, 25. Subsequent references to this work will be cited in text.

2. "A Revival of Radicalism?" *Dissent*, 10 (Spring 1963): 111.

3. Macdonald (whose 1948 critique of Howe's "cottonwool orotundities," cited in Chapter Three, still rankled) at once fired off a hilarious (and effective) reply: "This is singularly inept buffoonery, since the Sermon on the Mount is notably clear and simple . . . [but] *were* the Sermon woolly and pretentious in style . . . I should be right, since in that case the Sermon would not be the great moral message it is but a botch, and not only in style. . . . Speaking of style, I note that Mr. Howe has been converted to Christianity, since he refers to Christ as 'He.' (To me, he's 'he.') This shows what discoveries can be made if one pays

attention to style. And, on Mr. Howe's part, what an admirably subtle way of breaking the news!"—*Dissent*, 7 (Spring 1960): 216.

4. Lecture of 15 April 1994 at CUNY "Irving Howe and His World" Memorial Conference.

5. "Falling Out of the Canon," *New Republic*, 17 and 24 August 1992, 36. Subsequent references to this work will be cited in text.

6. *Eichmann in Jerusalem: A Report on the Banality of Evil*. Revised and enlarged edition (New York: Viking, 1964), 125.

7. Scholem also wrote: "Which of us can say today what decisions the elders of the Jews . . . ought to have arrived at in the circumstances. . . . Some among them were swine, others saints. . . . there were among them also many people in no way different from ourselves, who were compelled to make terrible decisions in circumstances that we cannot even begin to reproduce or reconstruct. I do not know whether they were right or wrong. Nor do I presume to judge. I was not there."—"Eichmann in Jerusalem: An Exchange of Letters between Gershom Scholem and Hannah Arendt," *Encounter*, 22 (January 1964): 52.

8. *Mr. Sammler's Planet* (New York: Viking, 1970), 22.

9. In this case, the magazine received many letters, but printed only one brief correction.

10. "'The New Yorker' and Hannah Arendt," *Commentary*, 36 (October 1963): 318. Subsequent references to this work will be cited in text.

11. "Arguments: More on Eichmann," *Partisan Review*, 31 (Spring 1964): 260.

12. "Record Straight," *Dissent*, 29 (Summer 1982): 383.

13. Letters from Readers, *Commentary*, 75 (February 1983): 5.

14. *Hannah Arendt/Martin Heidegger* (New Haven: Yale University Press, 1995), 78.

15. Richard Wolin, "Hannah and the Magician," *New Republic*, 9 October 1995, 31, 36. See also Wolin's *The Politics of Being: The Political Thought of Martin Heidegger* (New York: Columbia University Press, 1990). Another minor irony of the whole sordid episode is the suggestion, in Ann Birstein's "When the Wind Blew" (*Summer Situations*, 1972) that Alfred Kazin, who had made such a spectacle defending Arendt at the *Dissent* forum, may have done so partly because they too had once been lovers.

16. "The Negro Revolution," *Dissent*, 10 (Summer 1963): 214. Subsequent references to this work will be cited in text.

17. Howe's position on quotas was not consistent. In "Are American Jews Turning toward the Right?" coauthored with Bernard Rosenberg in *The New Conservatives*, ed. Lewis A. Coser and Irving Howe (New York: Quadrangle, 1974), Howe cites the use of quotas by the Israeli Labor party as evidence that there is no single Jewish position on quotas, and that opposition to them is not a requisite of Jewish self-respect. But back in 1949, in his book on the UAW and Reuther, Howe had sympathized with the forces opposed to race quotas, especially since the idea of special UAW board posts for Negroes originated with the Communist party.—UAW, 224–25, 231–32.

18. *Dissent*, 10 (Autumn 1963): 302. Further reflections by Howe on the subject of the Negro revolution may be found in the Summer 1964 issue of

Dissent, 279–95, a discussion by several participants of "The Negro Movement: Where Shall It Go Now?" See also "Richard Wright: A Word of Farewell," an essay first published in *New Republic,* 13 February 1961, and reprinted in C&A.

19. Ralph Ellison, *Shadow and Act* (New York: New American Library, 1966), 116. "The World and the Jug," as reprinted in *Shadow and Act,* includes both Ellison's original *New Leader* essay by that name and his later "rejoinder" to Howe in the same journal. Subsequent references to this work will be cited in text.

20. "A Reply to Ralph Ellison," *New Leader,* 3 February 1964, 12. Subsequent references to this work will be cited in text.

21. In his introduction to *Jewish-American Stories,* Howe alluded to "those niceties of Correct English which Gore Vidal and other untainted Americans hold dear" (15). Howe was bemused by Vidal's mocking reference to him as a "rabbi" in one of his (numerous) antisemitic outbursts. He thought of Vidal's antisemitism as distinctly American in character, "crackerbarrel elevated to literacy," as he once put it to me.

22. "New Black Writers," *Harper's,* 239 (December 1969): 141.

23. *Art and Ardor* (New York: Knopf, 1983), 96. Subsequent references to this work will be cited in text.

24. But in a 1993 "Afterword" to her essay, Ozick qualified: "I am ready, by the way, to yield to Irving Howe in what I am told is his continuing insistence that in his exchange with Ellison he was not approaching their discussion from any Jewish standpoint." In other words, Howe did not welcome Ozick's characterization of him as the prototypical Jew.—*Blacks and Jews: Alliances and Arguments,* ed. Paul Berman (New York: Delacorte, 1994), 74n.

25. "Radical Questions and the American Intellectual," *Partisan Review,* 33 (Spring 1966): 183, 318, 314. Subsequent references to this work will be cited in text.

26. "Is This Country Cracking Up?" *Dissent,* 14 (May-June 1967): 259, 262.

27. See also "An Exchange on the Left: Irving Howe vs. Phillip Rahv," *New York Review of Books,* 23 November 1967, 36–42.

28. "The second phase . . . took a sharp turn: away from the shapelessness of 'participatory democracy' and toward the rigidity of vanguard elites, away from the fraternal spirit of nonviolence and toward a quasi-Leninist fascination with violence" ("Historical Memory, Political Vision," 27).

29. Despite this condescending allusion, Howe made a point of consulting Hook in June 1967 when he was trying to put together an anthology of essays dealing with the question of the rights and limits of dissenting, revolutionary, and totalitarian groups in a democratic society.—Letter from IH to Sidney Hook, 6 June 1967. Sidney Hook Collection, Box 15, Folder 39 (Howe), Hoover Institution Archives.

30. In a balanced and discriminating essay called "The Poverty of Socialist Thought," Stephen Miller remarks that Howe "is forever backing into socialism—more often than not saying what socialism is not rather than what it is. . . . His writing is stronger when he deals with the betrayals of socialism than when he—wistfully, it seems—gives us visions of the future."—*Commentary,* 62 (August 1976): 32–33.

31. "Why Should Negroes Be above Criticism?" *Saturday Evening Post*, 14 December 1968, 10, 14–15.

32. "The New 'Confrontation Politics' Is a Dangerous Game," *New York Times Magazine*, 20 October 1968, 27. Subsequent references to this work will be cited in text.

33. Elsewhere Howe noted the absurdity of SDS declaring the United States to be "totalitarian" even as it managed to pour out of its Chicago office—"and through the postal system of this very 'totalitarian' country"—large quantities of material denouncing the society.—"A Word about 'Bourgeois Civil Liberties,'" *Dissent*, 15 (January-February 1968): 10-11. Subsequent references to this work will be cited in text.

34. Alfred Kazin recalls that during the sixties he and Muriel Rukeyser and Howe went to see Humphrey about the war and were told by the vice president, bitterly, "why don't you talk to *him* [i.e., Johnson]?"—*New York Jew* (New York: Knopf, 1978), 261.

35. "After the Mideast War," *Dissent*, 14 (July-August 1967): 387–88. Subsequent references to this work will be cited in text.

36. *New York Times Book Review*, 17 October 1976, 2.

37. Letter from Carl Gershman to EA, 25 September 1996.

38. "Vietnam and Israel," in *Israel, the Arabs and the Middle East*, ed. Irving Howe and Carl Gershman (New York: Bantam, 1972), 342. Subsequent references to this work will be cited in text.

39. "The Campus Left and Israel," in *Israel, the Arabs and the Middle East*, 428. Subsequent references to this work will be cited in text. (The essay originally appeared in the *New York Times* for 13 March 1971.)

40. Ruth R. Wisse, "The Big Lie: Reinventing the Middle East," in *The Middle East: Uncovering the Myths* (New York: Anti-Defamation League, 1991), 18–19.

41. He was brought to CUNY at the inception of the graduate program, by Helaine Newstead, its founder and first executive, and Leonard Lief, the chairman of English at Hunter.

42. "Adlai Stevenson: The Last, Sad Years," *Dissent*, 12 (Autumn 1965): 409–11. Howe's occasional softness toward conservatives did not, however, extend to such people as William Buckley, whom he dismissed as "an elegant jackanapes."—"William Buckley and the Price of Kicks," *Dissent*, 13 (January-February 1966): 93.

43. Samuel Hux, "Uncle Irving," *Modern Age*, 37 (Summer 1995): 334. Later in life, Howe would even come to speak with (qualified) approval of Kipling's "earned and measured conservatism that has reckoned the costs of civilization and takes them to be worth paying."—"The Burden of Civilization," 29.

44. See Lowell's poem of May 1968 called "The New York Intellectual," in *Notebook: 1967–68* (New York: Farrar Straus Giroux, 1969).

45. "If I were a Jew," Hardy told Israel Zangwill, "I should be a rabid Zionist."—Florence Emily Hardy, *The Life of Thomas Hardy: 1840–1928* (New York: St. Martin's, 1962), 328. Howe did not take notice of this intriguing remark.

46. *Thomas Hardy* (New York: Macmillan, 1967), xi. Subsequent references to this work will be cited in text.

47. The line was: "*geshtorbn der letster bal-tfile* ("the last *bal-tfile* is dead").

"Very gradually," Ozick writes, "through a series of feverish letters, the line evolved—from the editor's suggested line, to the poem's 'English equivalent' line, to that stage where the translator was ready to assume moral authority over the poem."—"A Translator's Monologue," *Metaphor and Memory* (New York: Knopf, 1989), 204.

48. At about the same time that Howe wrote this, Cynthia Ozick put into the mouth of her fictional Yiddish poet Edelshtein the following remarks: "Our reputation among ourselves as a nation of scholars is mostly empty. In actuality we are a mob of working people, laborers, hewers of wood. . . . Leivik, our chief poet, was a housepainter. . . . He could hang wallpaper. I once lived in a room he papered—yellow vines. . . . A good job, no bubbles, no peeling. This from a poet of very morbid tendencies. Mani Leib fixed shoes. Moishe Leib Halpern was a waiter, once in a while a handyman. . . . I beg you not to think I'm preaching Socialism. To my mind politics is dung."—"Envy; or, Yiddish in America," *Commentary*, 48 (November 1969): 48.

49. "Journey of a Poet," *Commentary*, 53 (January 1972): 76. Subsequent references to this work are cited in text.

50. See Ruth R. Wisse, "Found in America," *New Republic*, 18 and 25 September 1995.

51. "Without Gifts," *The Selected Poems of Jacob Glatstein*, trans. Ruth Whitman (New York: October House, 1972), 109.

7. In the Shadow of Decades

1. Howe and Michael Harrington actually edited an anthology called *The Seventies: Problems and Proposals* (New York: Harper & Row, 1973), a collection of essays from *Dissent* on matters of public policy. But, as Elliott Abrams pointed out in a *Commentary* review, the volume deals far more with the sixties than the seventies.

2. "Political Terrorism: Hysteria on the Left," *New York Times Magazine*, 12 April 1970, 27. Subsequent references to this work will be cited in text.

3. "On Sexual Politics: The Middle-Class Mind of Kate Millett," CP, 203. The essay originally appeared in *Harper's Magazine*, 241 (December 1970): 110–29.

4. Lecture of 15 April 1994 at CUNY "Irving Howe and His World" Memorial Conference.

5. In a letter of 5 January 1973 to Alvin Rosenfeld, Howe said that he had already written about 650 out of a projected 900 pages of his big book on the Jewish immigrant experience.

6. In the complementary sequel to this essay, Howe quoted with approval Northrop Frye's observation that Arnold gives primary place to the classics in education because he thinks of them "as the living powers of imagination that transform a class-ridden society into a classless one."—"Living with Kampf and Schlaff: Literary Tradition and Mass Education," *The American Scholar*, 43 (Winter 1973): 109.

7. In the "Kampf and Schlaff" sequel, Howe adds that "in the final analysis,

the survival of ethnic and racial subcultures depends mostly on whether those who grow up in them believe it valuable to preserve them. . . . It would be a dreadful form of intellectual condescension—and social cheating as well—if in the name of the autonomy of subcultures, we were to dissuade their members from trying to establish deep connections with the culture in which they are going to live" (111).

8. The essay is reprinted in *The Critical Point,* the text which I shall cite. Some foreshadowing of this attack may be detected eleven months earlier in Howe's essay on Jacob Glatstein, in which he recalls that he and Glatstein "quarreled once about Philip Roth, and now I suspect that he had the better of the quarrel."—"Journey of a Poet," 77. (In 1979, when he reprinted the original *New Republic* review, he acknowledged the disparity between it and the later essay on Roth's work as a whole: "Perhaps there are some points of conflict between the early review and the later essay; perhaps not. But nowhere is it written that critics cannot or should not modify their opinions as time goes by" [C&A, 38].)

9. One wonders if Howe had noticed a *New York Times* review by Fred Hechinger (16 July 1972) of Ernest Lehman's film version of *Portnoy's Complaint.* In the course of describing the film as antisemitic, Hechinger said that its racial thrusts at Jews sank "to the minstrel and watermelon level of insights."

10. In a spirited defense of Roth, Wilfrid Sheed wrote: "Howe says [Roth] lacks a culture, but we all lack one these days. That is his very material: the first generation to try winging it without a culture."—"The Good Word: Howe's Complaint," *New York Times Book Review,* 6 May 1973, 2.

11. In the very next issue of *Commentary,* Robert Alter, discussing Lehman's film of *Portnoy's Complaint,* asserted that "in the changed mood of the past four or five years, a negative complement of that sentimental myth [of the Jews as unique possessors of certain admired human qualities] seems to have gained at least limited currency, and we are at times encouraged to perceive as distinctly Jewish certain destructive character-types or qualities which are merely specific Jewish instances of a very widespread human heritage of blight and consternation. . . . A film like Lehman's on top of a novel like Roth's could exercise a certain limited accuracy of social observation and nevertheless have regrettably misleading implications."—"Defaming the Jews," *Commentary,* 55 (January 1973): 78–79.

12. Letters, *Commentary,* 55 (March 1973): 8, 12, 14.

13. *The Anatomy Lesson* in *Zuckerman Bound* (New York: Farrar Straus Giroux, 1985), 474.

14. Philip Roth, *Reading Myself and Others* (New York: Farrar Straus Giroux, 1975), 130. Subsequent references to this work will be cited in text.

15. "Tevye on Broadway," *Commentary,* 38 (November 1964): 73–75.

16. "On Lionel Trilling," *New Republic,* 13 March 1976, 29–30. Subsequent references to this work will be cited in text. One oddity of Howe's assessment of Trilling in relation to politics lies in something he does *not* mention: namely, Trilling's failure to resist (as Howe had done so abundantly) the New Left assault on culture itself. Norman Podhoretz, Trilling's student, had publicly accused his mentor of cowardice for refusing to dissociate himself from the radicalism of the sixties.

17. "Milton Hindus vs. Irving Howe," *New Boston Review,* 2 (January 1977): 7. Hindus's lengthy review of the book is the most biting that appeared, fiercely negative from beginning to end.

18. David Horenstein (who had remarried since the death of Howe's mother) was released from hospital in October of 1976 and seemed, for a time, to be regaining his lucidity.

19. See especially Alvin Rosenfeld, "Irving Howe: The World of Our Fathers," *Midstream,* 22 (October 1976): 84. Howe responded, in a letter to Rosenfeld, that this criticism was partly true, but that a writer cannot deal with what is beyond his reach, and so he had given some sense of religious institutions in the immigrant world, but little of their inner life.—Letter of 10 November 1976 from IH to Alvin Rosenfeld.

20. See, e.g., "The Fiction of Anti-Utopia," *New Republic,* 23 April 1962, 13–16.

21. Some sense of the relation that developed between Howe and Singer emerges from their discussion in "Yiddish Literature vs. Jewish Tradition: A Dialogue," *Midstream,* 19 (June/July 1973): 33–38.

22. "Yiddishkeit," *Commentary,* 61 (April 1976): 85.

23. In his later years, Howe tended more and more to use the term liberalism, uncritically, as a synonym for whatever is wise, good, and merciful. See, e.g., the essay "Literature and Liberalism" (C&A, 239–54). But of course it was not always so with him. Indeed, as late as November 1974 he pointedly put "the painful question: what inner failing of the 20th-century liberals has made so many of them vulnerable to the machismo swagger, the ideological bullying of authoritarian leaders?"—"Historical Memory, Political Vision," 25.

24. See also the 1988 essay "American Jews and Israel," 74.

25. Letter from IH to EA, 18 July 1977.

26. Letters from IH to Ruth Wisse, 20 March and 23 October 1976.

27. "The Limits of Ethnicity," *New Republic,* 25 June 1977, 18. Subsequent references to this work will be cited in text.

28. Letter from IH to EA, 28 March 1977. In fact, he wrote a "review" of this conjectural nonbook by one Northrop Kazin. "Kazin" began by calling Howe's *A Few Jewish Voices* a very thin collection of essays by a writer who had just become famous for a book that was anything but thin.

29. Letter from IH to EA, 12 December 1977. When his son finally did get a job, in spring of 1978, Howe said to me that for the first time in twenty-five years he wouldn't have to support a child, and that if I thought he liked the new situation, I didn't know anything about Jews.—Letter from IH to EA, 21 April 1978. Later, in 1984, when Nicholas Howe was denied tenure at Rutgers, his father again worked diligently to find him another position.

30. He likened his daughter to the kind of woman in Russia who, if her husband were sent to Siberia, would put the kerchief over her head and declare her readiness to go.—Letter from IH to EA, 25 May 1977.

31. Letter from IH to Ruth Wisse, 20 July 1976.

32. Letter from IH to EA, 25 May 1977.

33. See, on this subject, the debate between Hillel Halkin ["Philologos"] and Dovid Katz in "The Future of Yiddish," *Forward,* 16 August 1996.

34. "A Figure of Flawed Greatness," *Nation,* 23 September 1978, 277.

35. *Leon Trotsky* (New York: Viking, 1978), viii. Subsequent references to this work will be cited in text as LT.

36. "Writing and the Holocaust," *New Republic,* 27 October 1986, 36. Subsequent references to this work will be cited in text.

37. "The Problem of Pornography," *Dissent* (Spring 1978): 205.

38. "The Cities' Secret," *New Republic,* 22 January 1977, 55–56.

39. "The Right Menace," *New Republic,* 9 September 1978, 13, 16.

40. Letter to EA, 20 November 1979.

8. The Final Reckoning

1. Excerpts from this speech appear in "What Henry Heard," *New Republic,* 26 March 1977, 20–21. In his will, Howe left that part of his estate not bequeathed to individuals to *Dissent* and to the Democratic Socialists of America.

2. "I'm Not a Marxist," *New York Times Book Review,* 20 October 1985, 11.

3. "The American 80's: Disaster or Triumph?" *Commentary,* 90 (September 1990): 48.

4. *Socialism and America* (New York: Harcourt Brace Jovanovich, 1985), 49. Subsequent references to this work will be cited in text.

5. See Howe's early discussion of this problem in his analysis of Walter Reuther in the 1949 book on *The UAW and Walter Reuther.* There he describes Reuther as having to choose between "the lonely rectitude of radical politics or full participation in the union world, with doctrine struggling as best it could behind power and prestige . . . " (194–95).

6. See, in this connection, his letter to Sidney Hook of 26 November 1975, Sidney Hook Collection, Box 15, Folder 39 (Howe), Hoover Institution Archives.

7. In a lengthy note on the "brilliant masquerade" of Browderism, Howe recommends that American socialists employ something like the Popular Front strategy of the Communists, starting in 1935 and developed by Communist party boss Earl Browder. Dressing communism as "twentieth-century Americanism" (91), the Popular Front succeeded in penetrating the institutions and organizations of the New Deal, especially the Democratic party and allied local political groups. Unlike the socialists of those years, the Communists were flexible in dealing with local units or with CP members active in trade unions. (They saved their rigidity for defense of the Soviet Union, of the Stalinist terror—the forced collectivization which destroyed millions of peasants—and the Moscow trials.) Since the Popular Front strategy proved very successful in changing the CP from a tiny sect to a mass movement (until the Hitler-Stalin pact of 1939), Howe asks whether the same strategy could not be pursued by American socialists "in good faith and without Stalinist absurdities . . . out of an honest wish to advance the socialist idea by inching forward with the social reforms we associate with the welfare state" (103).

8. In an essay of 1981, Howe had defined an associated myth about America. It was the one that refused to recognize the working class as a major component of American society. Instead, the dominant American myth held

that America is a nation of independent craftsmen, small farmers, sturdy businessmen, all of whom succeeded through their own efforts and strength of character. This too began with Emerson ("Imagining Labor," 29).

9. "Thinning Ranks," *New Republic*, 25 November 1985, 34. A similar note is sounded by Sanford Pinsker in "Lost Causes / Marginal Hopes: The Collected Elegies of Irving Howe," *Virginia Quarterly Review*, 65 (Spring 1989): 215–30.

10. He even felt that he had a special, inside knowledge of Begin's nefariousness, for Begin was an ex-socialist, and it was axiomatic with Howe that ex-socialists made the worst reactionaries, bringing bad ingrained habits to a bad new ideology.—Letter from IH to EA, 18 July 1977.

11. "Israel: A Visitor's Notes," *Dissent*, 24 (Fall 1977): 360–61. Subsequent references to this work will be cited in text.

12. A few months later, in a review of *While Messiah Tarried: Jewish Socialist Movements, 1871–1917*, by Nora Levin, Howe remarked that Jewish socialism is "almost exhausted"; "in America it has been softened by time and liberal inducements; and in Israel it suffered a major political defeat last year, at least partly due to its own loss of conviction and morale."—*New York Times Book Review*, 22 January 1978, 10.

13. "I had no particular infatuation with Hebrew," he said in 1982 ("Range," 286).

14. "George Eliot and Radical Evil," SW, 352.

15. "'Peace Now' and American Jews," *Commentary*, 70 (August 1980): 17–18.

16. "'Warm Friends of Israel, Open Critics of Begin-Sharon,'" *New York Times*, 23 September 1982.

17. Ruth R. Wisse, *If I Am Not for Myself . . . The Liberal Betrayal of the Jews* (New York: Free Press, 1992), 79.

18. Letter of 15 February 1983 from Albert Glotzer to IH, Albert Glotzer Collection, Box 40, Howe Folder, Hoover Institution Archives. Copyright Stanford University.

19. Letter to *New York Times*, 26 January 1988.

20. "Notes from Jerusalem," *New York Review of Books*, 29 September 1988, 13. Subsequent references to this work will be cited in text.

21. By contrast, Philip Rahv, relentlessly dismissive of things Jewish (and Israeli), seems to have nourished a hope that the Marxist dream, dead in Russia and America, could be resuscitated in Israel. This may explain why, in his will, he left his money to the state of Israel. Howe left the state of Israel nothing except a painting by Hedda Stern, which he bequeathed to the Israel Museum in Jerusalem.

22. Carole S. Kessner, "From This Place and Time: An Interview with Lucy Dawidowicz," *Reconstructionist*, January-February 1990, 28.

23. See, in this connection, Howe's touching obituary for the *Jewish Daily Forward* in *New Republic*, 21 February 1983, 10–11.

24. Just how disingenuous was this cautionary note became clear when the Labor government of Rabin and Peres, driven by Peace Now ideology, supplied Arafat with arms for about 40,000 men even before the establishment of a new Palestinian state.

25. *The American Newness: Culture and Politics in the Age of Emerson* (Cam-

bridge: Harvard University Press, 1986), Preface. Subsequent references to this work will be cited in text.

26. See "The Plath Celebration," CP, 163. Howe might have noted similar self-pitying rhetoric in Coleridge, who said that slavery is a state of hopelessness, and therefore slavery to commerce, or slavery to opium are psychologically the same thing. Coleridge described opium as "the curse of my existence, my shame and my negro-slave inward humiliation and debasement."—*Inquiring Spirit: A Coleridge Reader*, ed. Kathleen Coburn (New York: Minerva, 1968), 19.

27. In September 1981 Howe delivered a lecture at Indiana University entitled "The End of Jewish Secularism," in which he says "farewell with love and gratitude" to secular Jewishness. The lecture was printed only posthumously, by Hunter College of CUNY in its Occasional Papers in Jewish History and Thought.

28. Letter of 18 August 1986 from IH to Ruth Wisse.

29. Letters of 22 January 1977, 18 July 1979, and 28 August 1979 from IH to Alvin Rosenfeld.

30. On this topic, see Yehuda Bauer, *The Holocaust in Historical Perspective* (Seattle: University of Washington Press, 1978), especially the chapter called "Against Mystification," in which Bauer stresses the uniqueness of the Holocaust, its difference from genocide, but also warns that to declare that there are no parallels to the Holocaust, and that the whole phenomenon is inexplicable, is equally an error and "mystification."

31. This passage is repeated, with only minor variations, as are some others from this essay, from Howe's major essay of the previous year on Primo Levi called "How to Write about the Holocaust," *New York Review of Books*, 28 March 1985, 14–17.

32. In his introduction to Howe's posthumously published collection of essays on fiction, Nicholas Howe says that his father rejected the original title as "portentous" (though it hardly seems that). The title *A Critic's Notebook* (New York: Harcourt Brace, 1994) was apparently supplied by the editor or the publisher. In a letter to Ruth Wisse in January 1990, Howe reported that he was working, albeit slowly, on a book about the novel as a genre, what he called *shtiklakh* of an impressionistic kind.—Letter of 30 January 1990 from IH to Ruth Wisse.

33. "The Human Factor," *New Republic*, 8 May 1989, 30. Subsequent references to this work will be cited in text.

34. "The Treason of the Critics," *New Republic*, 12 June 1989, 29. Subsequent references to this work will be cited in text.

35. "History and the Novel," *New Republic*, 3 September 1990, 29. Subsequent references to this work will be cited in text.

36. Letter of 30 January 1990 from IH to Ruth Wisse.

37. Howe was not entirely pleased by his less contentious later style. In March of 1991 he told me that he was getting old, but remained active, despite the loss of some of his old polemical vigor.—Letter from IH to EA, 21 March 1991.

38. "The Value of the Canon," *New Republic*, 18 February 1991, 41. Subsequent references to this work will be cited in text.

39. See letters of 26 November 1975, 10 November 1982, 17 December 1988, and 30 January 1989 from IH to Sidney Hook; and letters of 19 November 1982 and 7 February 1989 from Hook to Howe. Sidney Hook Collection, Box 15, Folder 39 (Howe), Hoover Institution Archives. In the 7 February letter, Hook could not resist telling Howe that "it cannot be news to you that you are more of an authority among those [in the cohort of Stanford curricular radicals] who consider themselves 'enlightened and new Left' among [sic] the humanists and social science faculty here than I am. Actually some of the faculty here who helped engineer the curricular coup . . . are graduates of the 60's, and a couple of them fall into the class you have immortalized with your phrase 'guerrillas with tenure.'"

40. "Mr. Bennett and Mrs. Woolf," *New Republic*, 4 June 1990, 26–28.

41. Morris Dickstein, "A World Away, a Generation Later," *New York Times Book Review*, 6 April 1997, 35.

42. Letter of 18 November 1944 from IH to Albert Glotzer, Albert Glotzer Collection, Box 12, Howe Folder, Hoover Institution Archives.

43. *A Surplus of Memory: Chronicle of the Warsaw Ghetto Uprising* (Berkeley: University of California Press, 1993).

44. *The Jews of Warsaw, 1939–1943* (Bloomington: Indiana University Press, 1982).

45. "The Road Leads Far Away," *New Republic*, 3 May 1993, 29–30. Subsequent references to this work will be cited in text.

46. Segev's book of 1993, *The Seventh Million: The Israelis and the Holocaust*, was systematically demolished by Shabtai Teveth, *Ben-Gurion and the Holocaust* (New York: Harcourt Brace, 1996).

47. Letter of 4 May 1993 from IH to Ruth Wisse.

48. Letter of 30 January 1989 from IH to Sidney Hook. Sidney Hook Collection, Box 15, Folder 39 (Howe), Hoover Institution Archives.

BIBLIOGRAPHY

Selected Works by Irving Howe

"Adlai Stevenson: The Last, Sad Years." *Dissent*, 12 (Autumn 1965): 409–11.
"After the Mideast War." *Dissent*, 14 (July-August 1967): 387–90.
"Again: Orwell and the Neoconservatives." *Dissent*, 31 (Spring 1984): 236.
The American Communist Party: A Critical History (1919–1957) [with Lewis Coser]. Boston: Beacon, 1957.
"American Jews and Israel." *Tikkun*, 4 (December 1988): 71–74.
The American Newness: Culture and Politics in the Age of Emerson. Cambridge: Harvard University Press, 1986.
"Are American Jews Turning toward the Right?" [with Bernard Rosenberg], in *The New Conservatives*, ed. Lewis Coser and Irving Howe. New York: Quadrangle, 1974.
"Arguments: More on Eichmann." *Partisan Review*, 31 (Spring 1964): 260.
Ashes Out of Hope: Fiction by Soviet-Yiddish Writers, ed. Irving Howe and Eliezer Greenberg. New York: Schocken, 1977.
"The Burden of Civilization." *New Republic*, 10 February 1982, 27–34.
"The Campus Left and Israel," in *Israel, the Arabs and the Middle East*, ed. Irving Howe and Carl Gershman. New York: Bantam, 1972.
Celebrations and Attacks. New York: Harcourt Brace Jovanovich, 1979.
"The Cities' Secret." *New Republic*, 22 January 1977, 55–57.
Classics of Modern Fiction. (ed.) New York: Harcourt Brace & World, 1968.
"The Concentrationary Universe." *New International*, 13 (September 1947): 220–21.
A Critic's Notebook, ed. Nicholas Howe. New York: Harcourt Brace, 1994.
The Critical Point. New York: Delta, 1973.
"The Dilemma of *Partisan Review.*" *New International*, 8 (February 1942): 22–24.
"Does It Hurt When You Laugh?" *Dissent*, 1 (January 1954): 4–7.
"An Exchange on the Left." *New York Review of Books*, 23 November 1967, 36–39.
"An Exercise in Memory." *New Republic*, 11 March 1991, 29–32.
"Falling Out of the Canon." *New Republic*, 17 and 24 August 1992, 35–37.
"The Fiction of Anti-Utopia." *New Republic*, 23 April 1962, 13–16.
"The First Ten Years." *Dissent*, 11 (Spring 1964): 150–52.

"The Frauds of Louis Fischer." *New International*, 7 (October 1941): 240–44.

"From Rebel to Bureaucrat." *New York Review of Books*, 24 October 1991, 52–55.

"Historical Memory, Political Vision." *New Republic*, 9 November 1974, 25–28.

"History and the Novel." *New Republic*, 3 September 1990, 29–34.

"How to Write about the Holocaust." *New York Review of Books*, 28 March 1985, 14–17.

"How *Partisan Review* Goes to War: Stalinophobia on the Cultural Front." *New International*, 13 (April 1947): 109–11.

"The Human Factor." *New Republic*, 8 May 1989, 30–34.

"I'm Not a Marxist." *New York Times Book Review*, 20 October 1985, 11.

"Imagining Labor." *New Republic*, 11 April 1981, 28–33.

"Immigrant Chic." *New York Magazine*, 12 May 1986, 76–77.

"Intellectual Freedom and Stalinists: Shall CP Teachers Be Prohibited from Teaching?" *New International*, 15 (December 1949): 231–36.

"The Intellectuals' Flight from Politics." *New International*, 13 (October 1947): 241–46.

"Is This Country Cracking Up?" *Dissent*, 14 (May-June 1967): 259–63.

"Israel: A Visitor's Notes." *Dissent*, 24 (Fall 1977): 359–63.

Jewish-American Stories. (ed.) New York: New American Library, 1977.

"The Jewish Writer and the English Literary Tradition." *Commentary*, 8 (October 1949): 364–65.

"Journey of a Poet." *Commentary*, 53 (January 1972): 75–77.

Leon Trotsky. New York: Viking, 1978.

"The Limits of Ethnicity." *New Republic*, 25 June 1977, 17–19.

"Literary Criticism and Literary Radicals." *The American Scholar*, 41 (Winter 1971–72): 113–20.

"Living with Kampf and Schlaff: Literary Tradition and Mass Education." *The American Scholar*, 43 (Winter 1973): 107–12.

"The Lost Young Intellectual." *Commentary*, 2 (October 1946): 361–67.

"Magazine Chronicle." *Partisan Review*, 16 (April 1949): 416–27.

A Margin of Hope: An Intellectual Autobiography. New York: Harcourt Brace Jovanovich, 1982.

"A Mind's Turnings." *Dissent*, 7 (Winter 1960): 31–38.

"Mr. Bennet and Mrs. Woolf." *New Republic*, 4 June 1990, 26–28.

"The Negro Revolution." *Dissent*, 10 (Summer 1963): front cover, 205–14.

"The Negro Revolution" (continued). *Dissent*, 10 (Autumn 1963): 301–304.

"New Black Writers." *Harper's*, 239 (December 1969): 130–41.

"The New 'Confrontation Politics' Is a Dangerous Game." *New York Times Magazine*, 20 October 1968, 27–29, 133–35, 137–40.

"'The New Yorker' and Hannah Arendt." *Commentary*, 36 (October 1963): 318–19.

"'1984'—Utopia Reversed: Orwell's Penetrating Examination of Totalitarian Society." *New International*, 16 (November-December 1950): 360–68.

"Notes from Jerusalem." *New York Review of Books*, 29 September 1988, 13–14.

"Of Fathers and Sons." *Commentary*, 2 (August 1946): 190–92.

"On the Significance of Koestler: A Reply by Irving Howe." *New International* (July 1947): 158–59.

"Our Country and Our Culture." *Partisan Review,* 19 (September-October 1952): 575–81.
"Periodicals." *Politics* (January 1947): 30–31 [as Theodore Dryden].
"Periodicals." *Politics* (March-April 1947): 63–64 [as Theodore Dryden].
"Philip Rahv: A Memoir." *The American Scholar,* 48 (Autumn 1979): 487–98.
"Political Terrorism: Hysteria on the Left." *New York Times Magazine,* 12 April 1970, 25–27, 124–28.
Politics and the Novel. New York: Horizon, 1957.
"The Problem of Pornography." *Dissent,* 25 (Spring 1978): 204–205.
"The Question of the Pound Award." *Partisan Review,* 16 (May 1949): 516–17.
"Radical Questions and the American Intellectual." *Partisan Review,* 33 (Spring 1966): 179–92, 312–24.
"The Range of the New York Intellectuals," in *Creators and Disturbers: Reminiscences by Jewish Intellectuals of New York,* ed. Bernard Rosenberg and Ernest Goldstein. New York: Columbia University Press, 1982.
"Record Straight." *Dissent,* 29 (Summer 1982): 382–83.
"A Reply to Ralph Ellison." *New Leader,* 3 February 1964, 12–14.
"A Revival of Radicalism?" *Dissent,* 10 (Spring 1963): 110–14.
"The Right Menace." *New Republic,* 9 September 1978, 12–17.
"The Road Leads Far Away." *New Republic,* 3 May 1993, 29–36.
Selected Stories: I. L. Peretz (ed.) New York: Schocken, 1974.
Selected Writings: 1950–1990. New York: Harcourt Brace Jovanovich, 1990.
"The Sentimental Fellow-Traveling of F. O. Matthiessen." *Partisan Review,* 15 (October 1948): 1125–29.
Sherwood Anderson: A Biographical and Critical Study. New York: William Sloane, 1951.
"The Significance of Koestler: An Exchange between Irving Howe and Neil Weiss." *New International,* 12 (October 1946): 251–52.
Socialism and America. New York: Harcourt Brace Jovanovich, 1985.
"Stalinism: The Murder Machine Adds Two Victims." *Labor Action,* 22 March 1943.
Steady Work: Essays in the Politics of Democratic Radicalism, 1953–1966. New York: Harcourt, Brace & World, 1966.
"The Stranger and the Victim: The Two Stereotypes of American Fiction." *Commentary,* 8 (August 1949): 147–56.
"Strangers." *Yale Review,* 66 (June 1977): 481–500.
"Tevye on Broadway." *Commentary,* 38 (November 1964): 73–75.
Thomas Hardy. New York: Macmillan, 1967.
"To Jerusalem and Back." *New York Times Book Review,* 17 October 1976, 1–2.
"Toward an Open Culture." *New Republic,* 5 March 1984, 25–29.
"The Treason of the Critics." *New Republic,* 12 June 1989, 28–31.
A Treasury of Yiddish Poetry, ed. Irving Howe and Eliezer Greenberg. New York: Holt, Rinehart and Winston, 1969.
A Treasury of Yiddish Stories, ed. Irving Howe and Eliezer Greenberg. New York: Viking, 1954.
The UAW and Walter Reuther [with B. J. Widick]. New York: Random House, 1949.

"The Value of the Canon." *New Republic*, 18 February 1991, 40–47.
"The Value of Taste." *Partisan Review*, 18 (January-February 1951): 124–26.
"Vietnam and Israel," in *Israel, the Arabs and the Middle East*, ed. Irving Howe and Carl Gershman. New York: Bantam, 1972.
Voices from the Yiddish: Essays, Memoirs, Diaries, ed. Irving Howe and Eliezer Greenberg. Ann Arbor: University of Michigan Press, 1972.
"Warm Friends of Israel, Open Critics of Begin-Sharon." *New York Times*, 23 September 1982.
"What Henry Heard." *New Republic*, 26 March 1977, 20–21.
"Why Should Negroes Be above Criticism?" *Saturday Evening Post*, 14 December 1968, 10, 14–15.
"William Buckley and the Price of Kicks." *Dissent*, 13 (January-February 1966): 92–94.
William Faulkner: A Critical Study. Chicago: Ivan R. Dee, 1991. (Originally published 1952.)
"A Word about 'Bourgeois Civil Liberties.'" *Dissent*, 15 (January-February 1968): 10–11.
"Word to Our Readers." (coauthored with other original editors of *Dissent*) *Dissent*, 1 (January 1954): 3–4.
World of Our Fathers. New York: Harcourt Brace Jovanovich, 1976.
"Writing and the Holocaust." *New Republic*, 27 October 1986, 27–39.

Works about Irving Howe

Alexander, Edward. *Irving Howe and Secular Jewishness: An Elegy.* Cincinnati: University of Cincinnati Judaic Studies Program, 1995.
Alter, Robert. "Yiddishkeit." *Commentary*, 61 (April 1976): 83–86.
Bernstein, Richard. [Obituary] *New York Times*, 6 May 1993.
Bloom, Alexander. *The New York Intellectuals and Their World*. New York: Oxford University Press, 1986.
Bromwich, David. "What Novels Are For." *New York Times Book Review*, 30 October 1994.
Cohn, Werner. "The Name-Changers." *Forum*, 50 (Winter 1983–84): 65–71.
Decter, Midge. "Socialism and Its Irresponsibilities." *Commentary*, 74 (December 1982): 25–32.
Draper, Hal. "A New Magazine Presents Itself to the Socialist Public." *Labor Action*, 22 February 1954.
Ellison, Ralph. *Shadow and Act*. New York: New American Library, 1966.
Glazer, Nathan. "Philistine Leftism." *Commentary*, 17 (February 1954): 201–206.
Glotzer, Al. "On Irving Howe." *Social Democrats Notes*, May 1993, 3–5.
Hindus, Milton. "Milton Hindus vs. Irving Howe." *New Boston Review*, 2 (January 1977): 7–10.
Hollander, John. Lecture of 15 April 1994 at CUNY's "Memorial Conference: Irving Howe and His World."
Hux, Samuel. "Uncle Irving." *Modern Age*, 37 (Summer 1995): 330–36.

Isserman, Maurice. *If I Had a Hammer . . . The Death of the Old Left and the Birth of the New Left.* New York: Basic, 1987.

Kramer, Hilton. "Irving Howe at Seventy." *New Criterion,* 9 (October 1990): 6–9.

Kristol, Irving. *Reflections of a Neoconservative.* New York: Basic Books, 1983.

Miller, Stephen. "The Poverty of Socialist Thought." *Commentary,* 62 (August 1976): 31–37.

Ozick, Cynthia. *Art and Ardor.* New York: Knopf, 1983.

———. *Metaphor and Memory.* New York: Knopf, 1989.

Pinsker, Sanford. "Lost Causes / Marginal Hopes." *Virginia Quarterly Review,* 65 (Spring 1989): 215–30.

Podhoretz, Norman. *Breaking Ranks.* New York: Harper & Row, 1979.

Rabinowitch, Alexander. "A Figure of Flawed Greatness [Trotsky]." *Nation,* 23 September 1978, 277–78.

"Remembering Irving Howe." Special issue of *Dissent,* 40 (Fall 1993): 515–49.

Rosenfeld, Alvin. "Irving Howe: The World of Our Fathers." *Midstream,* 22 (October 1976): 80–86.

Roth, Philip. *The Anatomy Lesson,* in *Zuckerman Bound.* New York: Farrar Straus Giroux, 1985.

Simon, John. "Irving Howe: A Triple Perspective." *New Leader,* 21 May 1979, 19–21.

Wald, Alan M. *The New York Intellectuals: The Rise and Decline of the Anti-Stalinist Left from the 1930's to the 1980's.* Chapel Hill: University of North Carolina Press, 1987.

Warshow, Robert. "'This Age of Conformity.'" *Partisan Review,* 21 (March-April 1954): 235–38.

Wieseltier, Leon. "Remembering Irving Howe (1920–93)." *New York Times Book Review,* 23 May 1993.

Wisse, Ruth R. "The New York (Jewish) Intellectuals." *Commentary,* 84 (November 1987): 28–38.

Wrong, Dennis. "Thinning Ranks." *New Republic,* 25 November 1985, 30–34.

Other Works Consulted

"Editorial Statement." *Partisan Review,* 4 (December 1937): 3–4.

Eliot, T. S. *After Strange Gods: A Primer of Modern Heresy.* New York: Harcourt Brace, 1934.

Gilman, Sander L. *Jewish Self-Hatred.* Baltimore: Johns Hopkins University Press, 1986.

Halkin, Hillel. *Letters to an American Jewish Friend.* Philadelphia: Jewish Publication Society, 1977.

Hook, Sidney. *Out of Step.* New York: Harper & Row, 1987.

Katz, Dovid. "The Future of Yiddish." *Forward,* 16 August 1966.

Kessner, Carole S., ed. *The "Other" New York Jewish Intellectuals.* New York: New York University Press, 1994.

Krupnick, Mark. *Lionel Trilling and the Fate of Cultural Criticism.* Evanston: Northwestern University Press, 1986.

Manuel, Frank E. *A Requiem for Karl Marx.* Cambridge: Harvard University Press, 1996.

Phillips, William. *A Partisan Review: Five Decades of the Literary Life.* New York: Stein and Day, 1983.

Rosenberg, Harold. "Does the Jew Exist? Sartre's Morality Play about Anti-Semitism." *Commentary,* 7 (January 1949): 8–18.

Trilling, Diana. *The Beginning of the Journey.* New York: Harcourt Brace, 1993.

Trilling, Lionel. *The Liberal Imagination.* New York: Viking, 1950.

Wolin, Richard. "Hannah and the Magician." *New Republic,* 9 October 1995, 27–37.

Wreszin, Michael. *A Rebel in Defense of Tradition: The Life and Politics of Dwight Macdonald.* New York: Basic Books, 1994.

Archival Sources

Lewis Coser Collection, Boston College Archives.
Albert Glotzer Collection. Hoover Institution Archives, Stanford University.
Sidney Hook Papers. Hoover Institution Archives, Stanford University.
Dwight Macdonald Papers. Yale University Library.

Oral Sources

Interviews of Albert Glotzer, Irving Panken, and Sylvia Panken by EA (September 1996).
Interview of Irving Howe by Robert Negin (November 1990).
Irving Howe Memorial Ceremony. 92nd Street Y Unterberg Poetry Center, 24 May 1993.
"A Memorial Conference: Irving Howe and His World." Graduate Center, City University of New York, 15 April 1994.
Oral History of the American Left, Tamiment Library, New York University.

INDEX

Edward Alexander is professor of English at the University of Washington. His books include *Matthew Arnold and John Stuart Mill; Matthew Arnold, John Ruskin and the Modern Temper; The Resonance of Dust: Essays on Holocaust Literature and Jewish Fate; Isaac Bashevis Singer: A Study of the Short Fiction; The Holocaust and the War of Ideas;* and *The Jewish Wars: Reflections by One of the Belligerents.*